Sports Reporting SECOND EDITION

Sports

Iowa State University Press / Ames

SECOND EDITION

Reporting

Bruce Garrison with Mark Sabljak

BRUCE GARRISON is professor of journalism at the University of Miami, Coral Gables. He is a former sports reporter for the *Knoxville News-Sentinel, Lexington Herald-Leader,* and *Hattiesburg American.* He is author of *Professional News Reporting* (1992), *Advanced Reporting: Skills for the Professional* (1992), *Professional News Writing* (1990), *Professional Feature Writing* (1989), and *Latin American Journalism* (1991). Garrison has also judged the finals of the Associated Press Sports Editors annual national sportswriting and reporting awards.

MARK SABLJAK is special events manager for Journal/Sentinel Inc., publisher of the *Milwaukee Journal* and *Milwaukee Sentinel* newspapers. As sports reporter and editor for the *Des Moines Register* and *Milwaukee Journal,* he has covered events from the high school to professional level. Sabljak, who holds a master's degree in communications from the University of Wisconsin-Milwaukee, has specialized in reporting economic issues in sports. His other books include *Who's Who in the Super Bowl* and *Sports Babylon.*

COVER PHOTO: Sports reporters on the sideline at a Miami Orange Bowl football game. (*Photo © by Michael DiBari.*)

TITLE SPREAD PHOTO: Sportswriters and photographers swarm New York Giants' players Carl Banks and Lawrence Taylor and head coach Bill Parcells on the field after the Giants defeated the Buffalo Bills, 20–19, at Super Bowl XXV in Tampa in 1991. (*Photo by Gin Ellis, NFL Photos.*)

Library of Congress
Cataloging-in-Publication Data
Garrison, Bruce
  Sports reporting / Bruce Garrison with Mark Sabljak. — 2nd ed. p. cm.
    Includes bibliographical references and index.
    ISBN 0-8138-1692-0
    1. Sports journalism. I. Sabljak, Mark. II. Title.
PN4784.S6G3   1993
070.4′49796 — dc20   92-40403

© 1985, 1993 Iowa State University Press
Ames, Iowa 50014
All rights reserved

⊗ Printed on acid-free paper in the United States of America

First edition, 1985
Second edition, 1993
Second printing, 1994

Contents

Foreword by BILL DWYRE

Executive Sports Editor, *Los Angeles Times*

It is August 9, 1991, as I write this, and I sit in my office in a blur of emotion. Piled around me are the solemn signs of an ailing business: resumes of former employees of *The National.* It failed recently, closed the doors and sent the talent packing with a couple of weeks' severance pay and "nice try" pats on the back.

The Days of Wine and Roses have become the days of vinegar and dandelions in the business of reporting and printing the news, and the grim reaper who walks the halls of publishing businesses these days certainly doesn't miss sports departments. Indeed, we live in a time of budget cuts, employee buyouts, and shrinking newsholes. And if you happened to be a member of the staff of *The National,* those things would have been the good news.

Unlike some other passings, *The National's* may not rest in peace among those of us who care about the sports-reporting industry. *The National* was to be the turning point in sports reporting, the final stone on the pile we have been building for so many years that we all hoped would someday rise up and show the world that what we do is significant, special, and more important to the daily readers of newspapers than upper exccutives of our publications care to admit.

As *The National* was being planned and promoted, its editor, Frank Deford, pointed out that sports sections all over America had been "newspaper publishers' dirty little secret." Publishers, he said, for years had been getting away with riding the heavy sports readership in newspapers to successful overall products while not paying enough dollars or recognition to the people responsible for those sports sections.

The National would change all that, Deford implied. It would be so good that the publishing world would have to sit up and take notice. Its momentum would upgrade the quality of all daily newspapers, which would be forced to compete to keep up.

Some 18 months later, *The National,* as well as Deford and his soapbox, were gone. Publishers everywhere, whose attention had been titillated at the beginning, said "I told you so" and went back to lying to each other about the readership of their editorial pages. The editorial types at *The National* blamed the production and circulation people for the death. Some of the rest of us wondered if the true cause of death hadn't been an acute overdose of optimism aggravated by naivete.

Whatever the cause, the departure of *The National* was a severe setback for those of us who, foolishly perhaps, wanted so desperately to have their field of endeavor raised a rung in status. I wanted *The National* to be superb, to show me new ways of doing things, to beat my writers on stories and to make me mad and motivate me to motivate my writers to beat them back. Never before had I seen such an impressive collection of sports journalism talent. Never before had my expectations been higher for the reinvention of America's sports pages.

And what did I get? A reinvented hockey box score.

But as I sit here in my blur, I realize that it is too easy to lay blame at the doorstep of the people who tried to make *The National* something special. They certainly had guts and a dream, and greatness seldom is achieved in anything without those ingredients. No, perhaps *The National* simply perpetuated the flaws that seem so evident in the last 10 years of sports journalism.

Sports sections in America have progressed only slightly in the last 10 years in the area where progress counts the most: the written word. It is unfortunate for newspapers that perhaps the one place where the written word has fared the best and been handled the most delicately is in a magazine: *Sports Illustrated.* Scattered among those beautiful color pictures are some beautifully reported and crafted words. And yes, some newspapers also do this well on a daily basis. Just not enough of them.

Generally speaking, America's sports sections are nicely packaged, nicely displayed, and nicely informational, but are poorly written. Even some of the larger newspapers seem to have settled on a formula of having one or two talented columnists and a supporting cast of sports fans turned hacks. Of course, I generalize, but I'm afraid that is pretty much the reality.

The proof of this is that so many sections seem to turn all their energy to the frosting while letting the cake get stale. While eager, young, inexperienced writers who could be shaped into something special sit around and get little or no direction or leadership, the layout and graphics people are figuring ways to package all this mediocrity into looking like something special. So the sports section becomes a lie, a fraud.

When a sports section has a fancy layout, nice accompanying explanatory graphics, and color pictures, the reader expects something special, something worth his or her time. The signals sent are clear: READ THIS!

But when the reading unveils an ordinary, lifeless, predictable piece, guess what happens the next time the reader sees the nice package? Fish-wrapping time. Or worse, cancel-the-newspaper time.

I'm not against art and graphics in the least — there's only one thing better than a great-reading sports story: a great-reading sports story that's well displayed. I'm just against art and graphics becoming the overwhelming priority of sports editors and their main assistants.

So read this book. Learn about reporting and writing. Take the examples to heart. Take nothing as gospel but take everything as the big puzzle of how to do this job correctly.

And keep the most important thing in mind: Newspapers are about the written word, first and foremost. Everything else is a reader aid, a help for the story, a guide to lead you to the story. If you need proof, just ask some experts to identify a list of five or so of the best newspapers in America today. Somewhere in that list will be the *Wall Street Journal*. Read it sometime soon, and notice how many pictures it runs.

Twelve-year National Football League defensive line veteran Dan Hampton of the Chicago Bears talks to reporters in the locker room at Soldier Field after a game in his final season before retiring. (*Photo by Bill Smith, Chicago Bears.*)

Preface

Sports is serious business in the mid-1990s. What was once fun and games is now much more than that. Experts say sports is a $50-billion-a-year industry in the United States. It fills much of the available time on television and is a major selling point for many newspapers.

Sports journalism is maturing in this final decade of the 20th century. It is adjusting to changing relations and standards involving sports and society. As the reporters responsible for chronicling the world of sports today, sports reporters come to their jobs with a wider view of the world and better tools with which to do those jobs.

In the eight years since the first edition of this book was published, sports journalists have continued to make positive strides toward full membership in the club of journalists. Sports journalists never quite got the respect they sought because they seldom deserved it, but the mid-1990s sports journalists are gradually earning some of that respect. Their aspirations to be full-fledged members of the club are not so wild and unimaginable as they were a generation or two ago. Better education and better tools are two of the reasons for this, and we hope this volume also will contribute to improvement of the craft.

As we noted in the first edition, sports journalism has changed in truly remarkable ways. Gone are the days of reporters and editors who served as cheerleaders for the home team. The contemporary sports journalist is serious, critical, and thorough. We feel an updated book is necessary to reflect these changes in philosophy, attitude, and day-to-day approach to sportswriting both for the beginning journalist interested in sports and for the veteran journalist seeking to expand his or her news gathering and writing horizons. This book reflects the experiences of two former sportswriters — one of us now teaching at a university and the other in a management career at a major daily newspaper — who are interested in evaluating sports journalism from a broad perspective. Reflecting our own priorities in sportswriting basics, this book is a new approach to sports journalism.

This book is about the most recent concerns and reporting strategies used in sports departments of leading newspapers. Our objective is to define these new techniques and their applications in sports journalism, illustrating them with real examples and explaining how they contribute to overall improvement of sports journalism today. We not only discuss contemporary approaches but also review traditional reporting tools and how each has been refined over generations of use. We also look at the special problems of sports reporting and possible solutions.

Because sports journalism is a broad topic appealing to people of many levels of experience in journalism, we have tried to make the book appropriate reading for a number of audiences: advanced college students who know the basics of news gathering and writing; beginning professionals, perhaps without a sports background, who need a handbook for reference when they find themselves covering sports part-time or even full-time; community newspaper reporters and editors who may serve as reporting "utility infielders" and cover all subjects; and veteran reporters who want to open new reporting horizons. We hope to discuss, for all our readers, the state of the art and the present situation of the sports journalist.

We believe that sports journalism requires a reporting-strategies approach, so we do not discuss sports journalism sport by sport. There is no need, for example, to discuss the differences in covering football and basketball games, because fundamentally, the observational and interviewing skills required are the same for both sports. Therefore, we include a substantial chapter on the game story. We discuss the interview, observation, and game stories — the true basics of sports journalism. We look at how to cover sports in the new areas of the courts, public opinion, and business and finance, and also as investigative projects.

Our goal is to contribute to the professionalization of sports journalism through expanding approaches and to instill a broader understanding of its impact, processes, and objectives, thus helping the sportswriter to do a better and more professional job.

Acknowledgments

A project of this size requires a great deal of help, and we would like to thank the individuals and institutions that have assisted us.

Two benchmark books introduced the broader social science approach to reporting and gave us the incentive to make similar applications to sports journalism. *The Handbook of Reporting Methods,* by Maxwell McCombs, Donald Shaw, and David Gray, and *New Strategies for Public Affairs Reporting,* by George S. Hage, Everette E. Dennis, Arnold H. Ismach, and Stephen Hartgen, suggested innovative approaches to general reporting, as well as to the specific area of public affairs reporting that made sense for sports journalists.

For their valuable assistance on the second edition, we thank:

Alan Prince, journalism professor in the School of Communication at the University of Miami, for his editing of each chapter and timely, sharp-eyed editorial criticism. Professor Prince is a rare jewel in journalism education. He made a major difference in the quality of this work. Our sincerest thanks to him.

Steve Doyle, assistant managing editor for sports, the *Orlando Sentinel* and 1989–90 president of Associated Press Sports Editors (APSE), for his availablity and willingness to provide information whenever requested.

Ed Storin, recently retired associate managing editor at the *Miami Herald* and present executive secretary of APSE, for making APSE newsletter backcopies available for reference.

John McGill, sports columnist for the *Lexington (Ky.) Herald-Leader* and longtime friend of the senior author, for his comments on sportswriting in general, for his specific comments on column writing, and for his general support for this project.

Michael B. Salwen, journalism professor at the University of Miami, for his editorial comments. Thanks also go to Professor Salwen for his coauthorship in conceiving, conducting, and writing the findings of the 1988 national study of APSE-member sports editors, which is discussed in depth in Chapter 15.

Kyu Ho Youm, journalism professor at the University of Miami, for his editorial comments.

Dale Bye, sports editor of the *Kansas City Star,* and Sandy Bailey, former sports editor of the *International Herald-Tribune* in Paris and now at the *New York Times,* for providing research material from the APSE writing and reporting contest in 1991. Thanks also to Dale Bye and his administrative assistant Cathy Lindstedt for providing *Kansas City Star* photographs for this book.

Michael DiBari, former photographer for the Kissimmee, Fla., *News-Gazette,* for his photographic contributions.

Miami Herald sportswriter Dan LeBatard for providing 1991 Cotton Bowl press materials.

Tom Snelling, NFL Photos in Los Angeles, for providing color photos and slides of National Football League players and the Super Bowl game in Tampa.

The public relations staff of the Miami Heat for providing press releases and other background materials.

Barbara Allen, public relations assistant for the Chicago Bears, for providing the color slide of a photograph by Bill Smith of retiring player Dan Hampton.

Susan Carpenter, public relations director for the Los Angeles Kings, for providing photographs of Kings' players meeting with sportswriters.

Dave Bergman, former photographer for the *Miami Hurricane* and 1991–92 editor of the University of Miami yearbook, the *Ibis,* for his photographic contributions.

Sherrie Lisitski, graduate student in journalism at the University of Miami, for her library research assistance.

Christina Henriques and Joanne Acosta, research assistants in the School of Communication at the University of Miami, for their library research and typing assistance.

Larry Wahl, associate athletic director at the University of Miami, for assistance on college athletics finances.

Gary Clark, chief of the Associated Press bureau for Florida, for providing information for Chapter 14.

Daniel G. Rubinetti, manager of media sales for SportsTicker, for providing information on SportsTicker services.

We continue to thank our research assistants for the first edition— Orlando Mellado, Jill Singer, and Jim Roth of the University of Miami and Joyce Dehli and Betsy Unger of Marquette University—for their tireless library work, typing, and proofreading.

We also thank Dean Edward Pfister at the University of Miami for his support through the School of Communication's resources.

We are grateful to the publications that have granted us permission to use their material.

And finally, we acknowledge the continuing support of Zoya Garrison and Mishi The Cat, and of Joan and Maggie Sabljak.

1 Introduction and History

Television cameras mix with still photographers and compete for prime sideline locations during a football game at Miami's Orange Bowl. (*Photo © by Michael DiBari.*)

St. Cloud High School, Fla., head football coach John Wal-laver answers questions from reporter Angela Melcher of the *Osceola News-Gazette* in Kissimmee, Fla. (*Photo © by Michael DiBari.*)

1

The Changing Nature of Sports Journalism

● *Miami Herald* sportswriter Scott Fowler, who normally spends time watching action on a basketball court, found himself recently in a law court, watching a different sort of action. He was assigned to cover a trial in which attorneys for a major college football program argued million-dollar damage claims against an artificial turf manufacturer and practice field contractor.

● Sportswriter Christine Brennan (1990) of the *Washington Post* served as a caddy during the Lady Keystone Open in Hershey, Pa., in an effort to get an inside look at the professional golf tour from the perspective of Tracy Kerdyk, a newcomer on the Ladies Professional Golf Association tour.

● *Boston Herald* sports writer Lisa Olson, on a routine National Football League game assignment, was allegedly harassed after a game by several New England Patriots players in the locker room while attempting to conduct an interview of cornerback Maurice Hurst. The case created an international stir and resulted in an independent investigation and NFL fines of thousands of dollars against team management. A week after Olson was allegedly harassed in Boston, another female reporter, Denise Tom, who works for *USA Today,* was kept out of the Seattle locker room by Cincinnati Bengals' coach Sam Wyche. That action also resulted in a large league fine (Donaghy 1990).

● Jordan Mendal (Wolper 1988), a student sportswriter for the Syracuse University *Daily Orange,* wrote a weekly satirical column called "Mendal's Madness." While he was on assignment after a game, several players pitched him into a shower and then poured soft drinks on his tape recorder and notebook. The players had been upset by some of his comments in his column during a losing season the previous year. Even the Syracuse coach at the time, Dick MacPherson, when he was asked about the incident by the newspaper's sports editor, said the writer had to take some responsibility for what happened. MacPherson said that writers were either on the team or off the team. The school's athletic director, Jack Crouthammel, said student journalists have to act like professionals if they want to be treated like professionals.

● At recent national meetings in Tampa, Boston, Redondo Beach (Calif.), and San Antonio, the nation's sports editors grappled with serious professional ethics concerns in attempting to revise and strengthen their national organization's ethical guidelines. The Associated Press Sports Editors, the nation's leading group of newspaper sports section managers, debated both new and old issues reflecting the changing world in which sports reporters do their work. Some of the issues were philosophical while others were practical, but the debate demonstrates great concern for increasing the standards of professional performance by sports journalists in this decade.

These situations represent the changing face of sports journalism in the mid-1990s. Sportswriters, journalists who report and edit the community's sports activity, have experienced a significant change in their roles since the late 1960s, particularly in the last few years. Sportswriters beginning careers in the mid-1990s will undoubtedly encounter similar situations. Sports coverage will continue to change; it is in the middle of a revolution. The sports department was for many years considered to be the "toy department" of the newspaper. Now the toy department has become legitimate (Freeman 1988; Garneau 1988).

The former toy department has also become a major industry. Sports in the United States has become a $50- to $60-billion-a-year business — one of the nation's 25 largest — which U.S. newspapers spent about $500 million to cover in 1988, according to two media observers (Shaw 1989; Rambo 1989). With numbers that large, it is easy to see how a one-time toy department has had to become a mature news gathering enterprise in only a few decades.

And the seriousness of sports today cannot be overlooked. Sports reporting involves litigation, crime, health, and international politics. Research has shown that Olympics and other international games reporting cannot be separated from politics (Salwen and Garrison 1987).

Ultimately, efforts to strengthen the sports department are designed to strengthen the role of the entire newspaper against other news media. Expenditures and improvements are implemented to attract readers. With so much competition for the leisure time of individuals in the mid-1990s, newspapers not only have to look at other newspapers but also at other news media and non-media leisure time activities as competition today. It is very difficult to get individuals to read in an age of television. It is even tougher to get the attention of a reader with so much other material available for them to read and with Americans devoting so little time to reading.

Trends in Sports Journalism

Sports sections in American newspapers are beefing up their products for the contemporary sports fan. Sports sections have always had strong followings in most cities, but that appeal has been rather narrow in terms of demographics. Sports section editors are broadening the appeal of their

The Nation's Top Daily Sports Sections

The Associated Press Sports Editors, the national organization of sports section managers, annually ranks the best sports sections. APSE rates sections for overall excellence, including quality of reporting, columnists, graphics, photography, scope of coverage, and effective use of resources. In 1992, the top sections were, in alphabetic order:

Top Ten Daily Sections Over 175,000 Circulation

Atlanta Journal and Constitution
Boston Globe
Chicago Tribune
Dallas Morning News
Detroit Free Press

Detroit News
Fort Lauderdale Sun-Sentinel
Orange County (Calif.) Register
USA Today
Washington Post

Top Ten Daily Sections 50,000–175,000 Circulation

Arlington Heights (Ill.) Daily Herald
Austin (Tex.) American-Statesman
Baltimore Evening Sun
Florida Today (Melbourne, Fla.)
Jackson (Miss.) Clarion-Ledger

San Antonio Light
San Francisco Examiner
Tacoma (Wash.) News Tribune
The Tennessean (Nashville, Tenn.)
Washington Times

Top Ten Daily Sections Under 50,000 Circulation

Albuquerque (N.Mex.) Tribune
Anchorage (Alaska) Times
Boulder (Colo.) Daily Camera
Gaston Gazette (Gastonia, N.C.)
Jackson (Mich.) Citizen Patriot
La Crosse (Wis.) Tribune

Marin Independent Journal
    (San Rafael, Calif.)
The Olympian (Olympia, Wash.)
Poughkeepsie (N.Y.) Journal
York (Pa.) Daily Record

product. Most significant are efforts to attract female readers. Women's sports are covered more often, and more women cover sports, too. *Presstime* staff writer C. David Rambo (1989) writes:

> In general, many of the gruff, grubby, home team-loving Oscar Madisons have given way to skilled young journalists who are just as much at ease reading the legal briefs in the recently settled Pete Rose gambling case as they are in covering play-by-play action of the Cincinnati Reds. "Sportswriters now have to be labor writers. They have to be cop reporters. They have to be economic reporters," says Gregory E. Favre, executive editor of *The Sacramento Bee.*
>
> The new breed of critical, erudite writer is asking tough questions about players' drug abuse, about their drinking, their spousal abuse and their spoiled-kid tantrums. Sportswriters, some bearing specialized titles like sports business reporter, are showing up at county council meetings to report on negotiations for stadium leases. They are asking college administrators about underhanded athletic-recruitment activities.

Sportswriters are also becoming less and less event oriented and more and more non-event, or process, oriented in their reporting. It is not sufficient to report only the results of a game, as many beginning sportswriters may believe. The game off the field or court is as important as the one on the field.

For example, the civil court case covered by Scott Fowler demonstrates a non-traditional milieu in which sportswriters will be following athletes more and more frequently in this decade. Jeffrey W. Wohler, sports editor of the *Oregonian* in Portland, says he wants to "bring journalism into the sports department." He says he wants his sportswriters as comfortable in the court room as they are in the press box (Rambo 1989).

Sportswriters are finding new methods to report stories they have covered for generations. Christine Brennan's participatory reporting at a professional golf tournament is only one of many such efforts, which have become more and more functional in sports features and increasingly necessary in serious investigations as well in recent years. When unable to get a story through the usual channels or sources, reporters are turning toward less conventional methods of news gathering, such as participation. These stories give new perspectives to old assignments, such as covering golf tournaments, motorcycle races, or even professional football. The story can be told from the inside out.

More and more women and minority reporters are interested in sportswriting careers, displaying talent equal to that of their white male counterparts. Slowly, locker rooms and stadium press boxes, formerly fortresses barring females, are responding to change and accepting women as equals. Growth in women's organized sports began gradually in the 1970s and rapidly picked up at the high school and collegiate levels. New interest in women's professional and amateur sports has developed as well at most metropolitan and community newspapers. Such developments have spawned such groups as the relatively new Association for Women in Sports Media and the Sports Task Force of the National Association for Black Journalists.

Controversy has always followed sportswriters. Sportswriters such as Lisa Olson, Denise Tom, and Jordan Mendal attract it because they try to do their jobs as objective reporters, not as leering women in a men's locker room or as cheerleaders for the school team. Athletes have long retaliated against writers they did not like for one reason or another. Some refused to talk (Steve Carlton, Philadelphia Phillies), others took action such as sending live rats to writers (Dave Kingman, Oakland A's) or dumping ice water on them (Guillermo Hernandez, Detroit Tigers).

It is difficult for sportswriters to provide balanced and incisive coverage with television and radio overshadowing print reporters. There are many problems that are rooted in the fundamental relationships of sportswriters and their sources. Veteran *Lexington (Ky.) Herald-Leader* sports columnist John McGill (1991) believes this firmly:

> [Today we see print] reportage balanced against TV reportage that tends to be more PR than journalism. Most coaches still cling to the idea that writers are either for or against them, and judge their worth according to how they fall in line. In TV, they've virtually had their wish come true. This obviously creates more tension between coaches and writers. With TV sinking so much money into sports, a natural conflict of interest has mushroomed, yet often TV "reporters" try to pass themselves off as journalists—hence the "soft" interviews and symbiotic relationships between coaches and TV announcers.

Tough ethical questions face sports editors and writers. They sensed the possible influence of freebies—free football tickets, free banquet tickets, free transportation to and from games—on their staff's reporting and have adopted codes of ethics to avoid possible damage to the credibility of the sports section. Newspapers have adopted similar policies, using newspaper-wide codes or national codes of organizations such as the Associated Press Sports Editors ethical guidelines or the Society of Professional Journalists code of ethics. An ethics policy is more expensive for the publisher and may drain a department's budget, but it can help to bridge the credibility gap.

As sports departments continue to redefine their roles in the mid-1990s, we must ask, "Where is sports journalism going?" Expect more in-depth reporting, expanded women's sports coverage, greater neutrality in covering local teams, more study of sports as business, more analysis of the influences of television on organized sports, and more involvement by women and minorities as sportswriters.

Wick Temple, former Associated Press general sports editor, feels that another change in the role of the sports journalist will be more movement away from serving as a cheerleader for the home team. While there are still many athletes and many in athletics management who maintain the traditional view that teams must be supported by the local media, the news media are abandoning that position and creating awkwardness in reporter-source relations at times. Temple (1977) told an Associated Press Sports Editors convention: "Sportswriters were cheerleaders for so long that coaches and players have come to expect newspapers to be a source of scrapbook material for them and a litany by which hero worshipers can stoke the fires of the hot stove leagues. It is going to take another decade for sports reporters to gain acceptance as journalists and put an end to the conception that they are publicity men and women." The rules that sportswriters play by, Temple said at the beginning of the modern era of sports journalism, have been changing. Sportswriting, he says, is "a whole new ballgame.

Critics of these changes in sports journalism, some of them sportswriters themselves, feel the pendulum has swung too far and argue that sportswriters, in their attempts to become more objective and thus more critical, have become rude and disrespectful. Sports officials have often gone even further in their criticism, calling sportswriters vengeful and spiteful.

Competing news media have forced changes in sportswriting. Until the late 1920s, sportswriters for newspapers had no competition in transmitting basic information to sports fans. As radio covered sports more and more, sportswriters became conscious of its impact and realized they had to provide more than just a description or chronology of the events of a fight or baseball game to satisfy the consumer.

The major development affecting sportswriting was the introduction of television sports in the 1950s. As both national and local sports telecasting grew—particularly baseball and football—sportswriters were again forced to adapt. Their stories became more insightful and interpretative, the emphasis less on the results of competition and more on *why* these results occurred. Afternoon publications, which were at a disadvantage covering most events because they were forced to write stories that would be read 24 hours later, began using a magazine style—more depth, more feature material, more analysis.

Writers continued to provide newspaper readers with *who, what, when,* and *where,* as well as *how,* but in smaller proportions. Television already did this instantaneously—and with pictures. No writer, even with a short deadline and overnight distribution to readers, can outperform the electronic media in transmitting results. The reaction of sportswriters was to develop probing analyses of events and to make a transition toward non-event-oriented sports coverage. Although features continued to play an important role, investigative, thorough reporting, which does not usually fit a broadcast format, became a larger part of sportswriting. Opinion, traditionally offered to readers through columns, continued to be emphasized, and more space was devoted to such subjective reporting.

Further influence of the electronic media is reflected in the growing emphasis in newspapers and magazines on women's sports and participant sports in the last decade. Television, for example, pumped money into women's tournaments such as golf and tennis tours, and this attracted better players and greater fan interest. For example, for the first time ever, a national network televised regular season women's college basketball in early 1991. Newspapers were forced to devote more coverage to these areas and to attempt to cover them even better than the electronic media. Previously, newspapers allocated their few columns of space to "legitimate" sports—meaning professional and college team and individual sports, and selected high school sports. Participant sports were seldom the focus of steady coverage until editors began to see them as another means to attract and serve readers, to add a dimension to sports reporting that is not provided regularly, if at all, by broadcasters.

Sports journalists of the mid-1990s will be involved in more in-depth reporting in their communities, focusing on serious topics such as sports injuries, gambling, regulation, drug abuse, and salaries. These topics will no doubt receive lengthy treatment developed from both traditional and non-traditional information gathering approaches. Reporters will continue to use interviews and observation. But they will also use innovative means of informing the sports reader to give a dimension of coverage not usually available in electronic sports journalism. For example, sports reporters will use more and more in-depth reporting techniques such as public opinion measurement, field experiments, and systematic document analysis—all topics discussed in this book. They will venture more and more into once-forbidden investigative reporting without the backup of news side reporters. The improved skills of sports reporters today will permit them to take on more difficult subjects on their own.

Such changes have been made by thousands of sports editors and many more sports journalists in order to place sports in the role of a dominating influence in the nation, Temple (1977) argues. And, he writes, sports reporters themselves are changing:

> Many bright, young writers are turning to sports as an ideal area to portray people and trends. The quality of applicants for sports department jobs is increasing as well. And women are applying in growing numbers.
>
> The sports reporters [of the 1990s] may not be distinguishable from their counterparts on any other section of the newspaper. They may dress like the political reporter, speak with the grammar of the book reviewer, have the same outside interests as the managing editor.
>
> Sports journalism no longer will be populated by scruffy ill-educated men who stand in long lines for a free lunch, write only stories favorable to the

teams they are covering and generally act like adults with a 14-year-old view of the world.

Qualifications of Sports Journalists

What does it take to become a sports journalist in the 1990s? The skills are not much different from those of other journalists, and perhaps are even tougher. You must know the business. And you must know journalism.

In 1990, the American Society of Newspaper Editors released a report indicating the priorities of its executive editors, editors, and managing editors in entry-level hiring. ASNE said it loud and clear: Today's reporters, including sportswriters and other specialists, must have writing skills, especially spelling and grammar knowledge. Furthermore, ASNE says internships, or experience, and knowledge of ethics play important roles as well.

Responsibilities of Sports Journalists

What are the daily responsibilities of the sports journalist? Most sports sections divide responsibilities in one of two ways. The traditional sports department required its sportswriters to be both sports reporters and copy editors; in other words, their roles within the department included both reporting assignments and desk work. In a typical situation, a reporter has specific beats or specializations. Because these beats are seasonal, there are less demanding periods that permit time for longer range reporting and office work. This approach is still common among small newspapers. Another system is becoming more popular in metropolitan daily sports departments with larger staffs. The sports department staff member works full time either as a reporter or as a sports desk copy editor. This allows greater specialization within, and full-time attention to, beats, even during off-season periods. It also encourages greater expertise in copydesk work, such as improving story content and structure, writing headlines, and designing layouts. This organizational model fits most large newspaper structures and seems to be the direction of department organization in the 1990s.

But in most sports departments, the journalist still works in a combination role as reporter and copy editor. On a typical day, a sportswriter for a morning metropolitan newspaper might follow a schedule requiring afternoon interviews and an evening game, plus several other stories before and after the game, during an eight- to nine-hour day. The afternoon daily sports journalist might have a bit more deadline freedom with some events, but the hours are just as demanding.

A small daily newspaper sportswriter's typical night at work before a morning edition could be as follows:

4 P.M.   Check in with the sports desk. For the next three hours, complete various copydesk assignments, make telephone calls, read the newspaper, write news briefs on local items.

6:15 P.M.   Drive across town to a basketball game, which starts at 7:30 and ends by 9:30.

9:45 P.M.   Gather the postgame statistics and complete the locker room interviews.

10 P.M.   Return to the office to write the game story, with an 11:15 P.M. deadline.

11:15 P.M.   After the deadline, return to the local desk for various late copy editing and production duties if it is a busy night.

11:45 P.M.   After the edition closes, take a late break and return shortly for late wire duty until the shift ends at 1 A.M.

1 A.M.   The department closes for the night with the paper going to press.

Beat responsibilities, as for any journalist, do not begin and end with an event or a season. After the World Series is over, for instance, a baseball writer cannot take a long break. Trades, free agent drafts, winter owner meetings, retirements, awards, and countless other off-season activities continue. The writer must monitor the beat even if there is no competition schedule to follow.

When the St. Louis Cardinals' regular season ends and his playoffs assignments are completed in October, Rick Hummel, the veteran Major League Baseball beat writer for the *St. Louis Post-Dispatch,* must gear up immediately for the free agent draft. With off-season front office changes, trades, and other daily activity as well, Hummel has little time off from the beat. If he is fortunate, he can take his accumulated time off in December or January before preparing for the new season. As winter activities come to a close, February spring training gets under way, taking him to Florida and on the road again.

Similarly, a writer assigned to a college beat does not let up when a season ends. Nor does the writer covering tennis quit when snow falls. Much significant news develops in the off season. Sports coverage, like anything else, is a full-time, seven-days-a-week, all-year job.

Technological Advances

Over the last two decades, technology has made the work of sports journalists much easier, although the job itself is more demanding. At the end of the 1960s, sportswriters were using the same technology as generations before them. But in the 1970s and 1980s, microwave and microchip technology changed the way reporters get their work done in what must be called a *revolutionary* manner.

Until this time, information was transmitted by teletype and telephone, and stories were typed and retyped. Technology began to affect sportswriting in the early 1970s. Equipment was designed to transmit photocopies of a page of copy by telephone lines from one telephone unit to another, making dictation unnecessary and on-location coverage much more efficient. Called telecopiers then, these fax machines are now common and are almost as important to sportswriters as their personal computers.

Dedicated electronic editing and reporting systems featuring video display terminals (VDTs) appeared. These systems were elaborate word processors for typesetting. Newspapers also began to use portable VDTs to transmit stories — electronically transmitting the original keystroke of a reporter in a stadium press box, or some other distant location, over telephone lines. This is changing in the mid-1990s to a new generation of computer equipment based on the personal computer. The typical desktop personal computer, linked with others in networks through telephone lines, is becoming the workhorse of the newsroom. Reporters now use tiny, but powerful, laptop or notebook computers for out-of-the-office work — both at home and on the beat.

The personal computer has simplified much of the work of the sports reporter, who is always inundated with statistics. Sports as well as news organizations are using personal computers for such tasks as statistical analysis of team and individual performance and financial management. This has resulted in faster, more accurate, and much more thorough coverage. Sports recordkeeping, as well, has been and will continue to be improved by technological advances. More and more newspapers have begun to use the computer for information storage and retrieval, a significant trend that will enhance the work of the sportswriter. Computers have also led to a new specialization in sports information graphics for sports journalists. Writing is only one way to tell the story. In addition to photography, informational graphics also depict how events occurred and other news.

Advances in telecommunications are making the work of sports journalists easier. Fax machines and cordless, portable, and cellular telephones make it possible for sports reporters to file stories, conduct interviews, and contact sources with an ease and speed unknown to earlier generations.

Satellite telecommunications technology has made it easier for reporters to see what is going on in the sports *world*. Most newspaper sports departments have one or more television sets linked to cable systems or satellite dishes to enable editors and reporters tied to the desk to witness what is happening not only down the street but thousands of miles away as well.

Production technology has brought changes to the newspaper industry as a whole in the past decade. Offset printing, the final step in photocomposition technology, has led to improved deadline schedules for sports sections—traditionally among the last pages produced—that permit printing the most recent news. Offset printing has also led to much higher quality printing precision and wider use of color in photography and other graphics. Coverage areas have widened. The increased speed provided by these technological developments enables sports journalists to prepare copy later and faster and still make deadlines. As long as press room and circulation needs, and other pressures, do not affect deadlines, sports reporting can be in the hands of readers faster, and in a more up-to-date and complete form, than could have been imagined by previous generations.

Newspaper publishers have always been willing to produce special sports sections if advertising was available to support them. In the mid-1990s, more sports "tabs"—as they are called because they are often tabloid size—are being published (Rambo 1989). There have been traditional special sections introducing the football season and special sections for professional golf tournaments, outdoor activities, and out-of-the-ordinary events such as the World Series or Super Bowl. Publishers and sports editors in many communities, acting on the high readership of sports sections, have in recent years added another dimension to coverage by publishing regular sports weekend sections. These enhanced sections contain more special stories, photographs, and graphics because they often have more space. They are regularly prepared and edited most often for Fridays.

Some critics would argue that such expanded coverage was forced by competition with electronic media. Perhaps so, but the fan wins through the additional in-depth advances on major games and tournaments, features on key individuals involved, and recaps of previous action. Thorough data can be provided, with statistics (e.g., standings and averages) that are not offered in regular daily editions because of lack of space. Sports journalists have been affected because of the need for additional feature-type stories. Space has become available for profiles and for investigative stories—more like a sports magazine approach. The "magazine" format adopted by some newspapers allows longer stories to be published in one piece rather than in a series. The increased space means the desk is allowed more latitude in layout and design as well, presenting a better total package. During the mid-1990s, more metropolitan newspapers will use this weekend magazine format, while smaller newspapers will also try to increase space either on a regular basis or with more frequent special sections.

More game-oriented and investigative sports stories are finding their way to the front page of the newspaper also. It was once uncommon. Now, it seems like a weekly occurrence. But the stories are not always about a local team winning a big game. As *Los Angeles Times* media critic David Shaw (1989) says, these stories are often about the serious side of life, not just the fun and games we enjoy. Shaw notes stories about financial problems of athletic programs, gambling, racketeering, drugs, lawsuits, political defections by athletes, sex crimes, strikes, and more. "Almost every day, it seems," he writes, "there's a new and important sports story outside the white lines of the playing field" (p. 1).

And more sports stories are winning national recognition such as Pulitzer Prizes for reporting. That was once a very rare occasion. In the 1980s, for instance, two medium-sized daily newspapers won the major awards for investigative reporting on sports problems on college campuses in Georgia and Kentucky.

Increased specialization in sports journalism has led to a proliferation of writers' groups in the 1980s and 1990s. Groups are devoted to the specialized concerns that are unique to the sportswriting beats, or jobs, they represent, from baseball to harness racing. These groups continue to grow in number and size as writers discover the advantages of sharing concerns with other reporters who do the same job at different newspapers. The major sportswriters' groups and associations in journalism according to Bill Dwyre (1988) are auto racing, baseball, bowling, boxing, college basketball, college football, golf, harness racing, hockey, outdoor, pro basketball, pro football, tennis, track, turf, and women sportswriters.

Several national publications have built their successes partly or completely on sports reporting. In the early 1980s, *USA Today* won immediate acclaim for its scope and depth of sports reporting. It continues to have a significant influence on national sports reporting. And in 1990, a new nationally oriented sports daily, *The National,* debuted in hopes of meeting the informational needs of sports fans in major metropolitan markets. Although *The National* lived barely one year before it closed in 1991, both publications took advantage of available printing technologies based on satellite transmissions to different printing plants across the country to get next-day news distributed while it was current for readers.

Sports section production has become an increasingly specialized effort. Broad skills are often not as preferred as those that are specific and deep. Even at small publications, specialized skills are more appreciated than they once were, and sports departments are working more often with other news departments such as the city desk, graphics desk, or business desk.

Changes in sports journalism are coming fast, perhaps faster than in other departments of media organizations. Print journalists feel it and have reacted to it. More and more Americans are spending leisure time on spectator or participant sports; interest in sports sections will grow correspondingly. As new issues surface, new strategies are being developed to handle them, and tested strategies are being refined to meet new needs.

References

Brennan, Christine. 1990. There's more to caddying than just carrying the bag. *Miami Herald,* August 19, 1D, 8D.

Donaghy, Jim. 1990. Year–1990 overview. Associated Press sports wire, December 11, n.p.

Dwyre, Bill. 1988. "A new phrase: Writers' groups." *APSE Newsletter,* December, 3, 12.

Freeman, Henry. 1988. It's time to put to rest toy department image. *APSE Newsletter,* June, 3.

Garneau, George. 1988. Get serious about the sports pages. *Editor & Publisher* 121 (May 7): 16, 37.

Huenergard, Celeste. 1979. No more cheerleading on the sports pages. *Editor & Publisher* 112 (June 16): 11.

McGill, John. 1991. Correspondence with author, January 19.

Rambo, C. David. 1989. Sports coverage plays a more vital role. *presstime,* October, 20–28.

Salwen, Michael B., and Bruce Garrison. 1987. Sports and politics: *Los Angeles Times* coverage of the 1984 Summer Olympic Games. *Newspaper Research Journal 8 (2):* 43–51.

Shaw, David. 1989. Taking sports seriously: It's over the fence, onto page 1. *Los Angeles Times,* June 23, 1–4.

Temple, Wick. 1977. Sportswriting: A whole new ballgame. *Bulletin of the American Society of Newspaper Editors,* September, 3–6.

Wolper, Allan. 1988. Campus journalism: Student reporters and abusive athletes. *Editor & Publisher* 121 (January 23): 20, 40.

Development of Sports Journalism in America

The development of sports journalism has paralleled the growth of the role of sports in America. For the first 150 years, Americans did not devote much attention to sports. Most leisure activity was recreational rather than highly competitive. But as the 18th century ended, a fascinating, geometric growth of sports and sports journalism began; sports has become a new force in American society. Sports journalism historians divide this development from the revolutionary era to the present into six different eras: (1) the pioneer era, up to 1830; (2) the period of acceptance, 1830–1865; (3) the era of consolidation and growth, 1865–1920; (4) the golden age, 1920–1930; (5) the perspective period, 1930–1950; and (6) the transition years, 1950–1970.

The Pioneer Era: Up to 1830

Early colonial America was not an era for sports. "Life was hard and exacting; the price of existence was never ending toil and vigilance. Forests completely surrounded the little settlement. Current religious views looked askance at anything that savored of play or worldly pleasure. What little play there was concerned itself with the activities of survival such as hunting, fishing, barn raisings and cornhusking" (Scott 1951).

Colonists later engaged in many recreational and leisure activities, such as boating, horse racing, cockfighting, shooting, and swimming (Weaver 1939), but these were seldom discussed in newspapers, which were dominated by political reporting. Of course, many activities considered sport today—such as hunting and fishing—were necessities in that era.

By 1815 industrialization in the East resulted in a shift from outdoor to indoor work and an interest in spectator sports. This led to the publication in 1829 of the first sports journal in the United States, the *American Turf Register and Sporting Magazine,* which was devoted to horse racing (Walsh 1966). This publication lasted for 15 years. A second major sporting publication, *Spirit of the Times,* began in 1831 and continued until 1901 (Mott 1962). It was edited by William Trotter Porter, who had founded the *American Turf Register,* and was called "an oracle in the sporting world" (Betts 1974).

During this period some newspapers covered certain sports, even if only on an occasional basis, such as horse racing, boxing, and wrestling. Newspapers made a boxer named John C. Heenan (the Benecia Boy) the first real hero of the ring (Betts 1974). Even some British publications wrote about sports in America (Mott 1962).

As religious sanctions lessened, allowing recreational activity on Sundays, participation and interest in sports grew. Team sports began to appear in urban areas, and more space was devoted to sports journalism in daily and weekly newspapers.

Social sanctions continued against certain sports, for example, boxing. According to Robert Boyle (1963), for some time boxing did not receive the upperclass approval that it received in England. But once it did, it became one of the leading sports subjects covered in newspapers. Horse racing had always been a major sport. Although it was popular as early as 1700 and well advertised in newspapers, stories on races were rarely published in the 18th century or early 19th century. During the 19th century, despite some protests about gambling, which was more popular at the end of the 18th and beginning of the 19th century than in the mid-20th century (Heath and Gelfand 1957), horse racing flourished. This stimulated an interest in reporting race results.

Other sporting publications as well as *Spirit of the Times* were begun in the 1830s, signaling the beginning of a new era in sports journalism. Although many were short-lived financial failures, their popularity forced general newspapers to give more space to major sports events. The *Spirit* was so well regarded that it "achieved a national reputation and was relied upon by newspapers everywhere. More than a hundred . . . extracts from its account of the Boston Fashion race [were published]" (Betts 1974).

In *Spirit of the Times,* William Porter published the sports stories of Henry William Herbert, who wrote under the pen name of Frank Forester, and John Stuart Skinner, who introduced the first racing column, "The Sporting Folio." (For more on Skinner, see William 1976.)

The Period of Acceptance: 1830–1865

Henry William Herbert's tie with William Porter gave the writer, who founded *American Monthly Magazine* in 1833, an outlet for his series of articles, beginning in 1839, on horses and horse racing. For 50 years, Herbert (writing as Frank Forester) described the life of the outdoors sportsman. His contribution, Frank Forester's *Horse and Horsemanship of the United States and British Provinces of North America,* published in 1857, is still viewed as an important study of thoroughbred and standardbred horses. He also wrote books from the 1840s through the 1880s on hunting, fishing, and field sports.

The period 1830–1865 has been described as "extremely important in the evolution of sports writing":

> The penny papers of this period were searching for sensational stories. Sports news, especially coverage of horse racing, cricket and — toward the end of the period — prize fighting, was used more often than ever before. The first sports papers, born in the last years of the Pioneering Period, flourished, patterned after English sports books and periodicals.
>
> The widespread opposition to sports had been dissipated, and by the 1830s, town ball and rounders were widely played. The emphasis had shifted to spectator events although outdoor recreation had come to be recognized as essential. The next decade saw growth of gymnastic societies and gymnasiums. Baseball clubs began to organize in 1845 and by the end of the period, hundreds of clubs had sprung up. A milestone had been reached (Heath and Gelfand 1957).

As early as 1835, the New York daily newspapers began to cover prize fights, racing, and early track, especially the *New York Sun, New York Herald,* and *New York Transcript.* Henry Chadwick began writing sports for the *New York Times* and *New York Tribune* by offering to cover and write about cricket and baseball for free. It was 1859 before he was hired (by the *New York Herald*) to cover baseball regularly. Considering baseball an American form of cricket, Chadwick longed for it to be sophisticated and gentlemanly. But baseball was destined to become quite different, very much a young man's sport uniquely American in nature (Cozens and Stumpf 1953).

The rise of baseball has been called "the most important development of the mid-nineteenth century" (Boyle 1963). An outgrowth of rounders, an English children's game, it was the first team game of the young nation. While many people think Abner Doubleday, a resident of Cooperstown, N.Y., was the creator of the game, Boyle (1963) and Scott (1951), among others, doubt the facts. Their contention, and that of most baseball historians today, is that baseball evolved through a series of developments in the first quarter of the 19th century. Doubleday's efforts are traced only to 1839 in upstate New York, while Boyle notes that in the 1840s "professional men and merchants with sufficient time on their hands began meeting on a vacant Manhattan lot to play baseball, and in 1845 they formed a club called the Knickerbockers." The club developed rules by 1846 that were generally used by other clubs. By 1858 the National Association of Baseball Players was formed to govern competition, and by 1861 there were teams in the major cities in the East.

Boyle observes that as baseball moved west from city to city it became popular in the sports publications of the age. The first news story of a game was apparently published in William T. Porter's *Spirit of the Times* on July 9, 1853 (Egan 1985). Under the headline, "Base Ball at Hoboken," this short story was printed with a boxscore: "Friend P. The first friendly game of the season, between the Gotham and Knickerbocker Base Ball Clubs was played on the grounds of the latter on the 5th inst. The game was commenced on Friday the 1st, but owing to the storm had to be postponed, the Knickerbockers making nine aces to two of the Gotham, the following is the score for both days . . ." (Egan 1985).

By the 1850s, Porter called baseball a "national game" and began to publish rules as well as some of the first box scores. He published the first woodcut (precursor to the photoengraving) of a game in progress and covered and reported the first convention of baseball players, in 1858, where it was decided that a game should end after nine innings and not after a team scores 21 runs.

The Civil War slowed the development of baseball, but the sport came back strong after the conflict ended. During the war soldiers often played the game as a diversion — southern soldiers learned it from their northern counterparts while being held prisoner and later took it home with them.

Although it is unclear exactly when Americans first played football, the sport was popular by the mid-19th century. It had developed from other sports, such as rugby, throughout the first third of the 19th century. By 1840, it was played in interclass games by students at Yale, Brown, Trinity, Amherst, and Harvard (at least until 1860, when the faculties at Harvard and Yale banned it). By the mid-1860s some space was devoted to football reporting. Boston-area newspapers, for example, described results, which were usually delayed because weekend editions were not published until later in the century (Weaver 1939).

Most reporters writing on sports during the pre–Civil War period were specialized in other areas or were general assignment reporters from the news departments. The only real sports specialist of the time was the horse racing writer.

The Era of Consolidation and Growth: 1865–1920

Technological developments in the Reconstruction Era changed sports journalism forever. The telephone (invented in 1876), the telegraph (modified by Thomas A. Edison in the 1870s), and the wireless (invented in 1895) revolutionized communication between reporters in the field and their news desks. The Associated Press hired Marconi in 1899 to transmit the first news report over his invention, the wireless, about international yacht races (Mott 1962). The typewriter, perfected in Milwaukee in late 1869, was one of the most significant developments affecting the work of the reporter. In addition, the web printing press, which speeded up newspaper publication, was developed in 1865.

As these and other changes in technology enabled reporters to do their jobs better, the coverage continued to become broader and more sophisticated. Mott (1962) writes that sports news developed remarkably during the turn of the century. The first step separating sports news from the rest of the newspaper was taken in the 1870s, when Joseph Pulitzer organized the first sports department in his newly purchased *New York World.* Mott writes: "By the end of the period [1872–1892] virtually all the great papers in the leading cities had 'sporting editors' with trained staffs; and though the sports section as such had not appeared, the *Herald, World,* and *Sun* would sometimes each devote a page or more to sports."

During this era other sportswriters became famous. Joe Vila from the *New York Sun* is credited with developing play-by-play summaries for football games. Damon Runyon's popularity grew from his writing for the *Denver Post* and *New York American.* Mott (1962) also observes, "Emphasis on sports was characteristic of the yellow press, which developed for that department a slangy and facetious style. This exploitation did much to promote national interest in league baseball and in prize fighting."

High interest in horse racing continued after the Civil War. In fact, many sporting journals emphasized races even during the Civil War. Betts (1974) observes that two of the three main sporting magazines were primarily devoted to horse racing since the "center of horse racing passed from an impoverished South to the more prosperous North and Midwest." At least four other widely circulated horse magazines debuted in the period. *Forest and Stream,* founded in 1873, concentrated on hunting, fishing, and other field sports. Interest in athletics in general was growing; baseball, football, and other team sports were particularly popular with people of all ages and socioeconomic levels. Journalists began to publish stories on these topics, also. Henry Chadwick produced the *Ball Players' Chronicle,* which did not last long but gave a definite "life" to baseball (Betts 1974). Francis C. Richter developed the *Sporting Life* in Philadelphia, publishing correspondents nationwide on a wide variety of subjects and claiming to be the largest circulating sports and baseball magazine of the 1880s, with about 45,000 copies.

The only competition was from the early versions of *The Sporting News,* begun by Alfred and Charlie Spink in St. Louis (and still published there today, with baseball, as always, its bread and butter). When Charlie Spink died in 1914, son J. G. Taylor Spink took over and ran the publication until he died on the job in 1962. Son C. C. Johnson Spink ran the *News* until he sold it in 1977 to the Times Mirror Co., which had resources for a complete modernization (Maier 1984).

Heath and Gelfand (1957) call the period 1880–1890 the dividing point between the 19th century's leisure-gentlemen style of living and the 20th century, which they characterize as the "new days of action." This change was partly the result of continuing urbanization and industrialization, particularly in the Northeast and Midwest, where innovative sports journalism was concentrated. Furthermore, sports were becoming organized. Sports organizations for professional and amateur athletes were created, leagues organized, and administrative offices established to supervise rules and policies. New sports were introduced at all levels of society. "By the 1880s, professional baseball established itself on a more secure footing; prize fighting gained a new grip on the popular mind in the meteoric rise to nationwide fame of John L. Sullivan; tennis and polo had been added to the more genteel sports of high society; competitive games caught on in the colleges and the armories" (Betts 1974).

It was also an era when women began to write about sports. Nellie Bly (whose real name was Elizabeth Cochrane), a highly regarded reporter for the *New York World,* wrote about prize fighting on occasion, and the *New York Times* reporter "Middie" Morgan wrote about racing and livestock activities in the period just after the Civil War.

One of the major sports events of the era was the prize fight, especially those involving John L. Sullivan. Newspapers sent reporters all over the world to cover his bouts. The *New York Daily Tribune* sent famed writer Arthur Brisbane to Europe to cover Sullivan. "Newspapers in New York, Boston, and other cities along the Atlantic seaboard disregarded the staggering cable tolls in their anxiety to give the subscribers an exclusive eyewitness description" (Frank 1944). The story played most prominently in that era, however, was a Nevada fight between Corbett and Fitzsimmons in 1897 (Mott 1962). During this period sportswriting about boxing may have peaked in appeal and coverage.

Baseball continued to catch the imagination of the American public. In 1869, the Cincinnati Red Stockings became the first professional team. At this time, the United States was developing into a major industrial nation, and millions of European immigrants were arriving to work in these industries. Many immigrants used baseball and other spectator sports attendance as a means of gaining social acceptance in their new homeland. Spectator sports became the most popular weekend activity, especially during the summer. The new wave in society in the last quarter of the century, sports became a safety valve for society—a form of acceptable entertainment. (Boyle 1963).

Because of this demand, other clubs developed and toured. In 1871 the National Association of Professional Baseball Players was organized. The National League was formed in 1876, the American Association in 1881, and the American League in 1900. (See Weaver 1939 for discussion of the origins of baseball through 1930.)

Football matured during the late 1800s and was immediately taken up at colleges and universities. During this period Americans began to modify the game from English to American rules. The first college game was between Princeton and Rutgers in 1869; the Intercollegiate Football Association was formed in 1876. The Midwestern teams Michigan and Minnesota, as well as Ivy League teams, dominated the development of the game in the 1870s and 1880s. But it wasn't until 1887 that football began to be accepted by players and spectators outside of colleges and universities, when the American Football Association and the American Football Union were established. By then, most large cities had football clubs. The National Football League, however, was not formed until 1921 (Weaver 1939; see also McCallum and Pearson 1973).

Concern for the physical condition of adults (because the conveniences of modern living such as trains and automobiles had changed an active lifestyle) spurred the recreational movement. Public facilities such as gymnasiums and beaches were developed for indoor and outdoor activities. YMCA and YWCA facilities were designed to provide common places for physical activity (Scott 1951). Journalists paid attention to this trend, and to the new sports that appeared. One new indoor sport was basketball, which was developed by James Naismith in 1891 as a winter indoor sport for his physical education students. It took hold immediately, with rapid growth in facilities and equipment. It grew so fast that Naismith was forced to expand the rules only a year later (Weaver 1939).

The nature of sportswriting and the tools that sports journalists used in reporting were changing as well as sports themselves. William Randolph Hearst started what has been called the first sports section in a daily newspaper in 1895 as a means to increase circulation of his *New York Journal* (Shirley 1985). At the beginning of the 20th century, the modern summary lead became a fixture. Up to that point most writing was chronological; reporters did very little reorganizing of material (Heath and Gelfand 1957). Gradually, other parts of the nation began to catch up with the East and Midwest in the development of sports journalism. As Betts (1974) notes, development of sports journalism was slow in the Far West, because settlement and the pioneer atmosphere continued through 1900. But not long after 1900, major newspapers in Los Angeles, San Francisco, and Seattle had their own sports departments. In the Southeast, economic and social problems resulting from the Civil War hampered acceptance of the modern athletic movement. By the beginning of World War I, however, many major southern newspapers were quite active in their coverage of sports and devoted ever larger amounts of space to sports news. This became an era characterized as one in which sports "had a remarkable development. It came to be segregated on special pages, with special makeup, pictures, and news-writing style" (Mott 1962).

Boxing remained a major area of sports coverage, although interest in newer sports, such as baseball and basketball, rapidly escalated. One of the noteworthy events of this period was the 23rd-round knockout of black heavyweight champion Jack Johnson by Jess Willard, cowboy boxer and the "white hope." Other sports, however, were beginning to attract attention. Bowling spread quickly; the American Bowling Congress was organized in 1895. There was increased construction of public golf courses and tennis courts. And baseball, with its new American League, began the World Series in 1905.

Another factor contributing to the growth of spectator sports in the early 20th century was the growth in technology. Regarding the impact of technology on sports and sports journalism, Betts (1974) says:

> In the twentieth century the rapidity with which one invention followed another demonstrated the increasingly close relationship between technology and social change. No one can deny the significance of sportsmen, athletes, journalists, and pioneers in many organizations, and no one can disregard the multiple forces transforming the social scene. The technological revolution is not the sole determining factor in the rise of sport, but to ignore its influence would result only in a more or less superficial understanding of the history of one of the prominent social institutions in modern America.

The wireless telegraph, which the Associated Press (AP) used to cover sports as early as 1899, remained important, especially in sending scoring summaries and racing statistics from city to city. Toward the end of the era, the telegraph was available just about anywhere sports competition and sports journalists were found. In 1916, for the first time, a play-by-play story was transmitted by AP from the World Series stadium to all points on the system—quite an extraordinary feat for the age (Cozens and Stumpf 1953).

Among the writers making reputations for themselves in this era were Arthur Brisbane (*New York Sun*), Charles Dryden (*Philadelphia North American*), Ring Lardner (*Chicago Tribune,* among others), Jack London (*New York Herald*), H. R. H. Smith (*New York Times*), Irvin S. Cobb (*New York Times*), and John H. Reitinger (AP). (See Frank 1944 for an edited collection of the works of writers of this era.) Dryden, who is credited as the originator of the distinctive and imaginative baseball writing language of the early 20th century, covered the Philadelphia A's. A number of these writers moved on to other writing careers, including Brisbane, London, and Cobb. In this age of sports journalism, unfortunately, most writing was unsigned, so the writers' identities are now lost.

By the period 1900–1920 many of the sports journals and magazines created in the 20th century had either died or were being published under new titles and management. At the same time general circulation magazines were beginning to take an interest in sports life. By 1920 articles on sports and recreation were popular reading in publications such as *Atlantic, Century, Harper's,* and *Scribner's,* and in mass circulation magazines such as *Collier's, American, Munsey's, McClure's, Everybody's, Saturday Evening Post,* and various women's magazines (Cozens and Stumpf 1953).

The Golden Age: 1920–1930

During what most sports journalism historians have come to call the golden age of sports journalism, radio was one of several new forces influencing sports journalism. Radio station KDKA in Pittsburgh announced election results in November 1920; less than a year later, in the summer of 1921, it was providing listeners with baseball scores. Soon a system was developed by which someone in the press box telephoned play-by-play results to a radio station studio where the game would be announced as it happened. This system enabled broadcast of the 1921 World Series (Towers 1981). And so an aspect of American society previously the exclusive territory of the print media (and primarily the reason for the growth of one major area of the newspaper) began to be shared.

This was an age of highly paid sports columnists. As well known as the people they wrote about during this era of Babe Ruth, Ty Cobb, and Bobby Jones were Damon Runyon, Heywood Broun (father of sportswriter and television correspondent Heywood Hale Broun), Ring Lardner, Grantland Rice, and Paul Gallico, among others. The success of sports journalism imparted a certain romance to the era and those who were part of it. Well remembered, for example, is Grantland Rice's famous *New York Herald Tribune* story about the Notre Dame victory over Army, 13–7, in 1924. Flowery and liberal with words and images, it still captures the reader's imagination:

> Outlined against a blue-gray October sky, the Four Horsemen rode again. In dramatic lore they are known as Famine, Pestilence, Destruction, and Death. These are only aliases. Their real names are Stuhldreher, Miller, Crowley and Layden. They formed the crest of the South Bend cyclone before which another fighting Army football team was swept over the precipice at the Polo Grounds yesterday afternoon as 55,000 spectators peered down on the bewildering panorama spread on the green plain below.

A cyclone can't be snared. It may be surrounded, but somewhere it breaks through to keep on going. When the cyclone starts from South Bend, where the candle lights still gleam through the Indiana sycamores, those in the way must take to storm cellars at top speed. Yesterday the cyclone struck again, as Notre Dame beat Army, 13 to 7, with a set of backfield stars that ripped and crashed through a strong Army defense with more speed and power than the warring cadets could meet.

Marvelous Backfield

Notre Dame won its ninth game in twelve Army starts through the driving power of one of the greatest backfields that ever churned up the turf of any gridiron of any football age. Brilliant backfields may come and go, but in Stuhldreher, Miller, Crowley and Layden, covered by a fast and charging line, Notre Dame can take its place in front of the field.

Coach McEwan sent one of his finest teams into action . . . (Rice 1954).

As they did with Notre Dame's Four Horsemen, headlines made heroes of Jack Dempsey, the ring champion of the decade; Bobby Jones, who came to dominate golf; Red Grange, the star of college football in the Midwest; and baseball's New York Yankees, with a roster full of Hall of Fame players who were celebrities in the western world. The sports content of newspapers was increasing. In the early 1920s, one midwestern newspaper devoted about 16 percent of news space to sports, compared with only 4 percent in 1890 (Boyle 1963). A study of 10 metropolitan daily newspapers shows that sports coverage in 1910 averaged about seven columns per week in each newspaper; this total expanded to about 10 columns in 1920 and 18 columns in 1930. The percentages of total sports content jumped from 9 percent in 1910 to 15 percent in 1920 (but dropped to 13 percent by 1930) (Towers 1981). The city editor of the *New York Herald Tribune,* Stanley Walker, said sports was second only to general news and that the readership for sports may have been even greater than for news at his newspaper. It was a period during which the sports section — a toddler at the turn of the century — achieved adulthood (Towers 1981).

According to Towers, sportswriters of the 1920s eventually came to be divided into two camps. Some sportswriters, typified by Grantland Rice and Paul Gallico, made athletes and sports bigger than life — the "gee whiz!" school of sportswriting. These writers dominated writing in the 1920s, an era of good feelings and boom times. Rice, Towers wrote, "was a relatively innocent man in a relatively innocent era." On the other side of the coin were the cynical "aw nuts!" reporters who were critical of their beats. William O. McGeehan, one of the "aw nuts!" school, wrote for the same newspaper as Rice, the *New York Herald Tribune.* The style and approach modeled by McGeehan and Westbrook Pegler became the trend of the 1930s and for many sports journalists of the 1990s, as well. (For more discussion, see Woodward 1949.)

John Kieran, who covered sports for a quarter century, wrote for the *New York Times* from 1916 to 1922, then for the *Herald Tribune* and the *American,* before rejoining the *Times* in 1927. At this time he began the *Times'* first signed daily sports column, "Sports of the Times," which is still being published.

Paul Gallico wrote for the *New York Daily News* for over a decade, 1923–1936, before leaving sports journalism for other writing pursuits. With a series of sports titles and other types of books totaling 27 volumes, Gallico exemplified the high-caliber writer attracted by the challenges of golden age sports journalism who eventually went on to other forms of writing.

Ethics became an issue in sports journalism in the 1920s. Sportswriters were charged with being influenced by both financial and emotional pressures. Some low-paid sportswriters earned extra income doing publicity work for team owners and promoters. This created what we now would label a conflict of interest, but it did not concern many at the time although credibility was at an all-time low. Emotional pressures were a different sort of problem. Sportswriters in the 1920s had much personal contact with the players they covered, particularly those in professional sports. Writers and athletes traveled together and spent much time together outside of work, making objectivity difficult. It was often hard to distinguish the journalist from the team employee (Woodward 1949).

Betts (1974) calls the end of World War I the turning point for sports and sports journalism. Sports, he says, became "an integral part of the business world, affecting varied areas of our economic system." The pageantry of sport had taken over the imagination of the public. Events such as the Kentucky Derby, Indianapolis 500, World Series, Soap Box Derby, and original four football bowl games on New Year's Day meant that sports journalism had a ready market for its product. (For more information about the golden age of sports journalism, see Lipsyte 1975.)

Then the stock market crash on October 29, 1929, changed not only American society in general but the role of sports and the nature of sports journalism.

The Perspective Period: 1930–1950

The economic disasters of 1929 and the resulting financial depression affected sports journalism both psychologically and financially. The bubble had burst — an era of successes and excesses ended abruptly and a grimmer reality ensued. It was the "final assault on the luxuriant verbiage of the 1920s sports coverage" (Towers 1981). The illusions about professional sports were replaced by reality and objectivity as the Depression deepened in the early 1930s, and McGeehan- and Pegler-style skepticism began to dominate sportswriting. These psychological effects are difficult to measure, but the financial ones are not. The journalism growth of the 1920s leveled off during the Depression. Newspaper circulation stopped growing, and advertising revenue declined (because of the influence of radio, as well as the Depression). As a result, stories were shorter.

The sportswriting period of the 1930s and 1940s was labeled the "Age of Reason" by former *New York Post* sportswriter Stanley Frank (1944). Frank wrote:

> The extravagant, ebullient treatment that typified sports writing of the 1920s vanished abruptly before breadlines and bankruptcies and bank holidays that were the evidences of a social revolution in the 1930s. A sense of the fitness of things tempered the writing that appeared with increasing frequency on the sports pages.
>
> For the first time, the men who reported sport began to suggest that some of the heroes had feet, as well as heads, of clay. Restraint brought mature objectivity and critical examination of methods and motives. The boys no longer were naive and they were not given to supporting promotions merely for the sake of boosting the business. Their growing prestige gave them a feeling of responsibility and they commenced to expose rascals and denounce skullduggery.

This new era of reasoned thinking, of perspective, dominated all newspapers.

During this period emphasis shifted from college to professional sports. Coverage expanded from the traditional professional baseball, boxing, and horse racing to include other professional sports, such as professional football and basketball.

Major writers of the period prior to World War II and through the beginning of the Korean War included Westbrook Pegler (*New York World-Telegram*), Arthur Daley (*New York Times*), Shirley Povich (*Washington Post*), Bob Considine (International News Service), Red Smith (*Philadelphia Record* and *New York Times*), Stanley Woodward (*New York Herald Tribune*), Edward Burns (*Chicago Tribune*), Dave Egan (*Boston Daily Record*), and John Kieran (*New York Times*). Many of the giants of the 1920s continued to write in this era as well. Grantland Rice, for example, who died in 1954 at age 73, was still producing six columns a week for the North American Newspaper Alliance at the time of his death.

Red Smith, long-time columnist for the *New York Herald Tribune* and the *New York Times,* started his career in the 1920s at the *Milwaukee Sentinel* and wrote later for the *St. Louis Star.* He wound up writing in New York at the end of World War II. Smith went to the *New York Times* when the *Herald Tribune* folded in 1966. Smith rose to national fame while at the *Herald Tribune,* but he won the Pulitzer Prize while at the *Times.* His death in 1982 ended a career of more than 50 years.

This was an era of passage. Ring Lardner died in 1933 at age 48. (See Yardley 1977 for more on Lardner.) William O. McGeehan died in 1933 at age 54, and Heywood Broun in 1939 at age 51. Many famous writers moved from sports to other positions in the news business. Pegler, for example, switched to the editorial page in the 1930s. Others became sports executives, as many major newspapers in metropolitan areas began to create positions through expansion at the end of the 1930s. These individuals handled administrative duties almost exclusively and left day-to-day editing and column writing to others.

Another major development was the decision by AP to create a separate sports wire for sports news beginning on the opening day of baseball season, April 16, 1945. This wire has been a major influence on the sports section. To expand the scope of newspaper coverage, from the largest dailies to small ones in non-metropolitan markets, regional sports wires were developed in late 1947 (Heath and Gelfand 1957).

Modern sports magazines appeared in this era. *Sport* began in 1946, and *The Sporting News* continued to grow despite competition from new, specialized sports publications. With an increase in public and private facilities for participant and spectator sports, specialized publications entered the marketplace, giving sports journalists still more outlets for their work. *World Tennis* was introduced, as was *Golf Digest* and the *Daily Racing Form*. Baseball magazines, a product of the 19th century, were still popular. Boating magazines, such as *Yachting,* were developed. Football, growing in popularity as a professional sport as well as a college sport, was represented by *Football Annual.* Other general publications for sports enthusiasts that were introduced in the 1940s included *Sports Digest* (1944), *Sport* (1946), *Sports Graphic* (1946), *Sports Album* (1948), *Sports Leaders* (1948), *Sport Life* (1948), and *Sports World* (1949). And not much later, in 1954, Henry Luce formulated what has become today's major sports magazine, *Sports Illustrated.*

There were countless major sports stories during the 1930s and 1940s. The Baer-Carnera heavyweight fight was a big story in 1934, as were the Louis-Schmeling fights in 1936 and 1937. Notre Dame football coach Knute Rockne died in an air accident in 1931. One of the major stories of the 1940s was the integration of professional baseball, when Branch Rickey hired Jackie Robinson in 1945. Coverage of this event, characterized by William Kelley (1976), was significant because Robinson "had broken one of the stiffest color barriers ever seen in professional sports." Black publications reported it as a historical event. In contrast, metropolitan newspapers tended to play the story as another sports story, with normal reporting. Pat Washburn (1980), writing about Robinson's first season, observed that sportswriters at times downgraded black baseball players, but the majority worked toward integration of the major leagues. In fact many, such as Damon Runyon, championed this cause. After some difficult seasons, blacks were no longer rare in the major leagues, and writers and editors finally acknowledged the important role superb athletes such as Robinson could play in professional sports.

At the time these changes were appearing in professional sports, Americans were becoming more interested in participant sports. In the New Deal era, "the average employed worker gained added leisure time because of increased industrial efficiency, legislation, and union agitation. By the end of 1939, a worker had one more day of leisure time than was available in 1929 and two days more than people working in 1890. Federal public works programs had placed heavy stress on recreational facilities, spending almost one and a half billion dollars by 1938" (Boyle 1963). Boyle observes that in the late 1930s the Works Progress Administration (WPA) built thousands of athletic fields and tennis, horseshoe, and handball courts, and hundreds of swimming pools, ski trails, and golf courses. The federal government purchased great amounts of forested lands for outdoors sportsmen, and national park attendance increased. States followed the lead of the federal government, doing much of the same thing at the state or regional level.

Daily newspapers and general consumption magazines paid more and more attention to these activities. It was a gradual increase, but one that reflected the change in attitude toward sports. By the end of World War II, Americans wanted not only to participate in sports on weekends and vacations but to read about these sports, as well. And the movement was just beginning.

The Transition Years 1950–1970

In the 1950s and 1960s, newspaper and magazine sports journalism adjusted to sports on television. As with the adjustment to sports on radio in the 1920s, in the late 1940s and particularly in the early 1950s, sportswriters were forced into a transition period by television and other developments in broadcasting and film. While listeners to baseball games on radio were sometimes treated to theatrical productions (in the late 1940s the Liberty Broadcasting System of Gordon McLendon took wire service reports and telegraph summaries of games in progress and combined them with sound effects to do "live" shows), live television changed sports coverage remarkably. Boxing was one of the first sports to be televised regularly. Gillette, which sponsored radio broadcasts, moved into television production sponsorship from 1946 through the 1950s. Late-1940s television sports coverage focused on basketball and bowling in addition to boxing, and it also looked at baseball. Special events such as the World Series and golf tournaments were covered on television by 1950. (For a discussion of this period, see Sterling and Kittross 1990.)

Television enhanced baseball's popularity in the 1950s and 1960s. Professional football particularly benefited from national television exposure in the same period. Prize fighting continued to be popular in the 1950s, with its new exposure on television backed by print coverage. Film and television attention brought the Olympics increased audience popularity. The Olympic Reporting Association was formed in 1956 at Melbourne, Australia, from seven major world press associations to cover the events more efficiently. Because of the increasing numbers of reporters, editors, cameramen and technicians, and other media workers, pooling became the rule for these "super events."

The rapid growth of sports broadcasting forced sportswriters to react. New tools assisted them in doing their jobs better. Enhanced communication allowed writers to transmit stories to the newsroom much more quickly. Teletype systems had been adapted to permit stadium-to-newsroom communication. Teletypesetting (TTS) systems developed in the 1950s by the wire services enabled national and regional copy to be edited and set in type without additional retyping in the composing room.

Associated Press sports editor Darrell Christian says the arrival of television required sportswriting to change its old habits: "TV has forced us [AP], and newspapers as well, to go behind the scenes. It has forced us into doing more key play stories, personality within the game stories, star of the game stories, to come up with the tidbits that the reader wouldn't know from TV. It's forced us to put the game in a larger perspective than who won or who lost. That's very difficult to do on an AP deadline. But we do it, and we do it well" (Grimsley 1988).

By the 1960s, sports and sports journalism were coming into their own. Sports publication circulation, as well as attendance, increased in the 1950s and 1960s. And because of new broadcasting outlets, radio and television audience numbers grew with each new season. Even the reserved *New York Times* ran three sports stories on its front page one fall day in 1962, when it judged as major stories the America's Cup yacht race, the New York Yankees' clinching the American League pennant, and a fight between Sonny Liston and Floyd Patterson (Boyle 1963).

It was another era of transition, perhaps the most important one for sports journalism. The range of sports stories broadened considerably in the late 1960s. Nationwide, women's sports received more attention, and more women began to take an interest in sports journalism careers. Interest grew in sports topics off the field and court; reporters began to look into boardrooms, courtrooms, and training rooms. Yet there was still an appeal in reading about the game. Instead of replacing newspaper and magazine sports reporting, television enhanced it. People who attended a game or watched it on television wanted to read about it the next day. In-depth reporting became the salvation of sportswriting (see Harriss et al. 1981). In the 1950s and 1960s, a new breed of journalists emerged. As many reporters from the golden age passed from the scene, we began to see the likes of Jim Murray (*Los Angeles Times*), Dave Kindred (*The National* and *The Sporting News*), Frank Deford (*Sports Illustrated* and *The National*), Dave Anderson (*New York Times*), and Tom Boswell (*Washington Post*). Most of these best-known sportswriters today seem to be following traditions established a generation or more before them, argues writer Peter Andrews (1987).

Television also expanded sports coverage. In the 1950s and 1960s, sports sections grew in both allotted space and scope. Melvin Mencher (1991) describes trends toward more analysis, more interviews, and new areas of coverage such as business, women's sports, and international sports. Participant sports continued to grow, he writes, and growth in the coverage of these activities skyrocketed, resulting in the development of special sections devoted to participant sports features and columns in the late 1960s and the 1970s. There was movement toward more objective (some call it negative) sportswriting in the late 1960s. This drift away from cheerleading, what some critics call blind support of area teams, flourishes in many metropolitan areas today. And in suburban and rural areas an emphasis on local sports continues to be a priority despite developments in wire service coverage.

The Contemporary Sports Journalist

A new era of sportswriters developed in the 1970s and 1980s, setting the stage for this decade. W. O. McGeehan and Westbrook Pegler led to writers like Red Smith. Writers such as Damon Runyon generated writers of the caliber and style of Jimmy Cannon. Arthur Daleys came from the mold of the Grantland Rices. Styles of the 1980s and 1990s, are represented by Jim Murray, Blackie Sherrod (*Dallas Morning News*), Skip Bayless (*Dallas Times-Herald*), Dave Kindred, John Shulian (*Philadelphia Daily News*), Edwin Pope (*Miami Herald*), and Mark Whicker (*Orange County [Calif.] Register*). For more biographical information on many of the famous writers, see Holtzman (1974). The styles and names are different, but a great new era of writers has developed.

References

Andrews, Peter. 1987. The art of sportswriting. *Columbia Journalism Review.* 26 (1): 25–30.

Betts, John Rickards. 1974. *America's Sporting Heritage: 1850–1950.* Reading, Mass.: Addison-Wesley.

Boyle, Robert H. 1963. *Sport: Mirror of American Life.* Boston: Little Brown.

Cozens, Frederick W., and Florence Scovil Stumpf. 1953. *Sports in American Life.* Chicago: University of Chicago Press.

Egan, Betty. 1985. Baseball meets the press. *Media History Digest* 5 (2): 60–64.

Frank, Stanley, ed. 1944. *Sports Extra.* New York: A. S. Barnes.

Grimsley, Will. 1988. AP and the sports explosion. *AP World.* 3 (Fall): 3–8.

Harriss, Julian, Kelly Leiter, and Stanley Johnson. 1981. *The Complete Reporter.* 4th ed. New York: Macmillan.

Heath, Harry E., Jr., and Lou Gelfand. 1957. *How to Cover, Write, and Edit Sports.* Ames: Iowa State University Press.

Holtzman, Jerome. 1974. *No Cheering in the Press Box.* New York: Holt, Rinehart & Winston.

Kelley, William G. 1976. Jackie Robinson and the press. *Journalism Quarterly* 53 (1): 138–39.

Lipsyte, Robert. 1975. *Sportsworld: An American Dreamworld.* New York: Quadrangle.

Maier, Frank. 1984. In service of "the game." *Newsweek.* 103 (24): 13.

McCallum, John, and Charles H. Pearson. 1973. *College Football U.S.A.: 1869–1973.* New York: McGraw-Hill.

Mencher, Melvin. 1991. *News Reporting and Writing.* 5th ed. Dubuque, Iowa: Brown.

Mott, Frank Luther. 1962. *American Journalism: A History, 1690–1960.* New York: Macmillan.

Rice, Grantland. 1954. *The Tumult and the Shouting: My Life in Sport.* New York: A. S. Barnes.

Scott, Harry Alexander. 1951. *Competitive Sports in Schools and Colleges.* New York: Harper.

Shirley, Bill. 1985. The sports editor: Once regarded as a stogie-smoking bunch of rapscallions, the boys in the toy department have joined the real world. *Los Angeles Times,* July 7, p. 3, pt. 3.

Sterling, Christopher H., and John M. Kittross. 1990. *Stay Tuned: A Concise History of American Broadcasting.* 2nd ed. Belmont, Calif.: Wadsworth.

Towers, Wayne M. 1981. World Series coverage in New York City in the 1920's. *Journalism Monographs* 73 (August): 4–5.

Walsh, Edward John. 1966. The preparation of sports writers. Ph.D. dissertation, Columbia University, New York, N.Y.

Washburn, Pat. 1980. New York newspaper coverage of Jackie Robinson in his first major league season. Paper presented at annual convention of Association for Education in Journalism, Boston.

Weaver, Robert B. 1939. *Amusements and Sports in American Life.* Chicago: University of Chicago Press.

William, Jack. 1976. John Stuart Skinner and early American sport journalism, 1819–1835. Ph.D. dissertation, University of Maryland, College Park.

Woodward, Stanley. 1949. *Sports Page.* New York: Simon and Schuster.

Yardley, Jonathan. 1977. *Ring: A Biography of Ring Lardner.* New York: Random House.

2 Traditional Reporting Strategies

Sportswriters on assignments such as this women's marathon in Miami must use their observational skills to supplement results summaries. (*Photo by the* Miami Herald *photography staff.*)

3

Sources

"People ain't gonna give you nothing no way. You gotta go get it." When Muhammad Ali, then known as Cassius Clay, made that statement in 1964, he was not referring to reporters. But he might as well have been. The majority of what the sports journalist reports is gathered by go-getting it.

Sportswriters cannot work without sources. A sportswriter might know quite a bit first-hand about a subject, especially from personal observation, but he or she cannot do the job without sources. Sources are people or reference materials with information reporters need for a story or for background (Ward 1991). This definition takes into account the increasingly helpful non-human sources, such as newspaper clips or "electronic clips" from data bases from a library, as well as magazine articles and legal documents. Some authorities, in fact, divide journalistic sources into two categories, human and physical.

In this chapter, we divide sources into another two categories—traditional and non-traditional. Traditional sources are those contacted through beats or assignments. Non-traditional sources include information gathered from precision journalism techniques such as surveys and polls or content analysis, freedom of information (FOI) access, anonymous sources, minority groups, and dissidents.

Studies of Sources

Most of the literature on journalistic sources concludes that a reporter is only as good as the source. Therefore, it is important to cultivate and maintain sources (Spikol 1981).

Everette Dennis and Arnold Ismach (1981) summarize key steps in dealing with sources:

1. *Make yourself known.* Reporters on beats or those who deal with the same sources repeatedly should visit and chat even when they aren't seeking specific information. Familiarity breeds rapport.

2. *Be pleasant.* It should be obvious that cooperation will go to the cheerful person more often than to the brooding or sour individual.

3. *Be considerate.* Many newspaper deadlines come at inconvenient times early in the morning and late in the evening. If you want to call a source at an odd hour, first make sure that it is necessary. If it is, explain why to the source and apologize for the intrusion.

4. *Become a good listener.* It is better to let your sources do most of the talking, even in idle conversation, than to bore them with your own unsolicited observations.

5. *Don't ignore underlings.* Even though your most important source is the high-level official, lesser assistants can be of great use as sources.

6. *Be straightforward.* A spirit of cooperation with sources doesn't mean compromising ethical or professional standards. You expect sources to be truthful with you; they will expect the same of you. Deception, or even fudging, is a sure way to end the relationship.

Much of a reporter's time is spent looking for and cultivating sources. Mencher (1991) describes a county courthouse reporter who spends a couple of hours a day chatting with clerks, testing their knowledge and reliability, and just passing the time of day with these regular sources. He also chats with guards, secretaries, and elevator operators.

Keeping and protecting the source are two of a reporter's major concerns. Sometimes a source will give a reporter the story only after the reporter promises not to tell where the information came from, both being aware that the source may not cooperate in the future if the name appears. Much of what the reporter deals in is give-and-take with sources, in each case balancing the needs of the readers against the need to maintain a source.

Reliability of sources is essential. Editors do not tolerate incorrect stories, so reporters must make sure that a source is giving correct information. Reporters must always be aware that sources are not working directly for them, that their paychecks come from another direction. Sources always have interests they want to protect and programs and ideas they want to push. The reporter who has to rely on transient sources for information on a breaking news story will soon find out that these people are notoriously inaccurate. Mencher (1991) says that someone who describes seeing an airplane crash in a ball of fire may not be relaying an event experienced three hours earlier, but scenes from television shows and movies seen over

Tips on Developing Sports Sources

Sports Illustrated reporter Bruce Selcraig lists six tips to sports editors that enhance his relationships with sports story sources (Smith 1987):

● *Be grateful.* "Most sources don't like to be thought of as merely news whores."

● *The truth test.* Routinely test your sources to make sure they are telling the truth. Ask questions to which you know the answers.

● *Tape recordings.* Sources use them also. Be careful of what you say just as much as you think a source is watching his or her words. "Do not ever say you are 'out to get' anybody." It is also illegal in some states to tape without consent.

● *Produce stories.* Sources can find you only if they see your name, or byline, in the newspaper.

● *Check a source's background.* Qualify the source, in other words. Check out the source's credibility with other reporters who may have dealt with the source.

● *Use police sources.* But don't impress them with how much you know. Police should be used as pitchers, not catchers. They often break promises. "When you have something they want, trade on an item-for-item basis."

the years. Basic verification of facts is always desirable.

Non-human, or physical, sources must not be overlooked. These include clippings from the newspaper library; the city directory, which lists residents' addresses, names, and phone numbers; and government reports. Most libraries are free to the public; librarians often welcome visits or calls from reporters, finding their questions challenging. Of course, even physical sources can be wrong. Errors in previous stories should not be repeated, so important statements should be double-checked or verified, if possible.

Using a Wide Range of Sources

A reporter must use a wide range of sources on most stories to get the complete picture of what has occurred, or is occurring. A single perspective can present a warped or biased point of view. Take, for example, the prospect of watching a football game televised with only one camera. It would be dull and omit much of the action. The same applies to a sportswriter's use of sources.

When the *Los Angeles Times'* team of sportswriters — Elliott Almond, John Cherwa, Alan Drooz, Bill Dwyre, Maryann Hudson, and Danny Robbins — wrote a series of articles about the death of Loyola Marymount University basketball star Hank Gathers, the team interviewed more than 100 people connected to Gathers or LMU. When *Austin American-Statesman* sportswriters Kirk Bohls, Reggie Roberts, and Suzanne Halliburton wrote stories about gambling by University of Texas football players, between 70 and 80 players and former players had to be interviewed.

But those two stories were not limited to human sources. The *Times'* team reviewed court transcripts and other documents. The Austin sportswriters also used the state's open records act to find documentation.

Solid sports reporting is hard work. It means finding the best and the most appropriate expert sources. It means finding the highest qualified authorities. It also means locating and persuading eyewitnesses and participants to become sources. And, of course, it involves using sources properly.

The Problem of Access to Sources

The single most important reporting problem facing sportswriters in the mid-1990s is access. There seems to be growing attention to the problem, but no ready solutions have been offered. Concern surfaced several times in the 1980s with a variety of causes, most of them related to locker rooms.

But there are other types of access problems. Reporters are having problems accessing public records. With growing computerization of rec-

KEY SPORTS BEAT SOURCES

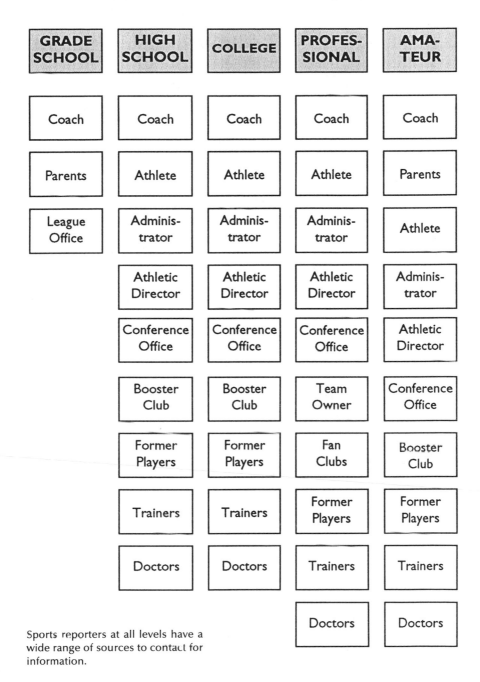

GRADE SCHOOL	HIGH SCHOOL	COLLEGE	PROFES- SIONAL	AMA- TEUR
Coach	Coach	Coach	Coach	Coach
Parents	Athlete	Athlete	Athlete	Parents
League Office	Adminis- trator	Adminis- trator	Adminis- trator	Athlete
	Athletic Director	Athletic Director	Athletic Director	Adminis- trator
	Conference Office	Conference Office	Conference Office	Athletic Director
	Booster Club	Booster Club	Team Owner	Conference Office
	Former Players	Former Players	Fan Clubs	Booster Club
	Trainers	Trainers	Former Players	Former Players
	Doctors	Doctors	Trainers	Trainers
			Doctors	Doctors

Sports reporters at all levels have a wide range of sources to contact for information.

ords, access becomes more complicated or impossible without a computer-literate clerk in the records office. Barriers to what were once easily reached athletes have been put up quietly. Today, more than ever before, sportswriters must contact athletes through formalized procedures such as sports information departments or press relations offices. Appointments must be made in advance. Preinterview screening occurs more often.

In short, the job is tougher than it used to be.

Gender is causing much of the attention and many of the access problems in recent years. Even though there are many more men than women sportswriters, men do not seem to experience gender-related access problems. Yet. As more women's professional sports leagues develop more public interest, the problem of locker room access to women's facilities will arise.

But in the mid-1990s, the concern remains on women's access to men's locker rooms. The recent case involving Lisa Olson, a sportswriter for the *Boston Herald,* and shortly afterward a second incident involving Denise Tom of *USA Today* pointed to the still-unreconciled problems involving privacy and the need for fast information on deadline following a game or tournament. While the harassment of Olson was well documented and the New England Patriot players involved were fined by the National Football League, and while the coach of the Cincinnati Bengals was fined for denying Tom access to the locker room after his team had played a game in Seattle, the problems of trying to report a story remain (for much more on this issue, see Lawrence 1990, United Press International 1990, Waterman 1990, Epstein 1990, Gordon 1989, and Bailey 1990).

Some athletic organizations have proposed or even instituted rules to settle the access problem. Most simply deny access to all reporters for a period of time or set up a separate interview facility. Some state legislatures have even debated proposed legislation assuring privacy to athletes but restricting the news media on deadline (Pieretti 1990).

Similar problems exist in solving computer access problems and intermediary barrier problems for sportswriters. These will take time to solve, until then, sportswriters needing information should anticipate problems on a case-by-case basis and try to remedy each situation ahead of time. Solutions will vary, but at least by expecting the problems, a sportswriter can likely get information needed through other means.

The Coach as a Source

In sportswriting, one thing is certain: The coach is the primary source of sports information on every level of team sports from grade school through college. On the professional level, the coach is still important, but the athlete is the main source. This difference occurs because the professional sports coach's influence (in terms of power over players, which is close to that of a dictator at beginning levels) is greatly diminished and the athlete is allowed more freedom, including the right to speak freely with the press.

Whether covering a specific beat or only doing occasional stories on a sports subject, the reporter must establish a working relationship with the coach because coaches not only can provide information on their own teams but other valuable information acquired through conferences and coaching organizations and their acquaintance with other coaches.

The coach is the primary contact because of his or her (1) knowledge of the subject, (2) position of responsibility, and (3) accessibility. A coach's knowledge is, of course, the most important. And a coach is usually responsible enough to answer questions with printable answers. Athletes, especially on the grade school or high school levels, have had little, if any, contact with members of the press. Their responses to questions may be inappropriate, unknowledgeable, or just plain wrong. Many reporters stay away altogether from interviewing grade school–aged athletes unless the athlete's parents are present to protect the reporter's reputation as well as the reputation of the young athlete. Even high school athletes are best interviewed with a parent or coach present to screen out statements that might later prove embarrassing to themselves or their teammates. This is not to say every athlete needs to be overly protected. For example, a high school senior basketball player who is being heavily recruited by colleges and has gone through many interviews may usually be interviewed without the help of an adult. But the high school sophomore who is experiencing his or her first interview after the first big game may need a coach or parent present to help handle the situation.

The accessibility of coaches also makes them the people most likely to handle questions. Coaches generally have office phones and hours when they can be reached. Student athletes, on the other hand, are usually unavailable because of class schedules and practice times.

Establishing and maintaining a working relationship with a coach is important, but it is not always easy. Coach Bobby Knight of Indiana University, for example, has an almost legendary inability to get along with the news media. During one basketball season, Knight even bypassed the traditional postgame interview session and instead handed out a mimeographed sheet of comments.

The reporter can take steps to establish and maintain a good relationship with a coach. First of all, early impressions are important. A reporter dealing with a coach for the first time should try to arrange for a meeting in person. A reporter who must phone instead must politely introduce himself or herself fully, ask if the coach has time to speak, and then explain what is wanted. Second, a reporter must learn about the coach and team before introductions. There is no poorer impression than that given by a reporter who has not gotten to know the subject by checking on the team's record or looking up the coach's background. If this is impossible, a reporter should apologetically explain that the information was unavailable and that the time spent answering questions is appreciated. Third, a reporter should be honest. If about to do a critical piece on a player or team, the reporter should let the coach know why the questions are being asked. This may result in a refusal to answer, but any information obtained by dishonesty will generally ruin chances of maintaining a decent relationship. Fourth, a reporter should keep in touch. Not every contact with a coach has to be story related. When covering a team or conference, a reporter should make a phone call or stop by occasionally during the off-season. When covering a conference, keep in touch with all the teams. One year's last-place team can be a contender the next year, and failing to maintain a relationship with a losing coach could prove disastrous in the future.

Remember that, while a reporter uses a coach to gain information, a coach concerned about a team's lackadaisical play may use the reporter, saying that the team is immature or lazy or even just plain inadequate. The coach knows that when the players read the resulting story they will get "psyched up." The reporter must be aware of being used and try to avoid stories that are only propaganda. In fact, no matter how hard a reporter works at a relationship with a coach, the reporter's aim and that of the coach are never, or seldom, the same. The reporter tries to present the facts as honestly and accurately as possible, while the coach's objective is to protect the team. Sometimes it is difficult to tell from a quotation whether the coach is winning; a losing coach will rarely come right out and say, "This team is terrible, they lack talent." Few, if any, coaches would hurt the team members by making this type of comment, so the reporter must provide the objectivity if there is indeed a lack of talent.

Most coaches, from amateur/grade school to big-time college professional levels, have one thing in common—they try to avoid the negative in dealings with the press. For example, a reporter for a major daily newspaper had a good working relationship with the coach of a local college soccer team. Both maintained frequent communication, and the coach would provide full information on game plans, scouting trips, and player progress. But on the day of a big match, the reporter opened the competing newspaper and found a story about how two of the team's top players had been suspended several days before. The reporter called the coach and asked why the fact wasn't mentioned in their several recent phone calls. The coach said that he would never volunteer such negative information, that it was up to the reporter to ask about it first. "I'm not going to hurt my team if I don't have to," the coach said.

The term "negative" has about as many different interpretations as there are coaches. Many coaches feel any fact is negative that isn't supportive or positive—the old "if you aren't for me, you're against me" attitude.

Kansas City Star sportswriter Ron Mott talks over starting lineups with O'Hara High School men's basketball coach Mark Nusbaum. (*Photo by Daniel Starling*, Kansas City Star.)

Other coaches are more understanding of the reporter's role, knowing the job is to report the facts, positive or negative. Coaches unhappy with "negative" articles have barred the offending reporter from covering the team or have refused to speak with the reporter. Indiana's coach Bobby Knight, critical of some articles by *Sports Illustrated* writer Curry Kirkpatrick, stopped a press conference after an important game and refused to answer further questions until Kirkpatrick left the room.

If the reporter is continually stressing the negative, the lines of communication may break down completely. Dave Begel of the *Milwaukee Journal* was once met with complete silence from Coach Bart Starr of the Green Bay Packers during a whole season after Begel had written several stories that Starr considered to be detrimental to the team. On a professional beat, it is still possible to cover a team even if the coach is not talking to the reporter. On a lower level, this may not be possible. The reporter must make the difficult ethical decision of what to report and what the long-term consequences will be.

The Athlete as a Source

Because athletes on different levels vary so much, it is impossible to generalize about them. Some obvious differences are age and education. Another is commitment. A professional athlete devotes many years to mastering a sport. The professional career is a period when the athlete makes the most money and gets the most attention. Because the time spent as a professional athlete is relatively short, athletes maximize their income by hiring agents to negotiate contracts, to establish and screen the media, and to help arrange speaking engagements and endorsements. Generally, a high school athlete has a different attitude toward participation in sports, thinking of it in many cases as nothing more than a hobby or means to become popular among peers. This changes somewhat as an athlete becomes a "college prospect."

Athletes on different levels, then, must be approached differently. But one rule pertains to all athlete sources: The reporter must be familiar with the subject in order to be respected by the source. Any athlete, no matter on what level, is likely to be a much better source of information if acquainted with the reporter. Reporters can facilitate this by being around the team as much as possible. If practices are open, they attend at least one a week. If the team has a media day, they go to it. If the school sponsors an awards celebration, they make reservations. Hopefully, the more the reporter's face is known, the more the athlete will feel comfortable and willing to provide useful information.

Credibility is also important to athletes, just as it is to coaches. When doing a story on an athlete, the reporter should explain what he or she is doing and why. Reporters should never mislead an athlete into contributing to a story that turns out to be a blistering attack on the team. Sometimes, of course, sticking to the intent of the story is not possible. In one case, a sports reporter decided to do a feature on a star player for the local major college basketball team. In the middle of the interview, the player became highly critical of some of the other players, saying they were the reason for the team's losing streak. When the reporter told his sports editor what the player said, he was told to print the critical comment immediately, not in a feature story but in a news story. When the player read the article the next day, he refused for several weeks to talk to the reporter, claiming he was betrayed.

Many coaches try to prevent reporters from gaining access to players, or they make access difficult. One of the most famous cases was that of Kareem Abdul-Jabbar. When he was attending UCLA and was known as Lew Alcindor in the 1960s, Alcindor was screened from reporters by his coach, John Wooden. High school coaches, too, have been known to screen their star players from the press to avoid the constant interference. This is especially the case with high school seniors who are being heavily recruited by colleges.

Many college coaches require all player interviews to be made through the school's sports information department. A sports information director (SID) handles arrangements for interview time, date, and place. To enforce the policy, players who do not follow the coach's rules may find themselves cut off from contact with the team. Although reporters are not legally bound by a coach's rules, it is generally easier for them to follow rules when simple feature stories with enough lead time are all that is concerned. But if there is a breaking news story (say, a teammate considering transferring to another school), going through the SID could cost valuable time, so a direct phone call to the athlete would be in order.

The press and athletes have common needs: Athletes need the press to keep the fans interested, and the press needs athletes to provide stories. Despite this, relations between athletes and the press have not always been smooth. Often, the frictions between the groups are merely personal. But in other more legendary cases, such as those of baseball players Mickey Mantle and Steve Carlton, an athlete's rancor toward certain reporters may spread to include most writers. Once, during spring training, Carlton even drew a black line around his locker area, forbidding reporters to step within. And recently, spring training has become a venue for athletes to take out their hostilities on reporters. Managers have lectured players about the media, saying the relations are simply "us versus them" and the news media are "them" (Fitzgerald 1989).

No matter how important the coach is as a source of information, readers want to know more about the athlete than about the coach. And the athlete usually provides the best material for interesting stories. Athletes come in all sizes and shapes, with differing backgrounds and dreams. Reporters must not rely exclusively on handouts or profiles provided by SIDs; they should get to know the athlete. What kind of family did the athlete come from? Did the athlete have to overcome any handicaps? Did the athlete have a pushy parent, an understanding one, or even an uninterested or negative one? Was the athlete a slow developer or a "natural"? Was the athlete highly recruited out of high school or overlooked? Did the athlete play many sports while young? Questions like these can lead to interesting angles for stories.

Although performance statistics are important tools for the sports journalist, it is the people involved who are interesting to readers. This is especially true in the less familiar sports, like field hockey and wrestling, where much of the story may end up as background. The reporter should focus at first on the person taking part in the sport, then add bits of information about the sport itself.

Other Useful Sources

Parents of young athletes sometimes prove to be better sources of information than coaches. A major college football or basketball coach, who may not have had much to do with the recruiting of the athlete (usually done by an assistant), often knows little about the athlete's personal background. On the high school and grade school levels, parents can be invaluable in verbalizing what their sons and daughters want out of sports (or what the parents want for them). Information from parents is also important for reporters to learn about athletes on the amateur level, where organized publicity usually isn't available. A speed skater competing in an out-of-state meet will generally phone his or her parents first with the results; in turn, the parents handle the media. For a background feature on a professional athlete, parents again should not be overlooked. Parents may provide valuable insights that the athletes themselves might not be able to offer.

As organizations become more media conscious, reporters find themselves dealing more and more with publicists or agents. Most colleges, even small ones, have someone serving as SID. All professional teams have publicity departments. Even amateur groups have found that one of the first permanent positions they need is that of publicist. In many cases, the publicist can be a valuable source of information. Generally, the publicist has an idea of what a reporter is looking for. And because many publicists travel with their teams, they become familiar with team members and story possibilities.

As in dealing with any type of public relations person, reporters must keep certain cautions in mind when dealing with sports publicists. Reporters must remember that, no matter what, publicists draw their paychecks from the sports organizations, and that may preclude them from freely providing negative facts. One reporter has found a way of getting around this problem by telling the publicist that journalists must know the bad with the good or the organization will not be fully trusted, and thus not fully covered.

Camaraderie among reporters and sister news organizations in news media groups can also become a source of information. When the Gannett Company's *Louisville Courier-Journal* conducted a recent investigation into the poor academic record of athletes in the University of Louisville basketball and football programs, it was helped by another Gannett newspaper hundreds of miles away for hard-to-get information for the series. For grade averages, admission test scores, and graduation rates for Metro Conference schools Memphis State, South Carolina, and Florida State, and for Southeastern Conference school Alabama, reporter Pat Forde called a reporter in Jackson, Mississippi, at the *Clarion-Ledger,* for help.

Exchange subscriptions to other newspapers and magazines can lead to possible story ideas. There is nothing better than the insight provided by a reporter actually covering a team. Newspapers covering the Big Ten Conference in football and basketball, for example, generally subscribe to the newspapers in the other Big Ten cities. Many newspapers exchange subscriptions at no cost for a period of time. Reporters can check such a plan through their managing editors or circulation departments. Sports magazines are also an important information source. A reporter covering a major college basketball team has a choice of weeklies such as *Sports Illustrated* and *The Sporting News,* national dailies such as *USA Today,* and annuals such as *Street and Smith Basketball Guide.* There are as many, if not more, publications for college football. Also, a reporter for a newspaper serviced by one of the wire organizations should be sure to let those responsible for handling copy know that he or she is interested in seeing anything on the beat.

Record books are also of great value, of course. Of varying quality, quantity, and frequency, they are available at almost all levels. Subsequent chapters of this book deal in depth with non-traditional story sources, such as surveys and polls. Freedom of information (FOI) rulings are playing a bigger part in sports reporting also, especially as economic and governmental factors, such as Title IX, take a larger role in shaping the future athletic plan for the United States. There are no limitations on who can file FOI requests (and in many instances, these requests are free of charge), allowing an individual reporter to make them.

The word "source" took on added meaning in the early 1970s, when "Deep Throat" of the Watergate investigation became famous. An unnamed source conjured up thoughts of clandestine meetings and secret code names. For a sportswriter, too, it is beneficial to have an "in" to a sports team, someone who can feed information without the coach or administration knowing. Usually, these sources are developed on the college and professional levels, where loyalty to the school, team, coach, and management is less critical. Often, these sources are developed by familiarity, with a reporter gaining a casual acquaintance with, for example, an athlete on a team and then establishing credibility to the point at which the athlete trusts the reporter enough to provide information. This information is usually not the scandalous Watergate type, but only an explanation of why a certain star player is not being fully utilized or why a certain substitute is not playing much.

The "dissident source" — a term coined for sources for political and racial issues — can be applied to sports reporting. Teams with many members, such as football, baseball, and soccer, will always include a few individuals disgruntled with their playing time or with the direction of the program; these players are naturals to cultivate as sources. Losing also has an effect on what players will say; often, a player who disagrees with the coaching may be willing to provide inside information. Many of the current recruiting violation stories have come from disgruntled players who were promised more playing time than they got or found the coach not to their liking. Assistant coaches in large programs have also been known to provide information to reporters. A reporter should remember that such a source of information has a reason for giving it, so the information divulged must always be carefully checked before being printed.

The two stories at the end of this chapter demonstrate excellent use of sources. The first story, by reporters Bob Young and Kent Somers from the *Arizona Republic* in Phoenix, shows how a variety of sources will be necessary for some stories. Their 68–column inch story, which included a chronology not included here, is part of a series of articles reporting an investigation into alleged violations of an Arizona conflict-of-interest law. The violations were made by the athletic director and an assistant athletic director at Northern Arizona University. This story is strong from several perspectives, including the significance of the subject matter. But it is also strong because of the variety of authoritative human sources interviewed and the public documents used.

Michelle Kaufman, a reporter and columnist for the *Detroit Free Press,* wrote a unique feature about Detroit-area professional athletes who are minority group members and their past and present encounters with racism in their community. The story was published on Martin Luther King Jr.'s birthday and carried a message of hope for the future held by the athletes despite the past experiences described in the story. The story opens with basketball star Isiah Thomas but covers a variety of personalities and sports through a series of vignettes based on Kaufman's interviews with the candid athletes.

SOURCE: The *Arizona Republic,* Phoenix, final chaser edition, page D1
DATE: Sunday, August 12, 1990
AUTHORS: Kent Somers and Bob Young; contributing to this article was John Doherty
HEADLINE: NAU officials' ties to agency may have broken state laws

Tom Jurich, athletic director at Northern Arizona University, and Rick Smith, an assistant AD, apparently violated state conflict-of-interest laws by using a travel agency they owned for athletic department business.

Jurich and Smith were part of an investment group that bought the Grand Canyon Travel Agency in Flagstaff in January 1986. After consulting with members of NAU's administration, Jurich said he divested himself of his interest in the business by June 1987. Smith remains a co-owner of the agency.

According to travel records obtained by *The Arizona Republic,* the NAU athletic department booked more than $155,000 in trips through the agency from 1986 through 1990, including a high of 55 percent of the trips booked in 1987-88 at a cost of about $87,000.

Travel agents usually earn at least a 10 percent commission, which translates into a profit of $15,500 from the NAU athletic department account.

Because NAU is a state university, its employees are subject to rules governing state employees.

State law requires state employees who have a substantial interest in a business to remove themselves from any decisions that involve the business and the state agency.

The law also requires any state employee who has a substantial interest in a business enterprise to sign a form disclosing the conflict. The form is to be placed in a public file.

In the summer of 1986, both Jurich and Smith made at least one business trip using their own travel agency, records show.

Additional conflicting questions arose during 1987-88 when Smith, who was recruiting coordinator in football from the fall of 1986 until he was named assistant athletic director in February 1989, used Grand Canyon Travel almost exclusively to book travel for recruits to visit NAU's campus, and for some coaches to visit or evaluate recruits.

During the past two years, the athletic department has booked 75 trips through Grand Canyon Travel at a cost of about $42,000.

"If there are facts indicating a potential violation of the criminal conflict-of-interest code, we would definitely be willing to review the case to determine if action should be taken," said Michael Cudahy, an assistant Arizona attorney general.

The penalty upon conviction would include forfeiting public employment. Someone who "intentionally or knowingly" violates the conflict-of-interest laws can be charged with a Class 6 felony. That carries a maximum sentence of 1.875 years in prison and a $150,000 fine.

Anyone who "recklessly or negligently" violates the conflict laws can be charged with a Class 1 misdemeanor. Conviction could mean a maximum of six months in jail and a $1,000 fine.

David Markee, the university vice president for student services who oversees the athletic department, admitted there was a conflict of interest when Smith was recruiting coordinator and was booking travel through Grand Canyon in 1987-88. But Markee said that situation was corrected, and that Jurich took proper steps to avoid potential conflict of interest on his part.

Smith's involvement in Grand Canyon Travel began in 1979 when he became a salesman for the agency, which was then owned by the Babbitt Brothers Trading Company.

In late 1985, an investment group called Black Rhino, of which Jurich and Smith were partners, agreed to buy the agency from the Babbitts and finalized the purchase in January 1988.

A Perception Problem

Although records show Jurich was assistant director of athletics drawing a salary of $30,000 when he and Smith purchased an interest in Grand Canyon Travel, Jurich says otherwise.

"I was not an athletic department official," he said. "I was a special assistant to (athletic director) Gary Walker, just working mainly with the booster club."

Jurich said there was no potential conflict of interest until he was selected co-athletic director along with Dave Brown in September 1986.

"Then once my roles changed, I began to see that it possibly could be a problem," he said. "I see it as more of a perception problem. I'm really sad I'm not in it anymore.

"I think it's a good business. I'd like to be in it someday, obviously not in the capacity I'm in now. But I felt it would not be a conflict because I would not let it get to be one."

Jurich originally told *The Republic* he decided in February 1987 to sell his share of the agency.

Asked why it took him five months after being selected co-athletic director to decide there was a conflict of interest, Jurich said, "It took us from September to January to find a buyer. There weren't a whole lot of buyers for a business that was losing money. It was a break-even proposition at best."

Although Jurich and Smith deny doing so, both were in positions to influence department employees to use the agency.

As co-athletic director, Jurich oversaw the football program while Smith was using the agency extensively. But Jurich and Smith said they never encouraged the use of Grand Canyon Travel.

"I can answer your question real simple," Jurich said. "Nobody (in the athletic department) has ever been pressured to use any travel agency in this town. They have free will to go wherever they want."

Files Raise Questions

According to state law, Jurich and Smith were required to sign forms disclosing their interest in Grand Canyon Travel upon purchasing the agency.

The Republic asked to examine the contents of the disclosure file, and after review by NAU's legal department, the file was turned over.

But unlike the rest of the disclosures, which were originals, Jurich's was a photocopy. He said he had signed the disclosure in March 1986, but unlike the majority of disclosures, there was no stamp of receipt by the university vice president's office.

Jane Manning, a spokesperson for the university, said Jurich's disclosure form had been placed in his personnel file. Only after *The Republic* filed a request citing Arizona public records laws did the university turn over portions of personnel files.

According to Manning, NAU's legal department made a photocopy of Jurich's disclosure form and placed it in the disclosure file before releasing it to *The Republic*. Jurich said he didn't know why his form wasn't in the proper file, because he signed it in the vice president's office.

There was no form on file for Smith, apparently a violation of the conflict-of-interest law. At the request of NAU attorney Steve Smith, Rick Smith signed a disclosure form on July 19, 1990, the same day reporters from *The Republic* viewed the file's contents.

"I thought I did sign one (earlier). I don't know what happened to it," Rick Smith said.

Markee said the files were not centralized and the disclosure procedure was flawed.

"No one asked for that (disclosure) file in the 10 years I've been at this university," Markee said. "So, if you're talking about the administration being ineffective in making sure it was in the right file, that's true."

A Big Jump in Business

During the 1986-87 fiscal year, the athletic department booked only four trips through Grand Canyon for a total of about $4,300. But the following year, the department booked 153 trips, running up the $87,000 tab.

That was nearly a year after Brown voiced his concern to the NAU administration about a potential conflict of interest involving Jurich, Smith and the travel agency in '86.

"He (Jurich) had to make a choice and he chose," Brown said. "Rick was a coach at that time and there was some discussion about that. Rick really had more dealings with it (the agency) than Tom. I did show concerns, and I voiced those concerns."

In 1988, department business manager Dug Tryon sent a memo to NAU's football staff telling it to discontinue booking travel through Grand Canyon Travel. But other coaches and administrators were free to use the agency.

Smith, who now is in charge of fund raising for the athletic department, continues as co-owner of the agency along with Dick Clark, a Flagstaff businessman and former president of NAU's booster club.

"In retrospect, there probably could have been (a conflict)," Smith said. "I had just become the recruiting coordinator and I went to (coach) Larry (Kentera) and said, 'Larry, there are some real logistical problems right now. I need to get tickets changed Saturdays and Sundays, I need to get the best deals and be sure of that because of the budget. Is it OK to go ahead and use Grand Canyon Travel?'

"The conflict, I thought, was if I used Grand Canyon Travel, which I never did for any of my business trips. There might have been one time I used it . . . I need to check on that."

Markee said Smith and Jurich never attempted to influence athletic department employees to use their travel agency.

"Is there a pattern of that?" Markee asked. "We did not (see a pattern) except that one error (1987-88), which we corrected . . . . We saw where a recruitment specialist, OK, was in error. And he was advised by his head coach (Kentera) to go ahead and use that (agency)."

Kentera tells a different story.

"I told him (Smith) to find out (from Jurich)," Kentera said. "I didn't care where he did his travel, but I didn't tell him specifically to use Grand Canyon. He said he checked on it and there was no policy against it."

Smith denies that he tried to influence any coaches to use his travel agency.

"Absolutely not," Smith said.

Coaches Lobbied

However, two former assistant football coaches said Smith often mentioned using the agency during staff meetings.

"He mentioned it in passing," said former NAU assistant Brad Childress, now an assistant coach at Utah. "He didn't want to be serious about it, but it was taken that way."

Another former coach, who requested anonymity, said Smith lobbied coaches to use Grand Canyon as early as 1985, when Smith still was a sales agent for the agency.

"I felt there was a conflict of interest and I didn't want to set myself up for problems," the former coach said. "I just felt like I wasn't going to be intimidated by anyone to do anything I didn't feel good about."

Several former NAU athletic department officials and coaches said there was subtle pressure because it had become apparent at the time that the use of co-athletic directors was not working out. Some department employees began aligning themselves behind either Brown or Jurich, who were involved in a power struggle for the job.

Smith said he doesn't believe there is a conflict of interest now, even though he continues as an owner of the agency and as an athletic department employee, because he makes no decisions about travel.

Markee and Jurich were asked what guarantees that Grand Canyon Travel is booking trips at the lowest possible fares.

Markee said it was in coaches' best interests to make sure they were getting the best value.

"If you were running an academic department and had a $4,000 budget, would you buy the highest priced tickets and have only half of your faculty travel?" Markee said. "It would be foolish. There's nothing to personally gain from it and everything to lose."

However, according to Flagstaff travel agents, the NAU athletic department account is lucrative, ranking among the top five accounts in the area.

Shortly after the Black Rhino group obtained Grand Canyon Travel, NAU's student union solicited bids for an on-campus travel agency, which was awarded to Grand Canyon.

Sam Wheeler, director of the campus union and student activities at NAU, said he was not informed that Jurich and Smith were involved in the ownership at the time the bid was awarded.

Wheeler said Grand Canyon was granted the on-campus agency because its bid was "head and shoulders" above others received.

After the on-campus agency was granted, the partnership that owned Grand Canyon Travel broke up. Clark and Smith took the off-campus locations and a third partner, Mike Howell, took the on-campus agency and renamed it Campus Travel Connection.

SOURCE: The *Detroit Free Press,* Metro final edition, page 1C
DATE: Monday, January 21, 1991
AUTHOR: Michelle Kaufman, *Free Press* sportswriter
HEADLINE: Athletes tell of racism, hopes for future

Isiah Thomas disguised himself as an ordinary black man last month, stuffed a thick wad of cash in his wallet, and headed out to mingle with the holiday shopping crowds.

The disguise, which sometimes includes fake facial hair, is a Christmas ritual. It allows Thomas to shop in peace, a luxury he treasures. Costumes also permit him to return—at least briefly—to a world he once knew. A world of bigotry.

On this day, when our nation commemorates the birth of Dr. Martin Luther King Jr., Thomas and other Detroit athletes share their reflections on racism, black pride and King.

"I wasn't treated like I'm normally treated," is the way Thomas described his shopping spree. "I was treated like I was before I became popular, before I had celebrity status. I wasn't wearing nice clothes, so when I went to pay for expensive gifts with cash, I got a lot of looks. When I walked into certain stores, people looked at me like, 'What are you doing here? If you're not going to buy, leave.' That's the real world. The world Isiah lives in isn't real."

Thomas doesn't face blatant prejudice when he's out of costume, but it doesn't surprise him that racial bias still exists.

"Our world and decision makers are still people from the '50s and

'60s," he said. "Just because blacks are allowed to vote and participate in the political process doesn't mean everything is fair and equal. We've seen changes, but we won't really reap the benefits of what Martin Luther King fought for until these decision makers have passed on. You can't tell me that a person who lived one way 40 years all of a sudden changes because some laws are passed."

> *"Being a Negro in America is not a comfortable existence. It means trying to smile when you want to cry. It means trying to hold on to physical life amid psychological death. It means the pain of watching your children grow up with clouds of inferiority in their mental skies."*
>
> —MARTIN LUTHER KING JR.

Nothing irritates Jerry Ball more than glancing in the rearview mirror of his black Mercedes-Benz and seeing flashing lights. Three times in the last year, the Lions' nose guard was pulled over for no apparent reason.

"I purposely don't have my windows tinted, and I don't wear any gaudy gold, but they still pull me over," Ball said. "A young black male can't have any fancy success without people being suspicious. It really p----s me off and I don't tolerate it. Every time, I told the policeman he shouldn't pass stereotypes, and they apologized."

Like Thomas, Ball sees racial discrimination at shops.

"I'll walk into an expensive store and the salespeople are just sitting there twiddling their thumbs," he said. "They just figure I'm some big, black guy who won't buy anything. Then I pick something off the rack and they start staring. Once I pull out my gold credit card, they realize I must not be a drug dealer or a shoplifter."

Ball also faces what he calls "sophisticated" prejudice in the business world.

Last year, Ball inquired about 10 acres of land in Beaumont, Texas, his hometown. He wanted to build a community center for neighborhood children. Researching prices as he always does, Ball learned that the land should cost no more than $2,000 per acre. The realtor found out an NFL player wanted the land and set the price at $15,000 an acre.

"Some people assume we're just dumb, black jocks and try to rip us off," he said. "I won't allow that to happen."

> *"In a multiracial society, no group can make it alone."*
>
> —MARTIN LUTHER KING JR.

One of Desmond Howard's favorite films is Spike Lee's "Do the Right Thing." Howard especially appreciated the scene where an Italian young man tells a black young man that Eddie Murphy and Michael Jackson are somehow different from other blacks.

"The same thing happens with athletes," said Howard, a wide receiver at Michigan. "As an athlete develops and gets more popular, people think he gets less black. It's like we turn gray. People around campus treat me nice, but if I wasn't a football player, I'm not sure it would be the same. I talk to non-athletes who are black, and they face things I don't."

Howard never thought much about race until his senior year in high school, when he read the lyrics of "Rightstarter," a rap song by the group Public Enemy. The words deal with black pride.

"I kind of woke up and started doing more reading on black history," Howard said. "My hero had always been Tony Dorsett, but I realized that there are 10,000 Tony Dorsetts out there and that I should look for inspiration from someone like Martin Luther King. He is a true hero. All they taught us in school is that he was a civil rights leader, led the bus boycott and went to jail. But there's so much more to the man."

Howard was disturbed when he got to Jacksonville for the Gator Bowl and realized that University of Mississippi fans wave rebel flags.

"My conscience wouldn't let me play under a Confederate flag," he said. "I'm sure these athletes were recruited by other schools, and they must know what the rebel flag stands for, so how could they go there? It would be like a Jewish student playing under a swastika. No way I could do it. I'm too proud."

> *"I have a dream that one day this nation will rise up and live out the true meaning of its creed: 'We hold these truths to be self-evident; that all men are created equal.'"*
>
> —MARTIN LUTHER KING JR.

John Salley grew up in Brooklyn, among Italians and Jews, but he didn't encounter much trouble until seventh grade. One day, Salley recalled, he and a friend were walking to school when they were approached by "30 Italian kids who wanted to kick our butts."

Fortunately for Salley, one of the kids was a home economics classmate named Patsy.

"Patsy told them I was cool, so they left us alone."

Today, Salley faces prejudice of a different kind.

"It's not up front, in my face anymore, but it still exists," he said. "Sometimes I'll walk in a place where I'm welcome, but there's a certain smell in the air that makes me uncomfortable. It's hard to understand unless you've felt it."

> *"He's allowed me to go up to the mountain. And I've looked over. And I've seen the promised land. I*

may not get there with you. But I want you to know
tonight that we as a people will get to the promised
land."

—MARTIN LUTHER KING JR.
From his last speech before
he was assassinated, April 4, 1968

Michael Cofer and Mark Aguirre are hopeful that the next generation
will be more color-blind.

"When you come into this world as a black baby, there are so many
challenges you'll have to face, and it's up to parents to educate their children and teach them to listen to all people," said Cofer, a Lions linebacker.
"We have to be able to socialize with one another and forget about color."

Aguirre grew up in a predominantly black area of Chicago, a few
blocks away from the border of Oak Park, a white suburb. It often puz-
zled Aguirre why none of his white classmates invited him over after
school.

"I couldn't capture what was going on at such a young age, but I look
back on it and I understand," he said. "It's sad. I can tell you one thing,
my daughter (Angelei) won't be prejudiced. She will love all people, and
hopefully, they'll love her back."

Reprinted with the permission of the *Detroit Free Press*

References

Bailey, Sandy. 1990. Orioles agree with papers on access issue. *APSE Newsletter,* January,
12.

Dennis, Everette E., and Arnold H. Ismach. 1981. *Reporting Processes and Practices:*
Newswriting for Today's Readers. Belmont, Calif: Wadsworth.

Epstein, Eve. 1990. Olson harassment. Associated Press sports wire, December 1, n.p.

Fitzgerald, Mark. 1989. "Us" against "them": Spring training is an increasingly hostile
time for newspeople as baseball players are encouraged to take it out on the media. *Editor &*
Publisher 122 (April 1):12.

Gordon, Lee. 1989. Vanderbilt/SEC access situation reviewed. *APSE Newsletter,* February, 5–6.

Lawrence, Rachel L. 1990. Reporter's choice. Associated Press sports wire, October 22,
n.p.

Mencher, Melvin. 1991. *News Reporting and Writing.* 5th ed. Dubuque, Iowa: Brown.

Pieretti, Fred. 1990. Locker room ban. Associated Press sports wire, October 17, n.p.

Smith, Mike. 1987. SI's Selcraig offers tips on developing news sources. *1987 Associated*
Press Sports Editors Convention Report, June 9–13, 11.

Spikol, Art. 1981. Non-fiction: Source spots. *Writer's Digest* 61 (4):6–8.

United Press International. 1990. *Post*'s Christine Brennan defends female reporter in
locker room dispute. United Press International sports wire, September 28, n.p.

Ward, Hiley H. 1991. *Reporting in Depth.* Mountain View, Calif.: Mayfield.

Waterman, Frederick. 1990. Reporter describes Patriots' sexual harassment. United Press
International sports wire, September 27, n.p.

4

Interviewing Strategies

Of the many possible sources of information—people, records and documents, first-hand observation—sportswriters depend on people the most. But people are also the most perilous and unreliable sources of information (Webb and Salancik 1966). Journalistic interviewing is one of the oldest strategies of reporting, dating from the early 19th century in American journalism (Nilsson 1971 and Brady 1977). Yet, while not a new strategy, interviewing techniques are constantly evolving.

As do writers in other departments of newspapers and magazines, writers of sports journalism depend on the interview for many of their most basic facts. Sportswriters conduct postgame interviews with coaches and players, interviews with visiting sports personalities for feature stories, interviews with principals in controversial stories for their opinions, and interviews with individuals for information upon which to base further interviews. Information is obtained by interviewing sources in person, over the telephone, and even by mail on rare occasions. Although a difficult skill to master, interviewing is essential for any sportswriter. Professional journalists are, of course, professional interrogators.

So, what is a journalistic interview? University of Oregon professor Ken Metzler (1989) offers a thoughtful definition. It is not enough, he writes, to say interviewing elicits information from a source for an unseen audience. Instead, Metzler tells readers, the journalistic interview also permits an exchange of information that produces "a level of intelligence higher than either participant could produce alone." Thus, the interviewer is more than an information processor.

The Need for an Interview

Some types of sports stories demand interviews, such as the locker room reactions of players and coaches, the personality profile, or the investigative series. In fact, the human element in many stories can only be obtained through interviews. At times, too, an interview is used to complement the reporting process. Sportswriters gather much of their information from non-human sources, such as reports or record books, and by their own observation, and follow up this research by questioning the individuals involved.

California State University at Sacramento professor Shirley Biagi (1986) lists five different types of stories that depend heavily on interviewing: (1) the basic news story, (2) news features, (3) profiles, (4) investigative stories, and (5) round-up stories.

Whatever the reason or type of story that calls for an interview to be conducted, the process involves following clearly defined stages.

The Interview Process I: Getting the Interview

Journalism professors George Killenberg and Rob Anderson (1989) suggest that an interview should begin with the "mirror" test. This is, simply put, a look into a mirror for introspection because, they write, "Everyone acquires attitudes, values, assumptions, and stereotypes that can be traced back to the formative years of childhood and family life. Our views of others are influenced by the socialized habits of behavior and perception."

After reporters understand their own orientations, they can turn their attention to getting started. In many cases, setting up an interview for a story can be as simple as informally approaching the subject. But sometimes it requires much more effort. The most direct method is to ask the person in advance for time for an interview. This can be done at practice, in the locker room, in a parking lot, or anywhere the reporter comes face to face with the potential interview subject. A letter (to set up an interview, or even to replace it) may be appropriate when personal contact is difficult, such as in out-of-town, or unusual in-town, situations.

Occasionally, potential sources are reluctant to be interviewed. In such cases it is helpful to go through a third person. When a timid high school student, for example, might not wish to talk to a reporter, then a coach, parent, or other individual can help. A third person can also help to contact hard-to-reach people, such as sports public relations specialists, promoters, athletic directors and managers, and coaches. Reporters should set up such interviews through secretaries, assistants, or other public relations spokespersons. Sports information directors often have the authority to arrange access to players. Coaches play this role at high school and junior high school levels, particularly with star players. Despite the help such third persons can provide, the first effort should be to contact the individual directly. Within the bounds of good judgment, it is best to avoid intermediaries when working at any but the highest levels in sports.

Persuading an individual to agree to be interviewed can be difficult. Not everyone wants to talk to reporters. Some people are intimidated by the process. Some are too busy. The problem, once a reporter requests an interview, is that the response is likely to be, "Why do you want to talk to me?" The reporter should have a ready answer and be prepared to defend the request for that individual's time and energy. Metzler (1989) suggests eight reasons why an individual should consent to an interview:

1. A chance to obtain recognition and publicity
2. A chance to tell his or her side of the story
3. A chance to be an "educator" (there's a little educator in everybody)
4. A chance to clarify positions or eliminate misunderstandings
5. A chance to influence or impress others
6. A novel experience
7. A touch of immortality, with words frozen into print
8. Sympathy with an altruistic and noble journalistic purpose (to educate the public)

The Interview Process II: Preparation

Research before an interview is advantageous, but because many interviews are spontaneous, sportswriters frequently do not have an opportunity to prepare. In such situations, a reporter can still draw upon his or her experiences to develop satisfactory questions. After a spectacular game, for example, there are always such standard question lines as the reactions of the individual(s) in the context of that particular event.

However, many interviews do permit preparation because they are set up in advance; a reporter at least knows he or she will be interviewing an individual or group. Any complete sports investigation or feature, advance, or other type of story draws upon information obtained during multiple interviews.

Consulting reference sources around the newsroom and in a library is a first step. A reporter can begin with the general topic and read it through, narrowing down to the specific interview. This funnel method, for example, might be used in preparing for an interview with a stock car driver. If the reporter has little or no knowledge of this style of automobile racing, such an interview will require a bit of preparation and research. Starting with automobile racing in general, a reporter can then seek material on stock car racing and finally material about the specific driver (which may be available in the newspaper's own library, press releases, and other printed sources). Obviously, it is important to use the most up-to-date sources to identify the right issues and make the information elicited from the interview as timely as possible. Many expert interviewers have pointed out that the quality of the research before an interview determines the quality of the interview.

A well-prepared interviewer enters an interview with major questions prepared in advance. Specific questions can be generated from the research in two steps. First, the questions are written down as they occur during research. Then, reviewing the list of questions, the reporter considers the order of the questions and the overall structure of the interview. The order of questions is important; for example, the most important and sensitive questions are not asked first. Some casual inquiries can break the ice and get the conversation going before the reporter moves on to the hard-hitting questions. Naturally, this step can be bypassed if time is short or the reporter is well acquainted with the source.

The structure of the interview and the context of the exchange should also be considered. What will the circumstances be? This might make a difference in the order of the questions and in how many questions are planned. Will follow-up questions be possible, for example?

If there is time, the revised list of questions should be typed. And these notes can be an asset. Most sources are impressed when a reporter obviously takes time and effort to prepare for an interview, and they may therefore tend to respond positively.

The Interview Process III: Asking Questions

Asking questions effectively is important in eliciting information from the source. A typed list gives a sense of security, especially if a reporter is inexperienced. But the questions must be good, effective, and probing.

Of the many decisions that a sports reporter must make about the interview question, one is the basic form: whether to use an "open-ended" question or a "closed-ended" question. Openness has to do with the form of the response, actually, and not the question itself. Open questions, also called free-response questions or unrestricted questions, invite the respondent or interview source to reply in his or her own words. Closed questions, also called restricted or forced-choice questions, ask the respondent to select a response from a series of alternatives that answer the reporter's question. The closed question thus controls the form, length, and content of the possible response. The classic example of this is the trial lawyer's instruction to a witness that he or she answer "yes" or "no."

These examples illustrate more fully the contrasting approaches:

1. (OPEN) What happens to the coaches in the athletic department when the football team has a losing season like this fall?

(CLOSED) When the football team has a losing season like the one this fall, do coaches blame themselves, each other, or someone else?

2. (OPEN) How do players on this team feel about attending the additional two team meetings a week?

(CLOSED) On this team, do most players feel they should attend the two extra team meetings a week, feel the meetings are not necessary, or do the players feel there needs to be more time spent on the practice field?

Five considerations are relevant to the choice of open- or closed-ended questioning of a source: (1) interview objectives, (2) the source's level of information and ability to answer, (3) structure or respondent opinions, (4) the source's motivation to communicate with the reporter, and (5) the reporter's initial knowledge of the four above characteristics.

In general, these guidelines should help produce effective interview questions:

1. Don't ask leading questions. ("It was a real surprise to win the game tonight, wasn't it, coach?") You'll likely hear the same words as a reply.

2. Watch qualifying words. Don't use words such as "always" or "never."

3. Avoid vague words.

4. Don't ask the same thing twice, in two different forms, unless the source has not responded to the first question.

5. Don't be afraid to ask basic questions. ("What is a nickel defense, coach?") Not understanding could lead to inaccuracies in the story, and reporters can learn from this as well.

6. Double-check spellings of names and other difficult or uncommon words. Double-check all figures. Ask the source to repeat them if necessary.

7. Go slow, be deliberate, but don't bore the source; go quickly, be efficient, but don't outrun the source. In other words, find the fine, middle ground in which to pace each interview.

8. Don't ask questions that can be answered with a simple "yes" or "no." To get a good quotation, ask, "How did your team's performance compare with other games this season?" instead of "Did your team play well tonight?"

9. Guard against distractions during the interview.

10. Avoid first person when possible; place the emphasis on the source, not the interviewer.

11. Avoid anonymous sources. They may damage overall story credibility.

12. With controversial material, use the two-source rule. Verify such

information from a second independent source before using it in a story.

13. Keep in mind that interviews are often only starting points. Follow up interviews with research and additional interviews. Try to supplement interviews with observation as well.

The Interview Process IV: Gathering Information

City University of New York professor Marvin Gottlieb (1986) argues that "there is probably no really good substitute for taking notes."

Should a reporter take notes? Yes. Use a tape recorder? Probably. Rely on memory? Not solely. Beginning reporters should try a combination of all three approaches. Not many sports reporters are given the gift of total recall. To fill in memory lapses, even if writing the story only minutes afterward, reporters should take notes and, when possible, tape-record the interview. Develop a shorthand style to make note taking more efficient, also. Or take a shorthand course at an adult education program at a high school nearby.

Years ago tape-recording all interviews was not mechanically possible. Even as recently as the early 1970s, small, lightweight cassette recorders were expensive, bulky, and not dependable. But today's microcassette systems are affordable, manageable in almost all situations, and operate quietly and unobtrusively. A source must be told that the reporter plans to tape the interview before the machine is turned on. If a source objects, the tape recorder should be put away. If taping is permitted, both source and reporter usually forget the recorder is there and get down to business after a moment or two.

To save time, it is also wise to take extensive notes. You should also note the tape location numbers, or indexes, when key points are made if it is not difficult to do. Indexing can, in fact, wait until later. The reporter should take notes as if the recorder were not there and then use the tape to fill in gaps, to double-check statements, and to obtain completely accurate quotations (see Abel 1969 and Morris 1973).

Some professionals think that setting up tape recorders uses too much valuable time before the interview and at times may also disrupt the interview. And some critics say tape recorders waste time after the interview, when specific portions of the interview needed for the story have to be found. Perhaps some of this time loss can be avoided with new, sophisticated recorders that have accurate indexes which count cassette revolutions. They also have built-in microphones and are small enough to be unobtrusive and easy to carry.

Astute sources notice problems that tape recorders can cause in the interview process, also. The late commissioner of baseball, A. Bartlett Giamatti (1988), told editors that young reporters especially suffer from the

Are You Responsible for What Sources Say (in Print)?

Alice Neff Lucan, assistant general counsel for Gannett Corporation, offers advice on what to do when a source says something potentially libelous during an interview: Be careful!

Lucan, writing in the *Associated Press Sports Editors Newsletter,* answered the question "Is my newspaper responsible for something someone says in a quote?"

"Yes," she says, "you are responsible for quoted material, unless some special argument diminishes your responsibility. At the outset, you are responsible for quoting a false and defamatory statement."

SOURCE: Alice Neff Lucan, "Sports writing truly mightier than the sword," *Associated Press Sports Editors Newsletter,* February 1988, p. 3.

convenience of tape recorders. He believes tape recorders have "ruined the young reporter's capacity to listen and choose the key phrase because once they turn on the machine they do not listen at all."

A beginner would be wise to try interviewing both with and without electronic support. Although a tape recorder might seem to be an inconvenience at first, as the reporter becomes more comfortable in an interview situation, the machine can be used more frequently. Also, for extremely important interviews or complicated material, it is prudent to use two recorders because of the possibility of mechanical failure (e.g., bad tape, malfunctions, or weak batteries).

When going on interviews, it is important for reporters to be businesslike and to dress professionally, but also to be friendly and pleasant, and to try to humanize the situation. An interviewer should not intimidate the source nor, on the other hand, permit the source to be intimidating.

A final word about gathering information: It is important to listen carefully and to let the source be the "star" of the interview. The interviewer shouldn't be afraid to divert from the list of questions, but only if it serves the interviewer's purpose and not the source's agenda. After the interview, the final comments and reactions sometimes provide the best information or quotations.

Types of Sports Interviews

There are different types of interviews. Some forms of interviews are used on a regular basis and some are used less regularly.

1. *Traditional in-person interviews.* This is the type of interview discussed so far. They are generally preparation-based interviews but are conducted in one effort.

2. *Depth in-person interviews.* These differ from traditional interviews in one major aspect: The depth interview usually requires more than one session, scheduled over several days, because it is difficult to complete a thorough session with a source (90 minutes to two hours) without tiring both interviewer and source. A series of interviews that may lead, for example, to a long article chronicling the career of a long-time high school coach should be divided into a number of sessions by subject, requiring several visits. The first session could be devoted simply to getting acquainted and some light questioning. A second session might be devoted to famous players and championship teams and a third to more philosophical topics concerning the sport itself, its future, and its personalities. Clearly, the depth interview requires depth preparation by both interviewer and source.

3. *Telephone interviews.* More interviewing is being conducted by telephone than ever before. With greater coverage commitments and tight

schedules, reporters must depend on the telephone, particularly when distance is a problem. This is a useful technique for gathering routine information, such as the results of road trips of local teams and checking up on the status of players. It is a distinct disadvantage, however, to use the telephone in gathering information for feature stories and other personal stories. The reporter should find a quiet place to call and try to find a telephone with a shoulder cradle to allow two-handed note taking or keyboarding notes directly into the computer. Some further useful tips for the telephone interview are to: (1) speak clearly and distinctly, (2) identify oneself and purpose early, (3) tell the source how much time is required, (4) use icebreakers as in an in-person interview, (5) avoid silences while taking notes, (6) provide verbal cues when listening, and (7) establish credibility early by bringing up mutual acquaintances (Metzler 1989).

4. *Background interviews.* These are often necessary but are certainly not preferred. A background interview generates information from the source in off-the-record form, which cannot be used for publication. If pressed, the source may upgrade the interview to publishable-but-unattributed status. This permits the reporter to use the information but not to attribute it to any named source. Neither is the reporter's choice, of course; news organizations constantly fight this concession but cannot do away with it.

5. *Question-and-answer interviews.* Question-and-answer (Q-A) interviews differ not in how they are conducted or what they cover, but in how the interview is presented and published. Q-A interviews found their niche in sportswriting because of the use of tapes, which assure accuracy and permit editing. Passages may be deleted with continuity in mind. There are no set organizational formats for the Q-A story other than the following basic outline: (1) An editor's note setting the context of the interview and providing necessary background not easily incorporated into the Q-A section; (2) moderate use of detail throughout that gives the reporter's impressions, inserted with parentheses to distinguish from the direct quotation; (3) *Q,* representing the question or questioner/interviewer, followed by the exact question asked. A name may be used instead; (4) *A,* the answer/respondent/source, followed by the verbatim response. Answers are occasionally edited, using ellipses or other punctuation, to allow more ground to be covered. These stories require tedious tape editing and transcribing, but occasionally they produce an effect that cannot be achieved through conventional story organization or interview forms (see Tienhaara 1980).

6. *Group or conference interviews.* At times the sportswriter, like other journalists, may be in a press conference situation where the interview is no longer a one-on-one situation. This creates different problems. The most obvious one is the lack of exclusivity to answers. This type of interview is usually more formal than the one-on-one, except for the group interview after an event, when chaos often reigns. The group interview

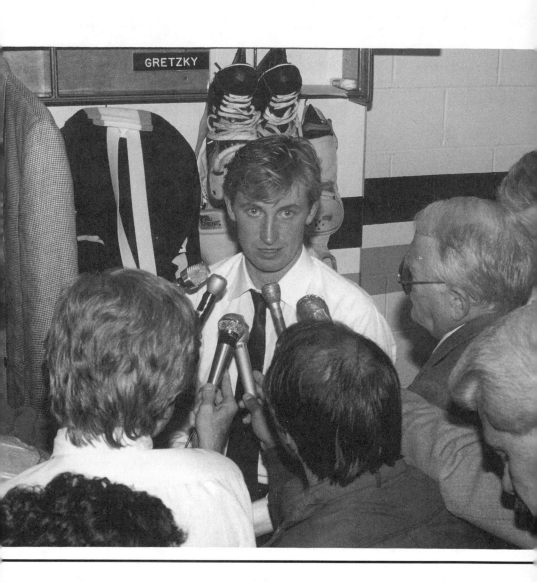

Los Angeles Kings hockey superstar Wayne Gretzky (center) responds to print and broadcast reporters' questions during a postgame locker room interview. (*Photo by Wen Roberts, Photography Ink.*)

allows less freedom in questioning. But because there are some questions that all reporters ask in one form or another (e.g., "How does it feel to break the team record?"), the best approach is to accept the conditions and get as much useful information as possible.

7. *Non-interview interviews.* An apparent contradiction, these interviews take the form of conversations rather than prepared formal interviews. This approach allows the reporter to remain in touch with a source. A brief telephone call to get an update on the status of an athlete's injury, for example, might not have any purpose other than touching base with him or her, but it could lead to something else. The majority of these source contacts will not produce much publishable information.

There are still other types of interviews, with other purposes. Charles Stewart and William Cash (1991) list some of them: information-giving interviews, information-gathering interviews, selection interviews, problems with source's behavior interviews, problems with interviewer's behavior interviews, problem-solving interviews, and persuasion interviews. Stewart and Cash clearly indicate that journalistic interviewing goes beyond the form we discussed, the information gathering interview. Occasionally, sportswriters become sources. To screen sources for interviews, sportswriters frequently use selection interviews. Problems can be solved through interviewing. And persuasive interviews can convince sources to participate in more thorough interviews or to provide other forms of assistance to the journalist.

Handling Quotations in Interviews

Once the source has given well-thought-out answers to well-prepared questions, a number of methods are available for handling the newly gathered information. Metzler (1989) lists five forms:

1. Direct quotations, which are exactly what was stated by the source, in phrases, sentences, or even entire paragraphs. They are punctuated by quotation marks and attributed to the speaker at the beginning or end of the statement, or in some non-obtrusive point in the middle. As Metzler points out, minor editing is generally permitted to make a quotation more readable as long as the meaning is unchanged. For example, an excited coach may say: "We just outscrapped and outplayed them in all departments tonight. *They* [who?] wanted to win a little bit more." To make the quotation more clear for the reader, the reporter can make the statement read "*Our team* wanted to win. . . ."

2. Indirect quotations, which are written without quotation marks, must have only minor deviations from the original statement. Write: He said that the team seemed to want to win more than the opponents did.

3. Paraphrased quotations, which represent what the source said but have been modified by the writer to shorten the story or to otherwise organize the information more efficiently.

4. Fragmentary quotations, which are combinations of paraphrased and direct quotations.

5. Dialogue quotations, which are quotations from two or more speakers, such as an exchange between a coach and a player. A tool of the novelist, dialogue is particularly effective when used sparingly and appropriately, such as in feature stories.

Metzler (1989) also lists why we use quotations in stories: (1) to establish authority in the story, (2) to provide human color to the story, (3) to provide authenticity to the story, and (4) to help readers with expressions and figures of speech.

First-Hand Observation and Interviewing

Direct observation will be discussed only briefly at this point, because the next chapter is devoted to a discussion of first-hand observation and observational strategies. But the processes of in-person interviewing and observation must be considered together. Jay Black (1978) stresses the importance of non-verbal cues when interviewing, stating that such cues are complex and subtle characteristics of the interview environment and often are "ultimately more significant than the verbal elements in determining the eventual success or failure of the interview." These cues include such things as non-verbal vocalizations and body movements, as well as non-verbal attributes such as personal appearance, attractiveness, height, skin color, and gender. William Rivers and Shelly Smolkin (1981) argue that observation also provides "liveliness" through detail.

While watching the source's non-verbal cues and listening to verbal ones, the reporter must also observe the environment during the interview. The athlete's home or the coach's office reveals much about the source. A few mental or written notes about the surroundings at the beginning, end, or during an interruption of an interview can enhance the story with detail. Such things as photos on desks and walls, framed awards or other citations, trophies, furniture styles, clothing, and other personality indicators contribute to the liveliness of the story.

Ethical Considerations in Interviews

A portion of Chapter 15 is devoted to the overall issue of professional behavior, but ethics of sports journalists must be a part of any discussion of

A Post-Interview Checklist for Reporters

Miami free-lance writer, attorney, and former journalism professor Alice Klement has developed a checklist for beginning reporters to use at the end of an interview. This list will help ensure that a good interview was conducted or, at least, identify shortcomings of the interview. For beginners, it would be helpful to apply this list to a just-completed interview for a self-assessment of strengths and weaknesses. Did the reporter:

1. Define and state clearly the interview purpose?
2. Demonstrate purposefulness (how)?
3. Prepare background data?
4. Open with an icebreaker?
5. Formulate and ask creative questions?
6. Probe where possible?
7. Seek specific details such as anecdotes and quotations?
8. Show sympathy or empathy if appropriate?
9. Listen carefully and ask follow-up questions?
10. Avoid filibustering (and did not bog down note taking)?
11. Ask tough "bomb" questions?
12. Recover, if appropriate, from a tense or hostile situation?
13. Conclude the interview gracefully?

SOURCE: Alice Klement, personal communication with the authors, March 1, 1989.

interviewing and interviewer–respondent, or reporter–source, relations. Peter Johansen (1976) argues that interviewing has an ethical impact at four key stages:

1. Does interviewing constitute an invasion of privacy? Where do sportswriters draw the line between the public and private lives of sources? What do you ask during an interview that might be considered an invasion of privacy? What would not be?

2. Is badgering acceptable if a source refuses to cooperate? How many times can a parent be asked to permit his or her child to be interviewed? How many times can a reporter ask a coach for access to a player? Should a reporter pay for an interview?

3. Should a reporter conduct an interview without identifying himself or herself as a journalist to the source? Should a reporter talk to a source to obtain information without making the purpose of the interview clear?

4. Should the source be told of possible consequences of an interview?

Johansen also says ethical questions arise in three other major areas: (1) the ground rules of the interview; (2) strategies, or ploys the reporter uses to obtain information in an interview such as putting words in a source's mouth; and (3) weighing the competence of the information gained.

Analysis of Stories Based on Interviews

The following examples from newspapers across the United States show how the sportswriter used information from an interview to enhance the story:

OBSERVING AND USING DETAIL. Description supplements the information obtained in an interview. It can help set the scene, provide mood, and if done well, paint a picture in the mind of a reader. Detail works well with other writer's tools in putting together the total story.

USING DIALOGUE. In the following example, notice how dialogue is used to strengthen the story, the same way a novelist might use it to recreate a conversation or to provide the sense of a conversation that may have occurred. In reading *San Francisco Chronicle* writer Jerry Carroll's story about Oakland A's manager Tony LaRussa, we can almost picture the conversation taking place between LaRussa, his wife Elaine, and Carroll. The subject is compelling enough — the LaRussas' animal-rights activism — but it comes alive by the interaction of quotations from the two primary sources of the story and the narration of the writer.

SOURCE: The *Miami Herald,* final edition, page 10H
DATE: Sunday, May 6, 1990
AUTHOR: Jerry Carroll, *San Francisco Chronicle*
HEADLINE: LaRussa's new pitch: Animal-rights activism; A's manager is
           devoted to cause, but not extreme

When Oakland Athletics manager Tony LaRussa was 10, a friend came over with a BB gun. Popping away at tin cans was interesting enough for a while, but pretty soon they looked for something more fun.

"I shot a bird on a chain-link fence," LaRussa says.

When the youthful hunter drew near to inspect his kill, he was swept by a wave of revulsion. "It was still quivering. I said never again."

LaRussa's wife, Elaine, has heard versions of this story from lots of men. "It's almost a rite of boyhood, the first tug on their conscience. They learn there really is such a thing as dying."

Many go on to develop a liking for blood sports and become hunters as adults.

Others, like LaRussa, 45, never overcome their disgust and horror at shedding the blood of another living thing. Some, like him, become vegetarians, but few opt for LaRussa's increasingly high-profile role in the animal-rights movement.

"It started about 15 years ago or so. I got off red meat first, then a few years later poultry. Then fish," he says.

The driving force behind the dietary switch and the couple's later involvement in the animal rights movement was Elaine, 45.

"We were living in New Orleans, and I saw a show on the public television channel called 'Pasture to Table,' " she says. "It showed the process of what the animal goes through. Seeing that really did something to me. I watched it with tears in my eyes.

"Life wasn't intended to be that way. I said I could never again be a party to this, and I was a vegetarian from that night. I told Tony, 'I will never cook meat again.' "

They could have pasta and rice and beans at home, but on the road finding something to eat wasn't always easy for LaRussa.

"Sometimes the games aren't over until 10 o'clock. The clubhouse spread is tough to eat and by the time you get back to the hotel things are closed." A lot of times he'd order a hamburger and just eat the roll, lettuce and tomato.

Elaine began joining humane societies and organizations dedicated to saving the whale, the sea otter, the dolphin and mountain lions.

"They're all endangered," says Tony, "whether they're classified as such or not."

"Before you know it," says his wife, "you belong to 50 different organizations."

Both regret the necessity to use leather products.

"There is no real alternative," says Tony. "The day there is some kind of synthetic baseball glove available and effective, I'll be the first to say use it." In any event, he says, leather is a byproduct of animals "slain for other purposes."

Elaine says, "I buy handbags as free of leather as possible. I wear leather shoes because I have not found dressy canvas shoes with heels I can go to a banquet in. And, anyhow, if I start being too far out, other people won't listen."

Baseball is full of good old boys who grew up hunting and trapping and count few experiences superior to having a buck in the cross-hairs. This leads to some, well, interesting exchanges between them and LaRussa.

"We have this ongoing dialogue. We kid in a good-natured way. They'll walk by and throw a hunting magazine on my desk. I don't see hunting as a sport. There can be no justification of hunting as a sport. It's not a fair competition."

Some of the A's tease LaRussa sometimes by wearing a T-shirt that shows a deer in the rifle sights. "I tell them they'd better take them home to wash. I tell them I'll burn them if I find them in their lockers."

LaRussa says he began going public with his feelings about animal rights three years ago.

"One of the reasons was the fur industry was giving the impression that anybody who was against the use of animals was some kind of extreme activist who had nothing else to do but go around and create havoc. I knew that wasn't true. I knew a lot of people — standard average Americans — who resented the fact that was the way we were being portrayed," he says.

"What I'm trying to do is create awareness. People say I'm trying to take choice away, which is total bulls---. I'm only trying to make your choice an informed one. That's what this country is all about."

Man is at the top of the animal chain, blessed with reasoning powers, LaRussa explains. "Doesn't that mean you have the highest responsibility to be the most compassionate?"

LaRussa says he is careful to avoid embarrassing the A's management with his views. "I don't ever want anyone to get the impression so much of me is going into this that I'm not taking care of what I'm supposed to do. I'm not on the phone soliciting other athletes or writing letters during the season."

But, he says, next winter he might begin asking other coaches and athletes to speak out on behalf of animal rights. "I'm sure the interest is there. I could name some guys on the club who share some of my feelings, but I don't want to speak for them."

Reprinted with the permission of the *San Francisco Chronicle*

INTERVIEWS AND FEATURE PROFILES. The basic element of a profile is an interview with the subject. In the first of the two following stories, *San Jose Mercury News* staff sportswriter Scott Vigallon profiles a San Jose State University starting quarterback who has been waiting for his chance to play for four years. The story is rich with quotations from the player and his head coach. These direct quotations make a major difference in an ordinary story, making it one that is highly personal, emotional, and detailed. In the second story, *Philadelphia Inquirer* sportswriter Bill Lyon writes about the return of Philadelphia 76ers coach Matty Guokas for a new season. In the story he fills gaps with precise quotations from interviews with the team owner and the coach himself. The quotations add authority to the story. They add personal flavor. The writer just about lets the owner and coach tell the story through their own words by identifying and capturing such rich, frequent quotations during his interviews.

SOURCE: *San Jose Mercury News,* morning final edition, page 4D
DATE: Thursday, November 8, 1990
AUTHOR: Scott Vigallon, *Mercury News* staff writer
HEADLINE: Martini finally has a season to savor; After 4 years in the shadows, SJS quarterback is in the spotlight

For four years, Ralph Martini's life as a quarterback had been haunted by bad timing. Now, in the fifth, Martini is having the time of his life.

"This is something I've dreamed about for a long time," Martini, the San Jose State quarterback said this week about his emergence as one of Big West Conference's top quarterbacks. "And I've worked hard for it. I don't want to sound cocky, but I deserve it."

Flip through the Ralph Martini History Book and you'll see his point. There's the chapter about earning a scholarship to Brigham Young in 1986 only to be switched from quarterback to tight end because the Cougars were thin at that position.

There's the chapter about being switched back to quarterback in 1987 only to get hurt and miss the season. There's the one about witnessing Ty Detmer's talents and transferring to SJS in 1988. There's also the one about being ready to take over at SJS the following year, only to see hot-shot junior college quarterback Matt Veatch come in and win the starting job.

But this season's chapter has been different. Martini, a fifth-year senior, is easing the pain of the previous four with his performance. Entering Saturday's game at New Mexico State, he has completed 57 percent of his passes for 2,469 yards and 18 touchdowns. He ranks 13th nationally in passing efficiency.

"I always believed I had the ability," Martini said. "I was just not given a shot. And, I was always in the wrong place at the wrong time."

Bad timing almost haunted him again this season. Veatch underwent elbow surgery last spring, and Martini emerged from spring practice as the Spartans' starter. However, when new Coach Terry Shea arrived, he declared the position open, and Martini had to win it again during preseason practice.

He did and has passed for 300 or more yards five times, including a career-high 442-yard performance last week against Fullerton State. Before 1990, his collegiate total was 969 passing yards, all achieved last season when he started two games and appeared in seven others.

Martini partially credits Shea for his improvement, saying his footwork, field vision and accuracy have all gotten better since Shea arrived. The main reason, Martini said, was simply a matter of playing time.

"For college football, you need a lot of snaps," he said.

Despite his relative inexperience, Martini has a good understanding of the offense, Shea said. The coach added that when Martini does make a mistake, he can take the heat.

"He comes off the sideline, and I'll put a hole right in his forehead with coaching points as to why he threw this pass and why he did this," Shea said. "And he doesn't blink. The players pick up on that. I've been around enough players where it's, 'The guy missed his block, and that's why I did it.' He doesn't fall into any of that escape."

Martini would like to fall into the hands of an NFL team next season. Shea said that in the past week, "a number of scouts" have inquired about Martini. Mel Kiper, an NFL draft analyst, said Martini is ranked 22nd among senior quarterbacks nationally and called Martini a "free-agent type."

Said Martini, "I'm not thinking about any of that right now."

Who can blame him? He's too busy enjoying his moment.

ETC.: SJS safety Hesh Colar will start Saturday, Shea said. Colar was suspended last week after being arrested Oct. 25 because of an incident outside of the Oasis, a downtown San Jose nightclub. Colar returned to practice Monday but had to get an academic matter cleared up before Shea would reinstate him for the game. Shea said the matter has been cleared up.

Finally, It's Martini's Season

In four years before the 1990 season, Ralph Martini changed positions, changed schools, redshirted one season and sat out another because of a transfer. He is now taking advantage of his first full season at quarterback. Here's a year-by-year look at Martini's career:

Statistics

1986 BYU TE 2 catches, 6 yards, 2 touchdowns
1987 BYU Redshirt
1988 SJS Transfer
1989 SJS QB 81 of 143, 969 yards, 7 touchdowns
1990 SJS QB 178 of 311, 2,469 yards, 18 touchdowns

SOURCE: *Philadelphia Inquirer,* final edition, page D1
DATE: Wednesday, May 13, 1987
AUTHOR: Bill Lyon, staff writer
HEADLINE: The right coach for the job

"The popular thing to do," said Harold Katz, "is not always the right thing to do. But I think this time we did both."

And so they have.

The 76ers—actually, their owner—re-hired Matty Guokas as coach. For two more years.

As has been suggested in this space for some time now, it is deserved. Sometimes, the best moves are the ones you never make.

So, at last, a cork can be stuffed in all that wretched, irresponsible rumormongering, all those incendiary "we hear" TV pronouncements.

So, once and for all: No, Gene Shue will not coach the 76ers next year.

Neither will Don Nelson.

Or Hubie Brown.

Or even Julius Erving.

The same tall, slender chap who has coached them the last two seasons will be back, the one who keeps his composure and his perspective, the one with the remarkable patience, the one who squeezed 45 wins out of an injury-depleted roster that missed more than 200 man-games.

He comes back because the owner thinks he is the right man at the right moment for this particular team.

"My main consideration," said Katz, "was how a coaching change would affect our players, who are new and young, and I concluded that we have to give this nucleus a chance for at least another year."

Translation: The team you see in May is going to be pretty much the team you see next fall.

"I anticipate only minor personnel changes," Katz said. "Obviously, if a superstar was suddenly available. . . ."

Not likely.

So, Matty Guokas will be coaching basically the same team. Minus Erving, of course. He says this is fine with him. Assuming they're healthy, of course.

"The more we can keep them together," Guokas said, "the better the chance to develop the chemistry."

The consensus is that neither the coach nor the players—because of persistent injuries—really had a fair chance to show what they can do this season past. So the owner is willing to give them another go.

There are a couple of other mitigating factors. Such as, for example, the lack of other options. Matty Guokas will coach basically the same team because little else is realistically available, specifically a guard to shoot from outside and a monster in the middle.

"It seems like we're always looking for an outside shooting threat," Guokas conceded. "And no one is just going to give you a center. Actually, if we could get another player like Tim McCormick, we'd be pleased."

The owner and the coach are in agreement on playing philosophy. They want an aggressive team and a running team, a team that not only fastbreaks, but runs after the other team scores.

"But to play that style, you need at least nine players," Katz said. "You just can't play up-tempo when only seven players are available night after night."

That was the case this season. But the owner and the coach say they are convinced that if Charles Barkley continues to improve, if David Wingate develops into the talent they expect, if Roy Hinson becomes more assertive, and if Cliff Robinson can avoid injury, then the Sixers can be legitimate contenders again.

The coach said that all the owner really wanted to know during their negotiations was whether the coach was enjoying his job. The coach said that, indeed, he was.

That seemed a curious word to use; there are a lot of words NBA coaches would choose to describe the madness that is their profession, but enjoyment might be the last one.

"Well, the season wasn't exactly a barrel of laughs," Guokas conceded, "but I like dealing with the players, I like the challenge, I like being one of only 23 guys with that job. And if you have any kind of competitive spark in you, well, the opportunity is there."

Asked to describe his philosophy in dealing with players, the present and future coach of the 76ers replied: "My approach is to treat everyone differently because everyone is different. Obviously, we all have rules we have to abide by as a team, but you make concessions. In cases of special requests, I don't think I said no to a player all year."

Which may help to explain the message that was left on the blackboard in the visitors' locker room in Milwaukee 10 days ago: "Dear Harold, Let Matty coach us next year. Charles Barkley."

To which the owner said: "I didn't poll the players about the coach."

Nor should he. This was a decision that spoke for itself.

Reprinted with the permission of the *Philadelphia Inquirer*

PRESS CONFERENCES OR GROUP INTERVIEWS. The following three stories, two from the *San Francisco Chronicle* and one from the Boston Globe, illustrate the type of information covered in group interview situations such as a press conference. These stories arc typical of interview situations when too many reporters seek access to individuals in the news on a single day such as when a big game will be played, immediately after it has been played, or when a major announcement is being made.

The first story, by *Chronicle* sportswriter John Carman, focuses on the former 49ers coach Bill Walsh and his career as a network television football analyst. Carman was unable to get information in a more exclusive environment so went to the press tour and briefing by the network. He was then able to pick the best quotations from Walsh to build his story.

The second story, by *Chronicle* sportswriter Ron Thomas, is an advance on an opening National Football League playoff game between San Francisco and Washington based on a press conference of 49ers coach George Seifert and his coaches. Unavailable under other more desirable circumstances, Thomas participated in the press conference and incorporated the best of the coaching staff's comments on the opponent and their own team into the advance that ran four days before the game.

The third story, by *Globe* sportswriter Joe Burris, is based on a common press conference type—the major announcement press briefing. Burris was present when the New England Patriots called the media to announce a new head coach for the 1991 season, former Syracuse University coach Dick MacPherson. He uses numerous quotations from three major participants in the press conference—the team's general manager, the new coach, and the brother of the new coach, a priest living in Boston.

SOURCE: *San Francisco Chronicle,* final edition, page E1
DATE: Wednesday, January 9, 1991
AUTHOR: John Carman
HEADLINE: TV jock Walsh picks the Niners

LOS ANGELES—Not to worry, says Bill Walsh. The 49ers are a virtual shoe-in to reach the Super Bowl.

The Washington Redskins, San Francisco's playoff opponent on Saturday, are well coached but lack the team speed to beat the Niners, the NBC Sports analyst and ex-49er coach told reporters during the network press tour here this week.

Ditto for another National Football Conference playoff contender, the Chicago Bears, Walsh said. The New York Giants are the fourth remaining NFC team, and Walsh said that without injured quarterback Phil Simms, the Giants "don't seem to be a team that was improving past the mid-point of the season."

But watch out, Walsh said, for the Buffalo Bills or Los Angeles Raiders. He said both are threats to give the American Conference its first Super Bowl victory since 1984.

"Either Buffalo or the Raiders can logically take on the 49ers and play very, very well, if not win," he said. "Both those teams are, contrary to recent years with the AFC, big, physical, strong, active teams. . . . The 49ers are not as strong as they were a year ago. They won more on skill this year than on their physical prowess, so to speak. So the 49ers would really be tested. It could conceivably be that the Raiders or the Bills are the strongest teams the 49ers would have played this year."

Super Bowl XXV will be televised January 27 from Tampa, on ABC.

Plans to Stay with NBC

Walsh is still waiting for his first crack at broadcasting a Super Bowl; NBC's turn in the rotation isn't until next year. Meanwhile, his name is bandied about for every coaching vacancy in the NFL, most recently at Tampa Bay.

Walsh apparently has been noncommittal about re-upping his NBC contract. But when he was asked about quitting TV to return to coaching, Walsh said, "I plan to stay with NBC" and added that "I don't expect" to be back in the NFL next season.

The qualifying words "plan" and "expect" could be classic dodges to leave Walsh room to maneuver. But he insisted that although he hasn't signed a new contract with the network, "we're going to be talking about that."

Walsh's abilities as a novice broadcaster were heavily criticized last year when he replaced Merlin Olsen as Dick Enberg's partner on NBC's top booth team. But his network boss, NBC Sports executive producer Terry O'Neil, said that Walsh has improved steadily.

"We're pleased with what he's done this year," O'Neil said. "Bill's grown. He's improved week to week. It's actually perceptible, we think. You know, he didn't win a Super Bowl till his third year as coach of the 49ers. I think it's unrealistic to think he would have hit his potential as a broadcaster any sooner than three years, at least.

"You only have to look at his recent couple of games. I mean, the Orange Bowl in Miami (between Colorado and Notre Dame) was a great example. Bill literally was coaching the Colorado team from the booth better than it was being done on the sideline."

Kudos to Seifert

Walsh, seated next to fellow NBC football analyst Paul Maguire at the Los Angeles press conference, tossed a bouquet in the direction of his 49ers successor, George Seifert, when he was asked for his coach of the year pick.

"I think George Seifert in the NFC, for sure," Walsh said.

"Well, there's a surprise," Maguire said sarcastically.

"I think Seifert has to get it," Walsh continued. "He's lost four games in two years, and won one championship. He's got the best record in the history of coaching at this point in his career. So at some point you have to acknowledge that.

"The team has done incredibly well, better than really any team in history. He has to receive a lot of that credit."

SOURCE: *San Francisco Chronicle,* final, page D1
DATE: Tuesday, January 8, 1991
AUTHOR: Ron Thomas, *Chronicle* staff writer
HEADLINE: Redskins will look different; Seifert says S.F. will need 'big' intensity to win

How high an intensity level should the 49ers reach for Saturday's playoff opener against Washington?

"As big as we can get it," coach George Seifert said during a press conference yesterday. "Super Bowl big? As big as it can get, because that's what we're going to need."

The Washington team the 49ers will face this week shouldn't be equated with the Redskins who lost at Candlestick Park, 26-13, in September. Joe Montana exploited that Redskins defense for 390 passing yards and two touchdowns, and he had plenty of time to do it, because he never was sacked.

Since then, Seifert said, Washington's defense has greatly improved. "They're beating everybody to the punch," he said. "When the ball is snapped, there's an explosion on the defensive side." That explosiveness has come mostly from a revamped defensive line and a linebacking corps that has revived the pass rush.

In September, the Redskins' starting linemen were ends Charles Mann and Markus Koch and tackles Tracy Rocker and Darryl Grant. One reserve lineman, Tim Johnson, hardly played because he had recently been acquired from Pittsburgh.

Another reserve, Eric Williams, was on the inactive list because he had been acquired from Detroit just a few days before the 49er game. And veteran lineman James Geathers, who had been signed as a Plan B free agent, was on injured reserve.

As the season went along, all three used their quickness off the snap to juice up the Redskins' pass rush. Although the matchup between 49ers offensive tackle Steve Wallace and Mann, a four-time Pro Bowler, still will be important, Seifert said, "The difference is the other guys have cranked it up. As we went into that (September) game, it was Mann that was the focal point. Now it's all of them. As a unit there's not a guy, but they're all very, very explosive."

Williams, whose father, Roy, played with the 49ers from 1958-64, eventually took the starting tackle job from Rocker, whose strong suit is running defense. Williams played very well until he injured an arch in the 15th game and went on injured reserve.

He was replaced by Johnson, who sacked Randall Cunningham twice in Washington's playoff victory over Philadelphia. Johnson and Geathers, whom 49er fans may remember as a former New Orleans starter, each had three sacks during the regular season. Fred Stokes, another sub, led the Redskins with seven sacks. Compared to recent years, it's a decidedly quicker group than in recent years.

Until last year, massive, ponderous Dave Butz was a fixture at tackle. He retired after the 1988 season and was replaced by Rocker. Johnson is much more mobile than both of them.

"I don't think he's as good as (Pierce) Holt and (Kevin) Fagan, but he's that size guy," 49er offensive line coach Bobb McKittrick said. "He's a 6-3, 260-pound guy instead of a 290-pound guy. He's just quicker."

The Redskins lost an excellent pass rusher when Dexter Manley was suspended for drug abuse last season and never returned to the team. Koch replaced him, and now Stokes replaces Koch on passing downs.

"Stokes is not as good as Dexter Manley, but he's quicker than Marcus Koch," McKittrick said. "And they've been bringing Geathers in (for Grant), and he's fresh."

Their efforts contributed to sacking Cunningham five times on Saturday.

"When Randall went back to pass, all of a sudden he's got all these different color uniforms in his backfield," Seifert said.

Three players have been the keys to the Redskins' improved pass coverage: linebackers Kurt Gouveia and Andre Collins, and cornerback Martin Mayhew.

In September, Collins, a second-round draft choice from Penn State who became an immediate starter, was playing in only his second NFL game and wasn't skilled enough at pass coverage to play in the nickel defense.

As the season went along, he developed into a rangy defender with enough speed to cover tight ends and play in the nickel. He also ranked second on the Redskins with six sacks and recently was named to a national publication's All-Rookie team.

Gouveia, a fourth-year player, specializes in pass defense and supplanted run-oriented Greg Manusky as the starting middle linebacker. (Gouveia also has distinguished himself by being a rare NFL player who enjoys doing needle point in his spare time.)

Mayhew was making only his second NFL start when John Taylor burned him for most of his eight catches for 160 yards and one touchdown. When the season ended, Mayhew led the Redskins with six interceptions.

"Their defense is just a heck of a lot better than when we played them the first time," Seifert said.

SOURCE: The *Boston Globe,* third edition, page 26
DATE: Tuesday, January 8, 1991
AUTHOR: Joe Burris, *Globe* staff
HEADLINE: Reporters flocked to unlikely source

FOXBOROUGH—At yesterday's press conference, there were three men drawing a swarm of reporters.

One was Patriots chief executive officer Sam Jankovich, who announced that Syracuse coach Dick MacPherson had been named New England's head coach. Another, of course, was MacPherson. But a surprising third was Dick's brother, Normand, a priest at St. Joseph's Parish in Old Town, Maine. He earned a place in the spotlight by making the announcement of his brother's hiring at Mass Sunday.

In fact, a few reporters phoned MacPherson's sister's home to try to confirm the church announcement. And ESPN credited him for making the announcement in its "SportsCenter" program yesterday morning.

Father MacPherson said that prior to Mass, he told the church lector, Louis Bates, and a few other members of the church who were in the sacristy at the time, of his brother's hiring.

"Then the lector said to the congregation, 'Please rise for our celebrant, the brother of the new Patriots' head coach,' " said MacPherson.

"I told the congregation that we were awarded a big Christmas present during Little Christmas," said Father MacPherson, who was somewhat shocked that the lector beat him to the punch.

"I was surprised he did it. I said to myself, 'Cripes, I thought I was going to say it.' "

He said the congregation was surprised as well, but greeted the announcement warmly. Well, at least some did.

"Some people said, 'Oh, what did he do that for?' " said Father MacPherson. "But everyone in Old Town knows Dick. It's his home church. After 1987 Syracuse's 11-0-1 season, he spent a lot of time at the local YMCA. He was very influential."

Asked if he had ever been in the spotlight, Father MacPherson said, "Oh, no. Some people felt that I came down here for that, but I really came to see our sister, who is in the hospital. The reporters called because they were having a tough time verifying the story."

After telling his own story, he spent much of the press conference talking about Dick, who used to get him Chicago Bears tickets while he was a priest in Chicago and Dick was an assistant freshman football coach at the University of Chicago. He has followed the teams his brother has coached—the Cleveland Browns, Denver Broncos and Syracuse. He even recalled times when they sneaked under the bleachers at the University of Maine's football stadium (about 5 miles from Old Town) to watch games.

Asked if Dick ever talked much about being head coach of the Patriots, Father MacPherson said, "Not that I know of. I got that out of my mind because I thought he was happy at Syracuse. As it turned out, he was. I remember the first time he showed me the Carrier Dome. I told him that I thought he'd go pro, and he said, 'No, this is my church.' "

In Father MacPherson's eyes, though, his brother made the right decision. "I think he knows there is a job to be done, and he knows how to get it done. I don't know what coaches he will find to help him, but I'm certain he will."

TELEPHONE INTERVIEWS. Sportswriters often depend on the telephone for information about competition involving local teams. In such cases, the coaches or other team representatives call in results and agree to be interviewed about the performance at the same time.

SOURCE: The *Miami Herald,* final edition, page 1D
DATE: Friday, February 9, 1990
AUTHOR: Gary Ferman, *Herald* sportswriter
HEADLINE: George blasts players, 'small-market' owners

New York Yankees owner George Steinbrenner Thursday blamed baseball's players union for the impasse in contract negotiations and blasted other owners for driving up salaries.

"The owners are putting out a proposal and the union isn't coming back with something concrete," he said.

Steinbrenner said he expects owners to be unified today at a meeting in Chicago to decide whether to institute a lockout when camps are due to open next Thursday. However, he criticized some "small-market" owners.

"I'm tired of hearing about all these guys in small markets crying about how much the so-called rich teams are making," Steinbrenner told *The Los Angeles Times.* "Don't look at me while you're crying about rising salaries."

In a telephone interview with *The Herald,* Steinbrenner said, "Those guys in San Francisco have to be stupid," referring to the $15 million contract given to first baseman Will Clark. "Clark is a fine ballplayer. But he isn't eligible for free agency for two years yet.

"When they point to the Yankees (for driving up salaries), it is pure bull. You look at the top 10 salaries in baseball and not one of them is a Yankee."

Reprinted with the permission of the *Miami Herald*

References

Abel, Friedrich E. 1969. Note-takers vs. Non-notetakers: Who makes more errors? *Journalism Quarterly* 46:811–14.

Biagi, Shirley. 1986. *Interviews That Work: A Practical Guide for Journalists.* Belmont, Calif.: Wadsworth.

Black, Jay. 1978. Reaping between the lines: Non-verbal cues to the journalistic interview. Paper presented at annual convention of Association for Education in Journalism, Seattle.

Brady, John. 1977. *The Craft of Interviewing.* New York: Vintage.

Giamatti, A. Bartlett. 1988. What's wrong with American sports pages? *Proceedings of the American Society of Newspaper Editors 1988.* Washington, D.C., April 15, 201–15.

Gottlieb, Marvin. 1986. *Interview.* New York: Longman.

Johansen, Peter. 1976. Interviewing. In *Handbook of Reporting Methods,* edited by Maxwell McCombs, Donald Lewis Shaw, and David Grey. Boston: Houghton Mifflin.

Killenberg, George M., and Rob Anderson. 1989. *Before the Story: Interviewing and*

Communication Skills for Journalists. New York: St. Martin's.

Klement, Alice. 1989. Personal communication with the authors, March 1.

Lucan, Alice Neff. 1988. Sports writing truly mightier than the sword. *APSE Newsletter,* February, 3.

Metzler, Ken. 1989. *Creative Interviewing.* 2nd ed. Englewood Cliffs, N.J.: Prentice-Hall.

Morris, Jim R. 1973. Newsmen's interview techniques and attitudes toward interviewing. *Journalism Quarterly* 50:539–42, 548.

Nilsson, Nils Gunnar. 1971. The origin of the interview. *Journalism Quarterly* 48:707–13.

Rivers, William L., and Shelly Smolkin. 1981. *Free-Lancer and Staff Writer: Newspaper Features and Magazine Articles.* 3d ed. Belmont, Calif.: Wadsworth.

Stewart, Charles J., and William B. Cash, Jr. 1991. *Interviewing: Principles and Practices.* 4th ed. Dubuque, Iowa: Brown.

Tienhaara, Barbara. 1980. Sports interviewing: Plimpton style. *Quill* 68 (10):22–23.

Webb, Eugene J., and Jerry R. Salancik. 1966. The interview or the only wheel in town. *Journalism Monographs* 2 (November): 1.

Professional tennis star Jennifer Capriati returns a shot at the Lipton International Tennis Tournament at Key Biscayne, Fla. (*Photo by Pete Cross, the* Miami Herald.)

5

Observation Strategies

Sports journalists depend a great deal on their ability to see what is going on around them. The most basic sports reporting assignment, covering a game, involves watching and recording what happens on the field or court. Reporters with fine-tuned observational skills will be able to watch and note not only the most significant elements of the game, but also more subtle actions that may affect the outcome. They may, at the same time a key play occurs, also see what is happening away from the center of action.

Sportswriters have to hone observational skills for stories that are not competition oriented also. During interviews, non-verbal cues may help a reporter decide whether a source is telling the truth, for instance. In writing a profile of an athlete, use of observational skills may help the story by providing rich description for mood, atmosphere, and background.

Strong descriptive writing depends on concentrated and careful observation. Developing an ability to see what is happening will lead to more color, or atmosphere, in spot sports news stories as well as in feature articles (Garrison 1989).

Perhaps the sports journalist with the most recognized observational skills is George Plimpton, a writer who has focused his work on just about all professional sports. His reputation has grown since his football book, *Paper Lion,* was published (Plimpton 1965). His first book, about playing for a baseball team during spring training (Plimpton 1961), set the stage for the heralded story of an ordinary guy who wanted to fulfill the dream of playing quarterback for a professional football team. With the cooperation of the Detroit Lions, Plimpton not only closely observed summer camp and preseason games, but actually got into a game to call five plays. His first-person observational skills used in writing those two books and the many books and magazine articles that have followed over the past three decades give readers a vivid impression of what happens on the inside of sports, from the locker rooms and practice fields (see also Plimpton 1978). Plimpton enriches his stories with detail through dialogue, descriptive reconstruction of scenes and settings, and unique creativity.

For the modern sports journalist, whether a Plimpton writing books and magazine articles or a sportswriter producing daily newspaper articles, observation strategies play an important role in overall reporting skills. To notice, with the full use of the human senses, the colors, sounds, smells, and textures of objects, leads to the use of richer adjectives and adverbs, more precise nouns, and overall stronger writing (Garrison 1989). Daniel Williamson (1975) recommends approaching an assignment with the idea that a reporter is the eyes, ears, and nose of the reader. Sportswriters must gather an assortment of information and compose a story from it, but, as a newsgatherer, the reporter has to choose the right information from his or her observations to create the correct image in the mind of the reader.

Need for Observation Strategies

Isn't it obvious that a sportswriter must observe what goes on around him or her? Yes. Isn't watching sports events always a large part of sports reporting? Of course. But because observation is so important, the more sophisticated and systematic reporters are about it, the more information their efforts will produce. And journalists sometimes forget that they can observe. As The Missouri Group (Brooks et al. 1988) states: "Some reporters look, but do not see. The detail they miss may be the difference between a routine story and one that is a delight to read." Powers of observation, the group of four Missouri professors says, work for reporters. What someone might call being nosy is the sharp journalist's simply noticing all that is happening. There are established ways to accomplish this, many of them developed in years of journalistic practice and others borrowed from social sciences such as anthropology, sociology, and psychology.

Validity is an important aspect of observational strategies. Often, observation serves as a reporter's "insurance policy." First-hand observation validates information from other sources. Reporters may find it not enough to rely on verbal responses. Close observation of sources can indicate to the reporter if a source is lying, holding back information, or behaving in any other inconsistent way. It can also clear up ambiguities.

Many times a reporter is unable to obtain information directly; reluctant sources or other situations may make information gathering through conventional procedures impossible. Beyond the interview and document search, one solution to collecting information is first-hand observation—simply watching what happens.

Non-participant Observation

Observation skills should be used together with information gathering skills such as interviewing and document searches. These three approaches seldom stand alone in a complete reporting effort. For example, some reporters rarely conduct an interview without noting details such as what the source wore, the environment of the conversation, and the source's facial expressions. William Rivers and Shelly Smolkin (1981) conclude: "Both the beginning newspaper writer and the newspaper staffer trying to switch from conventional newspaper style to the longer, more-demanding feature or in-depth article must accustom themselves to a new pace. They must learn the background that goes into writing lengthy articles." Much of this background is research, Rivers and Smolkin note, but they also point out that some is observation:

> Observation is vital to a true report. Like interviewing, direct observation yields liveliness—paragraphs that lend a lift and freshness. And woe betide the journalist who can't observe. Early in his career, Bruce Bliven had the good fortune to work under Fremont Older, a demanding San Francisco editor with "a personality so vigorous that you could feel his presence through a brick wall." Deciding that one dull reporter could write compellingly only by immersing himself in his subject, Older assigned him to write about the Salvation Army and gave him all the time he needed to research and write captivatingly. But after three weeks with the Army, the reporter turned in his usual flavorless stuff. "Didn't you observe anything?" Older bellowed. "At night, for instance, where did they hang the bass drum?" The reporter did not know. He was fired.

Concentration is essential because a reporter can become too familiar with his or her environment. Careful concentration on the immediate surroundings is essential when working on a story. There are many objects in an athlete's dorm room or in a coach's office that can compete for attention. These observation skills—noting detail and incorporating it into stories—are developed primarily from practice.

A second aspect of observation is perspective. The angle from which one sportswriter views a play may be different from that of another sportswriter; this can make a difference in the details observed. At a crowded press conference, a reporter with a close view of the subject might get more useful detail from facial expressions than could a colleague near the back. Being close may mean the most basic in reporting, too: The reporter can hear what is said. Cases of differing perspective have arisen countless times after controversial plays in games, and in recent years the whole situation has been further complicated by the addition of the instant videotape replay. The same problem is illustrated by two different camera angles replaying the same action.

Rivers and Smolkin (1981) have provided reporters with a list of the most common observation pitfalls:

1. Process of distortion. The reporter's perceptions can influence what is seen.

2. Emotional states. The reporter's emotional condition, or level of objectivity in observing the situation, can influence what is seen.

3. Significant details. Reporters often try to see too much and do not concentrate on the most important visual details. This certainly influences what is seen.

4. Distortions of perspective. A single perspective should be enhanced by a second or third perspective. Observing from only one angle can influence what is seen.

Journalists Mitchell and Blair Charnley (1979) point out still another aspect of observation, noting its importance in bringing color to a story with the addition of description: "The purpose of color is to take the readers to the scene, to provide the sensory stimulants that the reporter perceived. Its tool is putting into words what would have struck the observers—what they would have heard, seen, smelled, touched, tasted, and perhaps breathed." Charnley and Charnley advise seeking a "universal point of view," observing as the reader would have observed.

Ken Metzler (1989) recommends taking advantage of an identity as a reporter. Non-participation or minimal participation can be an advantage because the reporter's affiliation with a newspaper or magazine may provide a better perspective to witness an event or situation. This most clearly occurs when a sportswriter is given a press box, courtside, or ringside seat, or a sideline pass. A reporter's presence can change the situation, the ultimate being "media events"—events that occur only for the media's use, such as press conferences, grand openings, and special celebrity appearances. An effective reporter should be as unobtrusive as possible, taking notes only when it does not interfere. Taking too many notes can cause problems—for example, influencing the people being observed—and spoil the desired situation. Metzler also emphasizes the importance of concentration in order to memorize observations when note taking is not possible. Fortunately, when non-participant observation is important to a story, note taking is usually not a problem. But, it is important for a reporter to judge when not to take notes. Experience will teach this.

First-hand observation by a reporter can impart credibility to a story. There is no doubt that the eyewitness factor enhances the power of reporting. Everette Dennis and Arnold Ismach (1981) point out another advantage of personal observation — avoiding the errors that crop up when using intermediate sources to gather detail, such as telephoning eyewitnesses. When this is done, a reporter gives up any value in personal observation and must deal with potentially faulty memories, biases, misperceptions, and other forms of interference through which sources filter information.

But there are also disadvantages in gathering information by personal observation. Dennis and Ismach say observation is time-consuming, expensive (travel), sometimes potentially dangerous, and at times deceptive (because reporters can see only one perspective themselves). To avoid these problems, Dennis and Ismach offer these suggestions:

1. Train yourself through practice by reciting details such as contents of rooms and offices, or the appearance of friends.

2. Remember that your vantage point may obscure observation. Decide what you wish to observe and from what view.

3. Cross-check details with other observers.

4. Study non-verbal communication, such as manner of speech, facial expression, and body language.

5. Look for physical signs, such as nervousness.

6. Write down observations as soon as possible.

Participant Observation

The special instances of participant observation (called "participatory journalism" by some people), such as Plimpton's participating in the Professional Golfers' Association tour or competing as a professional boxer, are clearly not the everyday sort of observation-based reporting with which we are concerned. But participant observation at a regional or even a local level can be as useful as non-participant observation. Participant observation as an information-gathering tool has its roots in sociology and anthropology and has been accepted by reporters as a valid means of collecting information. (For some excellent perspectives of social sciences, see Whyte [1943] and Gans [1967].)

More than 50 years ago, New York sportswriter Paul Gallico got in the ring to box. Today, it is quite common to hear of young reporters who go back to school to describe our educational systems from the students' side, reporters who drive or ride in ambulances to learn the quality of medical services, or reporters who deliberately commit misdemeanors to get an inside look at county or state penal systems.

In sports journalism, participant observation is just as effective as a reporting tool. The advantage of coaching a team and writing about it, or working as a major league batboy, or even toting the golf bag of a touring pro on a PGA stop is to be able to convey the impressions and feelings of the direct experience to readers. Participant observation is observation in its purest form, because reporters cross the line from detached observation to involved observation, especially if sources do not know the reporter's real professional identity. Such unidentified participant observation can pose ethical problems, but the story may fall apart if the reporter's identity is known. This method should be used, therefore, only if there is no other way to get the story. For instance, if the source will not discuss some activity or concern or give honest and accurate answers, it may become essential to become an unidentified participant observer.

A reporter's undisclosed identification, however, can create restrictions. If hired as a ticket salesman for a collegiate athletic department, for example, a reporter cannot move easily into the athletic director's office to ask questions without blowing the cover. But the reporter can watch unfair, or even illegal, ticket sales or distribution policies if a key game nears with demand for tickets exceeding capacity of the stadium or arena.

It is preferable to operate as an identified reporter, as Plimpton does. The sources will eventually become accustomed to the observer reporter's presence and go back to their normal routines.

One of the advantages of participant observation is that it is an alternative to interviews with sources who are unwilling to talk to a reporter. An example might be individuals operating illegal sports gambling operations, involved in high-level big-money professional sports marketing strategies, or involved in management of public sports facilities and public monies. There is also less pressure on a reporter to depend on second-hand observation when participatory reporting is done (Ryan and Tankard 1977).

The perspective is unique. It is one thing to watch motocross racers from the judges' stand high above the track, but it is very different to take personal control of a powerful bike and race it through a trial heat. Even if you don't race, the perspective of just riding the motorbike around the track when no racing is going on is more than just watching someone else do it.

The work of a sports reporter may not be as well organized when observation is the method of information gathering. Whether participant or non-participant, observation lacks the clearly defined procedures of other reporting tools, such as interviewing or survey research. Matilda Riley and Edward Nelson (1974) state:

> [Observation] is defined broadly as diverse combinations of watching and listening—with questioning; with use of mechanical recording instruments, cameras, or other hardware; or with the artifacts of past interaction or any other pertinent data. There are no fixed boundaries. One can scarcely be surprised, then, that there [is] no clearly formulated methodology of sociological observation. Several strands of observational procedure [have been] adapted from anthropology, small group studies and various types of community stud-

ies and participant observation, each a particular hybrid of observation questioning, and documentary materials.

There are two general approaches to participant reporting by American newspapers and magazines. If resources permit, a sportswriter may become a participant. The writer then spends the additional time required for such participation and gives a full effort to becoming a part of the activity.

Sports reporting can turn the tables in a different way. If there are limited reporting resources or if the sports editor wants still another different perspective, an actual participant may become a reporter, writing about his or her experiences for publication. For example, Joey Meyer, basketball coach of DePaul University, wrote a column for the *Chicago Tribune* sports section during a basketball season. Roger Craig, manager of the San Francisco Giants, wrote nine stories — one column a day — for the *San Francisco Chronicle* (Stein 1986). Former Notre Dame lineman Steve Huffman wrote a first-person article for *Sports Illustrated* about his experiences on the team, including the controversial revelation that there were widespread use and sale of muscle-building steroids among players and that his coach, Lou Holtz, knew about it (Associated Press 1990).

On smaller newspapers, such as rural or suburban weeklies, it is not unusual to find the sportswriter of the newspaper also the high school football coach, or an assistant. While this practice creates some interesting stories, it can raise questions about conflict of interest.

Washington Post sportswriter Christine Brennan used participant observation in her story about Ladies Professional Golf Association tournament player Tracy Kerdyk. Brennan spent a week with Kerdyk, a beginner on the tour, at the Lady Keystone Open in Hershey, Pa. Brennan's story, distributed nationally by the Washington Post Service, was written first person and focused on her experiences as a caddy as well as on the players on the LPGA tour. The story is filled with Brennan's experiences and the interaction of the two individuals. Brennan tells readers that she has known Kerdyk since she was sportswriter for the *Miami Herald* and Kerdyk was a junior golfer in South Florida. The story is rich with direct quotations and descriptions difficult to get with a standard third-person approach. Readers are given insightful personal reactions to missed shots, gallery descriptions, and a strong look at life on the tour by a 24-year-old newcomer ranked 91st at the time, June 1990, on the LPGA money list. Brennan's story is quite long — about 85 standard newspaper column inches — and was published several weeks after the event. As a feature, it provides a diary-style look at a specific tournament, but also doubled as an advance for the *Post* for the LPGA Championship played at the end of July in the Washington area. Here is how the story began, but because of its exceptional length, it cannot be reproduced in its entirety here:

SOURCE: The *Miami Herald,* final edition, pages 1D, 8D
DATE: Sunday, August 19, 1990
AUTHOR: Christine Brennan, *Washington Post* sportswriter
HEADLINE: There's more to caddying than just carrying the bag

EDITOR'S NOTE: Christine Brennan, a former *Herald* sportswriter now writing for the *Washington Post,* caddied for Coral Gables' Tracy Kerdyk at the Lady Keystone Open June 1-3 in Hershey, Pa. Here is Brennan's account:

We trudged toward the 18th green, my golfer and I, our three-day, 11-mile journey over the emerald hills and valleys of Hershey, Pa., all but a few yards from being over. People in lawn chairs were waiting around the green. There were several hundred in the gallery and they were applauding. The cheering wasn't for the person loaded down with the bag, of course. That was me. It was for the woman carrying the putter I had just handed her.

The 18th is the place where dreams come true, or when they just get strung along for another week. It's where one pro golfer wins the tournament and where the others pick up their balls and walk off, dreaming about the day they will be in her place.

"Someday," said Tracy Kerdyk, the 24-year-old LPGA golfer I've known for eight years, since she was the only girl on the boys' golf team at Coral Gables High. "Someday, I'll walk up 18 and everyone will be standing there, cheering for me. I can't wait for the day that happens. I'll turn to look over my shoulder at the leader board and my name will be there, right on top. When that happens, I'll have tears in my eyes."

I turned to look at her as we walked up the fairway. The 35-pound bag riding on my right shoulder turned with me. I smiled. Tracy and I had discussed everything over three days: cute guys in the gallery, side bets on putts made and missed, if we'd have time to play tennis later, where we were going to eat dinner, when to take a bathroom break. Now, on 18, she suddenly turned sentimental. The good shots, the bad shots—they didn't matter anymore.

"In fact," she said, "I have tears in my eyes right now, just thinking about it."

Tracy was not among the leaders. Her name never made the big board that flanks the green. She was not going to win this golf tournament for which I was her caddie. She was simply going to finish tied for 54th, earn $679 and move on to the next stop on the tour.

Afterward, we went back to the hotel, changed, packed and checked out and still made it back to 18 in time to watch the leaders take that same walk and a woman named Cathy Gerring win the tournament.

Tracy has never won on the LPGA Tour, but she's in just her second year and she will win, because she is very good. Gerring is in her sixth year. Until Hershey, she had never won.

A Rookie at This

I have a few disclaimers to issue right off the bat. I took lessons as a kid, but I don't play golf now. I don't watch golf. And I don't do sand traps. Or at least, I didn't until this spring.

I'm a sports writer at *The Washington Post*. I play lots of sports for fun, but I observe for a living.

Almost a year ago, Tracy, then in the midst of a run that ended with her being runner-up LPGA Rookie of the Year, asked me if I wanted to caddie for her someday. Tracy is like a little sister to me. When she was in high school and I was beginning my career as a sports writer at *The Miami Herald,* she'd come by the UM press box to talk. One day she was depressed and thinking of giving up golf. I told her to give it a few weeks before she made up her mind. That was six years ago.

So she trusted me to carry her bag and play amateur psychologist for the week.

"As long as you don't mind that your caddie gives you absolutely no help," I said. No problem, she said.

Hills in Hershey are Murder

Tracy and I picked Hershey because the purse of $300,000 wasn't the tour's largest. Tracy did warn me that the hills of Hershey were murder. I bought a Lifecycle and started working out.

I liked the idea of caddying for her and having the opportunity to write about someone I first wrote about eight years ago. I deal with all kinds of professional athletes now, but I knew none of them as kids.

With Tracy, I did. My editor in Miami asked me to write a feature on the 16-year-old girl who was shooting 73s and beating the boys. When I went out to talk to her, I found a totally driven teen-ager with a list of goals. Her long-range goal was to make the LPGA Tour. . . .

Reprinted with the permission of the *Washington Post*

Unobtrusive Observation

This form of observation differs from non-participant or participant observation in that a reporter witnesses events without ever being a factor in the situation, without influencing the participants at all. To put it simply, the reporter becomes a part of the woodwork. The reporter moves among those at the event without the potential sources knowing that he or she is a reporter. An unknown or unrecognized reporter, such as a new staff member, can accomplish this type of observation more easily than a reporter of wide local reputation.

There is no intentional concealment of the reporter's identity or of his or her intent in this type of reporting. But Dennis and Ismach (1981) point out: "When reporters are on the scene of an event it is usually desirable for them not to call attention to themselves. Social scientists often seek methods of measurement that eliminate the experimenter effect."

There are various ethical considerations regarding unobtrusive observation as a reporting tool. Melvin Mencher (1991) notes that some journalists condemn this type of observation: "Their criticism stems from their concern about widespread intrusions into privacy by insurance firms, credit investigators, and the federal government. What right, then, should the journalist have to do what is his business to expose as a violation of privacy?" Such potential problems mean that decisions must be made about responsible reporting, Mencher adds. His advice: "For private activities, think twice; for official activities held in private, act in the public interest."

Ken Metzler (1989) says unobtrusive observation—"mouse in the corner observation"—is a good way to pick up color for a story. A feature story on a PGA tournament might be enhanced by watching it from the gallery; a reporter could tell the story about a players' strike better by talking to baseball fans at a local tavern and then portraying community reaction to the sudden interruption of the summer game.

Metzler (1989), Dennis and Ismach (1981), and others have suggested that reporters can conduct unobtrusive observation without watching people. For example, counting whiskey or beer bottles picked up after a college football game where alcoholic beverages are prohibited by state law may determine, in a rough way, the amount of drinking at the game. Another example of such "artifact" research is checking with building maintenance personnel to determine which glass needs to be cleaned the most at a school's hall of fame exhibits to determine which exhibits are among the most popular. Some reporters even venture into garbage dumpsters to research team business dealings by checking discarded correspondence and other papers. (See Metzler [1989], Dennis and Ismach [1981], and Webb and Campbell [1981] for other measures of human behavior that can be used as reporting tools.)

Systematic Analysis of Documents

One means of unobtrusively observing source activity is analyzing documents. Public documents, such as records of a stadium's operation by a metropolitan or county government, lend themselves to systematic content analysis. Although the procedure is a bit too involved to explain here, a number of excellent sources describe this procedure and its applications for journalists (Budd et al. 1967, Shaw and Wilhoit 1976, Krippendorff 1980, and Rosengren 1981). By deciding ahead of time what information is sought from the documents—in other words, what needs to be counted—a reporter can collect much more information than by using the usual read-the-document-and-take-notes procedure. This system is a means of handling the massive amounts of information in the minutes of stadium board meetings or in other similar records. Researchers have used document content analysis procedures for many years, and journalists are now applying these techniques. For the right story, a sportswriter should consider using this form of unobtrusive observation; it can yield much more information than less organized information gathering procedures.

Personal Experience Stories

Some sportswriting is based on personal observations through personal experiences unique to the writer. These special experiences are interesting enough to justify a story to permit others to share the experience. Personal experience stories are a major form of feature writing and often are used in magazine writing (Garrison 1989).

Personal experience stories are grounded in observational reporting, of course. These stories employ three major components, according to freelance writer Nancy Kelton (1988):

1. Point of view. What is the unique way in which the writer can present the situation?

2. Arrival at a basic truth. What is the point? What had been the conclusion from the experience?

3. Emotional involvement. Not only share your observations and experiences, but your emotional reaction to these observations and experiences.

The following story is an example of the sort of personal experience–observation reporting that has found its niche in sportswriting. By *Baltimore Sun* baseball writer Peter Schmuck, it is entertaining and insightful because he is able to share his reasons for becoming a sportswriter, his love for baseball, and the trials of having his unique last name.

SOURCE: The *Miami Herald,* final edition, page 13D
DATE: Sunday, February 4, 1990
AUTHOR: Peter Schmuck, the *Baltimore Sun*
HEADLINE: Yes, that is his name; No, he won't change it

EDITOR'S NOTE: Baseball writer Peter Schmuck recently left the *Orange County (Calif.) Register* to take a job at the *Baltimore Sun.*

BALTIMORE—First of all, let's dispense with the obvious questions.
Yes, it is my real name.
No, I never considered changing it.
And yes, it's kind of tough to order a pizza over the phone, which is one of the reasons I moved to Baltimore instead of Chicago.

Pardon the first-person narrative. It won't happen again, but when you arrive in a new city with a name like Schmuck, it's usually a good idea to explain yourself.

I'm one of the thousands of Southern Californians who watched the Macy's Parade on Thanksgiving Day and decided to move to a colder climate. Baltimore seemed like the perfect spot, though it would be even better if it had a giant inflatable Bullwinkle for special occasions.

I left California because I could no longer tolerate a state that once turned down my request for a personalized license plate on the grounds that my surname is "obscene and offensive to public decency." True story. You can look it up.

The Department of Motor Vehicles eventually relented, but it soon became obvious that there are better places to raise your kids than Southern California. I realized that about the time my 5-year-old son started greeting me with "Hey, dude" instead of "Hi, Dad."

There definitely are better places to cover baseball. For 11 seasons, I watched the Los Angeles Dodgers and California Angels combine to draw nearly 6 million fans a year. But I also watched about 5 million of them head for the parking lots in the seventh inning.

Even the night Jim Abbott pitched his first major-league shutout — matched against Roger Clemens, no less — it was just like clockwork. They came. They yawned. They conquered the urge to stay past 9 p.m.

Perhaps in an area that has nine major professional teams situated on the same 110-mile stretch of over-priced real estate, people can afford to be blase. Not so in Baltimore, where baseball is king and the Orioles are on the rebound. That's why I jumped at the opportunity to cover them for *The Sun.*

Baseball always has had a special place in my family history, though no Schmuck ever made it to the big leagues (unless you count Reggie Jackson). To my knowledge, no Schmuck ever even made it to the high school varsity. I certainly didn't.

My father, as a teen-ager growing up in St. Louis, used to work on Dizzy Dean's car. That ought to count for something. My brother was a promising young player, but traded his baseball future for a surfboard in about 1965. Only in California.

I had no baseball talent whatsoever, so I did the next best thing. I gained 40 pounds and became a sports writer. What a country.

There are certain advantages to having a strange name. No one ever forgets it, and even total strangers seem to know who I am whenever I do something stupid in traffic.

My brother got so tired of the constant ribbing that he changed his name to Paul Gilray and moved to a small town in Central California. But don't be fooled. He's just another Schmuck.

Reprinted with the permission of the *Baltimore Sun*

References

Associated Press. 1990. Notre Dame steroid use alleged. *Miami Herald,* August 22, 1C.

Brooks, Brian S., George Kennedy, Daryl S. Moen, and Don Ranly. 1988. *News Reporting and Writing.* 3rd ed. New York: St. Martin's.

Budd, Richard, Robert Thorp, and Lewis Donohew. 1967. *Content Analysis of Communications.* New York: Macmillan.

Charnley, Mitchell V., and Blair Charnley. 1979. *Reporting.* 4th ed. New York: Holt, Rinehart and Winston.

Dennis, Everette E., and Arnold H. Ismach. 1981. *Reporting Processes and Practices: Newswriting for Today's Readers.* Belmont, Calif.: Wadsworth.

Gans, Herbert J. 1967. *The Levitowners.* New York: Pantheon.

Garrison, Bruce. 1989. *Professional Feature Writing.* Hillsdale, N.J.: Lawrence Erlbaum Associates.

Kelton, Nancy. 1988. How to write personal experience articles. *Writer's Digest* 68 (1): 22–24.

Krippendorff, Klaus. 1980. *Content Analysis: An Introduction to Its Methodology.* Beverly Hills, Calif.: Sage.

Mencher, Melvin. 1991. *News Reporting and Writing.* 5th ed. Dubuque, Iowa: Brown.

Metzler, Ken. 1989. *Creative Interviewing.* Englewood Cliffs, N.J.: Prentice-Hall.

Plimpton, George. 1961. *Out of My League.* New York: Harper & Row.

———. 1965. *Paper Lion.* New York: Harper & Row.

———. 1978. Bozo the Bruin: "Lord, no more than five." *Sports Illustrated,* Febuary 6, 38.

Riley, Matilda White, and Edward E. Nelson. 1974. *Sociological Observation: A Strategy for New Social Knowledge.* New York: Basic Books.

Rivers, William L., and Shelly Smolkin. 1981. *Free-Lancer and Staff Writer: Newspaper Features and Magazine Articles.* Belmont, Calif.: Wadsworth.

Rosengren, Karl Erik. 1981. *Advances in Content Analysis.* Beverly Hills, Calif.: Sage.

Ryan, Michael, and James W. Tankard. 1977. *Basic News Reporting.* Palo Alto, Calif.: Mayfield.

Shaw, Donald Lewis, and G. Cleveland Wilhoit. 1976. In *Handbook of Reporting Methods,* edited by Maxwell McCombs, Donald L. Shaw, and David Grey. Boston: Houghton Mifflin.

Stein, M. L. 1986. Baseball manager learns a lesson. *Editor & Publisher* 119 (August 23): 16–17.

Webb, Eugene J., and Donald T. Campbell. 1981. *Unobtrusive Measures: Nonreactive Research in the Social Sciences.* 2nd ed. Boston: Houghton Mifflin.

Whyte, William Foote. 1943. *Street Corner Society: The Social Structure of an Italian Slum.* Chicago: University of Chicago Press.

Williamson, Daniel R. 1975. *Feature Writing for Newspapers.* New York: Hastings House.

3 Basic Story Forms

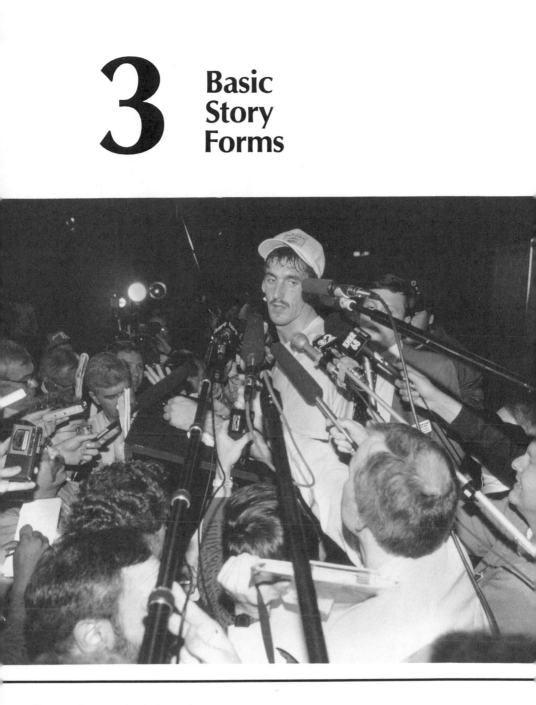

Sportswriters and photographers mob New York Giants' quarterback Jeff Hostetler in a special interview area after the Giants defeated the Buffalo Bills, 20–19, at Super Bowl XXV in Tampa in 1991. (*Photo by NFL Photos.*)

6

The Game Story

Almost the first thing that comes to mind when sportswriting is mentioned is the image of a journalist in a baseball park press box, on a football stadium sideline, or at a basketball arena courtside table. The journalist is rapidly taking notes about the action, perhaps even more quickly writing a story at his or her seat using a tiny portable personal computer.

Game coverage has never been the only aspect of sportswriting, but it continues to be the foundation of most sports sections. The serious sports journalist must know the mechanics of competition coverage to do a professional job and to succeed at the highest level. Learn the basics of covering a game, and mastery of the other types of sports stories will follow.

It is not unusual for a sportswriter to be assigned to write about several games in a single day, or to cover a tournament site involving as many as 16 teams, and to file stories on all games in one day. To accomplish this tall order, a sportswriter must know a great deal about the sport itself, the athletes, and the mechanics of getting the job done. This chapter, which focuses on the mechanics of covering sports competition, is not just a how-to-do-it for "gamers" (game stories), but it also discusses how to organize the reporting effort and how to prepare the story for publication in a short period of time.

Collecting Background

In any type of reporting, research is the most important aspect of preparation for an assignment, if the reporter has the time. Of course, a reporter may not know in advance that he or she will be covering a specific event—a tennis match or a baseball game, for example—and so cannot prepare. Instances when the reporter does not know enough about a sport to cover it adequately are rare, but in this era of increased attention to minor sports, a reporter might sometimes be in such a fix. When this occurs, a reporter can use several strategies. First is reading the literature of that sport such as rule books, magazines, and newsletters of organizations. If sufficient time or convenient literature is not available, the reporter should use human sources as educational tools. Talking to officials, scorers, statisticians, and managers of the event (and, in the case of minor sports especially, even the participants) is appropriate, before the action begins. Further explanations can be obtained afterward also. These experts can answer general questions about how the sport is played and the subtleties of the competition. Most people associated with a minor sport will be pleased to help in the spirit of boosting the sport or their own organization.

When preparation time is available to research a specific group of teams or athletes, sportswriters have a different set of problems. How does the reporter find out about them? Who are the record holders? Who are the potential stars? Reporters research these questions, reading books, magazines, and newspapers, including their own. Specialty magazines are particularly useful. In baseball, *The Sporting News* has been known as the "bible" of the sport. It prints individual and team statistics and minor league statistics and stories, too. Professional football has the *Pro Football Weekly* tabloid. For professional and college basketball, there are *Basketball Times* and numerous regional publications. For soccer, there are *Soccer Digest* and *Soccer America;* for tennis, *Tennis, World Tennis,* and *Tennis Weekly;* for hockey, *Hockey Digest* and the *Hockey News;* and for preseason looks at professional and college football and basketball, Street's and Smith's annuals. These specialty publications are produced months in advance, so the information in them is occasionally out of date.

Clipped stories from office files and electronic newspaper library data bases are extremely helpful for a reporter to learn of previous performances by the teams and the stars. Individuals familiar with the sport and the teams and players can provide records, starting lineups, changes in the status of players, and so forth. These individuals include coaches, sports information directors (SIDs), and even reporters from newspapers in areas the teams are from. Although the tendency of most sports editors and writers is to toss out any press releases coming in the mail as irrelevant hype, these mailings can provide useful background information for the reporter not informed about a team or player.

Continuity

The term "continuity" simply means placing the game story in context. A reporter should not write a game story without putting the event in some sort of bigger picture, which means preparation. What is the importance of the game or meet? What is the effect of the outcome in terms of wins and losses for the teams involved? How does it measure against other recent contests? How do the individual performances compare with other efforts? If the writer reports on the action of a single game only, the reader misses important and interesting background.

Pregame Arrangements

Sportswriters cannot walk into any situation and expect red carpet treatment. To ensure reasonable attention by the hosts at a stadium, arena, or field, at most levels of sports, an effort to make contact must be made in advance:

1. Amateur/high school level or lower. Unless it is a major event, most amateur leagues and sports organizations involving athletes of high school age or lower require little or no advance arrangement. With proper credentials from a newspaper or other publication, a reporter will usually be admitted at the gate. It is always best, however, to notify officials at the host school when a reporter plans to be present. This courtesy helps in long-term relationships with these sources.

2. Amateur/college level. The greater attention given this level of competition means it is more difficult to make on-the-spot arrangements to cover the events. Most institutions of higher learning have sports information departments that control all pregame arrangements. It isn't impossible to get into a game on the day it is played without advance arrangements, but, to avoid problems, reporters should call ahead to SIDs for tickets or passes to limited-space areas such as press boxes, locker rooms, and sidelines. At the same time, credentials for photographers and others on the reporting team can be obtained. Other arrangements, such as communications, are important also. A reporter facing a deadline at the end of a game or shortly afterward must have access to a telephone to get the results back to the office regardless of whether he or she is using a computer, facsimile machine, or voice dictation. If the game is an important one and there is just one telephone available, the newspaper may pay to have a telephone line installed for the reporter's exclusive use. If not, the reporter should arrive a bit early to find a telephone or even have someone such as a student stay on the telephone to keep it available and the line open. Many schools keep an office open after a game, providing a well-lighted place to work and a telephone.

3. Professional level. Collegiate level sports receive more attention from reporters than do high school level, and professional sports generally receive the most attention. Access is even more difficult to obtain, underlining the importance of the reporter's arranging in advance to be credentialed for news media areas and other limited areas such as the field or locker rooms. Arrangements must be made through public relations personnel days or weeks ahead of time. With the advance scheduling of professional teams, this is usually not a problem. For beat reporters, it is not a problem either. But for a one-time or irregular assignment, advance contact is necessary

Professional or college team media representatives will assist reporters in making advance arrangements if help is requested, particularly when reporters are on the road. It is part of their responsibilities.

At the Scene

The reporter should know the area—where telephones and facsimile machines are, the fastest way out of the parking areas, where work areas are, and where sources can be found. There is nothing more frustrating than learning that the custodian at a gym wants to lock the office in which a reporter planned to write the story or than finding out that a doorway is blocked or locked, preventing the reporter from getting to a coach whom another reporter is interviewing.

Once the reporter knows the layout of the facility, getting to know the sources is the next step. The reporter should introduce himself or herself to the official scorer of the basketball game or the chief statistician of the football game, for example, telling them that the figures will be needed afterward and making arrangements to see them at the end of the contest. The reporter should then introduce himself or herself to the coaches, if not already acquainted, in an opportune moment such as during warm-up drills. But do not interfere with game preparation. And the reporter should not forget assistant coaches. They are often the real authorities on specific aspects of the game, the specialists on the scene.

Finally, the reporter finds the place to watch the event, checks any available handouts, and settles down to record the action.

Keeping Play-by-Play Charts

Carefully recording game plays is crucial to writing a solid and complete game story. Readers of sports sections usually know the material well and will note slight inaccuracies and respond to errors. These critics will let the reporter know when the wrong player is named or the wrong point total is given.

Play-by-play charts are helpful and can reduce the errors that creep into game stories. These charts enable reporters to record play by play, score by score, and moment by moment what is occurring on the floor or field. Many different varieties of charts have been developed over the years, and some reporters even develop their own. Play-by-play charts for the major sports should include the following:

For basketball: For high school and college, there must be space for the complete box score, including field goals, three-point shots attempted and made, free throws and free throws attempted, fouls, assists, rebounds, and total points. There must be even more detail for professional basketball. There should be space for notes for the "running" summary of the game, such as who scored, what the score was at the time, the type of shot, and the time of the game when the score occurred.

For football: Just as for basketball, a football play-by-play card should be designed by quarters, allowing enough space for an average number of plays to be run by both teams. High school teams, for instance, run as many as 30 to 35 plays a quarter, including penalties. The sheets provide space for the down and yards to go, the yard stripe, the play description, the gain or loss, and any other relevant details.

For baseball: The standard baseball scorebook is the most common play-by-play sheet for baseball or softball. It permits an accurate method of listing players, positions, offensive efforts, pitching records, and other inning-by-inning information. Scorebooks, like other play-by-play sheets, vary depending on the publisher, so it is wise to evaluate several before making a purchase. Several scorebooks are large enough to permit use of a single book for each team regularly covered in a single season. This allows greater ease in recordkeeping and in comparing player efforts in several contests when writing a story.

It is difficult, though not impossible, to keep play-by-play charts for some sports such as swimming, track and field, soccer, and hockey. In these sports, note taking is even more important.

In addition to play-by-play summaries, some sportswriters keep their own game statistics. This is necessary for adequate fast reporting of major sports, such as basketball and football. With personal computers, teams can generate statistics more quickly, usually in time for reporters on short deadlines.

In basketball stories, for example, readers want not only scoring summaries but statistics such as turnovers, two-point and three-point field goal attempts, shooting percentages, rebounds, blocked shots, and assists. If there is no reliable source (and home team statisticians are not always reliable, because they tend to boost their own players), the reporter must keep these figures. Charts can be designed for this, too.

MIAMI HEAT VS. INDIANA PACERS
FRIDAY FEBRUARY 1, 1991
7:30 PM
MIAMI ARENA

MIAMI HEAT

HEAT (11-33)

No.	Player	Pos.	Ht.	Wt.
2	Keith Askins	G-F	6-8	197
4	Rony Seikaly	C	6-11½	252
11	Sherman Douglas	G	6-0	180
12	Vernell Coles	G	6-2	182
20	Jon Sundvold	G	6-2	175
21	Kevin Edwards	G	6-3	197
33	Alec Kessler	F-C	6-11	245
34	Willie Burton	G-F	6-8	219
41	Glen Rice	F	6-8	220
43	Grant Long	F	6-9	230
*44	Terry Davis	F	6-10	236
53	Alan Ogg	C	7-2	235
55	Billy Thompson	F	6-7	217

PACERS (18-24)

No.	Player	Pos.	Ht.	Wt.
4	Michael Williams	G	6-2	175
10	Vern Fleming	G	6-5	185
11	Detlef Schrempf	F	6-10	230
14	Randy Wittman	G	6-6	210
20	George McCloud	G-F	6-8	215
22	Jawann Oldham	C	7-0	215
*24	Rik Smits	C	7-4	265
31	Reggie Miller	G	6-7	185
33	Mike Sanders	F	6-6	215
41	LaSalle Thompson	F-C	6-10	260
44	Ken Williams	F	6-9	205
45	Chuck Person	F	6-8	225
54	Greg Dreiling	C	7-1	250

Head Coach:	Ron Rothstein	Head Coach:	Bob Hill
Assistants:	Dave Wohl, Tony Fiorentino	Assistants:	Billy Knight, Bob Ociepka
Trainer:	Ron Culp	Trainer:	David Craig
Injuries:	Terry Davis, turf toe (Injured List)	Injuries:	Rik Smits, bone chips, right elbow (Injured List)

*Injured List
****
PROBABLE STARTING LINEUPS

F	Long	F	Person
F	Thompson	F	Thompson
C	Kessler	C	Dreiling
G	Douglas	G	Miller
G	Rice	G	Williams

****
OTHER GAMES TONIGHT
Phoenix @ Philadelphia   Detroit @ Washington
Boston @ Charlotte   Sacramento @ Milwaukee
Chicago @ Dallas   LA Lakers @ LA Clippers
Golden State @ Portland
****
VISITING MEDIA: David Benner, Indianapolis Star; Steve Brunner, Indianapolis News; Mark Boyle, Pacer Radio; Dale Ratterman, Pacers PR Director

NBA

The Miami Heat
Miami Arena
Miami, Florida
33136-4102

(305) 577-HEAT

Pregame starting lineups, rosters, and other team information are often provided by professional and college teams for sportwriters assigned to cover the game. (*Reprinted with the permission of the Miami Heat.*)

At professional and college games, team publicists provide play-by-play summaries, such as this Statman II first-quarter summary from a Miami Heat NBA game, freeing reporters to take other notes. (*Reprinted with the permission of the Miami Heat.*)

108

```
---------------------------------------------------------------------
Heat    : Long        Thompson    Kessler   Douglas    Rice
Pacers  : Person      Thompson    Dreiling  Miller     M Williams


TIME   Miami Heat                      SCORE LEAD  Indiana Pacers
                                                   Start of Period: 7:39

       OPENING TIP Kessler vs Dreiling TIP TO: Miller

   JUMPBALL VIOLATION ON KESSLER
11:44   STEAL-Thompson                            M Williams BAD PASS TOW 1
11:39   Kessler BAD PASS TOW 1                    STEAL-M Williams
11:35                              0-2   -2  Person 3' RUNNING JUMP (M Williams)
11:35                                            20 SEC TIME OUT
11:35   Thompson S.FOUL (P1,T1)    0-3   -3  Person 1FT (GOOD)
11:15                              0-5   -5  Miller 6' RUNNING JUMP
11:18   20 SEC TIME OUT
11:18   COLES FOR DOUGLAS
11:18   Rice S.FOUL (P1,T2)        0-6   -6  Miller 1FT (GOOD)
10:25   Thompson 22' JUMP (Rice)   2-6   -4
10:12                              2-8   -6  Dreiling DRIVING LAYUP
09:45                              2-10  -8  Miller 12' BASELINE
09:45   DOUGLAS FOR COLES
09:45   Coles S.FOUL (P1,T3)       2-11  -9  Miller 1FT (GOOD)
09:20                              2-13  -11 Person SLAM DUNK (M Williams)
09:15   TIME OUT (1)
08:54                              2-15  -13 Thompson DRIVING LAYUP
08:36   Thompson 16' JUMP (Kessler) 4-15 -11
08:28   STEAL-Long                               M Williams LOSES BALL TOW 2
08:24   Thompson LOSES BALL TOW 2
08:19                                            TIME OUT (1)
07:55   Long SLAM DUNK             6-15  -9
07:44                              6-17  -11 M Williams LAYUP (Person)
07:18   SEIKALY FOR KESSLER
07:18   Douglas S.FOUL (P1,T4)     6-18  -12 M Williams 2FT (GOOD,MISS)
07:03                                            M Williams P.FOUL (P1,T1)
06:48   Douglas DRIVING LAYUP      8-18  -10
06:37                              8-20  -12 Person LAYUP (M Williams)
06:22   Douglas 6' JUMP           10-20  -10
06:09                             10-22  -12 Miller 21' JUMP (M Williams)
05:47   EDWARDS FOR THOMPSON
05:47                                            SCHREMPF FOR THOMPSON
05:47   Seikaly 2FT (MISS,GOOD)   11-22  -11 Dreiling S.FOUL (P1,T2)
05:45   STEAL-Edwards                            M Williams BAD PASS TOW 3
05:41   Edwards DRIVING LAYUP      13-22  -9
05:20                                            Miller TRAVELING TOW 4
05:03                                            FLEMING FOR M WILLIAMS
05:03   Seikaly 2FT (GOOD,GOOD)   15-22  -7  Schrempf S.FOUL (P1,T3)
04:53                                            Person OFF FOUL (P1): TOW 5
04:53                                            TIME OUT (2)
04:18                             15-24  -9  Fleming LAYUP (Miller)
03:31   Seikaly LAYUP             17-24  -7
03:24   STEAL-Edwards                            Fleming BAD PASS TOW 6
03:11   Seikaly LAYUP (Long)      19-24  -5
02:56   COLES FOR DOUGLAS
02:56                                            SANDERS FOR PERSON
02:56   Long S.FOUL (P1,PN)       19-26  -7  Schrempf 2FT (GOOD,GOOD)
02:40   Long 2FT (GOOD,GOOD)      21-26  -5  Sanders S.FOUL (P1,T4)
02:28                             21-28  -7  Dreiling SLAM DUNK (Schrempf)
02:05   Seikaly 6' HOOK           23-28  -5
01:59   STEAL-Coles                              Fleming BAD PASS TOW 7


01:55   Coles LAYUP              25-28  -3
01:29   BURTON FOR RICE
01:29                                            OLDHAM FOR DREILING
01:29   Long S.FOUL (P2,PN)      25-30  -5  Miller 2FT (GOOD,GOOD)
01:10   Burton 20' RT CORNER (Seikaly) 27-30 -3
:49.2   Coles LOSES BALL TOW 3                   STEAL-Miller
:46.0   Burton S.FOUL (P1,PN)    27-32  -5  Miller 2FT (GOOD,GOOD)
:34.1                                            ILLEGAL DEFENSE Schrempf
:19.5   THOMPSON FOR LONG
:19.5   Long FOULS (P3,PN)       27-34  -7  Schrempf (1+1) (GOOD,GOOD)

                        ----------------
                      End Of 1st Quarter (27-34)
                      Period Ended at 8:08

        BIG HOME  LEAD  0                  *LEAD CHANGES  0
        BIG VISIT LEAD 13                   TIMES TIED    0

     Heat      3  FOR   5 PTS      TURNOVERS  Pacers    7  FOR  10 PTS
            11/26 FOR  42 %      FIELD GOALS        11/15 FOR  73%
             5/6  FOR  83 %      FREE THROWS        12/13 FOR  92%
             O: 6 / D: 5        REBOUNDS           O: 0 / D: 10

     Seikaly        9        HIGH SCORER      12  Miller
     Long&Seikaly   3        HIGH REBOUNDER    4  Dreiling
     SEVERAL        1        HIGH ASSISTS      4  M Williams
```

Copyright (c) 1990 NBA Properties, Inc.   All Rights Reserved.

1ST QUARTER

02-01-91   Miami, Fl.
OFFICIALS: Bernie Fryer   Terry Durham   Woody Mayfield   TIME OF GAME:
ATTENDANCE:

VISITORS: Indiana

NO PLAYER		MIN	FG	FGA	3P	3PA	FT	FTA	OR	DR	TOT	A	PF	ST	TO	PTS
45 Chuck Person	F	9	3	4	0	0	1	1	0	1	1	1	1	0	1	7
41 LaSalle Thompson	F	6	1	1	0	0	0	0	0	0	0	0	0	0	0	2
54 Greg Dreiling	C	11	2	2	0	0	0	0	0	4	4	0	1	0	0	4
31 Reggie Miller	G	12	3	4	0	0	6	6	0	1	1	1	0	1	1	12
04 Michael Williams	G	7	1	2	0	0	1	2	0	1	1	4	1	1	3	3
11 Detlef Schrempf		6	0	0	0	0	4	4	0	0	0	1	1	0	0	4
10 Vern Fleming		5	1	1	0	0	0	0	0	1	1	0	0	0	2	2
33 Mike Sanders		3	0	1	0	0	0	0	0	0	0	0	1	0	0	0
22 Jawann Oldham		1	0	0	0	0	0	0	0	1	1	0	0	0	0	0
20 George McCloud		DNP-														
44 Ken Williams		DNP-														
14 Randy Wittman		DNP-														
TOTALS		60	11	15	0	0	12	13	0	9	9	7	5	2	7	34

PERCENTAGES: 73.3   0.0   92.3   TM REB: 1 TOT TO: 7 (10 PTS)

HOME: Miami

NO PLAYER		MIN	FG	FGA	3P	3PA	FT	FTA	OR	DR	TOT	A	PF	ST	TO	PTS
43 Grant Long	F	12	1	3	0	0	2	2	1	2	3	1	3	1	0	4
55 Billy Thompson	F	6	2	3	0	0	0	0	1	0	1	0	1	1	1	4
33 Alec Kessler	C	5	0	2	0	0	0	0	1	1	2	1	0	0	1	0
11 Sherman Douglas	G	8	2	4	0	0	0	0	0	0	0	0	1	0	0	4
41 Glen Rice	G	11	0	3	0	0	0	0	1	0	1	1	1	0	0	0
12 Vernell Coles		4	1	2	0	0	0	0	0	0	0	0	1	1	1	2
04 Rony Seikaly		7	3	4	0	0	3	4	1	2	3	1	0	0	0	9
21 Kevin Edwards		6	1	4	0	0	0	0	0	0	0	0	0	2	0	2
34 Willie Burton		1	1	1	0	0	0	0	0	0	0	0	1	0	0	2
02 Keith Askins		DNP-														
20 Jon Sundvold		DNP-														
53 Alan Ogg		DNP-														
TOTALS		60	11	26	0	0	5	6	5	5	10	4	8	5	3	27

PERCENTAGES: 42.3   0.0   83.3   TM REB: 1 TOT TO: 3 (5 PTS)

	BLOCKED SHOTS			SCORE BY PERIODS	1	2	3	4	OT	OT	OT	FINAL
Pacers	0	Heat	0	Indiana	34							34
				Miami	27							27

This report has been produced by STATMAN II (tm) 2.55.FWNP

Part of the statistics distributed to sportswriters by professional and college teams during a game is a box score. This one, provided by the NBA's Miami Heat, shows player statistics such as scoring at the end of the first quarter. (*Reprinted with the permission of the Miami Heat.*)

OFFICIAL SCORING SUMMARY
CORRECTED

MIAMI HURRICANES	vs.	TEXAS LONGHORNS
Visitors		Home

Date JANUARY 1, 1991   Site COTTON BOWL, DALLAS, TEXAS   Attendance 73,521

Score by Quarters	1	2	3	4	Final
MIAMI (9-2-0)	12	7	14	13	46
TEXAS (10-1-0, 8-0-0 SWC)	0	3	0	0	3

FIRST QUARTER		TIME	UT	UM

FIRST QUARTER

		TIME	UT	UM
UM---Carlos Huerta 28 yd field goal	(40 yds, 8 plays, 4:01)	8:53	0	3
UM---Carlos Huerta 50 yd field goal	(16 yds, 5 plays, 1:52)	5:26	0	6
UM---Carroll 12 yd pass from Erickson (Pass failed)	(9 yds, 2 plays, 0:17)	0:11	0	12

SECOND QUARTER

UT---Pollak 29 yd field goal	(46 yds, 9 plays, 5:01)	7:43	3	12
UM---Carroll 24 yd pass from Erickson (Huerta kick)	(21 yds, 2 plays, 0:48)	4:17	3	19

THIRD QUARTER

UM---Darrin Smith 34 yd interception return (Huerta kick)		11:46	3	26
UM---Hill 48yd pass from Erickson (Huerta kick)	(63 yds, 3 plays, 1:14)	6:09	3	33

FOURTH QUARTER

UM---Bethel 4 yd pass from Erickson (Kick blocked)	(77 yds, 12 plays, 6:28)	10:56	3	39
UM---Conley 26 yd run (Huerta kick)	(26 yds, 3 plays, 1:19)	9:23	3	46

Time of Game: Kickoff 12:51 PM   End of Game 4:12 PM Total Elapsed Time 3:21

Officials R---Jimmy Harper, U---Burton Williams, L---Billy Schroer,

LJ---Tommy Lorino, FJ---Joe DeLany, Jr., SJ---John Buoni, BJ---Charley Horton

Temperature 38°   Wind NNW 3-5 mph   Weather Humidity 43%, partly cloudy

At most professional and college games, official scoring summaries such as this one from a Mobil Cotton Bowl Classic are provided to sportswriters as part of the end-of-game handouts produced by sports publicists. (*Reprinted with the permission of the Mobil Cotton Bowl.*)

FINAL TEAM STATISTICS

	TEXAS Home	MIAMI Visitors
First Downs	20	16
Rushing	13	5
Passing	1	9
Penalty	6	2
Rushing Attempts	51	26
Yards Gained Rushing	232	106
Yards Lost Rushing	82	39
Net Yards Rushing	150	67
Net Yards Passing	55	272
Passes Attempted	18	28
Passes Completed	8	17
Had Intercepted	3	0
Total Offensive Plays	69	54
Total Net Yards	205	339
Average Gain Per Play	3.0	6.3
Return Yards	3	61
Fumbles: Number—Lost	2—2	1—0
Penalties: Number—Yards	8—68	16—202
Interceptions: Number—Yards	0—0	3—49
Number of Punts—Yards	5—203	5—192
Average Per Punt	40.6	38.4
Punt Returns: Number—Yards	1—3	2—12
Kickoff Returns: Number—Yards	7—124	2—82
Possession Time	34:52	25:08
Third-Down Conversions	2 Of 12	3 Of 10
Sacks By	4—22	9—64

As part of the final summary package of a major professional or college football game, detailed team statistics are provided by sports publicists for sportswriters. (*Reprinted with the permission of the Mobil Cotton Bowl.*)

FINAL INDIVIDUAL STATISTICS

TEXAS LONGHORNS
Home

Rushing	Att.	Gain	Lost	Net	TD	Long
Hadnot	17	102	1	101	0	26
Samuels	8	30	0	30	0	8
Brown	5	28	2	26	0	12
Saxton	5	33	10	23	0	24
A. Walker	3	3	4	-1	0	3
Davis	1	0	6	-6	0	-6
Gardere	12	36	59	-23	0	15
Totals	51	232	82	150	0	26

Passing	Att.-Comp.-Int.	Yards	TD	Long	Sacks
Gardere	16- 7 -3	40	0	10	8
Saxton	2- 1 -0	15	0	15	1
Totals	18- 8 -3	55	0	15	9

Pass Receiving	No.	Yards	TD	Long
Samuels	3	24	0	10
Kerry Cash	2	11	0	6
Davis	1	15	0	15
Keith Cash	1	8	0	8
Hadnot	1	-3	0	-3
Totals	8	55	0	15

Punting	No.	Yds.	Avg.	Long
Waits	5	203	40.6	57
Totals	5	203	40.6	57

Field Goals	Att.	Made	Long
Pollak	2	1	29
Totals	2	1	29

All Returns	Punts No. Yds. LP	Kickoffs No. Yds. LP	Intercepted No. Yds. LP
Samuels	1 - 3 3	3 - 70 29	-
Garza	-	1 - 0 0	-
A. Walker	-	3 - 54 24	-
Totals	1 - 3 3	7 -124 29	-

MIAMI HURRICANES
Visitors

Rushing	Att.	Gain	Lost	Net	TD	Long
Conley	3	38	0	38	1	26
McGuire	9	39	6	33	0	17
Patton	3	14	0	14	0	9
Johnson	4	15	5	10	0	9
Crowell	1	0	0	0	0	0
Erickson	6	0	28	-28	0	-2
Totals	26	106	39	67	1	26

Passing	Att.-Comp.-Int.	Yards	TD	Long	Sacks
Erickson	26-17 - 0	272	4	48	4
Torretta	2- 0 - 0	0	0	0	0
Totals	28- 17 - 0	272	4	48	4

Pass Receiving	No.	Yards	TD	Long
Carroll	8	135	2	24
Hill	1	48	1	48
Bethel	3	34	1	25
Spencer	1	25	0	25
Thomas	1	14	0	14
Chudzinski	1	7	0	7
Conley	1	6	0	6
Johnson	1	3	0	3
Totals	17	272	4	48

Punting	No.	Yds.	Avg.	Long
Snyder	5	192	38.4	46
Totals	5	192	38.4	46

Field Goals	Att.	Made	Long
Huerta	2	2	50
Totals	2	2	50

All Returns	Punts No. Yds. LP	Kickoffs No. Yds. LP	Intercepted No. Yds. LP
Williams	2 - 12 7	2 - 82 45	-
Bailey	-	-	1 -15 15
James	-	-	1 - 0 0
Smith	-	-	1 -34 34
Totals	2 - 12 7	2 - 82 45	3 -49 34

An important part of the final summary package of a major professional or college football game is the detailed individual statistics such as these from a college bowl game. (*Reprinted with the permission of the Mobil Cotton Bowl.*)

Lexington Herald Sports

	FG	FTM	FTA	PF	TP
Totals					

	FG	FTM	FTA	PF	TP
Totals					

Officials:

Although many colleges and professional teams provide play-by-play summaries for sportswriters, some reporters prefer to keep their own charts, such as this one for football.

FOOTBALL PLAY-BY-PLAY SCORE SHEET

Game at ....19......... Quarter.................. .... Sheet No................

.........VS.........

Down	Play	Rushing		Passes			Punts		K'Offs		Fumbles		Penalties	Scoring				Remarks
		Yard Stripe	Gain	Loss	Com	Not Com	Int	Dist	Ret	Dist	Ret	Own	Opps		T D	P A T	F G	Saf	

115

In football, the reporter might need the individual rushing totals of the major players or the individual passing performances of the quarterbacks for a story written on deadline. Team totals do not help, particularly if a coach rotates players frequently. A chart allows the reporter to record this information as it occurs, not as a time-consuming effort at the end of the game when the deadline is near. When the game is over, the running totals become individual totals for the game, and the job is already done.

Some shortcuts make this work more efficient. To avoid too much confusing note taking during the action, and thus falling behind, the sportswriter must maintain a high level of concentration and take advantage of natural breaks in the action (e.g., free throws in a basketball game, moving first down markers in football, warm-ups between innings, changing courts in tennis) to record what happened, using some special notation system and some type of shorthand. Note-taking tricks such as using the player's number instead of the name, using two pens with a different color of ink for each team, and developing codes for particular plays will cut the time it takes to record the action. Here is one sportswriter's way of doing basketball play-by-play:

Home	*Visitors*
12 +2 10df −1 12:02 H20−10	10 −2 10rb +2 11:55 H20−12

Translated, this means that player number 12 of the Home team made a field goal, was fouled by number 10 of the opposition, and was given a free throw that he missed. The 12:02 is the time remaining in the half, with the score (Home leading 20 to 10) the last number. When the action switched to the other end of the court, Visitor number 10 missed a field goal, got the rebound, and made the basket. Again, time and score are indicated. A beginner should practice keeping play-by-play charts on television games.

Typed play-by-play handouts are often available for reporters at half-time and game end at the college level and higher. These are produced by sports information department staff at the press table, often with a laptop personal computer. The more sophisticated colleges and universities and the professional teams have the staff and resources to provide such conveniences. Reporters covering high school or lower level competition will have to keep their own play-by-plays. Sports information play-by-plays have the advantage of freeing reporters from keeping statistics so they can observe other aspects of the game. But a word of advice: There is considerable variation in the quality and quantity of information contained in handouts, so the reporter must check them out ahead of time to see if the information is complete, reliable, and suits his or her needs. Someone may be brought along to keep statistics while the reporter keeps the play-by-play; this is especially helpful when the reporter is just beginning or trying out a new code system for noting plays.

The Best Vantage Points

Some vantage points for covering an athletic event are better than others, depending on the purpose of the story. The favorites are (1) with media in the press box or at the press table; (2) with coaches in the press box or at the press table; (3) at the sidelines, dugout, infield, or anywhere near the action; and (4) in the stands or elsewhere with the crowd.

At a major event, some newspapers position reporters in all these places to get the complete picture. A reporter in the press box, who has little diversion, might be assigned to write the game story. The reporter on the sideline of a football game might be assigned to cover the coaching strategies, the mood of the players, and other middle-of-the-action views in a feature story. And a reporter in the stands might be writing a feature on the fans.

Certain sports are better covered from certain places. Football, for example, is best covered from the press box. Some reporters prefer to walk the sidelines with the coaches, players, and officials, but the detail they gain is balanced by a loss in overall perspective. Basketball is best covered near the official scorer's table at the edge of the court. There is usually a designated area there for reporters.

For baseball, the location is less important, and there are several choices. Some reporters like the press box or the dugout, if allowed to be there. Some spend a few innings in each dugout during a game. Another good location is, of course, right behind home plate.

For tennis, the best location is at the net and near the umpire — so you can hear — at an officiated match. Swimming and track meets are best covered near the finish line, where the officials, judges, timers, and record-keepers are located. In golf, there is usually action all over the course. The reporter might walk the course, perhaps following a key player. Another successful way to watch golf is to stay near the finishing holes (17 and 18, or 8 and 9), watching the players as they arrive at these last greens. A sharp reporter will try to do both over a full day at the course.

The following two stories, by Michael Ventre, *Los Angeles Daily News* sportswriter, and Dan Le Batard, *Miami Herald* sportswriter, show how a complete playoff game story is written. Ventre reports on a professional football playoff game, and Le Batard shows how to write a championship college baseball game. Both stories are strong in providing context for readers.

Well aware that most people interested in this game have seen it live on television or at least have seen highlights before they read his story, Ventre takes a feature-oriented, second-day approach. This keeps his story, especially his lead, interesting to those already familiar with the outcome. His focus, instead, is to tell readers how and why the outcome occurred. What led to New York's convincing victory? How did the Giants dominate? Why were the Bears overwhelmed? He answers these questions. His lead tells you the game was won through the efforts of the New York reserve quarterback. He backs up his generalizations about the quarterback's sterling effort with descriptions of key plays and statistics. He uses direct quotations to provide additional analysis and explanation not available during the live network television coverage. As the story unfolds, Ventre focuses on reaction from players to the effort by the Giants and their substitute quarterback. Note how the story takes on a feature-analysis approach.

SOURCE: The *Miami Herald,* final edition, page 1D
DATE: Monday, January 14, 1991
AUTHOR: Michael Ventre, *Los Angeles Daily News*
HEADLINE: Giants rumble in battle of reserve QBs;
          Unbeaten Hostetler slices Chicago, 31-3

EAST RUTHERFORD, N.J.—When you are a run-oriented football team like the Chicago Bears, and the opposing team's backup quarterback gains more yardage rushing than your entire offense, it may be time to question your orientation.

Thanks to Jeff Hostetler and the New York Giants, the Bears are now in early hibernation. Hostetler, filling in for the injured Phil Simms, directed the Giants to a 31-3 victory over the Bears Sunday at Giants Stadium.

The Giants' victory sets up a showdown for a Super Bowl berth Sunday at Candlestick Park against the defending-champion San Francisco 49ers.

Hostetler, who is 4-0 as a regular-season starter, played brilliantly in his first-ever playoff start. He completed 10 of 17 passes for 112 yards, two for touchdowns and no interceptions.

"Jeff played like he was in a fantasy," said Stephen Baker. "It was extraordinary the plays he made. Scrambling, throwing the ball, he was making plays out of what wasn't there."

Hostetler also fooled the Bears with some nifty dashes that Simms couldn't have done with a motorcycle. Hostetler rushed for 43 yards on six carries, with one touchdown. That made him the game's second-leading rusher, behind teammate Ottis Anderson and his 80 yards on 21 carries.

The Bears? With pro bowler Neal Anderson in the backfield, Chicago rolled up a measly 27 yards on the ground. Anderson had 19 of that.

"The sad thing about the way we played on defense is that we expected Hostetler would be bootlegging and running and getting wide on us," said Bears defensive tackle Dan Hampton. "And he did it anyway."

While the Giants (14-3) marched confidently on the ground and in the air, the Bears (12-6) stumbled early and often. Much of it was due to the Giants' defense, which threw an unexpected 4-3 look at Chicago in an effort to spoil the Bears' appetite for the rush.

"Attack. Attack. Every time, attack," Giants defensive end Leonard Marshall said.

Said linebacker Lawrence Taylor: "I felt they weren't going to make any touchdowns on our defense. I don't see any team pounding it on our defense."

There was one play in particular that may have changed the game's tone. The Bears tried to pound it at the Giants' defense. The Giants pounded harder and won.

The situation: The Giants were ahead, 10-0, with 9:32 left in the second quarter. The Bears had a fourth-and-goal on the Giants' one. They opted to try for the TD instead of the field goal, despite John Madden's on-air protestations. Tomczak handed off to fullback Brad Muster. Muster was introduced to the Giants' 6-foot-4, 275-pound defensive end John Washington as he ran over the left side of the Bears' line. Washington stopped Muster cold, then danced up a storm.

Even though the Giants took over and were forced to punt, and the Bears then took over with good field position and got a field goal to cut it to 10-3, many Giants felt the message delivered by Washington's hit was more important than the score indicated.

"Whenever you have hits like that," Marshall said, "you can control the momentum."

Added Taylor: "I was praying for them to go for it rather than the field goal. There aren't many places you can run down there, and we had them all covered."

The Giants seemed to cover every avenue the Bears approached. Tomczak was 17 of 36 for 205 yards, with two interceptions.

In fact, New York jumped to a 3-0 lead on one of Tomczak's interceptions, even though he could hardly be faulted for this one. He threw to Dennis Gentry in the flat. The ball bounced off Gentry and into the hands of Giants cornerback Mark Collins. The Giants took over on the Bears' 34 and eventually got a 46-yard field goal from Matt Bahr.

On their next series, the Giants made it 10-0 when Hostetler threw a perfect lob into the corner of the end zone for Baker from 21 yards out.

After the aforementioned goal-line stand, and after Kevin Butler put Chicago on the board with a 33-yard field goal for 10-3, the Giants took over on their 20.

Hostetler's scrambling ability became painfully apparent to the Bears on this series. On fourth and one from the Chicago 32, Hostetler raced around right end for a 10-yard gain. Four plays later, on a rollout, Hostetler found tight end Howard Cross for a five-yard touchdown pass. The Giants entered halftime ahead, 17-3.

On their first possession of the second half, the Giants drove 49 yards and ended the drive with Hostetler's three-yard TD run.

Bye-bye Bears. Done in by a backup, who many doubted could lead the Giants to San Francisco.

"Some people have said that a team can't get to the Super Bowl with a backup quarterback," Hostetler said. "But if we win another game, we're there."

The Giants were successful on all four of their fourth-down conversion attempts. The Bears converted on only one of five on fourth down.

Here are the key fourth-down plays, all of which came in the opponents' territory:

Situation-Result

4th-and-14 at 28, Bears trailing, 3-0 Bears' Anderson 3-yard catch
4th-and-1 at 27, Giants leading, 3-0 Giants' Mrosko 6-yard catch
4th-and-goal at 1, Bears trailing, 10-0 Bears' Muster loses 1 yard
4th-and-1 at 32, Giants leading, 10-3 Giants' Hostetler 10-yard run
4th-and-6 at 35, Giants leading, 17-3 Giants' Hostetler 9-yard run
4th-and-goal at 5, Bears trailing, 24-3 Bears' Thornton 4-yard catch.

Reprinted with the permission of the *Los Angeles Daily News*

Le Batard writes a story about the favorite, also the home team, which loses to an underdog. The upset story is always interesting to read, and his story, like Ventre's NFL playoff game story, is filled with reaction, explanation, and play-by-play. Le Batard also gives readers a look ahead for the winning team in the game, which went on to the College World Series the following week. The story is strong because of its rich quotations combined with the details of how a favored team squandered offensive opportunities and lost to a virtual unknown. It is a classic theme in sportswriting.

SOURCE: The *Miami Herald,* final edition, page 1C
DATE: Wednesday, May 30, 1990
AUTHOR: Dan Le Batard, *Herald* sportswriter
HEADLINE: The Citadel shoots down UM hopes; No. 5 seed wins Atlantic regional

"Most people," University of Miami pitcher Jeff Alkire said softly Tuesday afternoon, "have never even heard of The Citadel."

Most people have probably never heard of Chris Coker, Tony Skole or Brad Stowell, either.

But the Crew Cut Kids from that unglamorous, unknown, underdog military school at Charleston, S.C., did the unbelievable Tuesday afternoon, winning the Atlantic Regional with a surprisingly easy 4-1 victory over the top-seeded University of Miami before 2,157 startled fans at Mark Light Stadium.

By beating UM ace Oscar Munoz (15-2), the fifth-seeded Citadel became the first all-military school to advance to the College World Series. And the clawing, biting Bulldogs did it by breezing through the double-elimination regional unbeaten, defeating mighty Miami twice. The Citadel (45-12) beat Miami, 6-2, Monday.

"They played relaxed," UM Coach Ron Fraser said. "They played like we usually do."

Miami, which ended the season 52-13, had not lost a regional at Mark Light since 1977. In the eight home regionals since then, Miami had gone 28-2—meaning UM lost as many regional home games to The Citadel in two days as it had lost to all of the playoff powerhouses over the last 13 years combined.

All in all, a pretty amazing Memorial Day Weekend.

Coker and Skole did the major damage Tuesday, each hitting a sixth-inning solo home run to left field. Stowell, by far The Citadel's worst starting pitcher, held UM to four hits over eight innings.

It was only Skole's third homer of the season, the others coming against East Tennessee State and Baptist College—teams most people probably have never heard of.

"I didn't run out of gas, I just got a couple of fastballs up and they hit them," Munoz said.

Stowell, meanwhile, came into the game with an earned-run average of 5.69 and a record of 4-3, and recent losses to Davidson and Augusta—teams most people probably . . . well, you know.

"We faced pitching a lot better than that this year," said UM first baseman Charles Johnson. "We were just trying to get it all back in one swing and you just can't do that."

Want an eloquent explanation for why UM lost?

Take the second inning.

And, for Fraser's sake, take it far, far away.

Miami's first two batters walked on eight straight balls from Stowell, an erratic sort who walked six batters Tuesday. Chris Hirsch then singled up the middle, loading the bases with no one out.

Mike Tosar, whom Stowell was trying to get to hit a run-scoring groundout, popped up to the shortstop instead. And then Gino DiMare, Miami's fastest player, grounded into a double play so routine it should have been served on a big silver platter.

Freeze-frame that critical second inning (the Bulldogs scored one run in the bottom of the inning) and it's clear why UM was eliminated.

Having to win two games in one sweltering afternoon, the Hurricanes merely melted like hot candle wax. Fraser said that the Hurricanes "did things they haven't done all year" in those painful 2½ hours Tuesday—things like popping up and hitting into double plays with the bases loaded. Missed opportunities hurt Miami throughout the regional, Fraser said.

"We made the routine plays under pressure," said Chal Port, The Citadel's crusty coach about to make his first College World Series appearance in his 26-year career. "I thought the crowd was somewhat harmful to Miami. They put a lot of pressure on those boys."

Pressure.

That was the operative word Tuesday. Miami, having to beat a team twice it had already lost to once, felt it in a big way. The Citadel, meanwhile, knew it had another game to play if it lost the first—a game which would be started by its ace Ken Britt (10-1, 1.97 ERA), a game which UM would have to start with an unproven reliever from its bullpen after having used Munoz in the opener.

"They were very, very loose," Fraser said. "They just went out and had fun. No pressure. We were the underdog."

Well, not quite. The Bulldogs were the undoubted underdogs and, as they poured onto the field past a dejected Fraser, even the UM coach couldn't help but feel good for them.

As the Bulldogs pounced on each other near the pitcher's mound in jubilant celebration, Fraser went over and interrupted the merriment. The cadets stopped their revelry instantaneously, as if in the presence of a drill sergeant, and gathered quietly around Fraser. He congratulated them and told them to "play like you did here today. Don't let the pressure and hoopla get to you in Omaha."

The Bulldogs aren't likely to let that happen.

"At a military school you are confronted with a lot of stressful situations," Port said. "It kind of conditions you under tension."

So, then, Chal, can your team go all the way?

"Oh, I don't know about that. We'll go all the way to Omaha. We may not win another game."

But that won't stop them from savoring the way they won Tuesday's.

After Miami's disastrous top of the second, The Citadel got two-out singles from Skole and Jason Rychlick and then a ground-rule double to right by Mike Branham. The hit would have scored at least two if it hadn't gone over the fence and, while Port argued that Rychlick should be allowed to score, he returned to the dugout laughing — symbolic of how loose his club was.

Miami tied it in the top of the sixth on a one-out double by Frank Mora to right, but The Citadel came right back in the bottom of the inning with the homers by Coker, with no outs, and Skole, with one out.

From there, UM went away quietly, going out in order in the seventh and putting just one harmless runner on in the eighth and ninth after The Citadel scored another run in the seventh on a two-out single to center by Coker.

Hank Kraft replaced Stowell after he gave up a leadoff double in the ninth to catcher Juan Flores, and retired three straight hitters.

"We didn't want the year to end here," said Flores, who as a senior played his final game as a Hurricane Tuesday. "We wanted to end it all in Omaha."

Yes, Jeff Alkire is OK today.

His ego is a bit injured after a 4-1 loss that eliminated UM, but his arm is fine.

Alkire kept UM alive Monday night by throwing a total of 14 innings — five in the first game of a double-header, nine in the second.

He said that although he was a little stiff Tuesday morning, he got up at 9:30 a.m. — just about nine hours after throwing his 191st pitch Monday night.

"My legs hurt the most," Alkire said. "I'm just a little stiff. I took a lap before the game and that was very hard. I was really exhausted."

Alkire said he could have pitched again in about four days. Alas, that won't be necessary.

Fraser said he thought about removing Alkire both for Alkire's well-being and the well-being of the team on 10 different occasions. But Alkire insisted his arm felt fine and the fact he continued retiring hitters supported that.

Covering Games by Telephone

Sometimes a sportswriter cannot cover a game in person because of varied and legitimate reasons such as limited staff, distance and expenses, or other priorities. Readers still want outcome information, especially on minor games not on television or radio. If coverage is not available through other means, such as from a reporter from another newspaper in the town where the teams are playing, a stringer, or a SID, a sportswriter will have to track down the information by telephone and write a story from that information.

Otherwise, arrangements must be made for someone—an official scorer, a student manager, an announcer, or another appropriate person—to call in the results. Selection of someone dependable will save time later, which is especially important under deadline pressure. If someone cannot be found to call, the reporter must find someone he or she can call for the results—a coach, SID, or other team representative. Telephone numbers and addresses should be kept on file; a good list would include home and office phone numbers of coaches and other officials and phone numbers of gymnasiums, press boxes, and other sports facilities. A reporter should also find out where teams stay when on the road, for quick answers if the arranged phone calls fall through. Coaches sometimes "forget" to call if their teams lose.

Once a phone contact is made, the first step is to get the scoring summary in agate form. The various types of standardized game statistics reporting forms are discussed below. Essentially, this means getting the full box score, a short box, or a line score. For speed, a reporter can type the information as it is received. Many newspapers have integrated the basic scoring summary formats into their personal computers and electronic editing systems, which means the reporter must only fill in the blanks. Because most summaries use last names only, the reporter must ask for the full names and positions of the key players in order to write the story as well as other details that do not show up in the scoring summary: What led up to the winning play? When did the play occur? And there are lesser details that enhance a story, the teams' nicknames, current win-loss records, and next opponents. Finally, the reporter should talk to the correspondent who was at the game. He or she might have a good idea for a story lead.

Scoring Summaries: Agate

Over the years, sportswriters have developed standardized scoring summaries for their own convenience as well as for that of readers. Since the 1983 revision, the *Associated Press Stylebook and Libel Manual* (Goldstein 1992) has maintained a separate section on sports usages. Part of that section is devoted to game story usages; it is a valuable section for begin-

Baseball and Basketball Box Scores

The *Associated Press Stylebook and Libel Manual* provides the following examples of two common box score game summaries:

BASEBALL

First Game

PHILADELPHIA	ab	r	h	bi
Stone lf	4	0	0	0
GGross lf	0	0	0	0
Schu 3	4	1	0	0
Samuel 2b	4	0	1	2
Schmidt 1	4	0	0	0
Virgil c	4	2	2	1
GWilson rf	4	0	0	0
Maddox c	3	0	0	0
Jeltz ss	2	0	0	0
KGross p	3	0	1	0
Tekulve p	0	0	0	0
Totals	32	3	4	3

SAN DIEGO	ab	r	h	bi
Flannry 2	3	0	1	0
Gwynn rf	4	0	2	0
Garvey 1	4	0	0	0
Nettles 3b	3	1	1	0
Royster 3	0	0	0	0
McRynl cf	4	0	1	1
Kennedy c	4	0	1	0
Martinez lf	4	1	1	0
Templtn ss	4	0	2	1
Bmbry ph	1	0	0	0
Lefferts p	0	0	0	0
Totals	33	2	9	2

```
Philadelphia        010  200  000-3
San Diego           000  200  000-2
```

None out when winning run scored.
E. Templeton, GWilson. DP—Philadelphia 2. LOB—Philadelphia 3, San Diego 6. 2B—Templeton, Gwynn. HR—Virgil (8).

	IP	H	R	ER	BB	SO
Philadelphia						
K Gross W,4-6	7 1-3	9	2	2	0	3
Tekulve S, 3	1 2-3	0	0	0	1	0
San Diego						
Dravecky L,4-3	7	4	3	1	1	2
Lefferts	2	0	0	0	0	1

HBP—Flannery by KGross. T—2:13. A—17,740.

BASKETBALL

LOS ANGELES (114)
Worthy 8-19 4-6 20, Rambis 4-6 0-0 8, Abdul-Jabbar 6-11 0-0 12, E. Johnson 8-14 3-4 19, Scott 5-14 0-0 10, Cooper 1-5 2-2 4, McAdoo 6-13 0-0 12, McGee 4-7 4-5 14, Spriggs 4-7 0-2 8, Kupchak 3-3 1-2 7. Totals 49-100 14-21 114.

BOSTON (148)
McHale 10-16 6-9 26, Bird 8-14 2-2 19, Parish 6-11 6-7 18, D. Johnson 6-14 1-1 13, Ainge 9-15 0-0 19, Buckner 3-5 0-0 6, Williams 3-5 0-0 6, Wedman 11-11 0-2 26, Maxwell 1-1 1-2 3, Kite 3-5 1-2 7, Carr 1-3 0-0 3, Clark 1-2 0-0 2. Totals 62-102, 17-25 148.

Three-point goals—Wedman 4, McGee 2, Bird, Ainge, Carr. Fouled out—None.
Rebounds—Los Angeles 43 (Rambis 9), Boston 63 (McHale 9).
Assists—Los Angeles 28 (E. Johnson 12), Boston 43 (D. Johnson 10).
Total fouls—Los Angeles 23, Boston 17. Technicals—Ainge. A—14,890.

SOURCE: Norm Goldstein, ed. 1992. *Associated Press Stylebook and Libel Manual*. New York: Associated Press, pp. 238, 240.

ners uncertain on how to write certain terms in their game stories. The section is also a definitive source for the basic scoring summary. The basic summary lists winners in the order of finish. The number indicating the place finish, AP says, "is followed by an athlete's full name, his affiliation or hometown, and his time, distance, points, or whatever performance factor is applicable to the sport. If a contest involves several types of events (such as a track or swim meet), the paragraph begins with the name of the event." The *Associated Press Stylebook and Libel Manual* also includes these key examples: baseball terms and box scores; basketball terms and box scores; boxing summaries; football terms, statistics charts, and scoring summaries; and summaries for golf, handball, hockey, racquetball, rowing, skating, swimming, tennis, volleyball, and water skiing.

Sports departments of many major newspapers, however, have developed their own summary styles over the years. Most small dailies and weeklies that run summaries and subscribe to a wire service will follow wire service style and adapt local statistics to that style. This tabulated information is commonly called "agate," named for the size of type in which it is usually set. Most newspaper stories are set in 8- and 9-point type (72 points equal 1 inch), while agate is usually set in 5½- to 7-point type. This saves space, which is the reason sports sections use it for box scores, standings, and other sports statistics.

There are at least six arguments for regularizing the style of sports statistics:

1. *Consistency.* Imagine the erratic appearance and reader confusion if the same newspaper reported baseball box scores in different ways in the same issue, or even in different issues.

2. *Readability.* When the statistics are reported in a consistent form day after day, readers can find information more easily. Readers learn to read a particular sports section and begin to expect material in a certain form and location. They learn the abbreviation "ab," for example, always stands for at-bats in a baseball box score.

3. *Speed.* From the sportswriter's point of view, consistent style allows greater efficiency in transmitting the results by laptop personal computer, by facsimile machine, or even by dictation. Electronic editing systems are formatted; that is, they are programmed for certain standard forms such as sports agate, so writers can simply fill in the blanks.

4. *Accuracy.* With a format to follow, information tends to be more accurate, because the reporter knows what to look for and how to record it. It is also easier to check for errors such as omissions and column totals that do not add up properly.

5. *Completeness.* When a reporter follows a specific format, important statistics are less likely to be left out, for example, the winning time in a 100-yard dash, the winning team, or the winner's first name.

6. *Continuity.* A regular format allows standardized reporting when several reporters cover the same event. Newspapers that do not have a set style are much less professional in their sports reporting.

Sports editors and sports copy/desk editors often prefer that a story accompanied by agate not repeat the information contained in the agate. Some repetition cannot be avoided, but it is sensible to avoid duplication as much as possible.

Daily newspapers are trying for greater standardization. The Associated Press Sports Editors organization is a leading proponent of this goal, which would facilitate wire service reporting and would improve coverage consistency.

There are numerous excellent sources of scoring summaries, such as the two wire service stylebooks (Goldstein 1992; Miller 1981), the NCAA and other sports organization statistical forms, and specialized magazines for specific sports.

Postgame Interviews

There are two types of postgame journalism. The first and most obvious, the one we are concerned with here, is getting the story from the participants. The second is the follow-up story a day or two later, after sources have had time to reflect on what happened, after coaches and players have looked at game films or tapes, and after injuries have been assessed.

First comes the immediate postgame interview, to be used with the game story. Quotations from the key players and coaches always attract readers. But the reporter has to know what to ask, and of whom, in the locker room. Too many sportswriters talk only to the coach or manager, ignoring the obvious source—the athlete. This pattern occurs particularly in amateur athletics, such as high school sports. There, coaches are viewed as the traditional, appropriate source of information about a team's performance.

A number of stories can come from locker room interviews. But too often the morning newspaper reporter is handicapped by too little time to get quotations, or other game color, so the game story suffers. An afternoon or weekly publication sportswriter has the advantage and can present in-depth information and details that were not available to the public in the morning editions or from radio or television.

Changes are occurring that affect the work of the reporter; a major one is locker room access. Because of the increasing number of women in sports journalism, more women need access to locker rooms to do their jobs. Some teams have put limitations on formerly open locker rooms,

Los Angeles Kings right wing Tomas Sandstrom (right) talks to sports reporters during a postgame locker room interview. (*Photo by Wen Roberts, Photography Ink.*)

however. In early 1991, the University of Hawaii athletic department, for example, closed its locker rooms to all reporters wanting after-game interviews (Associated Press 1991). Other schools and professional teams have considered and taken similar action.

Much of the current concern arose from the celebrated case involving the New England Patriots and *Boston Herald* sportswriter Lisa Olson. Several Patriots players harassed Olson in the Fall 1990 season during her attempts to conduct interviews after a game she was assigned to cover. Because of the prominence of this case, it is discussed in more detail in Chapter 15.

Covering women's sports such as golf and tennis has created similar problems for male reporters. Special rooms have now been set aside for interviews in an effort to equalize opportunities for all reporters. While this works in some cases, it has delayed interviewing and created difficulties for reporters pressed for time. Locker room access is important. When it is denied, the reporter can't record the moods, feelings, and actions of the coaches and athletes that can make the best-read stories in the entire sports section.

Locker room interviews are often an exercise in group (pack) journalism. When a number of reporters cover a game, they are all attracted to the same sources after the game. They must be present at these interviews, because coaches and players may not have, or may not want to spend, the time to talk to reporters individually. If a reporter has a perspective that other reporters do not have and wants to talk to the source alone, he or she will have to wait until others are gone or working on other interviews. Such a wait is sometimes worthwhile when an individual interview results.

A problem in interviewing athletes is their occasional lack of articulateness. Another is that some athletes are hard to interview because they do not want to talk to reporters at all. The temptation is to put words in the star's mouth, but this will not result in an accurate representation of the athlete's reactions. Another problem is the cliché. Many sources who deal with sportswriters on a regular basis have stock answers that are shallow and superficial. An alert and creative reporter presses beyond the standard quotation, asking a question with insight and creativity. Such a question is likely to elicit an interesting and quotable response that will make the story a winner.

In the following story by *Chicago Tribune* sportswriter Sam Smith, note how he uses postgame locker room quotations to strengthen his game story about the Chicago Bulls' victory over Seattle. The description of how the game was won is boosted to a higher level with reaction quotations from the team's coach, star Michael Jordan, and other key players in the game that evening. The story is filled with analysis of the meaning of the victory in terms of future performance by the team during the season.

SOURCE: The *Chicago Tribune,* final edition, page 3, zone C
DATE: Sunday, December 30, 1990
AUTHOR: Sam Smith
HEADLINE: Bulls lower the boom on Sonics; 5th straight win ends 11-3 month

The Bulls unwrapped their final package of 1990 Saturday night at the Stadium, a 116-91 victory over a Seattle team that gave away more gifts than Santa Claus.

"There were quite a few unforced errors," said Bulls coach Phil Jackson about Seattle's 22 turnovers, shared by nine players, which accounted for 31 Bulls points. "But our press also forced them into mistakes."

Michael Jordan with 31 points, Scottie Pippen with 22, Horace Grant with 16 and Bill Cartwright with 15 points and 13 rebounds made sure it was a sweet conclusion to 1990 as the Bulls moved to 20-9 with their fifth consecutive win and eighth in their last nine games.

Not coincidentally, all eight wins were at home as the Bulls completed their softest month of the season (11 of 14 games at home) with an 11-3 record.

So the Bulls enter 1991 starting Thursday night at Houston with eight of their next 13 games on the road and a good chance to find out whether December was just a time of miracles.

"We're about to see, aren't we?" said Jordan, who also had 10 rebounds.

The Bulls dominated the Sonics, who had won six straight but were completing an Eastern Conference road trip.

The Bulls led by 11 after one quarter with Cartwright scoring 13 points, then allowed Seattle to close within eight at halftime. But they flew away to a 17-point edge after three quarters and coasted down the stretch.

"I think we're feeling comfortable and falling into a good rhythm, especially with the home stretch we had," said Jordan. "But we have to make sure we play better on the road."

So the Bulls found out, after losing their first two home games of the season, that they could win at the Stadium.

They also found out:

—Cartwright remains their only strength in the middle. He is averaging 13.8 points and 9.6 rebounds in the last five games.

"I've been feeling good and moving well," said Cartwright, who carried the Bulls during a mostly sluggish first quarter against Seattle (12-14). "I'm just trying to get out there and attack early. We want to let teams know that everything they get, they're going to have to work for."

—Stacey King is not a starting power forward. Horace Grant returned to the starting lineup after a two-game stint with the second team and held Shawn Kemp to 13 points while scoring 16 and adding three blocks.

"It's nice to be back in there again with the guys I'm used to playing with," said Grant, who is expected to start Thursday. "Kemp's a strong, tough player, but I like that kind of challenge."

The Bulls also have seen Jordan resume his high-scoring ways, scoring more than 30 points in seven of the last eight games to move into the league's scoring lead.

And they'll all need to play good basketball to win on the road, where the bench players generally suffer. They've been inconsistent of late, with Cliff Levingston having his third scoreless game in the last eight Saturday, Dennis Hopson averaging 2.1 in the last seven games and Will Perdue all but eliminated from the rotation.

King showed some life with 10 points after two ineffective starts while B.J. Armstrong failed to reach double figures for the 12th straight game.

Yet that's less important than the play of Pippen, who has been on the best scoring streak of his career, averaging 20.6 points — plus eight rebounds — in his last 11 games.

But Pippen is shooting just 40 percent on the road, compared with 58 percent at home, and averaging 12.9 points away from the Stadium.

"I feel like I'm in a better rhythm now, although I couldn't get into the game in the first half," said Pippen, who had just four before halftime. But his 11 third-quarter points helped douse Seattle.

"In the third quarter we tightened up and played cohesive basketball," said Phil Jackson.

That's what they'll need to do in the new year now that the time for gift-giving is past.

Writing the Story

There are two kinds of game stories: a story written on deadline, also called the "A.M." story, and a story written within a short time period but without immediate deadline pressure, also called the "P.M." or non-daily story. There are, of course, two major approaches to writing these two kinds of stories, the first-day lead and the second-day lead.

After using the play-by-play charts, preparing a box or other agate, and conducting the postgame interviews, the reporter faces one more problem before turning the computer on: What to use and what to cut? A good reporter will always have too much to use, so he or she must evaluate and organize the information. This eases the pain of getting a story started on the computer screen, particularly for beginners. Selecting a lead may be the toughest decision; once it is chosen, the rest should follow naturally.

A solid sports lead, like any newspaper lead, tells one or more of these basic facts: *who, what, where, when, how,* and *why.* All this information need not be crammed into the first sentence, however. A well-crafted sports lead might consist of three or four sentences in two or three paragraphs. The major objective should be to establish the atmosphere of the game.

Phil Fuhrer (1975), sports editor of the *San Bernardino (Calif.) Sun-Telegram,* says a game story must include (1) analysis of the event, (2) quotations by the participants to back up the analysis, and (3) play-by-play reports as a setting both for the analysis and for the quotations. As Fuhrer notes, this approach to writing the story gives something to all readers — those who were present at the game, who heard it on radio, who saw it on television, and who were just aware of the score.

The *first-day lead* is more to the point and much more traditional in its approach: reporting results by emphasizing the outcome. But the direct approach sometimes does not work. With time zone differences and deadlines, a lead may have to be written while the game is still in progress.

Following are two first-day leads that were written about high school basketball games by Elaine Sung, *Miami Herald* high school sportswriter. These are straight summary leads that get to the point quickly, giving the outcome and the key contributors to the results.

Example 1

Freeman Brown and Donzel Rush each had 12 points to lead Carol City High to a 61-56 victory over Dillard Saturday night in the Dillard Holiday Tournament boys' basketball championship game at the Fort Lauderdale Dillard gym.

Carol City (7-4) trailed through the first three quarters, but crept back late in the third by going to the inside. The Chiefs tied the score at 42 with 19 seconds left in the quarter, but a jump shot by Warren Rosegreen gave Dillard (9-2) the lead again. (SOURCE: The *Miami Herald,* "Carol City wins; MHS finishes 3rd," Sunday, December 30, 1990, final edition, page 15D.)

Example 2

Katie Jenkins scored 14 points, 10 of them from the free-throw line, as Douglas High held off Miami High, 58-50, Wednesday night in the opening round of the Jim Kreul Holiday Basketball Classic at Douglas.

The 24-team tournament, in its inaugural year, is being held at five different sites in the Coral Springs area.

Douglas extended its unbeaten streak to 6-0; Miami High is 5-3.

The Eagles jumped to an 11-6 lead with a lot of give-and-take passing. Miami High was plagued with traveling calls in the first quarter and trailed, 21-12, after the first period. (SOURCE: The *Miami Herald,* "Douglas girls open Kreul tourney with a victory," Thursday, December 20, 1990, Broward edition, page 4D.)

The lead should get straight to the point; readers are quickly informed about what has happened in the game with no space wasted on feature angles or extraneous elements. They are still appropriate first-day, or morning edition, leads, when readers see a story on an event for the first time (Garrison 1990). They are particularly useful for readers who did not hear the game on radio or see it on television or in person. Many games are not broadcast, making first-day leads still useful tools in sportswriting in the 1990s.

The *second-day lead* goes further in providing a unique feature angle on the game, in incorporating the game outcome details into a feature format. This approach carries throughout the story and focuses on new elements of game analysis that did not surface in the first-day stories. The play-by-play, scoring, and other "results" details of the game take a back seat. Second-day leads often focus on the *why* element of the story, explaining why the results occurred. Often, when a game is televised or broadcast on radio to a large audience, print writers use second-day leads to keep their stories that appear the next morning or afternoon fresher for their readers.

Sportswriters must be careful, however, not to so overwhelm readers with the feature theme that the game itself is forgotten. The right mix is an ample amount of both. Take a look at these two inviting examples. The first, from Philadelphia, is by Tim Cowlishaw, *Dallas Morning News* sportswriter, and the second, about college baseball, is written by Barry Jackson, a *Miami Herald* sportswriter.

Example 1

PHILADELPHIA—For the third consecutive season, Buddy Ryan's Eagles lasted only 60 minutes in the postseason. No one knows whether Ryan will get a chance for a fourth playoff trip with Philadelphia.

Ryan's benching of Randall Cunningham for one series late in the third quarter will be second-guessed all winter by Eagles fans. But it was an instant-replay reversal just before halftime—a 10-point play as it turned out—that had the greater impact on Washington's 20-6 NFC wild-card victory at Veterans Stadium Saturday afternoon.

Washington (11-6) will play the New York Giants next Sunday if New Orleans defeats Chicago today. The Redskins will play at San Francisco Saturday if the Bears win. (SOURCE: The *Miami Herald,* "Skins ground Eagles; Ryan's fate in the air," Sunday, January 6, 1991, final edition, page 1D.)

Example 2

Before the weekend, Florida State Coach Mike Martin said this probably was the best team in his 11 years at the school.

Saturday, the sixth-ranked Seminoles finally gave Miami fans reason to believe him.

With familiar faces in new places, FSU beat the top-ranked Hurricanes, 6-2, before a stunned crowd of 6, 375 at Mark Light Stadium. The Seminoles rode the shoulders of starter Brad Gregory, an ex-reliever, and closer Ricky Kimball, a former starter.

Using a well-placed fastball and nasty curve, Gregory (1-1) snapped UM's 10-game winning streak and FSU's three-game skid against the Hur-

ricanes (46-7). (SOURCE: The *Miami Herald,* "6,375 watch Seminoles sty-
mie No. 1 Hurricanes," Sunday, May 6, 1990, final edition, page 1D.)

What happens after the reporter gets the right lead? The rest of the
story must be organized. There are three major options (Garrison 1990):
the chronological approach, the inverted pyramid approach, and the feature approach.

The *chronological approach.* This organizational form reports the
game story just as it occurred. Obviously, only a few games lend themselves
to this format, although at times it is an appropriate form for the second-
day story, setting up the circumstances and context for a big play at the end
of a game.

The *inverted pyramid approach.* This form, the most-used first-day
approach, is the most practical for the reader. It places the most important
events first, for example, those leading to victory, and then in descending
order of importance adds the rest of the game details.

The *feature approach.* This approach uses a particularly interesting
aspect of the game to start the story. The lead angle might not have occurred at the beginning of the game, nor does it have to be the most
important. This form is organized to explain the original angle of the story,
followed by other matters involving the game and integrating game details.
The following golf tournament results story by Dan Hruby, *San Jose Mercury News* sportswriter, shows a feature approach in the lead. His story is
about an unusual California pro-am golf tournament that pits men against
women for equal prize money. Note how he uses quotations to give the
story a feature flavor throughout, but only after setting up the story with
emphasis on the possibility of a woman beating men in the tournament
rather than the results of the opening day of competition—the approach
taken by an inverted pyramid story.

SOURCE: *San Jose Mercury News,* morning final edition, page 4E
DATE: Friday, December 14, 1990
AUTHOR: Dan Hruby, *Mercury News* staff writer
HEADLINE: LPGA's Johnston leads Spalding field by 1 stroke

Cathy Johnston says a woman can win the Spalding Invitational Pro-
Am Golf Tournament under way on the Monterey Peninsula.

But she has a lot of reasons why it isn't likely to happen.

Johnston, a five-year LPGA player, fired a 5-under-par 67 Thursday
to take the first-round lead and put herself in excellent position to become
the first woman to capture this $300,000 event.

Rick Rhoads, head pro at San Francisco Golf Club, checked in with a
68. Juli Inkster of Los Altos and Howard Twitty of Phoenix, regulars of
the women's and men's pro tour, shot 69s and former Monterey Bay Area

stars Bobby Clampett and Tim Loustalot were two of five players with 70s.

Johnston, Inkster, Clampett and Loustalot all played at Poppy Hills under ideal conditions. Rhoads played at Pebble Beach and Twitty at Spyglass Hill. The 90 pros and 270 amateurs play each of the three courses and then those making the cut finish at Pebble on Sunday.

Women have played in the Spalding, the only tournament to feature men playing against women for equal prize money, in 10 of the last 11 years. Although the women are given distance advantages off the tees, the highest finish by a woman has been a tie for fifth, by Jan Stephenson and Patty Sheehan in 1987.

"A woman can win here, but I don't really consider this a battle of the sexes," said Johnston, who scored her first victory this year, one of the LPGA's majors, in Pointe Claire, Canada. "If I have a good week and do beat the men, that's great. But I think all of us know the men have a lot more ability than the women. The men will shoot the low scores day in and day out."

Johnston, whose round Thursday included six birdies and one bogey, noted that the male touring pros outnumber the females in the Spalding. The men have a 30-4 advantage. And, generally, the men play the game better, she said.

"The men have by far a better short game," said Johnston, a former University of North Carolina player who'll turn 27 Sunday. "Their ball-striking is more consistent week to week. Except maybe for Betsy King and Beth Daniel, I think the men work harder than women pros. I'll probably get killed for saying it, but it's true."

The other two women pro entrants had problems.

Elaine Crosby shot a 77 and Deb Richard a 78, both at Poppy Hills.

Inkster, who took part of 1990 off to have a baby, has never put much emphasis on the men vs. women angle.

"I'm here to win the tournament, not beat the men," she said.

Rhoads agreed with Johnston that a woman could break through in the Spalding at any time.

"She can win if she is tough mentally and gets a hot putter on the last day," he said.

Rhoads, who said he caught the oft-difficult Pebble Beach course in a benign state, logged birdies on Nos. 3, 11, 16 and 17.

"Being a club pro, I only play about four tournaments a year, so I'm trying not to get too excited," Rhoads said.

Roger Maltbie, playing in his first event since shoulder surgery three months ago, struggled to an 83 at Poppy Hills.

Transmitting the Story

If a reporter is fortunate, there will be time to go to his or her office to prepare the story. But countless times the story must be transmitted from the scene or from another location. Over the years, this has been done in different ways. First, reporters used telephone and telegraph. Writers either called their offices and dictated or gave their copy to telegraph operators who retyped the stories on the wire directly to the newspaper office. In fact, dictating a story over the telephone, either from a typed piece of copy or from memory, is still done at times when other means fail or equipment is not available.

Some newspapers now depend on computers that speed up the process. When electronic editing developed to the point that it included portable personal computers and other portable terminals connected by telephone to a newspaper's typesetting computer, the need for dictating a story was eliminated at some newspapers. When a reporter is on the road, most newspaper editors require that stories be written by their reporters on laptop or notebook personal computers and transmitted by modem to a computer system at the newsroom.

Another method used when computers are not available is the facsimile machine, a machine that uses telephone lines to transmit copies of an original story from a sending unit to a receiving unit on the sports desk.

But whether the story is filed by telephone dictation, typed directly onto a personal computer, faxed, or sent some other way, reporters must still prepare the story in a press box, office, hotel room, or some other less-than-perfect environment. Typing with people reading over a shoulder, noise, interruptions, and other distractions are barriers to writing a good game story. To succeed in the final step in getting the event covered — submitting a story to the sports copydesk — a reporter must have carried out the steps of research, making pregame arrangements, and recording the action. Then there is a good chance of writing a story that will capture the mood, the color, the personality, the excitement, and the action of an athletic event.

References

Associated Press. 1991. Hawaii locker rooms. Associated Press sports wire, January 3, n.p.

Fuhrer, Phil. 1975. Need all elements in game story. *Ganetteer* 30 (17):3.

Garrison, Bruce. 1990. *Professional News Writing*. Hillsdale, N.J.: Lawrence Erlbaum Associates.

Goldstein, Norm, ed. 1992. *Associated Press Stylebook and Libel Manual*. New York: Associated Press.

Miller, Bobby Ray, ed. 1981. *The UPI Stylebook: A Handbook for Writers and Editors*. New York: United Press International.

7

Features
and Speciality
Stories

Feature stories are fun to write for many
sports journalists. A "fun-to-do-story" is the
attitude when journalists begin to work on a
feature story, a specialty story such as an
event sidebar, an advance on a big game, or
a follow-up story a few days after the game. These stories are often enjoyable because they give sportswriters so much writing flexibility and provide
a creative challenge. Features and specialty stories generally permit more
freedom in topic choice, story focus, range of potential reporting methods,
and variety in writing style.

These story types are discussed together in this chapter because each of
them provides an unconventional approach to the sports story. They are not
game- or press conference–based stories. Because they are enjoyable for
the writer, they should be more entertaining for readers, too.

Consider these recent varied topics and approaches:

● *Baltimore Evening Sun* sports reporter John Steadman traveled to
Charlotte, N.C., to write a feature profile on former Baltimore Colts
player Jerry Richardson, who, 30 years after playing in a league championship game for his team, has amassed a fortune in the fast food restaurant
business. He now seeks a professional football franchise for his city.

● *Kansas City Star* soccer writer Jo-Ann Barnas focused a feature
story on a professional soccer player who had not played soccer for eight

months because of a broken leg. The player, Kansas City Comets forward David Doyle, had injured his leg in a Major Indoor Soccer League playoff match against Wichita at the end of the previous season while chasing a ball. He had surgery and took a long route to the moment when he walked into the Soccer Dome and scrimmaged against teammates. Barnas captured that moment and the player's rehabilitation in her story.

● Dave Luecking, *St. Louis Post-Dispatch* hockey writer, developed a feature story on St. Louis Blues center Adam Oates after he was not selected as a member of the Campbell Conference team for the National Hockey League all-star game for the second straight year. Luecking's story described the high-caliber performance by Oates during the previous season and a half and Oates' reaction to being overlooked.

● *The Sporting News* sportswriter Jan Hubbard wrote a comprehensive feature about Golden State Warriors forward Chris Mullin, describing the influences Mullin's late father, Rod, had on the former St. John's All-American. Hubbard described Mullin's recent successes on the court but also told readers about Mullin's bout with alcoholism several years earlier.

● Samantha Stevenson, *New York Times* News Service writer, wrote a family-oriented profile of professional baseball and football star Bo Jackson. Stevenson visited Jackson in his rented home at Marina Del Rey, Calif., where Jackson and his family lived while he played for the Los Angeles Raiders. The story described Jackson's life as father of three children, his role as a husband, and how he fits it all into a dual professional sports career.

● *Richmond (Va.) Times-Dispatch* sportswriter Bob Lipper wrote a profile of Kansas City Chiefs running back Barry Word after his successful 1,000-yard season. Word had a spectacular team-record 200-yard performance in the final regular season game that took his team into the National Football League playoffs. Lipper outlines Word's winning ways in college and his time in prison for transporting cocaine. Readers learn about his exile from professional football before he returned to the league. The biographical article showed readers how Word survived a rollercoaster–like past six years.

● *Sports Illustrated* writer Alexander Wolff told readers how television networks and college athletic directors play a "dating game" in scheduling football and basketball teams. The school and network matchmakers combine teams with regional draws in lucrative markets for big money, but at the same time carefully watch the win-loss columns. His article showed how schools such as Georgetown University and Shenandoah College are paired on the basketball court.

● Tony Kornheiser, *Washington Post* sports columnist, wrote a spring training farce for the *Post*'s Sunday magazine. Touted as an "exclusive," the sports spoof said the Washington Senators would be returning to play professional baseball in Washington, D.C., after 16 years. Kornheiser was convincing in his 5,000-word feature. Some readers believed the outrageous story.

● Mike Conklin, *Chicago Tribune* sportswriter, wrote a feature about Army football star Bill Speier to describe how the lineman had his future interests focused on service in the Army and the great uncertainty at the time over the 1991 war in the Middle East. Just before the conflict between the allied forces and Iraq, Conklin told readers how Speier, a native Chicagoan, would serve for the next five years in the Army regardless of his potential future in the National Football League.

What Makes a Sports Feature Story?

Because of so much variety such as these examples show in feature writing, it is difficult to give a simple definition of sports feature writing. William Rivers and Shelly Smolkin (1981) say that features are different in intent from routine news reporting in that they are designed to capture the interest of the reader instead of simply to present information: "The feature reporter casts a wide net in search for facts, sometimes pulling in and using things a news reporter would consider frivolous. The feature writer's report provides a reading experience that depends more on style, grace, and humor than on the importance of information. This difference is reflected in the fact that those who produce features exclusively are called 'feature writers,' not 'reporters.' "

Feature stories are different from news stories in several ways. They include more "license" or freedom to deviate from conventional newswriting rules. This gives feature writing a strong creative element. Feature stories focus on the unusual and unconventional subject. These stories can become emotional from a standpoint of content, but also from the point of occasional personal involvement by the sportswriter. A strong sports feature will involve readers. These stories will elicit reader reaction because they can be "serious or light, timely or timeless, funny or sad, joyful or joyless. These articles tell us much about the human condition" in sports (Garrison 1989).

Professor Louis Alexander (1975) takes a slightly different approach, stating that features begin with reporting and writing and eventually tell the reader what an event was like and what it means. He says that attempting to formulate a careful, complete, and scholarly definition of feature writing would be impressive, but would be contrary to its nature: "A feature story provides a reader with the flavor of an event or the nature of a person, not just with the facts of what happened or to whom it happened. It carries the reader beyond the events and leads him to an understanding of them."

Others have pointed out that good features, about sports or not, must emphasize the unconventional, must have a unique quality. Thus, in sports

Unusual sports events, such as equestrian championships, make opportunities for sportswriters to produce
feature stories that explain the sports to readers unfamil-
iar with them. (*Photo by the* Miami Herald *photography
staff.*)

features we often see the odd or unusual. We read sports stories that are about funny events, as well as others that are about the pathetic. Feature stories may be about common subjects, as well, if written in an interesting fashion.

Daniel Williamson (1975) notes four key elements to a strong feature article:

1. The writer displays creative energy in terms of writing and organizing style, source selection, and packaging of information.

2. The writer treats the story subjectively, being more involved in the subject and permitting that to show in the article.

3. The writer must not forget the informative nature of news in favor of other considerations. The strong feature article contains a high element of news and information.

4. While accomplishing the first three writing goals, the writer must produce in an entertaining article.

Finding Feature Ideas

How are ideas for feature stories developed? Much of the routine news coverage in the sports section can generate ideas: the player on a hot streak, the coach of the winning team, the behind-the-scenes angle of a tournament, the atmosphere of a crucial conference game. The feature writer must identify the story idea. What makes a good story? What is the angle, or point, of the story? How can it be conveyed? A simple rule of thumb will help as a guide: A story that is interesting to the reporter might be equally interesting to readers.

By now it should be clear that there are as many feature ideas around any community as there are teams, players, and fans. Do not overlook good feature sources. Press releases can suggest legitimate feature ideas, as can sports publicists. Clips from other publications can suggest local applications of stories. People suggest ideas. All suggestions are worthy of consideration and many are worthy of developing when time permits.

Reporters should simply look at the world around them; many ideas occur to writers who are observant of their surroundings. Repoters should also listen carefully to readers for story ideas, read the work of other sportswriters for ideas that might be applicable, and use specialized publications (Garrison 1989).

Finally, editors, who are more experienced and knowledgeable than a beginning reporter, can provide winning sports story ideas. Besides, who said assigned stories are all bad? Successful features can come both from the assignment desk and from the reporter.

Writing Feature Stories

Refinement of the story idea is critical to a successful story. This is called giving the story focus or angle. With focus and an angle for a story, it is easier for a writer to decide what is relevant and what is not for the particular story. It helps the sifting process, when a writer begins to gather and eventually sort through information to produce the story.

In developing the story idea, Garrison (1989) recommends sportswriters take these three steps for success: (1) list research sources needed, (2) make a rough outline of the idea or article, and (3) list the possible interviews needed for the story.

Like any other sports story, feature stories vary greatly in length. Some of the very best feature approaches range from briefs that are only a paragraph or two long to full stories that run 10 to 20 column inches. And very effective feature stories sometimes require two or three times the conventional length; sports magazine features often run thousands of words.

Professor Benton Rain Patterson (1986) offers three basic rules for success in writing any type of feature article: (1) put people in the story, (2) tell a story, and (3) let the reader see and hear for himself or herself.

As with other forms of newspaper writing, many lead possibilities and organizational plans are suitable for sports features. Perhaps the most common lead is the summary lead, but it should not be the only one in a reporter's repertoire. Quotations that catch the essence of the story are particularly effective as feature story leads. Direct address leads (in which the reporter "speaks" to the reader) can catch the attention and eye of the reader. Question leads get a reader into the story quickly, but the question must be answered.

The feature story lead doesn't have to cram all the basic information into the first few sentences, however. Unlike straight news, where it is desirable to get as many of the traditional *who, what, where, when, how,* and *why* facts into the lead as possible, the feature story eventually tells the reader these story elements, but not at the beginning.

In feature writing, there is probably more freedom than in any other form of non-column sportswriting, and this means the potential for exciting and creative leads that sell the story right away. Below are two examples of leads.

Summary lead: Bob Ryan and Dan Shaughnessy, *Globe* staff writers covering the National Basketball Association all-star weekend in Miami, simply summarize an announcement by the league at the game, but the lead gives the basic *who, what, where,* and *when.* The *how* and *why* elements of the story come deeper into the text:

> MIAMI—The 1990 McDonald's Open will be played in Barcelona and will feature Patrick Ewing and the New York Knicks, NBA commissioner David Stern announced yesterday.

There had been much speculation that the fourth annual event would be played in Paris. The first Open was held in Milwaukee in 1987. Boston went to Madrid a year later, and the Denver Nuggets played in Rome this past year. (SOURCE: "Knicks will play in Spain," *Boston Globe,* Sunday, February 11, 1990, third edition, page 56.)

Delayed lead: The following delayed lead, written by *Boston Globe* sportswriter Will McDonough, tops a feature on play-calling by professional quarterbacks in the National Football League today. Note how he sets up a trend in football by giving the historical perspective for today's fans. The focus here is clearly on *what* in the first paragraph, while the *who, when,* and other elements are delayed several paragraphs:

It started back in the 1950s with Paul Brown and Otto Graham. Graham was the best quarterback in pro football. In his 10 years in the game, he played in 10 championship games. Some still say he is the best of all time.

Despite Graham's greatness, Brown, one of the great innovators in the history of the game, felt the coach should call the plays. To that point, quarterbacks called the plays. Brown started the change, and over the years it was adopted at all levels, from high school to the Super Bowl.

The reasoning is that coaches study the opponent all week, become expert on the strategy of the game and therefore know better than the quarterback.

But this year in Buffalo, all of that changed. "Our quarterbacks called most of the plays and they did a heck of a job at it," said Bills' offensive coordinator Ted Marchibroda.

How good a job? Buffalo led the league in scoring. (SOURCE: "Calling their own shots: Buffalo QBs score a direct hit," *Boston Globe,* Sunday, January 6, 1991, third edition, page 56.)

These leads reflect various combinations of the approaches listed above. The first is a straight, just-the-facts, spot news lead. Summary leads are highly functional and work best in non-feature settings. The second, delayed lead demonstrates how a feature story often begins. It does not have to get to the point right away. The lead serves a different function: It tries to hook the reader into reading a longer story to get to the point.

Although leads are important, it is equally vital for a story to carry out its promise with a strong organizational plan. This does not necessarily mean an outline, but the writer should think out the story and its flow before starting to write. Not being bound to conventional forms can generate problems in organizing the material. Many feature writers, however, use the straight news approach and inverted pyramid organization, in which the most important information is presented first and additional information follows in descending order of importance. Writers also use a chronological order, relating events by the clock or calendar. There are writers who use a suspense organizational plan, not telling the outcome until the end and, perhaps, surprising the reader.

Many writers say good feature material will "write itself." This may sound impossible to a beginning writer, but what these experienced reporters are saying is that some information can be effectively told in only one fashion, usually a rather simple structure that is not appropriate for all feature stories. The writer often does not use a summary lead but begins with a situation and describes it in detail. Such features often begin with a case study — a look at one team or one player — that is described in detail. The story then moves to more general descriptions of the league or the sport. These stories, like all features, are written so the reader can easily identify with the topic. Because many sports readers are active, stories should be written with this in mind.

Some stories are written in the question-answer style, but there is the risk of overkill. Although this organizational plan can be quite appropriate, sometimes the writer is too lazy to work out a more effective plan and turns an interview-profile story into an uninteresting Q-A format.

Regardless of the way the information is presented, feature stories must be creatively written. This is an opportunity to take full advantage of the colorful language, environment, and people who make up a sportswriter's world. What makes a good story? A well-written sports feature includes a clear story line, a subjective approach, an element of detail and information, an entertaining quality, a timelessness or a specific timeliness, a complete account in the story, and mechanically sound grammar and punctuation.

Features as Sidebars

Louis Alexander (1975) points out that sidebars are color stories, giving some of the flavor of an event beyond the facts. Sports sections, like other newspaper sections, run these stories above, below, or to the side of a straight news story, on the same page or on the jump page.

A common use of sidebars is to enhance event coverage by presenting angles and additional information not usually included within the scope of the event story. In a championship game, for example, one story usually tells the facts of the game. A sidebar or several sidebars focus on the winning team, the losing team, the home team, an exceptional or winning play, the coaches' reactions, the crowd and its reactions, and so on. The possible stories can range as widely as staff is available to write them. Most sidebars are written with a feature approach.

The following example is a reaction sidebar to the spot news announcement that Ferguson Jenkins was elected to the baseball Hall of Fame. The story, by *Chicago Tribune* sportswriter Robert Markus, provides reactions and comments from Jenkins' teammates on the day the announcement was made. Using the telephone interview effectively, Markus interviewed three key players during Jenkins' career from across the country and intertwined Jenkins' career statistics to back up their supportive quotations about the popular late-1960s and early-1970s Chicago Cubs pitcher.

SOURCE: The *Chicago Tribune,* North sports final, page 2, zone C
DATE: Wednesday, January 9, 1991
AUTHOR: Robert Markus, staff writer
HEADLINE: Former teammates laud Jenkins

Ferguson Jenkins spent Tuesday afternoon in an Oklahoma City hospital room visiting his wife, Maryanne, who is slowly recovering from a near-fatal auto accident she suffered a month ago.

When he returned to his home in Guthrie, Okla., the telephone was ringing. It was the sweetest sound the former Cubs pitcher has ever heard. It was notification he had been inducted into the baseball Hall of Fame in only his third year of eligibility.

Five minutes after getting the news from Jack Lang, secretary of the Baseball Writers Association of America, Jenkins was back out the door and on his way to New York, where on Wednesday he will be introduced at a press conference along with the other new members of the Hall of Fame.

Jenkins, whose lifetime record of 284-226 included six consecutive 20-win seasons with the Cubs, received 334 votes from the 443 Baseball Writers Association of America members.

"Isn't that wonderful?" exclaimed Don Kessinger, reached in his office at the University of Mississippi, where he is the head baseball coach. "I was hoping he'd get in. I was privileged to play shortstop behind him when he won 20 games six years in a row. Anyone who can do that is certainly a Hall-of-Famer."

Other former teammates were equally excited for the lanky pitcher, who is the only man in major league history to have more than 3,000 strikeouts and fewer than 1,000 walks.

"Fergie had the most outstandingly consistent control I ever caught," said Jim Sundberg, who was Jenkins' catcher on the Texas Rangers. "He had just amazing control and he was an amazing competitor. If he had the lead in the late innings, you could almost count on it being a win."

Sundberg grew up in Illinois and was a Cubs fan when Jenkins was throttling National League hitters for the Cubs from 1967 to 1973.

"He was one of the players on the top of my list," remembered Sundberg. "One of my greatest thrills was that in my first major league game in 1974, I caught Fergie and he threw a one-hitter. It was a swinging bunt by (Bert) Campaneris that Fergie tried to one-hand. He beat Oakland 1-0 that night."

"That's great," said Hall-of-Famer Billy Williams when he heard the news. Jenkins becomes the third Cub of that era to make the Hall of

Fame, joining Williams and Ernie Banks.

"He's about 6-6," observed Williams, "and I know he feels 10 feet tall right now. When I got that call from Jack Lang, it was really exciting. I wanted to share it with all the people who played the game."

"It's fabulous," agreed Ron Santo, the third baseman of that Cubs era. "I just talked to Fergie two days ago and I said, 'I have a feeling you'll make it. If they look at the record, you'll be in.' He didn't think he would be. He said, 'They've got Gaylord Perry, Rollie Fingers and Rod Carew.' He was concerned."

Jenkins also undoubtedly was concerned that the only hint of scandal that touched his otherwise illustrious career might come back to haunt him.

In 1980, he was found guilty of cocaine possession in Canada and, even though the judge, because of the pitcher's previous exemplary record, gave Jenkins an absolute discharge—which meant he would not have a criminal record—Jenkins feared some writers might use the incident to vote against him.

Obviously that didn't happen. Jenkins came to the Cubs in 1966 after a year and a half with the Phillies, and then-manager Leo Durocher put him right into the starting rotation.

Starting with 1967, Jenkins won 20 or more games for the next six years. After slumping to 14-16 in 1973, he was traded to the Rangers, where he won 25 games and Comeback of the Year honors.

After eight years with the Rangers and Boston Red Sox, Jenkins finished his career with the Cubs. In 1982, he was 14-15 with a 3.15 earned-run average for a team that won only 73 games. He was released in spring training of 1984 after going 6-9 in his final season.

He always felt that given the chance, he could have won the 16 more games that would have made him a 300-game winner.

But he had already done enough. He ended up with 3,192 strikeouts and only 997 walks, an unparalleled feat.

"You win as many as he won," said Santo. "You win 20 games six years in a row in Wrigley Field, that's a Hall-of-Fame pitcher."

Other Sports Feature Story Forms

There are many other forms of feature stories. Although a complete discussion would require too much space, we will take a look at some important types.

COLOR STORIES. Color stories focus on a subject and provide much descriptive detail. This detail contributes to the atmosphere for another story, so color stories are often used as sidebars. There is no real formula for the color story; it can have any organizational plan and any type of lead. Color stories focus on events much of the time but not always (Garrison 1989). A good color story? At a tournament, it might be a story about local cheerleaders winning the cheering trophy. At a championship game, it might be a story on the crowd. At a Friday night hometown football game, it might be a story about the individuals who have operated the Booster Club concessions all season.

Miami Herald sportswriter S. L. Price, as part of his coverage of the U.S. Open tennis championship in New York, wrote this story under the label "U.S. Open Notebook" to give readers additional color about the tournament. This story, in addition to his center court match coverage for the day, places a spotlight on one player, Zina Garrison. Note how this feature, as a color story should do, gives details through direct quotations, specific physical descriptions, re-creation of scenes—all this lets the reader "see" what happened rather than just read about it. Starting with Price's lead, you can "see" Garrison as she suffers from her injured ankle.

SOURCE: The *Miami Herald,* final edition, page 7D
DATE: Thursday, September 6, 1990
AUTHOR: S. L. Price, *Herald* sportswriter
HEADLINE: Sanchez ousts ailing Garrison

NEW YORK—The ankle was throbbing and Zina Garrison could barely move. She hadn't been this frustrated in a long time. A voice went through her mind and it said, "Quit." When she talked about it later, there were tears in her eyes.

"I thought about it during the first set," Garrison said. "But I like playing. I have a very high tolerance for pain. I just wanted to stay out there and finish. I wanted to at least make her work for the money she was getting."

So Garrison, seeded fourth, made Arantxa Sanchez-Vicario of Spain work Wednesday, but in the end the work wasn't so hard. Sanchez, seeded sixth, beat Garrison, 6-2, 6-2, to move into the U.S. Open semifinals for the first time.

Friday, Sanchez will meet top-seeded Steffi Graf, who routed Jana Novotna, 6-3, 6-1, earlier Wednesday.

It wasn't an easy loss for Garrison to take. She had come in playing the best tennis of her life. She had beaten Monica Seles and Graf at Wimbledon. But in her first-round match against Beate Reinstadler of Austria, Garrison sprained her right ankle. She had it taped for her next three victories, but the tape began to irritate her Achilles tendon.

Garrison's doctor tried to persuade her not to play Wednesday. "I was really close," she said. "If I didn't have a day off (Tuesday), I probably would not have been able to play. I just wanted to go out there and try."

But it was obvious that something was missing from Garrison's serve-

and-volley game; her serve didn't sting and her volley didn't exist. She stayed on the baseline, hoping Sanchez would make mistakes.

"I was really surprised because she was not coming in all of the time," said Sanchez, who suffered a sprained left ankle in July.

Later Wednesday, Garrison pulled out of doubles with Patty Fendick, who is having bad luck with doubles partners. Fendick's mixed-doubles partner, Ken Flach, walked off the court during a match Sunday, resulting in a default. Flach was fined $2,700.

"I was probably the last on the list of girls who would play with him," Fendick said. "He'll have problems finding another partner now."

For Graf, the elimination of Garrison would seem to further smooth a path already made glassy by the upsets of Seles and Martina Navratilova. "There is nobody to stop her from winning this championship," Novotna said.

Asked about Sanchez's chances against Graf, Garrison said, "I don't think she played that good. She definitely would have to step it up another two paces to play Steffi. She was letting me play, not really going for her shots."

Graf, however, said that Sanchez "looks stronger in this tournament than Zina did. She is more consistent. She will fight for every point. She won't give me anything like other players do."

Sanchez, who upset Graf in the 1989 French Open final, sees it exactly the same way. "She knows I'm tough and I know she is the best," Sanchez said. "But I don't have anything to lose and I'm going to play my game. And the way I play, I think I can beat her again."

No. 1 seed Ivan Baron of Plantation beat Narathorn Srichaphan of Thailand, 6-3, 6-4, in boys' singles Wednesday to earn a stadium-court match today against No. 15 Andrea Gaudenzi of Italy.

Reprinted with the permission of the *Miami Herald*

PERSONALITY PROFILES. Personality profiles look at the individual, in most cases focusing on one person. These stories "sketch" someone in the news, usually an individual who has performed exceptionally or for some other reason has been singled out. The profile is devoted to explaining why the person is special. These stories may illustrate success or failure, happiness or sadness. Personality profiles often contain the impressions of others about the subject. The stories traditionally contain anecdotes that place the subject in his or her natural context. Profiles of this type are often connected to current events with a news peg, such as a recent activity or experience that serves as the rationale for the story. A strong personality profile might be a story about a coach winning his or her first championship, a player leading the conference in scoring, a longtime referee about to retire, or an injured star player.

The following profile, by *Baltimore Evening Sun* sports reporter John Steadman, is the traditional success story. This sports profile takes a slightly different twist, however, on the sports success theme of boy-be-comes-star-athlete. In this case, Steadman's story shows how a star athlete became a millionaire based on his hard work and business abilities after his athletic career ended. The story tells readers how this man, former Balti-more Colt Jerry Richardson, wants to own a National Football League franchise in his hometown of Charlotte, N.C. It is an appealing story that is well written with details and meaningful direct quotations.

SOURCE: The *Miami Herald,* first edition, page 7D
DATE: Sunday, May 13, 1990
AUTHOR: John Steadman, *Baltimore Evening Sun*
HEADLINE: Ex-NFL star dreaming of a grand empire

CHARLOTTE, N.C.—Some men reach the summit. They scale the precarious Mountain of Success, which translates to wealth, prestige and social acceptance. Then they pound their chests, become enthralled with self-importance and forget old friends.

An exception to such a dreadful scenario is a tall, well-groomed southern gentleman named Jerry Richardson, whose achievements read like a tale lifted from a pulp magazine fiction story. Richardson is the catalyst in the move to build a $125 million stadium in Charlotte that hopefully will house a National Football League expansion team. Gover-nors, senators and business leaders court his friendship.

Had it not been for the Baltimore Colts, it is doubtful if Richardson could have attained such affluence and renown. But the most important quality he offers is basic humility. What he has accomplished does not get in the way of kindness and consideration for others.

Richardson, after catching a touchdown pass in the Colts' NFL title win over the New York Giants in 1959, took the championship check of $4,674.44 and turned it into an investment that has carried him to multi-millionaire status. His net worth cannot be assessed and if it could, he would be the least impressed.

The money from the victory over the Giants was used by Richardson to buy a Hardee's franchise in Spartanburg, S.C., where he cooked and waited tables. Then other purchases followed, slowly but deliberately, un-der the corporate name of Spartan Food Services. Today he is president of TW Services, a New York Stock Exchange–listed company with $3.3 bil-lion in annual revenues.

Included in his network of holdings are 456 Hardee's Restaurants in 10 states, 213 Quincy Family Steak Houses, 989 Denny's Restaurants, 266 Denny's Restaurant franchises, 90 El Pollo Loco Restaurants, 87 El Pollo Loco Restaurant franchises as well as the Canteen Corp. The Richardson roster varies from between 108,000 to 114,000 employees.

Not bad for a kid out of Wofford College, whose father was a barber in Fayetteville. Richardson was selected as a "future" on the 13th round in the 1958 NFL draft, the same year the Colts picked Lenny Lyles, Ray Brown, John Sample, John Diehl and Floyd Peters. As a rookie, he caught a 12-yard scoring toss from John Unitas in the 1959 finale with the Giants and was a backup for two seasons to Raymond Berry and Jim Mutscheller.

"From my family's point of view," he said, "the reason we're even in position to seek an expansion franchise is the money we received when we won the championship in Baltimore. It was the down payment on the first restaurant. That was the beginning and I am deeply grateful to have been so fortunate. I've never forgotten what it meant."

Richardson's wife, the former Rosalind Sallenger, originally from Florence, S.C., went to a then all-girls school, Winthrop College, in Rock Hill. They have three children, sons Jon and Mark, both former football players at North Carolina and Clemson, respectively, a daughter, Ashley Richardson Allen, and five grandchildren.

Jerry and Rosalind Richardson reside in Spartanburg, S.C., have a summer home at Lake James, N.C., and enjoy a quiet lifestyle.

"He doesn't like recognition," said Max Muhleman, the sports marketing expert who is one of his advisers. "The man is conservative, low-key and has no personal vanity. He just enjoys his family, working and being physically fit."

So, obviously, Richardson is not one of those All-America bores who stands around dominating the conversation by reflecting on his achievements. Son Mark tells of when he wrote to outline what he had been doing and where he thought they were on the Carolina pro football project.

"I got a note back from him telling me I had written a good letter but I used 'I' four times and that was four times too many. Then he signed it, 'Love, Dad.' He just can't stand anyone using the pronoun 'I.' In all his conversations, he constantly says, 'we, we, we' and never uses the first person. My impression is it comes from playing a team game like football."

The respect Jerry Richardson, 53, earned led him to being invited to join the board of directors of the National Bank of North Carolina and Istotechnologies Inc., plus chairman of the board of Winchell's Donut Houses. He is a trustee at Wofford, his alma mater; Saint Mary's College in Raleigh; and his church, St. Paul's Methodist, in Spartanburg.

If Richardson wins an expansion franchise, he will be only the second former player to own a team in the 70-year history of the NFL. The first was the esteemed George Halas, founder, general manager, player and coach of the Chicago Bears.

It all started for Richardson with that check for $4,674.44 he took home from the 1959 championship game.

Reprinted with the permission of the *Baltimore Evening Sun*

HUMAN INTEREST STORIES. Human interest stories may also be personality profiles. But as Rivers and Smolkin (1981) state, the human interest story "should engage the reader emotionally, stimulating or depressing him [or her], angering or amusing him [or her], awakening sympathy or distaste." These stories are not the usual day-to-day features, because they require special circumstances. The reader's personal involvement depends on a combination of factors. The reader must be able to identify with the subject. The writing must be simple, without complex organization or confusion. These stories may depict, for example, the fight of the paralyzed athlete, the effect on a team of the loss of a teammate, the difficult training before a winning effort, or the cooperative efforts of a community organization to send a deserving athlete to a competition. When done well, these stories are the most widely read of any in the sports section.

The key to successful human interest sports features is the human element (Garrison 1989). These stories display a range of emotions — horror, amusement, excitement, joy, depression, sympathy, sadness, anger — and help readers to associate with the story being told. A strong human interest feature does three things: (1) It describes an extraordinary experience; (2) it shows how people have coped with a problem common to many people; and (3) it focuses on a timely issue of wide regional or national concern.

The following story by Mark Newman, *San Jose Mercury News* sportswriter, focuses on the anniversary of the Loma Prieta earthquake in California at the beginning of the 1990 World Series in the San Francisco–Oakland Bay Area of California. Many Americans remember the startling live television coverage of the earthquake in 1989 just as a World Series game was to begin at San Francisco's Candlestick Park. A year later, Newman picks up on this human interest theme in his story. Tragedies of this magnitude bring memories to people, and the return of the World Series a year later made this story one that had to be written.

SOURCE: *San Jose Mercury News,* morning final edition, page 5D
DATE: Friday, October 19, 1990
AUTHOR: Mark Newman, *Mercury News* staff writer
HEADLINE: Memories surface as series returns to scene of the disaster

It would have been one thing to simply acknowledge the anniversary of the Loma Prieta earthquake, to simply remember the victims and the heroes of that night.

Now, as if by design, the World Series has returned to the Bay Area for another tangible reminder of what happened.

"I'm sure there will be some sharp memories," said Fay Vincent, the baseball commissioner. "It's something we shared."

Vincent arrived in the Bay Area from Cincinnati on Thursday along with the baseball entourage for tonight's Game 3 between the A's and the Reds at the Oakland Coliseum. It is where the first two games of the last

World Series were played, a time of festivity and innocence, of half-black and half-green ball caps. For those such as Vincent who return as visitors, it still might be impossible to look upon these next games routinely.

"The issue has come up a lot in the past year because so many people ask me about it, and because I frequently see people who played a role in those events," Vincent said. "It certainly was one of the greatest challenges of my life. I'm pleased we got through it, and I'm pleased with the decision we made."

Vincent said before Wednesday's Game 2 at Riverfront Stadium that there was scheduled to be some type of commemoration that night, for the quake had struck exactly one year earlier. As it turned out, no such feature was included in the pregame ceremonies. Baseball officials said some commemoration is more likely to take place before Game 3, given the fact that it happened here.

The quake, which measured 7.1 on the Richter scale, shook Candlestick Park for 15 seconds about 20 minutes before Game 3. What was supposed to be a wondrous showcase for Bay Area baseball turned into a nightmare. From that moment on, never in this century did a World Series mean so little.

Vincent, who recently had been appointed commissioner after Bart Giamatti's death, postponed the game. There was a 10-day hiatus before play resumed, and Vincent remembers how close he came to going home.

"It was close," he said. "If we could not have played at Candlestick, or if the community didn't want it, then we wouldn't have played it. I didn't want to move it."

As for the decision to send the sellout crowd home Oct. 17, Vincent said: "The real issue was that we knew there were major problems in the community. The decision to cancel was so people could be on their way driving while there was daylight. Once it became clear there was major dislocation, it became clear we needed people to move. I think it was the correct judgment and I canceled it as soon as I could.

"As for me, I didn't know enough to be frightened during the earthquake. I got so busy in the two weeks, there wasn't really a significant effect on me that way. To those of us who went through it, it won't be forgotten."

Vincent said he has developed a close relationship with various Bay Area officials, and he said Major League Baseball in the past year raised "a substantial amount" of money for area relief work.

"I see the community through the Oakland and San Francisco teams," Vincent said. "There are some continuing ties because of this. I felt the real hero of that World Series was Cmdr. (Isiah) Nelson. His death during the past year was perhaps the most disappointing thing to me, because he was a good friend. He was a real part of this."

Vincent worked with Nelson, of the San Francisco Police Department, in an effort to resume the Series.

While Vincent talked about coming back to the Bay Area, Cincinnati players said they had not given the quake much thought.

"We go out there three times a year for each team for as long as I can

remember, and there's been earthquakes, but nothing major like last year,"
Reds' pitcher Rick Mahler said. "It's something you absolutely have no
control over. It's nothing you concern *yourself* with."

In the following human interest feature, *San Jose Mercury News* columnist Mark Purdy writes of his personal feelings about the end of Chicago's Comiskey Park. Human interest stories are often personal, and his
emotional reaction to Comiskey's demise makes compelling reading. Many
readers will identify with him. They will remember their visit to Comiskey,
or their own feelings when other old baseball parks closed, perhaps one
near them. Readers will, like Purdy does, lament progress and long for the
old times when life was simpler and perhaps easier.

SOURCE: *San Jose Mercury News,* morning final edition, page 1E
DATE: Friday, September 28, 1990
AUTHOR: Mark Purdy, *Mercury News* sports columnist
HEADLINE: They're wrecking a relic

A friend is dying this weekend. I don't want to be there. I wouldn't
feel like cheering.

That is what will happen Sunday afternoon, on Chicago's south side.
Comiskey Park will die, as thousands applaud. The oldest ballpark in the
major leagues is being euthanized. It will be replaced next season by a
spiffy new concrete stadium across the street. A capacity crowd will send
off the old brick park with speeches, standing ovations and fireworks.

Oh, yes. The White Sox also will play their final baseball games on
the site.

Sorry. I don't want any part of it. I'll say goodbye, but I won't cheer. I
wouldn't cheer if they took a wrecking ball to the Smithsonian Institute,
either. Comiskey was built in 1910, four years before Babe Ruth first
stepped on a major league field and 29 years before the Hall of Fame was
opened in Cooperstown. That's how old Comiskey is.

A few years ago, I wrote about my affection for the rusty hulk, noting
that I would rather spend an afternoon with Comiskey Park than an
afternoon with Bo Derek.

"What are you — perverted?" asked a colleague with whom I shared an
office. "No," I answered. "Bo is a fad. Comiskey is tradition."

"Huh?"

"Never mind."

With Comiskey being put to sleep, only three of the classic stadiums
will remain. Yankee Stadium doesn't count, because in the mid-70s, it was
remodeled into an ersatz shell of its former self, sort of a Universal Studios

version of Yankee Stadium. That leaves Fenway Park, Tiger Stadium and Wrigley Field to remind us of the days when stadiums didn't all look like concrete ashtrays for Andre the Giant.

But of all those old parks, Comiskey is/was the best. No arguments, please. I'll admit it is an emotional thing. For me, Comiskey was the place where I first learned to love baseball. In 1970, when I arrived in Chicago as a college freshman, I was a virtual blank canvas in terms of the national pastime. My dad was a great sports fan, except when it came to baseball. He never took me to a major league game as a child. College football and basketball, yes. Baseball, no.

Consequently, when I left my small Ohio home town to attend school in the big city, I was curious to check out both Comiskey and Wrigley Field. A new pal, Rock, soon set me straight. He had grown up on the north side of Chicago, supposedly Cubs territory. But he loathed Wrigley.

"Comiskey is more real, because the fans are more real," Rock explained. "Cub fans are like weekend hippies. They come to games because it's fashionable."

He was correct. It is too simple to say that Comiskey is more blue-collar than Wrigley. To me, it is more about attitude than about collars. Fans usually reflect the stadium they patronize. If the old ballparks were pieces of clothing, Fenway Park would be a trendy pair of faded L. L. Bean chino slacks. Tiger Stadium would be a worn leather motorcycle jacket. Wrigley Field would be a neatly pressed old tuxedo.

And Comiskey Park? It would be a ragged pair of veteran blue jeans, the kind you never want to throw out of the closet. Always comfortable. Never pretentious. The stadium's features — basic brick outer walls, ethnic concession stands, picnic area directly behind a screen in the left field wall — attracted the kind of people who savored baseball most.

Over the next few days, you will hear and read about the momentous events and personalities that characterized Comiskey. That is fine. The list is an impressive one, from Shoeless Joe Jackson to Joe Louis to the Beatles.

But if you never were there, nothing will quite convey the rank-and-file energy that infested the stadium.

It was at Comiskey Park, for example, that the practice of calling home run hitters back out of the dugout for an "encore" tip of their caps first began. Surrounded by such stuff, it was easy for an 18-year-old college student to get caught up in the mix. It also helped that Dick Allen came along in 1972 to hit 37 home runs. During a student strike that spring, in protest of Nixon's latest Vietnam escalation, bonfires burned in the barricaded campus streets. "So," a friend said, "do you want to go to the revolution tonight? Or do you want to go to Comiskey?"

I think that's the moment I knew I would become a sportswriter. The revolution may have been exciting, but Comiskey was hardly boring. Opening day of 1973 was one of those typically charming Chicago spring afternoons where a jet stream breeze was blowing off Lake Michigan and the wind chill factor hovered in the 20s. The park was barely half full. Vida Blue of the A's was mowing down the Sox. A group of us had played hooky from biology class and were seated along the first-base line.

As we sat and shivered, a gaggle of longhaired men made their way down our aisle, carrying a portable beer cooler the size of a Volkswagen. They were vaguely familiar. Then it hit me.

"Look," I said. "That's Alice Cooper."

"Sure," said Rock, who was sitting next to me. "Alice Cooper at a White Sox game."

But as the group sat down in front of us and began popping open 16-ounce beverages from the cooler, my pal realized I wasn't joking. At that juncture in American history, I couldn't imagine Alice Cooper coming to any other baseball stadium except Comiskey.

"Who you picking this season?" I asked.

"I like the A's," Alice said. "They've got the best pitching."

Alice always did know his baseball.

Still, he wasn't the weirdest person at Comiskey, not by a long shot. There was the voodoo lady, for example. We discovered her one hot August afternoon in 1983, the White Sox's last championship season. I was living elsewhere by then, but had organized a field trip to Comiskey with some friends. We sat behind home plate. Two rows ahead of us sat a woman who began plucking out her hair, strand by strand, each time Sox designated hitter Greg Luzinski came to bat. Then she would begin to chant gibberish and clench the hair in her fists.

"YABBBAWEEGEEEEJ!" the voodoo lady yelled in the second inning.

Luzinski swung. The ball exploded off his bat. The left fielder looked up. The people in the lower deck looked up. The people in the upper deck looked up. The ball hit the roof.

"BABAWEEWEWEEKABING!" screamed the voodoo lady.

We promptly moved to the bleachers. Other people will remember Luke Appling and Nellie Fox when the old ballyard shuts down Sunday afternoon. I'll remember the voodoo lady and the other wonderful people I met at the best ballpark on earth.

Goodbye old friend. I'd also rather be at Bo Derek's funeral than yours.

Advances as Feature Stories

The basic advance story is not necessarily a feature story. Many advance stories simply tell the reader specifics about an event that is to happen in a day or two, such as a meeting of lease directors or a game between two undefeated teams. The story is usually short; information is often attributed to a source. A straight news advance tells the reader the basic *who, what, where, when, how,* and *why.* There will be no mercy for a

Los Angeles Kings head coach Tom Webster (far right) responds to a reporter's question during the team's annual preseason media day, always a good source of "advance" feature stories on teams and individual players and coaches. (*Photo by Wen Roberts, Photography Ink.*)

careless sportswriter who writes an advance about an important game that does not give the starting time or the location. The format for such stories is simple. It is most often written in inverted pyramid form, providing the reader with the most important information first. Details follow in descending order of importance.

Most advances for sports sections have to offer more. Not only does the story provide the basics of the upcoming event, but it does so within a feature story framework — looking at some element of the event, such as a player, team momentum, a streak of injuries, or the coaches. The advance built into a feature format sets the stage better, building interest in the event and also building readership for later stories about it.

The following advance for an upcoming sports event from *Philadelphia Inquirer* sports reporter Ron Reid is much more developed than a typical advance because it uses the feature approach. Reid tells readers that the Olympic Festival is about to begin in Minneapolis, but he gives his eastern readers a dose of Minnesota midwestern living. This lead gives more of the flavor of the event. With direct quotations and description, this story is interesting and inviting for readers.

SOURCE: *Philadelphia Inquirer,* final edition, page C5
DATE: Friday, July 6, 1990
AUTHOR: Ron Reid, *Inquirer* staff writer
HEADLINE: Athletes converge for Minneapolis' big sports party

MINNEAPOLIS — The Olympic Festival opens today, giving the nation a view of its emerging Olympians and a heady dose of civic pride — Minnesota style.

Only here can you watch the splendid skills of the likes of Jackie Joyner-Kersee while learning that the largest carp ever caught in Minnesota weighed 55 pounds, 5 ounces; that water skiing and the Nerf ball were invented here some time ago; the morel mushroom is the official state fungus and the common loon is the official state bird. The official purpose of an Olympic Festival is twofold: to give aspiring athletes the chance to hone their skills against one another; and to familiarize the world-class competitors among them with the routine of an Olympics.

Some national sports governing bodies even use the competition as their qualifying trial for the Olympic Games.

But a festival also demands a few modest raves about anything worth bragging about from its army of local volunteers. In this particular year, Olympic Festival executives and volunteers are hoping their event won't be overshadowed by the Goodwill Games, which start July 20, so they are only too willing to tell you, for instance, that Minnesota has 12,034 lakes of 10 acres or larger, and more shoreline than California and Oregon combined.

Toward greater recognition, Minnesota will be helped by about 3,100 athletes gathered here to run, jump, throw, swim, skate, sail, shoot, spike, paddle, punch, pirouette and otherwise go for the gold over the next nine days, performing for teams designated the North, South, East and West in 37 sports.

The roster of athletes includes such international competitors as Joyner-Kersee, the heptathlon world-record holder and two-time Olympic champion, and Hollis Conway, the high jump's Olympic silver medalist, who set the American record of 7 feet, 10 inches in Festival competition a year ago.

The track and field competition also will include Villanova middle-distance runners Kathy Franey, Michelle Bennett, Kate Fonshell and Mike Seeger.

Carol Lewis, the Willingboro native and two-time Olympian whose better-known brother, Carl, is promoting his book, will carry the family name in the long jump, while Vince Labosky, the 1990 national champion from Tabernacle, heads an impressive field in the javelin.

There are about 120 athletes from Philadelphia and its suburbs scheduled to compete in the Festival, a preponderance of whom (27) will be in the women's field hockey tournament.

Figure skating also has drawn its usual large representation from the University of Delaware Skating Center, coached by Ron Ludington.

Calla Urbanski of Wilmington, and her partner, Mark Naylor, from Harrisburg, will shoot for their second straight Festival title in the pairs competition. Their chief rivals are Elaine Asanakis, also of Wilmington, and Joel McKeever, her partner from Dallas.

Skating also claims the youngest Festival participant in Nicole Bobek of Colorado Springs, Colo., a 4-foot-11, 90-pound, 12-year-old who is entered in the women's singles.

Youth similarly will be served in swimming, with entrants restricted to top athletes, 18 and under, without previous national-team experience. Their meet, on Sunday, Monday and Tuesday, will be the first ever held in the new University of Minnesota Aquatic Center—one of 23 Festival venues throughout the Twin Cities.

Diving competition starts in the same facility on Thursday, when Allison Maisch, 23, of Cherry Hill, hopes to improve one spot on the silver medal she won at last year's Festival in Oklahoma.

The basketball competition will be headed by a bevy of collegiate stars, 25 of whom played last season at four-year colleges or universities. Among their number: Villanova's 6-6 center Calvin Byrd, who will be joined on the East team by the Wildcats' 6-10 incoming freshman Anthony Pelle, from the Bronx.

In boxing, Philadelphia's Marcel Brown, a contender in the 112-pound flyweight division, will fight his first bout on Sunday, his 21st birthday.

Competition also starts on Sunday for Philadelphia's Mike Rafferty, 19, in the 125-pound featherweight division.

The Festival's most interesting athlete may be a weightlifter. He is Roberto "Tony" Urrutia, 32, the three-time world champion who defected from his native Cuba in 1980, when the island nation's team was training in Mexico City for the Moscow Olympics.

Now residing in Hollywood, Fla., Urrutia was forced to live three months in a car after he first came to the United States. He will compete in the 82.5-kilogram (181-pound) class.

NOTES. ESPN will televise 30 hours of Festival competition starting with figure skating, men's basketball, boxing and synchronized swimming tomorrow from 4 p.m. to 7 p.m. and 9 p.m. to 11 p.m. The cable network plans to feature 11 of the Festival's 37 sports during its telecasts.

Members of the Philadelphia Sports Congress, hoping to bring the Festival to Philadelphia in 1993, 1994 or 1995, are on hand to observe the operation of the event in the Twin Cities.

Follow-up Features

Follow-up features accomplish much when done properly. These special stories are done one or two days after the event. Follow-up stories may highlight news not known the day of the event or even the day after it. Who won is no longer news, so the focus can turn to the *how* and the *why.*

The follow-up feature incorporates all the elements of feature stories in much the same way as does an advance feature. It ties up any loose ends, emphasizing the remaining significant news. The writer can focus on detail that was not possible to give the first day because of space limitations or other reasons, and usually can emphasize quotations and the impressions, reactions, and feelings of those involved. These stories also provide opportunities to give readers new information (injury reports) and new looks at and interpretation of old information (such as critical plays). Yet, there must be a link to the original event for the reader who has not had a chance to see the first-day coverage (Garrison 1989).

This type of writing is common among magazines that have deadline problems. Publications such as the *Sporting News* and *Sports Illustrated,* although weeklies, cannot compete with television and daily newspapers for breaking or spot news, so they must take the follow-up approach by offering something new to readers on events that have already occurred. The same problem, of course, exists with small newspapers published once or twice a week.

Following is an example of a second-day follow-up feature by *Miami Herald* football writer Greg Cote. Cote's story is a recap of the Miami Dolphins season that had ended two days earlier in the National Football League playoffs. In his story, Cote assesses the loss but also the gains made by the team throughout the entire season. He focuses on the thoughts of the team's leader, Coach Don Shula. Cote addresses what the team must do to improve for the coming season, as well, using Shula and his own expertise in the analysis.

SOURCE: The *Miami Herald,* final edition, page 1D
DATE: Monday, January 14, 1991
AUTHOR: Greg Cote, *Herald* sportswriter
HEADLINE: It's over . . . now Dolphins look ahead; Pass rusher is Shula's top priority as draft, Plan B awaits

His Super Bowl dreams freeze-dried just 24 hours earlier, Dolphin Coach Don Shula said in a post-mortem Sunday that the season-ending loss to Buffalo didn't change his opinion about good things accomplished . . . or deficiencies that still exist.

"The whole year overall was really a positive step in the right direction," Shula said. "But we also realize we still have a long way to go in a lot of areas."

The Dolphins erased last year's 8-8 record and four straight seasons of playoff-less football with this year's 12-4 regular season and 1-1 playoff run finished by Saturday's 44-34 loss at snowy Orchard Park, N.Y.

But the way a merry season ended — with Jim Kelly beating Dolphin blitzes and recalling Miami defensive lapses past — only underlined for Shula what his club's main needs are as he ponders the upcoming Plan B free-agency period and draft.

"Pressure on the quarterback, from the interior line or from an outside rush," is what Shula said when asked his priority for improvement.

A sack-getter and heat-bringer, whether outside linebacker, defensive end or nose tackle, is expected to be Miami's priority in April's draft.

End Jeff Cross had 11½ sacks this year but a tepid 2½ the second half of the season.

"We didn't see any letdown in effort from Jeff," Shula said. "People just started paying more attention with double-teams."

Nobody picked up the slack. Shula particularly seeks more sack pressure from his outside linebackers; starters David Griggs and Hugh Green combined for 7½ sacks.

Not trusting the base defense to pressure Kelly and the Bills is what led Miami to gamble with a blitz package that failed Saturday.

But will the remedy arrive via the draft? Trouble is, the league's inbred parity system fixes to slap Miami a little bit, draft-wise. Success this year means the Dolphins (barring a trade-up) will select 24th of 28 teams in the draft, after getting the ninth pick each of the past two years.

Moreover, Miami does not have a second-round pick this year (that was traded away in the Tim McKyer deal) — so a trade-up is likelier; Miami will need to make its first choice count.

The draft still looms distantly, however. More pressing is the Feb. 1 Plan B deadline, when all teams may protect 37 players and expose all others to free agency.

"We haven't gotten into that yet. We will now," Shula said. "There are going to be some tough decisions for us to make as far as who to keep. As far as who to go after, our idea is to be aggressive. We've used Plan B to our advantage."

Miami's activity in the two years Plan B has been in effect included two gem-signings last year in blocking fullback Tony Paige and inside linebacker Cliff Odom, who emerged as valued starters.

Shula said an emphasis again, in both Plan B and the draft, would be to increase the size and brute force of the Dolphins. Leaping strides were made in this area last year with the signing of Paige and Odom and then the drafting of offensive linemen Richmond Webb and Keith Sims.

Plan B presents some intriguing decisions for the Dolphins this year. Perhaps the single biggest tough call is outside linebacker Eric Kumerow, the 1988 No. 1 draft pick who towers 6-7 but has added only millimeters to the defense.

Kumerow this season had one tackle on defense, apart from slightly more productive special-teams play. "He was here and healthy and competed but didn't do the job for us," Shula said.

Neither did 1987's top two draftees, defensive end John Bosa (injured all year) and outside linebacker Rick Graf (holdout/injured/unproductive). They also live on the Plan B bubble.

Shula referred to all three, but doubtless to Kumerow most of all, in saying, "Our investments didn't pay off . . ."

Dead-wood players to lop off and needs to address are issues for Shula and staff in the coming weeks. They'll be personally scouting two college all-star games, the East-West Shrine and the Senior Bowl, over the next two weeks.

This much is evident as coaches weigh current Dolphin personnel by position area:

● Quarterback and running back are fairly set. Dan Marino reasserted himself as a clutch-time champ. Shula loves Paige's blocking. And Sammie Smith emerged late, with 282 tough yards the final three games. Said Shula: "Sammie made giant strides during the season to be the kind of back we wanted him to be."

● Offensive line is another area that elicits a Shula smile. He couldn't be more pleased with the top-pick, tackle Webb, who will be named UPI's AFC rookie of the year. "You couldn't ask a young player to come in and do a better job. Outstanding," Shula said. "And at a position where we really needed the help."

Second-round pick Sims, the 305-pound guard, was hampered by a midyear knee injury ("I don't know if he was ever 100 percent after that," Shula said.), but hopes still reach the clouds.

"With a year under Keith's belt—he has to make sure that belt doesn't get any bigger—he and Richmond should be there for a long time," Shula said.

The coach also lobbed bouquets at his other starters on the NFL's youngest offensive line, as well as to veteran backups Roy "End Zone Dance" Foster and Jeff Dellenbach.

Clearly, "We'll continue to work in the direction of an improved run and a balanced attack," Shula said.

● Receivers? This may be an area of need. Marks Brothers Clayton, 29, and especially Duper, 31, won't last forever, and younger wideouts James Pruitt and Tony Martin still must demonstrate they are of Marksian stock.

● Defensive line seeks more punch, and the linebacker row seeks more youth. Outside-LB Hugh Green and insiders Odom and Barry Krauss are thirtysomething; whether Miami can squeeze another solid starter's year from Odom and Green is questionable.

● The secondary is not a targeted area as far as a new-personnel infusion, but, as Shula said Sunday, "We need better coverage."

Miami seeks an upgrade at backup cornerback, where Paul Lankford and Rodney Thomas are marginal.

● Special teams also are an area of Dolphin need when it comes to return men. Miami averaged only 18 yards on kick returns and six yards on punt returns.

Reprinted with the permission of the *Miami Herald*

References

Alexander, Louis. 1975. *Beyond the Facts: A Guide to the Art of Feature Writing*. Houston: Gulf.

Garrison, Bruce. 1989. *Professional Feature Writing*. Hillsdale, N.J.: Lawrence Erlbaum Associates.

Patterson, Benton Rain. 1986. *Write to be Read: A Practical Guide to Feature Writing*. Ames, Iowa: Iowa State University Press.

Rivers, William L., and Shelly Smolkin. 1981. *Free-Lancer and Staff Writer: Newspaper Features and Magazine Articles*. 3rd ed. Belmont, Calif.: Wadsworth.

Williamson, Daniel R. 1975. *Feature Writing for Newspapers*. New York: Hastings House.

Columns
and
Columnists

Almost all sportswriters and many readers, at one time or another, have dreamed about writing their own columns. Some realize their dreams, achieving the level of prominence and expertise necessary for a regular column. Being a sports columnist, even at a local level, can be a glamorous and rewarding career. The column style of writing, which differs from the routine reporting discussed so far, has been common in most newspaper sports sections for several generations, dating more than a half century back to the eras of Grantland Rice and Jimmy Cannon. Personal columns afford writers visibility, because the columns often command the best story locations in the sports section. Many columns are found on the front page of weekday editions and on the first or second pages of Sunday sections. Columns also allow writers much more writing freedom than is permitted rank-and-file reporters.

Columns are expected to contain personal opinion and analysis. Readers expect columns to be subjective in nature—in contrast to daily reporting, which strives for objectivity, or fairness, in content. Some columnists, however, choose to retain a neutral, objective approach, but most offer their personal perspective.

In sports journalism, a handful of columnists have become the best in the business. Their skill at choosing subjects, crafting sentences, and using the best image-filled words have made them superior. America's best columnists are not only read in their own hometown newspapers, but they are read in newspapers across the country through syndication and news serv-

America's Top Sports Columnists

Some of the best-known award-winning sports columnists today include:

Mitch Albom, *Detroit Free Press*
Dave Anderson, *New York Times*
Furman Bisher, *Atlanta Constitution-Journal*
Thomas Boswell, *Washington Post*
Mark Bradley, *Atlanta Constitution-Journal*
Bill Conlin, *Philadelphia Daily News*
Peter Gammons, *Boston Globe*
Joe Gergen, *Long Island (N.Y.) Newsday*
Rich Hofmann, *Philadelphia Daily News*
Steve Jacobson, *Long Island (N.Y.) Newsday*
Dave Kindred, *The Sporting News,* St. Louis
Tony Kornheiser, *Washington Post*
Bernie Lincicome, *Chicago Tribune*
Mike Littwin, *Baltimore Sun*
Leigh Montville, *Boston Globe*
Jim Murray, *Los Angeles Times*
Edwin Pope, *Miami Herald*
Mark Purdy, *San Jose Mercury News*
Ron Rapoport, *Los Angeles Daily News*
Brian Schmitz, *Orlando Sentinel*
Dan Shaughnessy, *Boston Globe*
Blackie Sherrod, *Dallas Morning News*
John Shulian, *Philadelphia Daily News*
Art Spander, *San Francisco Chronicle*
Shelby Strother, *Detroit News*
George Vecsey, *New York Times*
Bob Verdi, *Chicago Tribune*
Mark Whicker, *Orange County (Calif.) Register*

SOURCE: Based on APSE awards over the past decade.

ices. Many of these top sports columnists today will be familiar names to sports fans and sportswriters alike. They are the trendsetters. They are often the opinion leaders on sports issues of the day.

Jim Murray is the undisputed dean of sports columnists in the 1990s. Murray, who has won nearly every major sportswriting award for the *Los Angeles Times,* perhaps capped his career in 1990 by winning the Pulitzer Prize for commentary. Sportswriters rarely win the Pulitzer Prize, so this honor shows just how distinguished the work of Murray has been throughout his career.

Qualities of the Columnist

Like Los Angeles' Jim Murray, it takes a special writer to be a sports columnist. Widely read sports columns need time for development. This "cultivation" gives time for readership growth (Harris et al. 1981). People must become acquainted with the writer and the nature of the column. According to Harriss et al., there are at least four characteristics of a good columnist:

1. The writer must have something to say. The writer must have resources to provide material for columns and knowledge to draw on for ideas.

2. The column must be interesting. Terrific material can fall flat if it is not written in a manner that strongly appeals to readers.

3. The column should be entertaining. Most of the time columns are handled as feature material.

4. The column and columnist must be durable. This is the "acid test." Columns must maintain quality and also be regular in terms of publication. The challenge is to retain high quality day after day without losing freshness and, eventually, reader appeal.

A higher level of expertise is required of columnists than of regular sportswriters. Readers expect something special, something unique that is not available elsewhere in the sports section. This often comes from the unique sources the columnist has cultivated. Another element is the columnist's special knowledge in one or more areas, which comes from education and experience. Very few beginning sportswriters enjoy the luxury of a column. On small newspapers, such as community or suburban weeklies, the position of columnist may come with the position of sportswriter on a one- or two-person sports staff, but on most newspapers, and most certainly on dailies and major weeklies, it is an earned position. Most sports columnists have sportswriting experience before they begin columns, and many also move into administrative positions in their sections, such as sports editor or assistant sports editor.

Life as a Sports Columnist

Although an earned privilege in the sports department, writing a column is difficult and demanding. Some sports columnists write as many as five columns a week or more than 200 a year. This amount of material is staggering—in terms of 700- or 800-word columns—enough to fill a book each year. Even a weekly columnist writes 50 or more columns a year.

Quantity is not the only concern. A columnist must produce high-quality material regularly. The quality of the column is a challenge. Few average sportswriters produce that many high-quality stories. Although everyone experiences highs and lows in writing, a columnist must be consistent in his or her work. Readers expect a certain approach and technique after they become familiar with a column. Column writing is also a regular business. A column is usually written to appear on a specific day (or days) of the week. A weekly column might be required each Wednesday for Thursday publication, for example, or might have to be ready by Thursday for Saturday production of a Sunday edition.

Thus, columnists must create ideas and write on schedule, even when they don't feel like writing. Some columnists solve this problem by having an extra column or two ready in case a dry spell hits or for when they must travel. A column that is not regularly published cannot develop a following as easily: Readers can't find it unless it is published the same day and located in the same place.

Column writing requires more original reporting than a beginner might imagine. A columnist has a reporter's instincts. A successful columnist frequently works from the field rather than depending on the telephone. Such a writer provides depth and perceptive analysis, using expert observation skills, interviewing in person, and personally investigating documents and other forms of public records. The columnist becomes a refined reporter; although he or she is writing subjective material much of the time, the work must be researched and organized ahead of time, not afterward. Underlying all this, of course, is a solid base of knowledgeable sources who trust the columnist with valuable information and access to that information.

If a sportswriter can handle the pressure of the job, the rewards can be great. Some sports columnists, the most widely read ones, are heavily recruited and paid very well. If they are good, they sell newspapers and may justify their high income on sales alone. But it often takes an entire career to reach that level.

Throughout the 1980s and into this decade, sports editors, their writers, and newspaper management debated the merits of high superstar columnist salaries. "Are these people worth all that money?" moderators asked at countless seminars and professional meetings. Obviously, the writers think their publishers are getting value for their dollar. They argue that the hard work, high standards, and substance in their work pay off in many intangible ways. Yet their critics say superstar columnists are often a morale problem for staffs, and they can ruin departmental salary and travel budgets. For the most part, the writers get what the market dictates they are worth. As *Dallas Morning News* editor Burl Osborne once said, "An excellent columnist is the whipped cream of a good sports section. Any decision on spending money is based on a decision that you expect to get value from it" (Radolf 1984).

The intense competition that once existed between Osborne's *Dallas Morning News* and the crosstown *Dallas Times Herald,* which closed in 1991 after losing the battle for supremacy in Dallas, is often noted when this issue is discussed in the industry. The competition for readers was strong enough that the *Morning News* hired the highly regarded columnist Blackie Sherrod away from the *Times Herald* for a large-sum, long-term contract. To many at that time, it sounded like a deal given to a professional athlete, not a sportswriter. It was not long afterward that Skip Bayless, the rising star columnist at the *Morning News,* was hired away by the *Times Herald* (Fitzgerald 1985; Haughton 1985).

Life as a columnist is not all writing and balancing bank accounts. It can get rough. Columnists who are widely read are often controversial. They write what they feel even if it is not the popular point of view. The competition for readers is often high pressure, leading to errors or bad judgment. It can also lead to rivalries that resemble schoolyard jeering. In Boston, for instance, former *Boston Herald* and *The National* columnist Charles Pierce attacked in print the ethics of *Boston Globe* columnist Bob Ryan in response to a Ryan column. Ryan had, Pierce said, criticized the ethics of a former *Herald* writer who became a sports agent (Radolf 1989). Of course, readers may benefit when such rivalries find their way into the newspaper because they make for lively reading. And, in the case of the Boston rivalry, the discussion even reached local radio sports talk shows.

Controversial columnists are often justifiably critical of the athletes and coaches they cover. Even student sports journalists can catch some of this heat. Student sports columnists at Duke University's *Chronicle* were given a 10-minute, profanity-laced lecture by an irate source for their unfavorable coverage. The critic? He was none other than head coach Mike Kryzyzewski. One columnist graded players' performances but the coach and his team got angry at the newspaper's sportswriters (Associated Press 1990).

Detroit Free Press sports columnist Michelle Kaufman caught the wrath of a reader after writing a tongue-in-cheek column about being a female sportswriter in the mostly male world of sports. Kaufman told readers that she really enjoyed her work writing sports despite the wisecracks she hears about going into men's locker rooms. Her column, reprinted in Chapter 15, discussed the general problem of women reporting about men from locker rooms before the issue exploded weeks later with the controversy surrounding the New England Patriots and *Boston Herald* reporter Lisa Olson. Kaufman's Detroit critic sent her a five-page, handwritten letter telling her to quit her job. "Don't you know when you're not wanted?" he wrote (Kaufman 1990).

Columnists must have thick skin to receive criticism like that, but it is part of the territory of being a columnist. So are other forms of harassment. Mitch Albom, also a *Detroit Free Press* columnist, had water dumped on his head by Detroit Tigers relief pitcher Willie Hernandez. The pitcher said it was Albom's column that turned fans against the pitcher and resulted in booing each time he played at home (*Editor & Publisher* 1988).

Major Types of Sports Columns

Dozens of types of sports columns are written today, but seven major forms will be discussed here.

ESSAY WITH CURRENT EVENTS–ISSUES APPROACH. Most sports columnists use this style. The essay, a form with roots in literature, has been adapted to column writing of all types. Essay columns, as William Rivers (1975) notes, generally are leisurely and informal. Essay organization is simple format, including a general introduction, a discussion with evidence or arguments supporting points made in the introduction, and a summary conclusion or ending (Garrison 1990). Most writers have been introduced to this approach in basic composition courses.

The main reason the essay is so widely used is that it lends itself to presentation of spot news within the column. Many sports columnists attempt to discuss breaking news in their columns or to use their essay-style columns to comment on breaking news.

Some essay columns are humorous. These are among the most entertaining columns to read, but they are very difficult to write. Finding the right material for humor is a challenge, and few writers can maintain a consistent level of good humorous or light material. Most sports columnists use humor only occasionally, thus avoiding the constant pressure to come up with an amusing column each deadline. Many sports columnists use humor in their writing as a tool when making a serious point. Satire, understatement, storytelling, and other techniques are not only attention-arousing devices but sometimes are the only appropriate means for getting a point across.

The following essay column, written by *Miami Herald* columnist Edwin Pope, the Associated Press Sports Editors Red Smith Award winner in 1989, demonstrates the current events–issues essay column with his description of opening day at a South Florida race track. Pope is effective in

A Sports Columnist Talks about Writing Columns

By John McGill, *Lexington (Ky.) Herald-Leader* sports columnist

In writing a column, you are presented countless opportunities for criticism—of waste, impropriety, arrogant behavior, and the like. You even have a chance to write about more mundane subjects such as an analysis of why a team won or lost—and it's your obligation to take on these subjects. You should, in fact, welcome such opportunities.

It's important, however, to also comment when something happens or someone reflects the ideals that sports are supposed to be about. If you focus on the negatives, you offer no guidelines for what sports should aspire to, and you can unwittingly dilute the impact of your valid criticisms by gaining a reputation for focusing only on the bad.

In other words, there's little sense in bemoaning the bad if you haven't celebrated the good. As personal examples, I once wrote on the riots preceding the 1989 Super Bowl, comparing the glitz and money around the game against the violence and anguish of the impoverished in Miami—but stressing that this was a microcosm of ills in our society as a whole. Conversely, I once wrote on the death of Bill Veeck, a baseball owner who never forgot the fan and who, unlike the bottom-line, corporate-tinged ownership that pervades the game today, never lost his sense for fun and a more humanistic approach to life.

It's as important for a columnist to encourage those who reflect positive aspects of life as it is to expose and criticize those who fail to measure up. In both cases, the bottom line is the same: You are writing from a philosophical base (whatever that may be in your own case) that not only offers a multi-faceted view, but enables you to avoid the trap of merely criticizing for criticism's sake.

SOURCE: John McGill, personal communication with author, January 19, 1991.

commenting on a current major sports event in his region, and he uses his personal observation to supplement his opinions. And he is still a reporter, using direct quotations from individuals he interviewed on the scene.

SOURCE: The *Miami Herald,* final edition, page 1D
DATE: Tuesday, January 15, 1991
AUTHOR: Edwin Pope, *Herald* sports editor
HEADLINE: Iffiest 'season' opens cloudily at Gulfstream

The Season opened overcast.

Like the world.

The Season is South Florida's tag for the choice cut of the horse-racing calendar. It usually arrives with bugles and drums.

Monday's music at Gulfstream Park sounded altogether too martial.

Usually, The Season signals tourists winging in like descending angels, fortified with gobs of greenbacks squirreled away during months of toil for one grand blowout in the sun.

Monday wasn't usually.

Monday's clouds were immensely more than meteorological. The overall pall over Gulfstream arrived as the darkest in decades.

The Season started under skies gray as smoke, a recession too real for South Florida despite national economists' arguments, and the possibility of cataclysm in the Mideast.

"I'm here because I'm always here," said a red-sweatered grocery man, Paulie Zimmerman, 46, from Utica, N.Y. "Besides, the grandstand admission is free, and they have a big giveaway on mutuel tickets. But this isn't the party it usually is."

To be sure.

For one thing, maybe incidental to the large scheme, Florida racing is coming out of the first year since World War II when Hialeah did not run a meeting.

We should only hope that is no omen.

Hamstrung Hialeah won't run this year, either. Under economic and military circumstances alone, that may turn out to be John Brunetti's smartest move as owner.

Meanwhile, Gulfstream, and this is as usual, threw in its heaviest promotional drive, and fans responded in encouraging numbers — for the opening at least.

The inaugural crowd of 20,620 was larger than last year's attendance of 18,686.

"It is now post time!" track announcer Ross Morton boomed at 1:01 p.m.

Into the lead bounced four-year-old gelding Flawless Stone. Jockey Larry Saumell choked the rest of the first-race field with heel-dust the full 1 1/16 mile and paid $17.40, $9.00 and $7.60.

The Season was officially on, for better or worse, through May 12.

"I haven't the slightest idea how the winter will go," said Doug Donn, Gulfstream president and general manager. "I'm as worried about the Mideast as everyone else is, for reasons that have nothing to do with business. As for The Season, people always have needed diversion, and that's the business we're in."

Reprinted with the permission of the *Miami Herald*

Mitch Albom, APSE award-winning columnist for the *Detroit Free Press,* was not afraid to express his opinion after the untimely death of college basketball star Hank Gathers during a game was shown repeatedly on local and network television in Detroit. The expression of opinion by experienced observers is one of the real selling points for columns. That experience has to be combined with a talent for writing and the statement of personal opinion in an eloquent manner. But all this does not stop Albom from being a reporter. Note how he combines his opinion with well-reported facts.

SOURCE: The *Miami Herald,* final edition, page 6D
DATE: Thursday, March 8, 1990
AUTHOR: Mitch Albom, *Detroit Free Press* columnist
HEADLINE: An unforgettable image; Gathers' death shouldn't have been put on TV

He began to die in a grotesque fashion, dropping to the floor, convulsing as his teammates stared in horror. Like many people, I cannot get the image of Hank Gathers out of my head. The question is: Should it be there in the first place?

Ask television. Gathers, a powerful center for Loyola Marymount, was not the first athlete to die of heart trouble after physical exertion. Why, two years ago, Pete Maravich, a name more famous than Gathers', expired in a similar fashion.

But America did not buzz about Maravich the way it does this week. The reason: 30 or 40 seconds of footage that aired on TV news across the country Sunday night, showing Gathers collapsing in a heap, his mother running from the stands. The look on her face. The violent jerking of his body.

That footage did not belong on TV. Not in my opinion. No way. The story could have been told without it. Hank Gathers was not a president. His death did not bring down a political regime. It was a tragic slice of the real world that demanded a real tug of ethics. Yet few TV stations chose not to run it.

"It's a news story," I was told when I called Detroit stations. One weekend anchor said, "If we didn't air it, our viewers would have been cheated."

Cheated? Of what? Voyeurism?

I don't buy it. There are lines in everything, including journalism. Are they not crossed when it comes to a young man's life, his dignity, the grief that a broadcast might cause his family or friends? There are only so many subjects you can hide behind the curtain of "I'm only doing my job."

Does death now fall into the category?

"I think there have been more gruesome things on the air," said John Walsh, managing editor for ESPN, which brought the story nationwide Sunday night. "Our policy is to warn people beforehand if something might be offensive. And we did that."

Yes. This is a tidy tradition. We warned you. But in truth, such warnings often serve to whet the appetite, to make you curious. You end up watching anyhow. Meanwhile Sunday, ESPN also had a camera at the La Salle game, when Lionel Simmons, a close friend of Gathers, was told of the death. Simmons wept. The camera whirred. News? Or staged tragedy?

Now, please. I am not placing print on some holy perch above TV. Many newspapers, including the two Detroit dailies, ran still photos of a dying Gathers on the front pages of their sports sections. I don't like that, either.

But in this case, the footage was incomparably more disturbing. Especially Gathers convulsing on the court, and being wheeled to an ambulance. Some stations stopped the tape before that. Others did not. They ran it four and five times in the next 24 hours. Their justification was often to point to previous tragedies and say, "Well, it's not as bad as that."

That is not an answer. Nor is citing the recent footage of executed Romanian president Nicolae Ceaucescu and saying: "That was worse."

That was also different. His death signaled the end of a political era, it changed an entire nation. Ceaucescu's corpse became a national symbol.

Hank Gathers was not a symbol. His death was medical and personal. It deserved some privacy. Sure, he was a great player and a good pro prospect. But to equate his fall, newswise, with that of a Romanian dictator, is to balloon the importance of the NBA draft shamefully out of proportion.

Now, I know TV is a visual medium—at its best, a great one. And I know this is a hard call. But somewhere, someone has to make it. Someone has to say, "We're not going with this. It's wrong. I don't care what the other stations are showing."

That takes foresight. Courage. It also takes time. TV pictures are so powerful, they can glorify a moment or rape it. Yet the weighty decisions to air footage are often made—as they were Sunday night—by harried young producers who have little time to catch a breath, let alone debate ethics.

And then there is the question of competition. Few stations want to be caught with their footage down. Said a candid Eli Zaret of Channel 2: "You get too esoteric in this business, you'll hurt yourself. . . . Everybody this morning is talking about, 'Did you see what happened?' What if the person said, 'No. I watched Channel 2 and they didn't show it'? Then you'd have made a horrible decision."

I credit Eli with honesty. But a horrible decision? I don't think so. In dilemmas like these, maybe it's best to ask yourself a question you learned in kindergarten: Is it right or is it wrong? Somewhere inside, there should be a flame of conscience that separates the two.

That Gathers footage—which some stations, unbelievably, are still showing—did little more than shock people and haunt his family. Can you imagine if you were a friend, living miles away, who flicked on the TV and watched that tragic footage?

Sure, it brought home the tragedy of playing athletics with a heart condition. But did we really have to watch a man die to learn that? Have we grown that thick?

Or have we just grown that insensitive? There are some TV people who swear America wants to see this kind of tragedy. And others with a late-blooming conscience who now say, "Maybe we shouldn't have shown it." But the fact is, at the moment of truth, everybody did.

Sadly, that tells you all you need to know.

Reprinted with the permission of the *Detroit Free Press*

ITEM OR ANECDOTE COLUMNS. Columnists find this approach effective when their news gathering has resulted in a long list of short, perhaps unrelated, items. Such a column might include three or four topics of some substance—with, say, three to five paragraphs each—that are not connected. Or, in even more fragmented columns, one- or two-sentence pieces of information are connected by transitions and various style devices.

Many sports editors find this approach useful in integrating news of the day from the various wire services; instead of using half a dozen or more wire shorts (one- or two-paragraph stories), the copy editor or a reporter rewrites the material into a summary column about sports people, places, and events. For example, the *Columbia Missourian,* a community newspaper produced by the University of Missouri School of Journalism, finds this approach helpful in combining local and wire news on a regular basis under the column heading "Briefly." The *Chicago Tribune*'s regular items column is called "Bits & Pieces." The *Los Angeles Times* calls the column "Morning Briefing."

SPECIALIZED OR TOPICAL COLUMNS. Many popular columns fit into this category, and most newspapers publish one or more on a weekly basis. To study the topical or specialized column, we must consider the various beats organized by the sports editor for reporters. At many newspapers the best reporters on the major beats are provided opportunities to write regular columns on material routinely gathered from their day-to-day activities. For example, pro football writers write a pro football column from material that never really fit into a spot news story; the tennis writer might have a Sunday tennis column; and the reporter covering swimming might write a

The performance and activities of women's professional tennis stars such as Monica Seles are often the subjects of columns. (*Photo by Bill Frakes, the* Miami Herald.)

Saturday or weekend swimming column. A number of newspapers have found that this approach encourages creativity and enhances and expands coverage on the more important beats.

Just about all major daily newspapers publish an outdoors column on Saturday or Sunday. This is a prime example of the specialized or beat topic that has evolved into a regular column, in this case focusing on participatory sports. In the *Chicago Tribune* sports section, for example, Ed Sherman and Skip Myslenski both write "On Colleges," John Husar writes "On the Outdoors," Don Pierson writes "On Pro Football," Sam Smith writes "Bulls/NBA Report," Jerome Holtzman writes "On Baseball," and Barry Temkin writes "On High Schools." And all those columns each appear in a single Sunday section.

A new type of specialized column, which has begun to catch on in recent years, is the radio and television sports column. As has been pointed out, radio and television sports broadcasting has changed professional and amateur sports, as well as sports reporting itself. In reaction, many newspapers have decided to acknowledge this reality by offering their readers radio and television information, such as decisions to black out viewing areas or to telecast certain games (Haughton 1990). It is a functional approach that is appealing to readers. At *USA Today,* for example, Rudy Martzke writes a "Sports on TV" column at least four times a week, complete with latest sports television programming news and listings of daily and weekend sports on national television. At Atlanta, *Journal-Constitution* sportswriter Prentis Rogers writes a daily sports-on-TV column. But Jack Craig, *Boston Globe* TV sports columnist, is the dean of the specialized craft, writing about sports on television since 1967 and regularly since 1969. His column runs three times a week (Haughton 1990).

Still another specialized column that has developed in recent years is one on sports medicine. One of the most popular sports medicine columns is "Dr. Jock," written by Dr. David Bachman and Marilynn Preston for Tribune Media Services, Inc. Another specialized column is one by Hal Lebovitz, who regularly writes "Ask the Referee" for *The Sporting News.* These columns take a participant approach, written for those who run or have other sports interests and the accompanying common medical problems.

HOW-TO-DO-IT COLUMNS. How-to-do-it columns are seldom written by sportswriters but instead by non-journalists with expertise in specific sports. These columns require special credibility and knowledge, and let's face it, the athletes are the ones who can tell how it should be done. Few sportswriters are so athletically skilled as to be able to teach a sport. But some are, and when this rare combination occurs, the newspaper and its readers are fortunate.

Column Writing for Small and Large Papers

By Steve Clow, *Los Angeles Daily News*

Big or small newspaper, big or small market, big or small travel budget, there is one big problem for all sports columnists: ideas. Good ideas. Inventive ideas. Ideas they can pull off. Ideas that lead to other ideas.

In a workshop on column writing, Mark Whicker of the *Orange County Register* via Philadelphia, Dallas, and Winston-Salem and Tim Ellerbee of the *Anderson (S.C.) Independent-Mail* via Macon and some small Georgia newspapers agreed that the worst feeling is to wake up and not know what they will write about that day.

So how do they avoid the dreaded idea slump?

"The key in my situation is organization and planning," Whicker said. "I read the schedule weeks in advance. I know what I'm doing between now and August. But there's always room for flexibility if somebody [in sports] gets fired or there's a strike."

Ellerbee, who became a full-time columnist in January after 4½ years as sports editor, sits down every Sunday night and plans for 10 columns. "You know three people won't return phone calls, but you might end up with five good columns out of it."

They agreed that columnists in smaller cities have a tougher time because they have fewer big events to write about. Ellerbee recently got four columns out of a visit by Tree Rollins of the Atlanta Hawks to a basketball camp in his area.

Whicker said of his *Winston-Salem Journal* days: "I was dying during the summer. I was even sorry to see the stock car races leave."

The columnists spoke on several other matters. Their views:

● **Editors Assigning Columns:** "My editor doesn't really assign me columns. When SMU got the death penalty, he called me and asked me if I wanted to write about it. I said yes, but if I had said no, it would have been OK," Whicker said.

● **Beat Writers Writing Columns:** "You wonder if you want a guy criticizing [Clemson football coach] Danny Ford, then getting him on the phone and asking him who's starting at quarterback," Ellerbee said. "I don't know if you're not putting yourself in jeopardy."

Whicker said that a beat writer may be more qualified to write opinion about a team than a columnist, who isn't around all the time. "But there's no BBWAA [Baseball Writers of America Association] for college football writers if Clemson decides to freeze out beat writers," he said.

● **The Use of "I":** "I'm not one of those people who believes you should outlaw the personal pronoun, but it's offensive all the time. I-I-I . . . it's not good writing," Whicker said. "Look at your great Op-Ed columnists. William Safire doesn't say, 'I went over and had lunch with George Shultz.' "

● **Sports Talk Shows:** "It's a real fringe element, at least back East," Whicker said. "These people have extremely strong opinions or are extremely drunk. They spend 20 minutes on hold. I've got more important things to do with my time."

● **Deadlines:** "I solved that by moving to a place where we had three extra hours to write and one edition," Whicker said.

● **Travel:** "We're working toward a larger travel budget," Ellerbee said. "I hope to get one up that I will control. We need to be at the Super Bowl."

● **Prep Columns:** "We have 42 high schools that we cover," Ellerbee said. "There are times when [commentary] is merited, times when you refrain. Whicker said it's a no-win situation. "You can't glorify them or put them on a pedestal. If you make fun of it, they'll burn your house down."

● **Whicker on Other Columnists:** "I like Dave Kindred, Bob Verdi; Ed Fowler of Houston is very underrated. Patrick Reusse is very underrated. He just moved from St. Paul to Minneapolis."

● **Ellerbee on Other Columnists:** "I read every column I can. I like Dave Kindred."

SOURCE: 1988 APSE Convention Report
Associated Press Sports Editors, p. 10.
Reprinted with the permission of Steve Clow and APSE

Most how-to-do-it columns take close looks at specific activities in a certain sport. Although these columns are ordinarily short and may even be ghostwritten, they remain popular and are given space by many newspapers because readers want such material and also perhaps because syndicated material like this is less expensive than something originated locally. For a more complete look at the wide variety of columns currently written by sports specialists, see a recent edition of the *Editor & Publisher Annual Syndicate Directory,* published each summer by *Editor & Publisher.*

READER FORUM COLUMNS. More and more, newspapers are giving space for readers' letters to the sports editor or to others on the staff. Some newspapers print the letters only when there is space. Others organize letters and outside commentary into reader forum columns that generally consist of comments on the product of the sports staff (a feedback mechanism) or on happenings in the sports world.

Other newspapers have taken this concept one step farther. Some metropolitan newspapers, as well as some of the better small dailies and weeklies, have a regular column written by a series of guests (non-staff individuals) on topics of their choosing. Arranged for by the sports editor or another reporter in advance, these columns allow readers to present their views in an organized fashion and in more depth than they could in ordinary letters to the editor.

ADVICE-TO-PARTICIPANTS COLUMNS. Some columns are designed to advise readers on sports or recreational activities. Like the sports medicine or the how-to-do-it columns, these columns answer specific questions from readers on a multitude of topics. Many times they are likened to "Dear Abby" or other personal advice features, but they are geared to the specific needs of athletes and sports consumers. One example is "Participant Sports," a once-a-week, 500-word syndicated column from Tom Hagin.

SPORTS TRIVIA COLUMNS. Long a popular feature of many sports sections, sports trivia columns are written to accomplish several objectives. With the right material, such columns can be very informative, particularly for sports records fanatics, by providing answers to questions on a wide range of topics such as terminology, traditions, records, and rules. They generate more interest if they include facts on local or area teams as well. These columns can settle issues raised in telephoned or written queries. And they certainly allow interaction and reader involvement with the sports section. For an example of this, read "The Answer Man," a question-answer column written regularly by John Duxbury for *The Sporting News.*

Writing Sports Columns

Whether a part-time writer who contributes a column to a community weekly newspaper sports section or a veteran metropolitan newspaper sports editor who has written a column for many years, a writer must complete certain steps in taking the column from idea to publication. There are six primary considerations in getting a column off the ground.

1. *Developing sources.* Material must steadily filter into the columnist's files. One way to get a column started is to give serious consideration to suggestions by sources and to information provided by sources. Columnists should cultivate sources by working closely with them to gain their trust as well as to verify their tips and information. A columnist cannot have too many sources.

2. *Developing ideas.* Many ideas come from working with sources. But the columnist cannot be dependent on any one source for column ideas, especially if writing anything close to a column a day. He or she must look at a variety of publications, people, and kinds of activities. Old ideas can be put in a new, timely perspective. Columnists should not be afraid to try something different, innovative, or creative. They eventually develop the ability to sort out good ideas from poor ones.

3. *The right attitude.* A columnist must write authoritatively and confidently, conveying this certainty to the reader without being pretentious or pompous. A columnist should reflect self-confidence in his or her knowledge and writing.

4. *Creative approaches.* It is very important for the columnist to renew readers' interest by doing things differently from time to time. Columnists, like other writers, are prone to writer's block and get into creative ruts. To force themselves out of this, they can mix things up by changing reporting style, writing style, or general presentation. They can get out of the office and work in the field or try a special series of columns. New sources are helpful in areas in which the columnist has felt safe and comfortable with old ones.

5. *Writing from a local angle.* For most columnists, this is not very difficult. But they often forget the surrounding area in an effort to get something "bigger." They should include local people, places, and events in the column. Statewide writers should look within specific regions. Regional writers within a state should look in various communities. Writers serving a large community should look into neighborhoods and suburbs. This approach cannot miss.

6. *Considering impact.* At times, the sports column can have a surprising impact on a community. Respected columnists can and do influence policymaking and general community sentiment about current issues. What the columnist writes is often what people then discuss. It is a considerable responsibility for the writer.

Most columnists write their individual columns as sportswriters handle a feature story or other article of moderate length. Most columns are in the 600- to 900-word range, which is a considerable length. Many columnists write a single column in one sitting. To get a little ahead, some write two at a time or try to write more than one per day. Some put their columns together a piece at a time, if the material is not affected by a wait. How a columnist writes a column depends on the style of writing, the type of column, and the topic.

A final point to consider is the view of the writer. Many columnists write in first rather than third person. Usually, it can be argued, writing should be in third person to minimize the importance of the reporter. But in personalized sports column writing, many writers use a first-person approach, with the pronoun "I" used throughout the column. Others, however, feel uncomfortable writing in first person. There are even arguments for using the second-person, or direct-address, approach, but fewer columnists use second person than first or third person.

Subjectivity is an important consideration. Most sports columns are read for opinion, for the reactions of the columnist. So the standard objective approach is often forsaken. But just as some writers prefer third over first person, some attempt to keep their personal opinions out of their columns. Either way is appropriate, but beginning columnists should try to be consistent in approach.

Perspectives in Column Writing

There are three types of sports columnists: the syndicated or national columnist, the regional columnist, and the local or community columnist. Each must be aware of differing audience needs.

Syndicated columnists are the most widely read because their work is produced for a number of publications. They are the best known. Among the most widely syndicated columnists in the mid-1990s are Dave Anderson and George Vecsey, who write "Sports of the Times" for the New York Times News Service; Jim Murray, Los Angeles Times News Service; and Thomas Boswell, Washington Post Writers Group. Their material must have broad appeal because of the various types of publications that buy and publish their work. What is written for an East Coast newspaper must be equally interesting for West Coast readers. What is written for the metropolitan reader must interest the rural reader. What is written for an American League East Division fan must appeal to the National League West Division fan as well.

Regional and local columnists often do not have as many resources, such as travel expense budgets, and must handle their columns differently. They must, sometimes not by choice, narrow the perspective of their columns. The range of topics may not be limited, but the development of these ideas may be restricted by a lack of opportunities and resources. Regional columnists write for metropolitan newspapers, or perhaps a chain of weekly newspapers. Their work may be distributed to several newspapers owned by the same company. Because metropolitan newspapers with large circulations often serve entire states or parts of several states, the columnist becomes regional.

The local or community columnist caters to the smallest area and probably has the narrowest range of prospects. But this columnist has the advantage of writing for an especially interested group of readers who know the material, which allows writing in more detail than is possible in national or regional columns. But these columnists, especially those writing for small daily or weekly newspapers, suffer most from lack of resources, even resources as basic as long distance telephone or facsimile machine access.

Who Writes Columns?

Most successful columnists are, first of all, individualists. They observe from a different angle, talk to unconventional sources, write the forgotten side of a story. They are not afraid of doing something differently.

Second, good columnists are discriminating reporters, able to perceive differences that others might not notice. They are writers who provide new insights in situations. They think about the story in an intellectual way and stretch their writing beyond the superficial approaches many other writers offer. Their work is the product of their experience and special abilities.

Third, sports columnists must be able to analyze. Their work reflects a skill at breaking the whole into parts, such as the key plays of a game or the reasons contributing to a decision by a longtime coach to retire. Good columnists also pull seemingly unrelated parts together into a synthesis not found in the work of other writers.

Fourth, good columnists bring their experience as sportswriters to the column, that special knowledge from beats and other assignments that make them uniquely qualified to write columns. The reporting skills are refined and developed as information gathering tools—the special sources, the ability to gather facts and cultivate pools of information others only think about. Their writing skills are polished and show creativity and originality.

So who, exactly, writes columns? At least four groups of journalists are sources of sports columns.

1. Sports editors and other administrators. The most common column is the one authored regularly by the editor. In many cases these columns are not daily but appear more than once a week. On large newspapers, columns

may be written by other administrators in the department, such as assistant sports editors, Sunday editors, and special weekend section editors.

2. Beat reporters. Another common approach is to assign major beat reporters to columns, perhaps on a less-frequent publication basis than the sports editor's column. These columns may appear as a group on Sundays, or be spread throughout the week as space permits. Some large newspapers with many columnists will do both.

3. Invited specialists. Some newspapers employ a widely known authority on a topic as a contributing editor or columnist about that topic.

4. Unsolicited specialists. Some newspapers use unsolicited columns sent to the newspaper from various sources on a regular basis. Smaller newspapers, especially, use these columns, which usually come from the public relations department of a large firm, the public information office of a government agency, or a similar institution.

These regular releases make good columns for newspapers with limited budgets because they offer authoritative information. Many newspaper editors delete from such material any commercial references or other text that only serves the interests of the source. An unsolicited conservation agency column, for example, can have enough good material in it for a once-a-week outdoors column.

The two columns below illustrate the best of column writing in sports. *Orange County Register* columnist Mark Whicker also writes for *The Sporting News.* His column below comments on the end of the college basketball season, the National Collegiate Athletic Association men's tournament, tournament eligibility, scheduling, and other issues that always seem to become important at Final Four time each spring. Blackie Sherrod, the veteran columnist for the *Dallas Morning News,* writes about National Football League Commissioner Paul Tagliabue's edict telling Jerry Glanville to stop his cutting remarks about other coaches or be fined.

SOURCE: The *Miami Herald,* first edition, page 1D
DATE: Friday, March 30, 1990
AUTHOR: Mark Whicker, *Orange County Register*
HEADLINE: Here's how best team can win

For CBS, the 1990 NCAA Tournament is already a wrap.

Tate George beating Clemson with zeroes on the clock . . . Kenny Anderson tying Michigan State even later than that . . . Paris McCurdy grinning as the foul shot that beats Oregon State reaches midflight . . . All sorts of No. 44-related pathos involving Loyola Marymount . . .

Now if you can't put together a "music piece" out of that, maybe you should go work for the MacNeil-Lehrer NewsHour.

This just might be the year that everyone sees the NCAA Tournament for what it is — a rollicking three-week miniseries, not a championship. It's been a while since the tournament determined the best team, and now it doesn't even pretend to.

Only one of the top eight seeds (Nevada-Las Vegas) has survived to the Final Four. Fortunately, three of the four have at least won something to qualify themselves — UNLV and Arkansas won the Big West and Southwest regular season and tournaments, and Georgia Tech won the ACC tournament.

Then there's Moby Duke, which hasn't won the NCAAs but has provided the comedy segment of the program in the last two Final Fours. Despite winning neither the ACC regular season nor tournament, Duke got a No. 3 seed in the easy East.

The Big Ten placed seven teams in the 64-team bracket, and only two survived the first weekend, and those two had to win overtime games to do that. The fact that Big Ten Commissioner Jim Delany is the chairman of the selection committee means nothing in itself. The favoritism is institutional, not personal.

The first CBS-televised game of the tournament was a first-round matchup between Ohio State (Big Ten) and Providence (Big East). Ohio State was 16-12. Providence was 17-11. Together, they were 8-18 against the other NCAA Tournament teams.

That same night, Indiana (Big Ten) lost a first-rounder to Cal. Indiana was 18-10, and 2-10 against the other six Big Ten teams in the tournament. The Hoosiers played one non-conference game outside the state line.

Kansas State (Big Eight) was 17-14. North Carolina (ACC), which eliminated top-seeded Oklahoma, went 19-12 and lost twice to Maryland. Villanova (Big East) was 18-14 and went from Dec. 30 until deep February without winning (or losing) two in a row.

Ohio State, Providence, Indiana, Kansas State, North Carolina and Villanova deserved these playoffs about as much as the Kings deserve the NHL playoffs.

Why them and not Southern Illinois, 24-game winner and regular-season champion of the Missouri Valley? Or Long Beach State, which went 23-9 and beat Texas and Purdue?

Because of a diabolical little thing called "strength of schedule."

It sounds OK. Who can argue with rewarding those with the guts to play the big boys? Why validate a club that plays Hawaii-Loa, Hawaii-Pacific, Florida International, St. Leo, UDC, Virginia Tech, North Carolina, Northern Iowa, Florida and De Paul in its non-league schedule, for instance?

Well, that team was Georgetown. And Jeff Sagarin's computer, which closely parallels the NCAA's, says Georgetown's schedule-strength rating was 81.46, 11th best nationally.

How can that be? Because the Hoyas get scheduling credit for playing Syracuse, Connecticut and other Big East schools twice each. They do not do so by choice. They are contracted to do so. This is known as having your cake and eating everyone else's, too.

It would be fairer to judge schedule strength by the games one does not have to play. In this way, Loyola Marymount would have gotten the high seed it deserved. The Lions went 23-5 and played LSU, LaSalle, Oregon State, UNLV, Xavier and Oklahoma in non-conference. They should not have been penalized for playing Portland, Gonzaga and St. Mary's twice apiece. After all, they had to.

Still, Sagarin rated LMU 12th overall, which did not stop Delany's committee from seeding it 11th in the West.

Eight Big Ten teams had a schedule-strength record of 80-plus. (LMU's was 74.85.) So did six ACC teams. So did six Big East teams. Meanwhile, UNLV ran a gauntlet of NC State, Kansas, De Paul, Loyola Marymount, Arkansas, Oklahoma, Oklahoma State, Arizona, Louisville and Temple and barely squeezed into the 80's, at 80.08. Do we want an equitable NCAA field, with actual regular-season winners getting a seeding break? Does it matter? If so, here's how:

1. Reduce the schedule-strength formula to non-conference games.

2. Give automatic NCAA Tournament bids to regular-season winners of the 32 conferences. This year, James Madison won the Southern Conference and Southern Illinois won the Valley, but both lost conference tournament finals in home-court situations (at Richmond and Illinois State). Both were left out. The regular season is two months; the league tournament is three days.

3. Give automatic NCAA bids to tournament winners of the 28 highest-rated conferences. Those conferences that still refuse to hold tournaments (like the Big Ten) could qualify their second-place team.

4. Seed the regular-season champs at the top and the tournament champs at the bottom. Those two groups will make up 60 teams, maximum. This year, it would have been 47.

5. Pick enough at-large teams — the Dukes, Syracuses, Kansases, UCLAs — to fill the field to 64. Use the computer to determine them, with the revised schedule-strength rating. Seed these teams in between the conference and tournament champions.

6. Freeze the number of eligible conferences at the current 32. If a new conference forms, it cannot join the mix until another one disbands, which, in the case of the Sun Belt and the Atlantic 10, is quite likely.

Relax, CBS. Your music pieces would endure. So would the fun.

SOURCE: The *Miami Herald,* first edition, page 6D
DATE: Thursday, September 20, 1990
AUTHOR: Blackie Sherrod, *Dallas Morning News*
HEADLINE: This rule's so bad it makes you gag

Oh, it is not without precedent. Some may remember another time when grown men made fools of themselves under kindred circumstances. This was in the day of the infamous Southwest Conference "gag rule," in which coaches and officials were absolutely forbidden to make any comment about the conference or its inhabitants or any of its action that could be considered negative.

This high drama took place in a Lubbock motel during a league meeting. Southern Methodist University was slapped with some punishment and its coach, Hayden Fry, was warned by conference moguls to make absolutely no comment to the press after he left the dock.

But instead of issuing one "no comment," getting in his car and driving back to Dallas, Hayden visited the motel suite reserved for media interviews. There he sat for maybe an hour, answering "no comment" to several hundred questions. It got to be ridiculous, of course.

Hayden, have you stopped turpentining your cat?

"No comment."

Hayden, do you actually think Howard Grubbs (the SWC secretary) looks like a monkey?

"No comment." On and on. By going to the extreme, the coach was illustrating the absurdity of the "gag rule." People began to laugh at it, which is the surest form of genocide. Soon after, the inane gag was removed.

That memory arrived with a depressing thump this week when NFL Commissioner Paul Tagliabue issued an edict of similar silliness. He told Jerry Glanville to stop those cutting remarks about other coaches or he would give him a swift kick in the pocketbook. Presto, we're back in kindergarten again.

There has always been delightful popoffs around the league. Buddy Ryan comes immediately to mind. Sam Wyche is no slouch, nor is Mike Ditka. Bud Grant, in his day, had a sly way with a dig. So did John McKay. But apparently their cuts didn't stir enough resentment to prompt the league to insert its iron hand, like in the case of Glanville.

Glanville started his feisty routine while coaching in Houston, instantly riling traditionalists. His feud with Chuck Noll made headlines, as did his squabble with Wyche. Matter of fact, Glanville gave an all-time response when someone sought his reaction to Wyche's censuring barb.

"I don't think any less of Sam Wyche than I did before," said Glanville. A classic, worthy of Dorothy Parker or Groucho Marx.

Obviously, Glanville answers hath not turneth away wrath. Last week Glanville, now at Atlanta, referred to Jack Pardee as "a jerk" among a few other biting remarks. Tagliabue, taking an interlocking grip on his scepter, warned Glanville that any further wisecracks would bring a fine.

"I reminded him, at the league meeting in March, the competition committee and the owners told me to crack down on what they believed was unsportsmanlike conduct, uncalled-for, flip remarks by coaches," the commissioner said.

What of those wonderful exchanges between Ditka and Ryan, better by far than Abbott and Costello? Might a coach even refer to another coach's waistband?

"I imagine that would fall in this category," said Jimmy Johnson with a grin, "although I wouldn't know what you are referring to." You may remember that the Cowboys' coach referred to Ryan's "big fat butt" in last year's Cowboy-Eagle hassle.

"They're trying to keep it out of the wrestling image," Johnson said.

Well, it just could be the rasslers have a protest of their own. What of the showboat footballer who, when involved in a tackle or fumble recovery, leaps up, dashes to an unoccupied portion of the field where he will not have to share the stage, raises his arms in a victorious "Y" and invites the crowd to congratulate him? Or all those weird celebratory gyrations in the end zone after a score? Dangerous Danny McShane, while making off with the world heavyweight champeenship of Western Utah and a sizable portion of Whipper Billy Watson's left ear, never pulled such antics, although I'm sure he wished he had.

Reprinted with the permission of the *Dallas Morning News*

References

Alexander, Louis. 1975. *Beyond the Facts: A Guide to the Art of Feature Writing*. Houston: Gulf.

Associated Press. 1990. Duke—Student Paper. Associated Press sports wire. January 17, n.p.

Editor & Publisher. 1988. Pitcher apologizes for dumping water on columnist. 121 (March 19): 15.

Fitzgerald, Mark. 1985. SPORTS plays a major role in Dallas newspaper battle. *Editor & Publisher* 118 (October 26): 28, 35.

Garrison, Bruce. 1990. *Professional News Writing*. Hillsdale, N.J.: Lawrence Erlbaum Associates.

Harriss, Julian, Kelly Leiter, and Stanley Johnson. 1981. *The Complete Reporter*. 4th ed. New York: Macmillan.

Haughton, Jim. 1985. His friends call him: 'The richest sportswriter in the business.' *Editor & Publisher* 118 (June 15): 34.

———. 1990. Sportswriters who cover tv sports. *Editor & Publisher* 123 (October 13): 16–17, 58.

Kaufman, Michelle. 1990. Correspondence with authors, September 20.

McGill, John. 1991. Correspondence with author, January 19.

Radolf, Andrew. 1984. Superstar sports columnists: Are they worth six-figure salaries? *Editor & Publisher* 117 (December 8): 12.

———. 1989. Barbs in Boston: Sports columnists of rival newspapers question each other's ethics. *Editor & Publisher* 122 (April 1): 41.

Rivers, William. 1975. *The Mass Media*. 2nd ed. New York: Harper & Row.

9

The
Big
Event

The world of sports is filled with major
events—think about it for a moment. We
picture the megaevents: the Super Bowl,
World Series, Kentucky Derby, NCAA Final
Four basketball, a heavyweight boxing
championship, the Masters, the Stanley Cup. But there are other big events
on a smaller scale. At a regional or state level, there are state championships in high school football and basketball, amateur golf tournaments,
marathons, baseball tournaments, and so forth. Even some routine regular
season games between intense rivals can take on the aura of an end-of-the-
season championship.

Any newspaper, from the smallest weekly to the largest daily, has big
events in sports to cover. Such events might take many forms: a state high
school basketball tournament, a running race that draws tens of thousands
of competitors, an annual event such as the Rose Bowl, or an Olympic
games. Reader interest is there. The sportswriter has to satisfy the interest
with a super effort. No matter what the event might be, successful reporting
requires a plan. These strategies must be crafted months ahead of time. In
the case of the Super Bowl, coverage of some newspapers is determined
well before even the teams are decided.

In other cases, such as when a local team qualifies for the state tournament, editors may have only days to determine their plan. Many of the
questions editors ask themselves are the same no matter how much planning time exists before the big event. The questions include: How many

reporters should cover the event? What does the budget permit? Which reporters and editors should go? How should the event be illustrated? Photos? Graphics? Should the newspaper concentrate on just the local angle, or should the total event be covered? Different events require different decisions.

Planning the Coverage

Depending on size and deadlines of the publication, big events are covered in different ways. For a small-circulation daily or weekly newspaper, a big event can be a state high school basketball tournament, but only when the local team makes the tournament. For a middle-sized–circulation daily, a big event may be broader in scope. It could include a national or regional small college wrestling tournament held at a nearby community college or a national tournament 1,000 miles away. However, for the large-circulation daily, it can be just about any national sports event such as the Super Bowl, a major international event such as the Wimbledon tennis tournament, or even a running event sponsored by the newspaper itself that draws tens of thousands of entries.

While each big event has unique coverage characteristics, they all have several things in common. First, they are important to the newspaper's readership, events that are expected to be given special treatment. Second, each requires careful advance planning to come up with this special treatment. In fact, the planning stage of big event coverage may prove more important than the actual coverage. How is this possible? Consider this example.

A reporter is covering the championship game of the state high school basketball tournament. The game begins at 7:30 P.M. With each game about 90 minutes long, the reporter will have only a half hour before the newspaper's regular 9:30 P.M. deadline. But at the end of regulation time, the score is tied and an overtime period is played. Because the reporter cannot finish his or her story by the 9:30 deadline, he or she calls the copydesk and advises an editor that the story will be late. Someone on the copydesk calls the production department to ask if it is possible to hold the edition by a half hour. But the production people say, "Sorry, we can't do it. The circulation trucks need to roll on time to meet the delivery schedule." This situation could have been avoided if someone had consulted the production department ahead of time and discussed the possibility of the game going into overtime. Because of the strong local interest in the story, also, it is likely that advance planning for a long game would have permitted more flexibility to get the story in the 9:30 edition.

Thus, planning is the key to big event coverage. And planning means a team effort, involving all phases of the newspaper, including the editorial, photography, art, advertising, production, circulation, and promotion departments. Leaving any of these groups out could spell disaster.

When should big event planning begin? The sports department staff should determine well in advance what it hopes to accomplish in its coverage. First, the department should review past coverage and determine whether it was truly special, or left something to be desired. Were there too many reporters at the event, leaving the copydesk short of personnel to handle editing? Was the coverage adequate in terms of stories but lacking photographs, graphics, or original artwork? Did the deadlines imposed by the production department make it impossible for the all-important postgame interviews to be included in the coverage?

Problems such as these can often be avoided through teamwork, but unless they are anticipated well ahead of time, they may occur year after year. After all, while the sports department is gearing up for the big event, all departments are working on the regular daily editions. And when the big event is over, it will be quickly forgotten, replaced by another day's events and another edition.

Added to teamwork is another element—time. All the planning in the world will not help if the departments involved are not given adequate time to react to the additional demands. Newspapers have limited human resources, set by daily newspaper production needs. Added workloads required by the special big event coverage require advance planning to fit the extra work into the schedule. Let's follow the planning as it pertains to each department in the newspaper.

THE SPORTS DEPARTMENT. The planning effort must begin in the sports department, which provides the reporters to cover the event and should have the best understanding of the event and the audience that the newspaper will try to satisfy with its coverage. The appropriate beat reporter might initiate discussions as time nears for the event, quickly involving his or her editors. The sports editor sometimes handles the task, meeting with assistants and those who have covered the event in the past, in addition to those who will be covering it in the future. The sports editor may name a "point person" to coordinate coverage.

For example, at the *Milwaukee Journal,* coverage of the newspaper's big fall promotion, the Al McGuire Run, is centered in the sports department. The run, held annually, draws nearly 30,000 runners and walkers, ranking it among the largest such events in the nation. All newspaper departments are involved, with a member of the sports department coordinating the overall interaction of departments.

THE ADVERTISING DEPARTMENT. Although the advertising department may seem to have the least to do with actual event coverage, its contribution can play a large role. Special event coverage usually requires special page space needs, and news space in most newspapers—often called the newshole—is determined by the amount of supporting advertising. That is not to say the news department itself cannot order extra space. Many newspapers have a space "bank" from which editors can "withdraw" additional columns or pages for special planned or even unexpected uses. In the case of a big event with a date set well in advance, it may be possible to coordinate with the advertising department for extra advertising-supported space to allow even better coverage. Often, this means requesting one or more "open" pages, or pages without advertising, in addition to the usual space requirements for a given day. For the *Milwaukee Journal*'s annual run, editors sought to publish additional finish-line results in the newspaper the day after the event. The advertising department, meanwhile, seeing an opportunity to sell ads in the next day's edition, targeted businesses such as running shoe stores, health spas, fitness equipment stores, and sports medicine clinics, among others, to buy ads.

The advertising department is interested in generating additional revenue from the run-related ads, and the sports section will find it easier to ask for additional space to publish results in a section that is enlarged by a larger-than-usual ad lineup. Advertising's involvement in event coverage, therefore, can be extremely helpful. It can provide not only added space needs after the run, but also before the run. The advertising department can also attempt to sell ads around special prerace coverage, either on the sports pages or in a special big-event advance feature section.

The advertising department's cooperation, however, requires the most lead time. Special advertising efforts, such as in the *Journal*'s Al McGuire Run coverage, are planned many months before the event. Advertising is set well in advance because of the needs of the advertising business. Advertisers plan annual budgets carefully and need more lead time than sportswriters would generally consider adequate. Advertisers look at the needs of their own businesses, then look next to the newspaper's schedule and potential audience. An auto dealership, for example, may determine in December that its best bet for advertising is during the football season (which is also the new-car season) and may place the major part of its advertising during that time. If advertising from auto dealerships is expected for a spring project, say, a special auto racing section, the advertiser will probably need to know months before to revise its ad budget.

And while lead time is helpful for the advertising department, the big events that occur with little possible lead time—such as the state tournament trip—should not be planned without consultation with the advertising department. Excitement in a community over the local team's trip to the state championships may provide the opportunity for the ad department to sell "Go team go" ads and generate additional space for the sports department news coverage.

THE GRAPHICS DEPARTMENT. Because sports events normally provide some of the most exciting of all visual possibilities, the graphics department plays a key part in any big event team effort. Graphics include not only traditional sports photography but also computer-generated graphics such as information charts, maps, or diagrams. And today, especially at large newspapers, original artwork such as drawings and paintings are used more and more to illustrate and supplement major event coverage. The sports department editor or an appointed person should confer with the head of the graphics department well in advance of any big event to critique the previous year's coverage and plan upcoming coverage. Use of these varieties of graphics requires much advance time, of course, because graphic artists must have adequate time to create.

A note of caution: Maintaining good relations among all departments in a newspaper is critical. This means understanding the unique problems of each department and working to avoid placing unnecessary burdens on a department. While the big sports event may be capturing the attention of most of the sports readers, the graphics department is also required to serve all other news departments (and on small newspapers, non-news departments such as advertising and promotion) of the newspaper to which the big event may mean very little. Communication between departments is required to avoid potential conflicts.

Planning with the graphics department can overcome numerous problems, including deadlines. If the state high school basketball tournament is played in a city other than the newspaper's own, special transmitting equipment, labs, or even transportation arrangements may be needed to get photos and other graphics to the publishing site quickly. Planning can also solve personnel problems. If the sports department's photography needs are to be greater for an upcoming special event, rearranging work schedules in the graphics department may be required. Planning can also determine photographic subjects. Events like a state basketball tournament provide not only game-related pictures of athletes but feature shots of cheerleaders and hometown fans with banners, costumes, and even painted faces.

The cooperation of the graphics department can be crucial. In the case of the *Journal*'s run, here's what happened: After a meeting including the sports department representative, the newspaper's managing editor, and photo desk and photo department personnel, plans were made to obtain permission to put a photographer atop a tall building along the race route for a dramatic overhead shot, to place a special truck in front of the lead runners to get action shots, to rent a "cherry picker" crane to get another high-level shot along the route, and to place photographers at the finish line to get head-on shots of the winners. In order to make the press run for a special edition published only minutes after the race ended, photographers had to arrange for special parking to speed their film to the darkroom, even beginning the developing process in the car as it headed back to the newspaper.

Photography of a big event poses a special challenge for a newspaper that cannot afford the time or money to send a staff photographer. A sports journalist may have to take on the task of photographer to make sure the event is properly covered. Standard equipment for a photojournalist is a 35-millimeter single-lens reflex camera, which many newspapers loan to staff members. Most major journalism schools have classes in photojournalism, and potential or working reporters should take at least one course. Also, trade schools sometimes have evening classes, and some large camera stores run classes or clinics. There are also many books on photography, some even specializing in sports photography. A knowledgeable camera store salesperson should be able to suggest an appropriate book in stock or be able to order one. The local library should have books and magazines with tips on capturing sports events on film.

As with the reporting, planning is the key to photography and graphics success. Check out the situation for photography at the big event ahead of time. Is a special pass necessary to get near the action for photos? What is the lighting like in the facility? (Lighting determines the type of film to be used.) If time is crucial, what facilities are available for developing film and then having it delivered to the newspaper?

The public relations or publicity staff in charge of the big event can help in obtaining credentials and suggesting where film developing is possible. Other full-time photographers can give tips on lighting and ideas on where to sit for the best photos. Newer arenas, for instance, have automatic ceiling flash systems that photographers can use. Familiarity with the camera is also crucial. It is beneficial to practice by photographing a "practice" game well ahead of the event and having an expert critique the work.

In addition to photographs, graphics for the event previews and actual coverage can be greatly enhanced by the art department. Graphic artists can provide logos to emphasize special coverage of an event well in advance. For a state high school basketball tournament, they can generate maps showing where the teams have come from. They can develop special page layouts for event coverage pages. Graphs and charts can visually present material such as offensive and defensive averages and other statistics in an understandable and appealing manner. The use of computers to generate artwork for newspaper pages has led to a greater diversity in the look of sports pages.

THE PRODUCTION DEPARTMENT. The newspaper business is loaded with deadlines, and the production department is most involved in setting and keeping those deadlines. The example of the 7:30 P.M. state tournament final going into overtime showed the importance of informing the production department of the potential timing of the event. Production and news executives can order a "hold" on the presses to allow for any overtime possibility. Management can also schedule added personnel, such as might be needed to prepare photos or full-color graphics for the printing process.

THE CIRCULATION DEPARTMENT. A 14-year-old newspaper carrier may be just as critical to the big event coverage as a seasoned sports columnist at the event. If the carrier does not get the newspaper to the reader, all the time spent on planning and execution is wasted. Generally, it is up to production to coordinate late press runs and delivery, but communication between the editorial and circulation departments can improve the situation and even lead to additional readership opportunities.

In the case of the newspaper with statewide circulation that is covering a state high school basketball tournament, this may mean holding the regular early edition intended specifically for the towns participating in the tournament final so that a later edition, with the game story in it, can be delivered.

In the case of the *Milwaukee Journal*'s Al McGuire Run, the circulation department has trucks ready to rush just-off-the-press copies to the postrun ceremonies.

PROMOTION OR MARKETING SERVICES DEPARTMENT. If a newspaper has spent time and energy planning special treatment of a big event, the newspaper should boast about it. That's a job most newspapers give to their promotion or marketing services department. This department can promote the special coverage in many ways, through radio and television ads, special cards on newspaper boxes, posters located at dealers, and, of course, through in-newspaper ads. Promotional efforts of sports stories at the *Philadelphia Daily News,* for example, have boosted street sales for the newspaper (Haskin 1986). Similar efforts by hundreds of other newspapers have been successful, also.

OTHER PLANNING CONSIDERATIONS. The sports department must deal with other advance planning considerations. While promotion entices readers with ads detailing special upcoming coverage, the sports department itself can build to a climax by running special advance news and feature articles. For example, one newspaper built up to its Olympic coverage by running occasional "target" stories, chronicling the stories of local athletes attempting to qualify for the games. In advance of a state high school tournament, a newspaper might run a "Tournament Trail" column, providing features, anecdotes, and comments from experts and players. Such a feature can use material drawn from games leading up to the tournament.

Allocating reporters within the sports department is a problem that requires planning. If there is a special section with added space planned before an event, an editor may hand out assignments as far as a year in advance to allow reporters to work them around their daily assignments and schedules, thus reducing the amount of work right before the event.

Requirements for event coverage may need advance administrative attention. Credentials, such as game and parking passes, usually must be ordered well in advance. Some events make provisions for last-minute arrangements, especially for the reporters of a just-qualified team, but others, such as the Olympics, require the requests many months in advance. Equipment may be needed to transmit stories from the tournament or event site, and additional devices may have to be rented. Often, newspapers will install special telephone lines at the site of the event. For example, if telephone lines are to be located courtside for the state high school basketball tournament for reporters and graphics artists to use to transmit stories and graphics with portable computers, these have to be ordered in advance.

Finally, do not forget about advance arrangements for housing and transportation. At crowded events, this is critical. Even at less-crowded events, it is wise to purchase tickets in advance to save on fares, if possible, and to reserve nearby rooms early to cut down on transportation time to and from the event site. Reporters who do not plan ahead on housing and transportation will invariably spend more money and time than they need to do. Savings of time means more time to write and report. Savings of money means more can be done at the event or more money remains for subsequent assignments.

In summary, special coverage requires planning and teamwork. Leaving out any one member of the event's "team" can lead to a breakdown in all the other areas.

THE INDIVIDUAL REPORTER. Sometimes the event passes by so smoothly that everyone wonders what all the fuss was about during the planning process. But when a reporter, minutes before deadline, is in the middle of 300 other reporters in a crowded New York press box at the U.S. Open tennis tournament with no telephone to send the story, as happened to one reporter from a major metro newspaper, or when a local reporter covering the nation's top cross-country ski race wakes up the morning after the event to find his or her circulation department wasn't notified to deliver newspapers to the event's headquarters site, missing the opportunity to sell to thousands of participants and fans, it becomes apparent that the most important step, planning, must be taken first.

When all advanced planning has been accomplished, it is up to the reporter or reporters covering the event to provide the best possible material. The key to informative and exciting articles from an event is individual planning and research. The sports editor should inform the reporters of their assignments early, to allow them to begin researching their particular areas.

Let's use the example of the U.S. Open tennis tournament, held in August and September each year at Flushing Meadow in New York City. Although the situation there causes unique problems, methods of planning its coverage can be applied to any event, even a local golf tournament. The reporter assigned should immediately begin to make a file of stories that pertain to the event. Clippings and electronic data base searches from the newspaper's library or information center will reveal what past coverage has included. Books on the sport and even the specific event give background on previous winners. The wire services will usually transmit articles in advance that pertain to the event. A reporter should leave a note with the copydesk editors explaining the assignment and asking for copies of such stories.

In the case of the U.S. Open, the publicity department of the U.S. Tennis Association has proved helpful, not only providing credentials and tips on where to stay, but also producing early press releases that include information for backgrounding the event. The reporter must be sure to be on the mailing list of such a sponsoring or support organization. Several magazines and tabloids produced by tennis associations and other publishers are sources of stories about the Open and the players and personalities who will be involved. Such background sometimes is difficult to obtain at the event, so a reporter should be prepared to take along a file of clips. This allows the reporter to change from a story about a specific match to a feature on a past winner, for example, without spending hours researching the subject.

Some reporters today also do research from remote sites by computer, linking their portable laptop personal computers to electronic data base services such as CompuServe, Prodigy, or SportsTicker for current results and information as well as services such as Dialog or Vu-Text for archival research such as stories from previous tournaments. Although this can be expensive, it is a solution to research on the road at a big event.

What does the reporter from a distant newspaper cover at an event of national scope, such as the U.S. Open? Most events will have at least one local angle. Obvious stories about the local athlete who qualified for the tournament can trace his or her path to getting into the field. A further search and some telephone calls may turn up a local tennis official who will be working at the Open as a linesman. Even a local family that plans its annual vacation around the event may make a good feature, especially if the family is a hometown tennis-playing family.

If this is a first-time assignment, a reporter should also seek help in advance on how to cover the event, possibly from a fellow staff member who has covered it in the past. For example, a reporter who covered several U.S. Opens had found that the press box at the tournament, located high above the court, was too far away to catch expression and color in a match below. That reporter suggested that a new reporter covering the next Open purchase a sideline ticket to get closer to the playing surface. If no one on the staff has covered the event before, a reporter can call someone at another newspaper. The fellowship among newspaper reporters will usually yield some helpful information.

The Event

All the planning is over when the reporter finally arrives at the event. The excitement and pageantry may just about overwhelm a first-time reporter. It is important that the reporter get quickly to the task for which he or she is paid and for which the newspaper has probably spent hundreds or even thousands of dollars for special sections, promotions, travel, and accommodations. The temptation for someone covering the U.S. Open the first time may be to see the town and live it up a bit before the first scheduled story must be written. But the personal side to a trip should never interfere with the task itself. The results a reporter obtains at the big event may determine whether he or she will ever cover such an event again. Many a reporter has had his or her professional reputation made — or broken — while covering such a high-visibility event.

The reporter's situation can be likened to a football game, in which the players invariably say they are eager to get that first "hit" to jar them back to reality and do away with jitters. The reporter can go through the same process, getting that first "hit" by introducing himself or herself to fellow reporters and to coaches and officials, by asking a question at the press conference, by taking notes of the activities, and by scheduling personal interviews with participants immediately. Usually, it helps to arrive early and to get in the routine of filing stories. This can help smooth out rough edges with less danger of trouble when it counts most.

Upon arriving at the national event, reporters should contact the local press officials to receive any needed credentials that haven't been mailed, to pick up any recent press material, and to let the officials know they are present. At regional tournaments of the National Collegiate Athletic Association basketball tournament, for example, a press center is set up that provides a meeting place for reporters and acts as a central spot for the volumes of material that college sports information offices provide. Some reporters like to simplify matters, carrying only notebooks and pencils to a game site. Others feel the more material they bring, the better. The way a game develops may remind a reporter of a similar game in the past. If material on that game is available to the reporter, it can provide facts on which intelligent questions can be based during the postgame press conference. And that press conference may be the single most important activity for the reporter covering the big event.

PACK JOURNALISM. The term "pack journalism" grew out of political campaign coverage in the United States, particularly of those candidates on the presidential trail. Reporters climb onto buses or airplanes and follow the major candidates around the country in "packs," filing in and out of the vehicles. Some reporters have been criticized for allowing themselves to be influenced by their fellow reporters in such pack-style events.

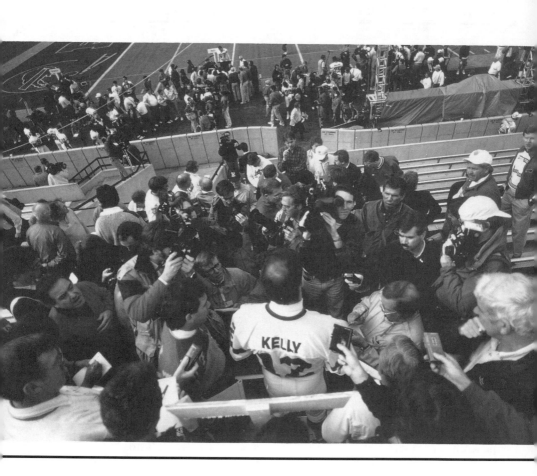

Few major sports events command more media attention than the Super Bowl. Here, sports journalists assigned to cover Super Bowl XXV in Tampa crowd around Buffalo quarterback Jim Kelly in a section of the stadium during media day. On the field, other players and reporters hold similar sessions. (*Photo by NFL Photos.*)

The big sports event, by its nature, attracts the interest of a large number of people in a city, a state, or the nation, and this attention attracts the news media in large numbers. Super Bowl XXV in 1991, played in Tampa, Fla., drew 3,000 reporters and other media professionals (Haughton 1991). Just four years earlier, Super Bowl XXI, played in Pasadena, Calif., drew about 2,200 credentialed news media representatives (Haughton 1987). The NCAA women's Final Four in New Orleans in 1991 drew more than 300 credentialed media representatives (Wilson 1991). The more members of the news media, of course, the wider the coverage of the event. The number of reporters at an event not only has an effect on the mental outlook of any reporter covering it, but can also physically prevent a reporter from coming up with the stories he or she may want to do.

Access to sources is the major reporting problem at big events. The players, especially the key ones, will be protected. Exclusive interviews will probably not be permitted. Coaches will be available only in controlled situations such as daily press briefings. Other access is likely to be prohibited to allow preparation for the event. And afterward, the demand by reporters for direct quotations and reaction-type commentary from the participants will require press conferences instead, or in addition to, regular locker room interviews. Reporters will have to be aggressive to get their questions asked in all circumstances. Big events are not for the timid.

At an event like a state high school basketball tournament, a personal interview with a coach whom a reporter has interviewed many times before may not be possible when dozens of other reporters are seeking an interview with the same individual. The availability of players is limited, as well, and event officials may set predetermined times for media interviews. In a half-hour press conference, a reporter may find he or she is never picked to ask a question or that an answer to a personal question needed to make a story complete is impossible to get in such an atmosphere. It is difficult to fight pack journalism; every reporter at a highly reported event will be trying to do essentially the same thing. A newspaper, however, can add a personal touch to big event coverage by organizing a short "notes" column as part of each day's coverage package, with anecdotes of "life at the event" written in a chatty style and relating personal experiences such as those with restaurant service and taxi cab drivers. These tiny portraits of the event can be contributed by everyone on the reporting and graphics team, of course. And the "notes" will give readers a deeper impression of what is happening there.

EFFECTS OF TELEVISION. Almost every big sports event is covered by broadcast or cable television. The impact of television cannot be ignored. Television, especially at the commercial network level, means major money to the organizations that provide the competition. Because of this, the networks can change the rules of the game. From television timeouts to when the games are played, television makes a difference to fans and print sports-writers. The World Series, for instance, used to be played only in the day-time. Now its weekday games are during prime time, and weekend games are often also at night. These changed deadlines have made life almost unbearable for print sportswriters. Because the games are at night and often end near midnight in the East, filing stories becomes a nightmare (Fitzgerald 1986).

Ranging from the Super Bowl to regular season high school football and basketball games, television will affect the reporting strategy of print sportswriters at a big event. The growth of cable television and its all-sports networks, such as ESPN, and the apparent insatiability of regular network television for sports coverage mean that television is a factor that must be considered in a big event coverage plan. Most newspapers are discovering that, instead of trying to find ways to overcome television, newspapers are best suited to providing the in-depth and localized coverage that a mass television broadcast cannot provide. Television coverage is more concerned with the actual event — the match, the game, the race — than with the steps leading up to it or those immediately afterward. Unlike television, newspa-pers can offer detailed previews. And even though a network may have 20 or more cameras at an event such as the Super Bowl, limited television time means there are places cameras probably won't be present, such as the pregame interview and postgame press conference. A newspaper reporter, on the other hand, has the time to talk to person after person, to present short comments from many individuals, or to present a lengthy interview with just one person. Newspapers can localize a national big event by con-tacting local people (e.g., politicians, celebrities, and other sports figures) and asking them to predict the outcome of the event.

Reporters can also use the telephone to contact individuals throughout the nation for their predictions about an event, again something television will generally not have the time to do.

THE PRESS CONFERENCE. It is particularly important that the skill of inter-viewing (see Chapter 4) be mastered. But it is also important that the re-porter understand the nature of the big event press conference. It almost never fails. A reporter sits through an hour-long press conference before a big game and decides, after 55 minutes, there's just nothing that's been said that's worth using in his or her story. Then, suddenly, a comment triggers a thought: "Hey, that sounds exactly like what he (the coach) said three years ago before his team won his last title." And that recollection may lead to more questions and a good story.

Because of the large number of reporters covering the big event, press conferences have become commonplace. Most reporters moan about sitting through them, promise their colleagues they won't show up, and then reluc-tantly do so anyway, groaning all the way through. They are there because of the fear that something *newsworthy* might occur. It is the sort of event that a reporter must attend, even if nothing significant is said. Some announcements will be newsworthy. Many pregame press conferences include distribution of prepared statements and likely have the opposing coaches, plus a key player or two, to answer a short round of questions (Mencher 1991). A press conference should be used as background to get such mundane questions out of the way, such as, "What defense will a team use?" or "What is the mood of the team?" A reporter can ask more detailed and specific questions in any possible personal interviews. A reporter who does not attend a press conference may end up asking the same questions later in a personal interview, to the annoyance of the source.

The press conference also works to the source's advantage because there is some control over what questions will be asked—and answered. A particularly tough question can be sidestepped, and if the reporter is not called on again, a follow-up question may not be possible (Dennis and Ismach 1981). There are two important rules to follow at a press conference: Don't be shy, but don't be greedy.

The number of reporters converging on an event may be intimidating, but less is gained by attending without also asking questions. Asking a question early and loosening up may make it easier to ask the tough question later. There's also a point at which a reporter can become an irritant to the sources and fellow reporters by asking too many questions.

Reporters can spice up the story built around the press conference by providing observational details: What was the setting—a small, cramped locker room, or a spacious concert hall just next to the playing field? How were the sources dressed—in fine clothing or casual attire? What was the attitude of the source—did the attitude grow antagonistic as the press conference went on, and, if so, why?

It is a good assumption that a sportswriter's readers will have seen all or part of the event on television. This will have an effect on how a story is written after the event has occurred. Reporters have to dig for elements of the event that did not get emphasized or covered on television. It pays to monitor television coverage if possible. Some football press boxes, for example, have closed-circuit television. To get the edge on television at a big event means providing readers with analysis and interpretation of what occurred. This means finding expert sources who can explain what occurred and why. It is the sportswriter's job to translate it for readers for the edition. A good place to start, of course, is the post–big event press conference.

The postevent press conference varies in format and location from event to event. Many big events have a single interview room where the opposing coaches and key players appear on a regular schedule. If this interview session is going on at the same time as the locker room is opened, reporters must make a choice. Many newspapers assign extra reporters just to watch the game and then gather quotations in the locker room, either to be used by the lead story reporter or for special locker room sidebar stories.

BIG EVENT COVERAGE. The Super Bowl provides a particularly good example of how a big event is covered. Thousands of sports journalists, print and broadcast, cover the event each year. There is perhaps more written before this single game than before any other event. Roy Blount Jr. (1978) calls the Super Bowl the "Hyperbowl" because of its usual extravagance of media coverage, parties, and dollars spent — on bets and scalped tickets. Blount says there is "no way to cover the Super Bowl. It's like trying to knit a sweater for a man permanently buried under three tons of wool. If you try to knit a sweater big enough to fit the pile of wool, you feel overextended. If you try to guess and knit a sweater to fit the man, you feel you haven't risen to the occasion." Blount laments the usual less-than-stellar game and the obligatory next day headline "Super Bowl Not So Super."

Groups of reporters literally charter airplanes to get to this game. About 70 reporters from Buffalo used a chartered jet to travel to the Tampa Super Bowl in 1991. About 30 buses were required to move the sports journalists from site to site during Super Bowl week. A registration center is created for the news media at major events such as a Super Bowl. In Tampa, it was in a convention center. Reporters and other media staff members registered on arrival, received credentials, and moved into a "news bullpen" of tables and chairs and screened booths (Haughton 1991).

After decades of trying, some newspapers have acknowledged that their Super Bowl coverage needs to be a little "soft" but can also have the bite of some hard news stories. Bill Dwyre, executive sports editor of the *Los Angeles Times,* had 20 staffers covering Super Bowl XXI in Pasadena, Calif. (Stein 1987). He said, "We have to give readers a certain amount of soft stuff — profiles, features and notes — but we're also using this week to produce some journalism. We're going after hot issues like drugs and the NFL labor situation" (Stein 1987). Other newspapers used creativity in their feature coverage, with the *San Francisco Examiner* giving one writer $500 and the assignment to find cheap lodging, cheap food, and a cheap ticket to the game. The writer's column "Super Bowl on a Shoestring" ran daily.

Many newspapers will publish special sections in advance or on the day of the Super Bowl, hoping to capitalize on reader — and advertiser — attention. The *San Jose Mercury News* produced a 36-page tabloid for Super Bowl XXI as a guide for television viewers (Stein 1987). That newspaper produced an 88-page game guide and a 24-page wrap-around section for the day after Super Bowl XIX at Stanford Stadium in 1985. The day of the 1985 game, the newspaper had 40 reporters and 14 photographers assigned to work on the special section. The *San Francisco Examiner* produced an 82-page souvenir magazine for readers (Stein 1985).

Even smaller newspapers can find ways to cover the big event. The

New York Giants linebacker Lawrence Taylor (wearing a hat) is the center of attention during pregame interviews at media day for Super Bowl XXV in Tampa. Mass interview situations such as this are common at big events. (*Photo by NFL Photos.*)

Pasadena Star-News sports editor was able to get only one photographer onto the field of a game played down the street in his newspaper's town. But because photographers from the *New York Daily News* needed a darkroom to transmit photos back to their newspaper, the *Star-News* allowed use of its darkroom in exchange for the opportunity to augment its photo coverage with photographs by the *Daily News* (Stein 1987).

Speed is the key to photo coverage and, although the process is still time-consuming, new technology is cutting down the time needed to shoot, develop, and transmit photos. For Super Bowl XXV, the Associated Press used PhotoStream picture-a-minute digital photo delivery. The choice of color photos taken and transmitted by the AP was greatly enhanced by the PhotoStream system. "We were able to select, edit and transmit color pictures in numbers never possible in past Super Bowls," said one AP official, who estimated 20 color photos were delivered before the game was over and nearly 40 during the hours following the game (Associated Press 1991).

Coverage such as that provided to readers by the *Los Angeles Times* and *San Jose Mercury News* is obviously a result of huge sports department staffs. But even smaller newspapers can provide the blanket coverage of their own big event, by following the pattern of the bigger newspapers in planning. Editors and reporters should sit down and brainstorm all the possible stories and columns that can be written about the event, remembering to step back enough to see the entire picture of the event and how it fits into the context of overall society. Then, story choices should be decided, graphic coverage should be considered, assignments made, and the entire plan written up and circulated among all departments in the newspaper.

After the Event

When the big event day is finally over, the natural reaction is to sit back and relax and quickly try to forget how much work was put into coverage. But instead, while the event is still fresh, editors and reporters should write notes on how they feel the coverage could be improved. These notes need not necessarily be acted on immediately but should be kept for consideration until the first planning session is held for next year's big event, by which time everyone's memory of the event and its coverage problems and possibilities might otherwise be a blur.

The period immediately after a big event also offers good feature possibilities. For example, the state high school basketball tournament can be followed by a story on the hometown parades, visits with the governor, and school pep rallies for the winners. A national wrestling tournament held at a local college can lead to a story on the experiences of tournament organizers, meet officials, and even those housing the athletes.

One of the most effective postevent articles is the reporter's personal

Kansas City Star sports copy editor Mark Holland (right) works at his computer terminal in the newspaper's office. Holland is one of many behind-the-scenes sports journalists who work to get the sports section published on deadline during a big event. (*Photo by Daniel Starling,* Kansas City Star.)

reminiscences—behind-the-scenes anecdotes, dramatic moments, humorous sidelights that did not make the previous articles. A reporter who covered both the Boston Marathon road race and the American Birkebeiner cross-country ski race in northern Wisconsin, considered the biggest events of both sports in the United States, wrote an article comparing the two events, talking about the similar personalities and hardships at the two widely separate events.

Covering a U.S. Open Tennis Tournament

Newsday, the daily tabloid newspaper serving metropolitan New York that is based on Long Island, covers the U.S. Open tennis tournament at nearby Flushing Meadow each year as a local event. Even though the U.S. Open is an international tennis event, it is a major local event for *Newsday* and its sports department. On men's championship Sunday, the newspaper staffs the tournament to cover the championship match, but also plans its "notes" column called "Aces and Faults," and plans a feature sidebar on the winning player.

Although this tournament runs two weeks and has two major finals played on different days—the women's final is the day before the men's—the newspaper devotes considerable space to the event each day, especially on the championship weekend. The stories, written on deadline by three different reporters and illustrated amply with staff photography, are reprinted below. The lead story, by Pat Calabria, is just over 1,000 words in length. The notes column by John Jeansonne is much briefer, containing four different items and the scorecard (the day's results) at under 600 words. The feature sidebar by Joe Gergen on winner Pete Sampras and a historical perspective on winners of the tournament runs just under 1,000 words. In all three stories, notice the wide use of direct quotations and detail. These characteristics of the stories add much to their success. But also consider the work required by the reporters to get the information in the short time frame of reporting and writing on deadline.

SOURCE: *Newsday,* Nassau and Suffolk edition, page 82
DATE: Monday, September 10, 1990
AUTHOR: Pat Calabria
HEADLINE: Sampras, pure and simple; Low-key 19-year-old sweeps flamboyant Agassi

The U.S. Open champion was not dressed in shades of electric lime yesterday. Nor was he attired in hot lava. Instead, the only trace of neon that Pete Sampras wore could be found on his face. It was just his smile that glowed.

On a day when he became the youngest men's title-holder in the history of the tournament by demolishing flamboyant Andre Agassi, the California teenager finally allowed himself a sparse show of emotion. That was as big a surprise as the victory itself.

"I'm usually low-key," Sampras said, by way of apology. "That's more my personality. I can't help it."

But a 6-4, 6-3, 6-2 victory that required a mere 1 hour, 42 minutes — and filed him in the lore and legend of the sport — finally wrung an expression of satisfaction from the kid. On an afternoon when he became the first American champion since John McEnroe in 1984 and the most unheralded winner in perhaps 33 years, it was Sampras' only concession.

He fired 13 more aces, bringing his total to 100 for his seven matches at Flushing Meadow. He added 12 more service winners. He was not broken the whole match.

"It was," Agassi said, "a good old-fashioned street mugging."

That's a description Sampras, Mr. Vanilla, would never have thought to use. But it fit. Just 28 days past his 19th birthday, Sampras nudged from the record books the name of Oliver Campbell, who was 19 years, six months when he won the Open's 10th edition in 1890.

He also administered one of the most lopsided defeats in the Open era against a favored opponent who had dropped only two sets in the tournament. Sampras was only the No. 12 seed, and not until yesterday, in his first appearance in a Grand Slam final, did he emerge as a star.

"I'm just a normal 19-year-old with an unusual job, doing unusual things, like I did today," he said. "That's me."

Certainly, the surprised crowd of 20,746 appreciated the freshness Sampras brought to the Stadium Court. He was profuse in his praise of Agassi, the fans, his parents and anyone else he could think of. In contrast to the rainbow of colors in Agassi's wardrobe, Sampas was outfitted in basic white.

That suits him, too. Probably not since unseeded Mal Anderson of Australia won the championship in 1957 has a player of so little stature come out of the blue to win the Open. That was back in the era of white balls and court etiquette that Sampras seems to have sprung from, too.

In other words, he's no Agassi. And Agassi, it turned out, was no Sampras.

Agassi did not serve an ace all day. He won only three points on Sampras' serve in the first set, and only five in the second. He didn't hold his first break point on Sampras until the first game of the third set.

"If Pete did anything out there," Agassi said, "it was that he encouraged me to work on my serve."

It's Sampras' best weapon — reaching a top speed of 120 mph — and the one he used to eliminate McEnroe in the semifinals, No. 3 seed Ivan Lendl in the quarterfinals and No. 6 Thomas Muster in the fourth round. It was almost assuring when Sampras said he had never served better.

After breaking Agassi for a 2-1 lead in the third game of the match — the game that decided the first set — Sampras held his serve by blasting three straight aces. After breaking Agassi for a 3-2 lead in the second set,

Sampras polished off the next game with a service winner.

His gifted volleying kept Agassi pinned to the baseline. When Agassi tried to rip passing shots past him, Sampras was perfectly positioned to slap winners across the court. True to form, he broke Agassi for 4-2 in the third set, held serve and broke Agassi for the match. "Today was the best I could possibly do," he said, "and it couldn't have come at a better time."

Or at a worse time for Agassi, who was frustrated in a second attempt to win his first Grand Slam title, after losing the French Open final to Andres Gomez. It hurt.

After all, Agassi's rise a year ago was overshadowed by Michael Chang's upset victory at Roland Garros. Now Sampras has come out of the woodwork to also surpass him in Grand Slam success, if not yet in the rankings.

Indeed, Sampras will occupy the No. 6 spot on the ATP computer today—two notches below Agassi—a long way from No. 89, where he started the year. He never won a tournament before February, and now he has won three. The $350,000 winner's share he received nearly doubled his 1990 earnings.

"It's been great," Sampras said of his two-week fantasy. "I've had a great time. Now I just want to let it soak in."

It wasn't easy to keep his sneakers on the ground. His parents back in Rancho Palos Verdes, west of Los Angeles, were having a difficult time as well. Sampras' father, Soterios, refuses to watch his son's matches because they are too taxing on his nerves.

Sampras guessed that, under the circumstances, they decided to tape the championship match. That appears to be the family's way of coping with success. When the great champion Fred Perry suggested in June that Sampras soon would win Wimbledon, Sampras said: "Fred, you're out of control."

Sampras promptly lost in the first round. But that was then and this is now, and Sampras is the winner. "This is the ultimate," he said. "Whatever else I do in my career, I'll always be a U.S. Open champion."

MATCH STATS

Sampras		Agassi
53	1st Serve Percentage	77
13	Aces	0
12	Service Winners	9
1	Double Faults	1
27	Placement Winners	10
34	Unforced Errors	28
13	Service Games Held	9
0	Service Games Broken	5
100	Total Points Won	74
62	Advance to Net	7
39	Net Points Won	5
	Time of match 1:42	

SOURCE: *Newsday,* Nassau and Suffolk edition, page 83
DATE: Monday, September 10, 1990
AUTHOR: John Jeansonne
HEADLINE: Aces and Faults

A New Beginning

Pete Sampras' coach of two years, Joe Brandi, 46, of Puerto Rico, greeted Sampras after his U.S. Open victory with the words: "Pete, your work has just begun." Brandi, ironically, has been working with Sampras at the tennis academy of Nick Bollettieri, coach of Andre Agassi, though Bollettieri made it clear he could take no credit for Brandi's or Sampras' success yesterday.

Paying the Price

"I had a really long talk with Pete last December," Brandi said. "I said, 'Pete, if you want to be a champion, you have to pay the price off the court as well as on the court. And if I am going to travel with you—you know I have a wife and two kids—you're going to do what I tell you.' Pete's very mellow. But at the same time, he is like concrete." Brandi said a breakthrough in Sampras' commitment to tennis came after Sampras was injured in February at the Lipton tournament in Florida, returned to Bollettieri's academy and worked on his conditioning as well as his tennis, concentrating on "return of serve, slice backhand and getting closer to the net."

On the Path of Progress

While Agassi sequestered himself in Westchester County throughout the two-week Open, Sampras stayed at the players' hotel in Manhattan and ate breakfast daily at Wolf's Sixth Avenue Deli. When an acquaintance from Los Angeles spotted Sampras yesterday morning in the hotel lobby and said he hadn't seen him at the deli, Sampras said he had eaten at an upscale hotel instead. "I'm moving up in the world," he said.

Navratilova's Slam Dance

Martina Navratilova teamed with Gigi Fernandez to win the Open women's doubles championship, ending the Grand Slam bid of Jana Novotna–Helena Sukova in the process. For Navratilova, 33, it was her 54th Grand Slam title, leaving her eight short of the record held by Margaret Smith Court. "I'm too far away from that to think about it," Navratilova said. She laughed. "But I'm going to play doubles till I'm 50."

Navratilova was reminded that Ivan Lendl has said he intends to begin playing doubles to improve his net game. "Mixed doubles with Lendl?" Navratilova said. "I don't think so. If I missed, he'd sic his dog on me."

Asked whether the women, who received Open prize money equal to the men, should play best-of-five matches, Navratilova said: "You pay for quality, not quantity. You don't pay Elton John for how long he's on the stage; you pay him because he's Elton John. The men got more attention here, basically, because John McEnroe came back from the dead. We got more at Wimbledon."

SCORECARD
Featured Results

Men's Singles Championship
    Pete Sampras (12) d. Andre Agassi (4) 6-4, 6-3, 6-2
Women's Doubles Championship
    Fernandez-Navratilova d. Novotna-Sukova 6-2, 6-4
Senior Men's Doubles Championship
    Stockton-Gullikson d. Edmondson-Stewart 6-7 (3-7), 7-6 (7-5), 6-4
Boys' Singles Championship
    A. Gaudenzi (15) d. M. Tillstroem (13) 6-2, 4-6, 7-6 (7-3)
Girls' Singles Championship
    Magdalena Maleeva (1) d. N. van Lottum (5) 7-5, 6-2

SOURCE: *Newsday,* Nassau and Suffolk edition, page 83
DATE: Monday, September 10, 1990
AUTHOR: Joe Gergen
HEADLINE: Sampras provides a sense of history

Long before he made history at the U.S. Open, Pete Sampras had a sense that life on the planet, as well as his chosen sport, did not begin with him. Among the complaints lodged against his generation is its lack of appreciation for and understanding of the past. It is Sampras' approach to tennis, as well as his game itself, that sets him apart.

Not only is Sampras the youngest male player to win America's national championship, but he was younger than his opponent in yesterday's final. And Andre Agassi is as current as the sport allows, the player who most embodies now. Add the fact that Sampras never finished high school and it might be assumed that the range of his interest and knowledge did not extend beyond MTV.

Lo and behold, the depth of the 19-year-old Californian does not stop with his second serve. As much as his ascent at the National Tennis Center was a stunning revelation of ability, his reaction to the breakthrough was becoming and evocative. It was just the way he might have imagined the modest stars of an earlier era accepting their success.

"I've always looked up to the older guys, like Laver and Rosewall," Sampras said in the glow of his 6-4, 6-3, 6-2 thrashing of Agassi. "I really enjoyed that era. I have tremendous respect for those guys, I really do. I think all those Australians were class individuals, and I would like to be in that category."

Fittingly, Sampras lit up the Open like a rocket, which happens to be the nickname of his personal favorite. Although he is too young to have seen Rod Laver at his peak, even on television, he remembers watching tapes of the man's matches against compatriot Ken Rosewall in the WCT finals in Dallas almost two decades ago. The tapes were the gift of a coach who was working on the youngster's footwork when he was 14 and in the throes of a metamorphosis from baseline moth to serve-and-volley butterfly.

He was mesmerized by Laver. "I thought he could do it all, on any surface," Sampras said. "Stay back if he wanted, come in if he wanted. He just seemed like a class player."

Ironically, Sampras was first touted as a future champion on the grass at Wimbledon, but it is on the hard courts in his native country where he stamped himself as a star of the present. "I'd like to think grass is my best surface," he said, "but it's going to take me some time to play on grass. I've been playing on hard courts for the last 10 years."

And, yes, he said it might be even a greater achievement to win Wimbledon because of all the tradition associated with the tournament. This is in sharp contrast to Agassi's proclamations of love and devotion for the U.S. Open, understandable in view of his distaste for grass and white clothing.

Of course, the two players share little more than an age group and a country of origin. Although Sampras wields a modern composite racket, he has a collection of the old wood models back in the family garage at Rancho Palos Verdes. There are players on the tour today who aren't even aware that rackets once grew on trees.

Agassi may be one of them, although that may be nothing more than a stereotype. But it's safe to say his knowledge of tennis history is less than acute.

Among those who participated in the victory presentation after the French Open final, where Agassi finished second to Andres Gomez of Ecuador, was Jean Borotra. A former French and Wimbledon champion, he was one of the celebrated Three Musketeers who dominated men's tennis in the post–World War I era. The French media asked Agassi his feelings about meeting such a legend.

"Oh, that old guy?" Agassi replied. "I didn't even know who he was."

After yesterday's defeat, the 20-year-old would-be champion remains a legend only on Madison Avenue. Sampras said that Agassi's time would come, that he was too good not to win a Grand Slam title sometime soon. And Agassi agreed. "I'm getting closer all the time," he said.

Yet he was beaten to the punch for the second time. Only last spring, he was beaten to the French Open title by a younger American, Michael Chang. And now he finished second in the U.S. Open to still another younger Yank, Sampras. Of all the kids aspiring to fill John McEnroe's sneakers as the next great American player, Sampras came the farthest the fastest.

He didn't win his first pro event until the U.S. Pro Indoor in Philadelphia seven months ago, defeating Gomez in the final. "Probably, he's very underrated in America with the likes of Agassi and Chang," Gomez said at the time. "But I have to say when asked who's the best that Pete is. His game is complete, and I don't think Chang and Agassi will ever be serve-and-volleyers."

And perhaps they never will be Open champions. Sampras might have been just another baseliner if he didn't decide along with his coach at the time, Pete Fisher, that he wasn't progressing with his two-fisted backhand game at the tender age of 14. So he spent a year learning to rally one-handed and working on what he called a "terrible" serve. Now he stands as the heir to McEnroe, the first U.S. champion with the strokes to succeed on all surfaces.

So return with us now to those thrilling days of yesteryear when tennis players wore predominantly white clothes and short hair, applauded their opponents and accepted victory with grace. Return with us now to yesterday.

Copyright 1991, *Newsday* and *New York Newsday*
Reprinted with the permission of *Newsday*

References

Associated Press. 1991. AP transmits via PhotoStream from Super Bowl. *AP Log,* February 4, 4.

Blount, Roy. 1978. Hyperbowl: Can mortal journalists cover the Super Bowl? *Columbia Journalism Review* 16 (6): 36.

Dennis, Everette E., and Arnold Ismach. 1981. *Reporting Processes and Practices: Newswriting for Today's Readers.* Belmont, Calif.: Wadsworth.

Fitzgerald, Mark. 1986. A Series played for TV. *Editor & Publisher* 119 (December 6): 18, 51.

Haskin, Don. 1986. Sports promotion boosts street sales. *Editor & Publisher* 119 (November 8): 24.

Haughton, Jim. 1987. More than 2,200 were credentialed for this year's Super Bowl. *Editor & Publisher* 120 (February 14): 16–17.

_____. 1991. Covering the Super Bowl. *Editor & Publisher* 124 (March 9): 14–15.

Mencher, Melvin. 1991. *News Reporting and Writing.* 5th ed. Dubuque, Iowa: Brown.

Stein, M. L. 1985. Super Bowl produces Bay area media blitz. *Editor & Publisher* 118 (February 16): 22.

_____. 1987. Covering the Super Bowl. *Editor & Publisher* 120 (February 14): 14–16.

Wilson, Austin. 1991. Final Four Tenth Anniversary. Associated Press sports wire, March 26, n.p.

4 Advanced Reporting Strategies

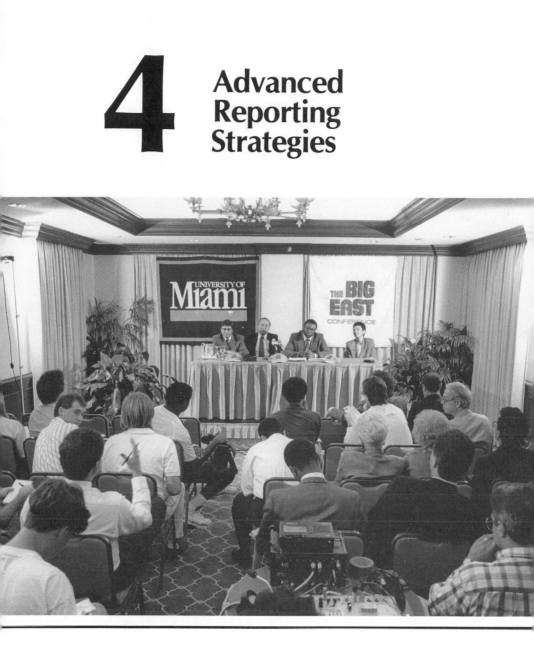

Press conferences are often the means by which sports organizations release information about investigations and new developments. At this press conference in Miami, University of Miami coaches and Big East officials announce to a collection of reporters the school's decision to join the conference. (*Photo © by Dave Bergman*.)

10

Investigative Sports Reporting

The amount of sports investigative reporting has grown in the past decade. More and more often, newspapers are investigating stories that involve athletes, athletic programs, sports agents, gambling, sale and use of illegal drugs and the abuse of legal drugs, illegal or unethical business deals, fraud, sex scandals, political defections, and athletic organization rules cheating. But a field that was once dominated by news reporters "loaned" to sports departments is now being dominated by skilled reporters within sports departments. Sports investigative reporting is *the* growing specialization in sports journalism in this decade.

In the past decade, the *Washington Post, Philadelphia Inquirer, Newsday, Chicago Tribune, Dallas Morning News, Atlanta Constitution,* and a handful of other major daily newspapers hired specialists to conduct investigations into the sports business, college athletics, and other social, economic, and even political problems in the once seemingly innocent sports world. These newspapers, known for being among the elite in producing daily and Sunday sports sections in the United States, heralded the arrival of the growing sports investigative reporting specialization.

Entering the 1990s, more newspapers became involved in serious investigative sports journalism. The short-lived *National,* based in New York, gained a fast reputation for its work by Pulitzer Prize winner Jeffrey Marx. Newspapers in Phoenix, Los Angeles, Detroit, Boston, Louisville, Austin, Tex., Birmingham, Ala., and Pittsburgh were recognized as leaders in high-quality investigative reporting on sports subjects.

Even small- and medium-sized daily newspapers with limited financial and human resources began to devote energies to important investigative stories. The *St. Paul Pioneer Press Dispatch, Florida Times-Union* in Jacksonville, Colorado Springs *Gazette Telegraph, Spokane (Wash.) Spokesman-Review, Albuquerque Tribune, Lexington (Ky.) Herald-Leader, Macon (Ga.) Telegraph and News, Austin (Tex.) American-Statesman, Dayton Daily News,* and other small- and medium-sized dailies have gained reputations for quality investigative efforts.

In the 1990s sports world, numerous important sports stories require the time and patience of an investigative approach. If a sportswriter simply views sports as a big business, dozens of investigation ideas will surface. The problems and abuses of the business world do not stop when the businesses involve professional or amateur sports. These serious subjects require time-consuming reporting to be done right. As one sports editor recently said, these writers "turn over a whole lot of rocks and see what develops" (Shaw 1989a). These stories cannot be written after a handful of interviews or a few hours out of the office. They require work. Lots of it. Some dramatic recent examples:

● The *Lexington (Ky.) Herald-Leader* investigated recruiting improprieties in college basketball, including cash payoffs by boosters to players for its home team, the University of Kentucky Wildcats. The series won a Pulitzer Prize.

● The *Atlanta Constitution* investigated charges that illegal payments were given to University of Georgia star Dominique Wilkins and his mother by a sports agent while Wilkins was still playing at Georgia.

● The *New York Times, Sports Illustrated, Cleveland Plain Dealer, Dayton Daily News, Cincinnati Post,* and *Cincinnati Enquirer* did the ground-breaking investigations into the gambling and tax problems of baseball star Pete Rose (Shaw 1989c).

● The *Los Angeles Times* published a massive 10,000-word analysis of the cause and circumstances of the death of college basketball star Hank Gathers, attempting to answer numerous questions by interviewing more than 100 people and reading 2,000 pages of depositions of those involved, only one week after Gathers' sudden death in March 1990.

● The *Dallas Times Herald* and *Dallas Morning News* both investigated the violations of NCAA rules at Southern Methodist University, which ultimately led to the "death penalty" for the school and the temporary end of its Division I-A football program (Fitzgerald 1987).

● The recently closed *Dallas Times Herald* investigated irregularities at Texas A & M University, leading to the resignation of the head football coach.

● The *Arizona Daily Star* in Tucson investigated the University of Arizona athletic department and found numerous serious violations. The reporting won a Pulitzer Prize.

But critics often ask: Should the sports department do these difficult, often complex, investigative stories? Are sportswriters professionally prepared to do these types of stories? (Fitzgerald 1985, Shaw 1989a, Shaw 1989b, Shaw 1989c). These questions must be considered before a sports editor attempts to look into a story that needs an investigative approach. Some of the best newspapers have resisted setting up full-time sports investigative "teams" even though they do investigative reporting on a regular basis. The *Los Angeles Times,* for example, originally decided against a team approach to its investigative sports reporting (Shaw 1989b) before creating a four-person team (Dwyre 1991).

Not everyone likes investigative journalism of any kind. For many readers, it is fine for the news pages, but they often object when investigations begin to filter onto sports pages and take the "fun and games" out of the sports section. An editor must remember that many sports section readers react adversely, especially if these stories concern home teams. To many people, a thorough, tough investigative piece "contaminates" the generally entertaining sports pages, no matter how well it is written and reported (Shaw 1989b).

"Cheerleader" or home team booster-oriented sports section readers feel the local sports section has no business investigating the home teams. When the *Lexington (Ky.) Herald-Leader* ran its investigative series on college recruiting, which included unfavorable disclosures about the local University of Kentucky basketball team, readers reacted in large numbers. In response to shocking stories that said Kentucky players accepted cash from boosters, readers organized a boycott of the newspaper, canceled subscriptions, circulated petitions, and called in complaints (*Editor & Publisher* 1985a). A sports section editor must also be certain that there are good, sound reasons for publishing a critical investigative story so criticism from readers and the sources can be answered. Craig Stanke, a sports reporter for the *Fort Lauderdale Sun-Sentinel,* agrees that the effects can be disheartening. "If (your reporting) gets a coach fired, it's a tragedy (to readers), and your own sports department gets down on you," he told an Investigative Reporters and Editors (IRE) national convention panel on investigative sports reporting in Chicago. "We have some difficult questions about how much we can dig into, how much we can investigate and at what point we go overboard in covering things, and being unfair to our readers who want to read the sports pages for entertainment," he added (Fitzgerald 1985).

Because investigative reporting is more common today, some sources have become accustomed to its hard give-and-take. But sports reporters, who are probably more comfortable with event-oriented coverage such as writing about games, have to be reminded that their eyes should be open to more than just who scored and what yardline the ball is on. A potential investigative story may be found on just about any sports beat, from Little League to the professionals. Several areas are appropriate for sports section investigations:

- recruiting of athletes for high school and college programs and the promises made to these athletes
- high school and college sports boosters programs
- agents and their relations with college student athletes
- privately funded foundations that aid sports programs
- drug use by athletes to increase strength and pain endurance
- drug test cheating to protect eligibility
- gambling and point-shaving
- business practices of professional and college teams
- professional labor negotiations

Who should do the investigative story? Not every sports reporter should attempt to be an investigative reporter. Many reporters have had no experience with investigative pieces. Usually, these stories require more experienced reporters, including reporters with expertise in the subjects involved. But inexperienced reporters can learn.

Beat reporters, who have the most sources, may find it uncomfortable to play tough with their contacts, knowing that once the story is over they will have to deal with these people again. An editor may choose to form a partnership, one reporter from within the beat and one from without, to allow the beat reporter to have input and yet not bear the entire responsibility of the investigation. Or an editor may choose to bring in a sportswriter from a different beat to avoid damaging fragile source–reporter relationships on the beat producing the investigation.

Some newspapers team one sports reporter with a non-sports reporter more knowledgeable about investigative techniques. The sports departments of many newspapers do not permanently assign an individual as an investigative reporter but designate a member of the sports department to investigate a particular story. A newspaper may also borrow a reporter from the news department. And some newspapers regularly rotate reporters through different departments, including sports, for experience. These rotations create opportunities for reporters to learn.

A full-time investigative reporter's usefulness within a sports department obviously depends on the potential stories. For most sports departments, an investigative reporter would be an expensive luxury. At most newspapers, regular staff reporters with beat responsibilities occasionally take on investigative stories as part of a team when the story warrants it.

Unqualified sports reporters, trying to do their best on a story that requires deep investigation, often make mistakes that lead to problems. The inexperience of most sports reporters in doing investigative reporting is the reason behind the doubts of many critics about investigative sports reporting. Investigations, if not done carefully, can cause big credibility problems for newspapers, as they did for the *Arizona Daily Star* in Tucson. The newspaper, which had earlier won a Pulitzer Prize for investigations of the University of Arizona athletic department, got into trouble because it made reporting errors in a different investigation of the University of Arizona basketball team. The newspaper incorrectly accused the Arizona coach of a conflict of interest, saying that a company which paid the coach as an advisor was awarded the team's uniform contract. The "massive" magnitude of the error—the description by the newspaper's managing editor—led to the resignation of the reporter who wrote the story and the sports editor of the newspaper (Healey 1985, *Editor & Publisher* 1985b).

Los Angeles Times media critic David Shaw (1989a) was concerned enough with the problems of improperly prepared sports reporters in handling complicated investigative stories that he wrote a critical analysis concluding that many off-field stories are "fumbled" because writers do not do enough digging for information. Although he concedes that most newspaper sports sections "have improved enormously over the past 30 years," he says the problem is in what the sections do not do. "Most sports sections still do very little investigative reporting, and almost all are woefully inadequate in covering the business side of sports" (Shaw 1989a).

Defining Investigative Sports Reporting

What is investigative reporting? Specifically, what is investigative sports reporting? It is an approach to reporting that reflects a combination of reporting methods. The term "investigative sports reporting" actually refers to an age-old technique simply applied to the context of sports. John Behrens (1977) uses the terms "investigative reporter," "muckraker," "scandalmonger," and "typewriter guerilla" interchangeably. But investigative reporters, as we have come to define them in the past two decades since the famed Watergate investigations by the *Washington Post* and other newspapers, are reporters who deal with (1) a subject that involves obstacles to gathering information with conventional reporting tools, and (2) a story that fully explains or explores the significance of a subject (Bolch and Miller 1978).

Therefore, investigative reporting is more thorough, complete, and deeper than ordinary reporting. This definition allows for stories not only on politics or crime but also on topics that require arduous research but do not reveal immoral or illegal activity.

Bob Greene, legendary investigative reporter for *Newsday* and former president of the association of Investigative Reporters and Editors (IRE) adds further elements to this definition. He says investigative reporting focuses on significant materials that someone is trying to hide, and the findings are the reporter's own work rather than leaked material (Dennis and Ismach 1981). IRE's own book on investigative reporting says all reporting should be investigative in nature. Greene says it is "simply old-fashioned, hard-nosed reporting. What delineates it from other forms is the nature of what is being reported and the amount of original work involved" (Ullmann and Colbert 1991).

Another experienced investigative reporter defines it this way:

> Investigative reporting is nothing in the world but good reporting. Now there are nuances that come in, I'll concede that. Investigative reporting requires more documentation than a lot of the run-of-the-mill work because you are frequently dealing with a person's livelihood, with his reputation, more than in a routine news story. You have to be much more careful of the damage you can inflict and that makes you cautious. It makes you look for any additional back-up material you can find — documentation, verification, from other sources if you can find it written (Bolch and Miller 1978).

The Associated Press Sports Editors encourages investigative sports reporting. APSE feels, however, that "pure and truly significant investigative reporting is rare. . . ." APSE explains that "investigative work should rely on reporting of facts discovered or uncovered by the author rather than reports from anonymous sources offering unverified statements of fact." APSE further tells members that "relying solely on quotes from an FBI source does not make a story 'investigative.' Doing the work the FBI would do in order to build a story would be investigative." APSE encourages its member newspapers to do investigative sports reporting that shows initiative, documentation, resourcefulness, and original reporting "in uncovering newsworthy and significant facts and developments that otherwise might not have been reported" and that have impact and bring changes (Associated Press Sports Editors 1991).

Methods of Investigative Reporting

The methods of investigative reporting are virtually the same methods as all other forms of reporting, involving interviews, observation, and documents. Investigative reporters are often highly skilled interviewers — detectives, if you will. But they also know how to follow a trail on paper, in a computer data base, and in government files. Carl Bernstein put it best when he said:

> The one thing that so-called investigative stuff is, is actual painstaking work. It's hard work in the sense that people like Sy [Hersh], Woodward, and myself and I'm sure others, spend a lot of time with records and going through

ten thousand pieces of paper and whatever to find a certain little thing. Such work requires patience certainly if you want to do a definitive piece whether it be on the Washington Redskins or Watergate (Behrens 1977).

The key words in Bernstein's definition are "painstaking work," for, if beginners listen to the best investigative reporters, it quickly becomes clear that the glamour that comes from breaking a big story is preceded by many hours of developing sources, tracking down leads, writing requests for records, searching files, interviewing, and then rechecking facts.

Two top investigative reporters, in fact, liken their task to that of archeologists, lawyers, and historians (Benjaminson and Anderson 1990). The work is painstaking, careful, logical, and complete. Good lawyers do it in preparing for trial, archeologists do it in examining the ruins of ancient civilizations, and historians do it in analyzing the past. Unlike most historians, however, investigative reporters do their work while the subjects of their research are still around to see the results. Although historians face problems of incomplete and lost records, current investigators must face outright hostility and obstruction. Generally, the corrupt do not fear the judgment of history as much as they fear exposure, prosecution, conviction, and disgrace. That is why they conceal their activities, and why reporters often must go to unusual lengths to uncover them. Investigative reporting, then, is simply the reporting of concealed information.

The reason investigative work is so painstaking is simple. If you make a mistake on the yardage of one pass during a football game, hardly anyone will notice. But if you make a mistake on a key question in an investigative story—for instance, whether a member of the athletic department's administration knew of a player's ineligibility to play in a big game—you leave yourself or the newspaper open to strong criticism, damaged credibility, and possible legal action in court.

The difficulties posed by an investigative story are not the only obstacle. Sociologist Michael Schudson (1978) suggests that there are barriers to investigative journalism within the newspaper itself. For one thing, investigative reporting is time-consuming and, therefore, money-consuming. One newspaper, for example, freed a member of its staff for three months for an investigative project that was never published. Not many newspapers can afford to do that. Schudson also points out that appointing investigative reporters establishes a staff elite potentially in conflict with the generally democratic newsroom. And the work is hard and seldom glamorous; thus, many investigative reporters eventually become disillusioned.

It is important that the right person be chosen for the job of investigative reporter. One editor listed the following characteristics he looks for in investigative reporters: "What you look for more than anything else is enthusiasm, willingness to work and work hard. Because that's what it really is: hard work. Interest. A desire to know something about everything and to be able to see a story. A real desire for accuracy. To be right and be first. Competitive spirit. Energy, a lot of energy. All these things" (Bolch and Miller 1978). Harry Rosenfeld, assistant managing editor of the *Washington Post,* outlined the reasons he chose Carl Bernstein for the Watergate story: "We made careful, meticulous assignments, calling first for personnel records and selecting those with skills to track down, while keeping mature perspective. We especially looked for persons who were error-proof. We laid it all out for them. We anticipated violent denials and assaults on our paper. In short, from beginning to end, we knew where we were at" (Behrens 1977).

Because an investigative story is in the sports rather than the political realm is no reason to make a less careful choice of investigative reporter. In fact, investigative stories within the sports pages have sometimes led to violent attacks and even death threats against the reporters and the newspaper. The depth of emotion that sports activity arouses in the public makes these stories all the more emotionally charged and controversial. Once the subject is selected, an investigative reporter is ready to tackle either a pre-existing story or to come up with a story that requires investigative reporting techniques. More often than not, the reporter is faced with a situation that already exists. Bolch and Miller (1978) point to seven possible sources of an investigative story:

1. *The beat.* This is the most usual place to find an idea for an investigative story. The reporter, during regular rounds, may be taken aside by a source and asked, "Did you hear about . . .?" One editor says having a beat is of inestimable value in producing such story ideas, adding, "You know the little cracks and corners and where the bodies are buried. You learn how to get the information you want" (Bolsch and Miller 1978).

2. *Tips.* Tips usually come from anonymous sources and usually by phone. Out of the clear blue, a reporter may get a call from someone with important information on a certain situation or person. It is important for reporters to remain patient on the telephone, not dismissing a caller because he or she isn't known or seems like a "crazy." Obviously, the tipster's story must be thoroughly checked out before it goes to print.

3. *Known tipsters.* Reporters may be given a tip from someone they know. Frequently, as Bolch and Miller (1978) point out, tipsters have a self-serving motive that must be kept in mind. But once understood, this motive does not necessarily lessen the value of their information. Just as government officials who are fired or eased out of office are frequently interviewed both on and off the record, so should be coaches, athletes, and other athletic officials in the same situation. For example, once a disenchanted key recruit leaves a team because he says he is not getting enough playing time, he is no longer influenced or intimidated by his coach. The player may talk candidly and honestly with a reporter about team problems.

4. *Intuition.* A veteran reporter is occasionally faced with a situation that doesn't *feel* right. Bolch and Miller (1978) cite the example of an investigative reporter who looked closely at federal grant programs because he found a good deal of them "a waste of money" and, in one such look, found illegal political patronage existed in filling staff positions.

5. *Patterns.* Reporters with experience on a beat will notice out-of-the-ordinary occurrences that are more than just coincidental. They will see patterns that emerge, such as a manager of ticket sales at a major university who favors certain groups or individuals when tickets arc in great demand but in short supply.

6. *Reporters' files.* Investigative stories can come from reporters' files put together years before. One reporter said, "I began building a file on money in politics back in 1963, way before it became a fashionable topic. I don't recall what triggered my idea that this might be a good topic, but I must have noted an odd contribution that shouldn't have been" (Bolch and Miller 1978). These files over the course of years are a potential basis for investigative stories.

7. *Stories leading to stories.* An investigative situation may actually spring from an innocuous routine story. Bolch and Miller (1978) give the example of a reporter who found it odd that a charity telethon raised only $700. Rather than follow it up, the reporter merely gave it a brief mention. Another reporter, more alert, began a probe that led to the removal of the charity's director and top officials.

8. *Public documents.* Sports operations leave the same sort of "paper trail" as other organizations. A sports investigative reporter will seek these public documents and use them as part of his or her search for information.

One model that illustrates the process behind an investigative story is offered by Paul Williams (1978). The first step, *conception,* includes many of the same sources we have already discussed, as well as reading (information taken from other newspapers and magazines), legwork (ideas gained from work outside the office), related angle (an idea developed while working on another story that is filed for future research), and new breaks or tips.

After conception comes the *feasibility* stage, in which the reporter checks out the problems and possibilities of the story idea. At this point, the reporter usually sends a memo to the editor describing the story's potential, the investigative assumptions and problems, the possible sources of information, the leverage and resources needed to see non-public records, and an assessment, if the story pertains to an individual, of the target's ability to resist investigation.

At the first *decision* stage, the paper's editor decides whether to undertake the project and defines the goals to be accomplished by running the story. The *planning and base-building* stage includes establishing files and forms to compile information and deciding on investigative activities such as checking records, interviews, processing data, reading references, and assigning special responsibilities. The *original research* stage involves the three major forms of research techniques—records, interviews, and observation. At the *re-evaluation* stage, the reporter and editors look at progress and decide whether to proceed with the investigation. If it is decided to proceed, it is time for the reporter to conduct the key interviews, trying to get answers to the central questions that have arisen. Then the reporter and editors again evaluate the information and decide whether to go on to the final stages, *writing and publication.*

Using Public Records

Sports organizations, like other organizations, keep records. They leave a "paper trail" or, these days, a "computer data base trail." If the organization is public, then the paper-computer trail is the sportswriter's to follow. The first commandment of investigative reporting is to get the records (Ullmann and Colbert 1991). A piece of paper from a government source may be "the smoking gun," as some put it; that is, the conclusive piece of evidence in an investigation. Or it can be the key to other information, the piece needed to convince editors to go on with an investigative story or series (Williams 1978).

There are three types of records: (1) records the law entitles the public to see, (2) records the law prohibits the public from seeing, and (3) records not mentioned by the law. Williams says good reporters do not admit the existence of the second category. As far as reporters are concerned, the only important distinctions among the three kinds of records involve the best methods to get them and the relative difficulty of doing so.

Recordkeeping is fairly standard from city to city, county to county, and state to state, but the laws governing access are dissimilar and change often. How can a reporter find out which records are public? Fellow reporters are a great asset to the novice investigative reporter. For example, if a reporter is seeking a city property tax form, a quick check with the city beat reporter can usually generate instructions on how to get the form.

Even when a certain record is public, a reporter may have a hard time getting a copy from a clerk. Many clerks guard their files zealously and may even challenge reporters to take them to court before removing a record from its proper file. It is important to know the prevailing state or federal records laws before you challenge for records. A different approach involves befriending the record-keeper. Being a friend rather than an enemy can expedite the research. A reporter on friendly terms with a clerk has a powerful ally in the use of records, the search for more records, and determining the existence of other forms of hard evidence.

Anatomy of
an Investigation:
Conducting Your Own

By Don Collins, *USA Today*

"Whatever you do, don't talk to reporters."

Atlanta Journal-Constitution reporter Chris Mortensen, laughing, said that was the admonition his lawyer gave him as they left the courtroom during the trial of sports agent Jim Abernethy.

Mortensen and *Newsday* reporter Danny Robbins spoke at a seminar at the APSE [Associated Press Sports Editors] convention, "The Anatomy of an Investigation."

The first half of the seminar dealt primarily with Mortensen's investigative work on sports agents. Robbins took the second day to explain how he reported a series of stories on basketball player Lloyd Daniels.

Mortensen and Robbins took the audience through case studies of each of their investigations, rather than deal with general principles of investigative reporting.

In his reporting on agents, Mortensen said he started after receiving a tip. Most of his reporting was done by phone. "I got great support from my editors," Mortensen said. "If I had to meet someone face-to-face, I was gone."

Mortensen's work aided in 11 states establishing legislation governing agents, and 11 more have pending legislation.

"I don't care if the reporting helped clean up the agent business," Mortensen said. "What I care is that we reported what was happening."

Tim Tucker, *Atlanta Journal-Constitution* executive sports editor, was involved with Mortensen on most of the editing on the series. He said: "We didn't set out to do a five-part series or to win awards. It was just a matter of following a news story."

Robbins encouraged reporters to work the edges of stories and use resources such as the legislative services of the NCAA.

SOURCE: Don Collins, "The anatomy of an investigation: How to conduct your own," in *1988 Associated Press Sports Editors Convention Report*, p. 7. Reprinted with the permission of Don Collins and APSE

There are many different types of records, including:

1. Voter records and driver's license and motor vehicle license records.
2. Records of vital statistics such as birth, death, marriage, and divorce.
3. Charity records (most states require annual reporting of income and expenditures).
4. Land ownership, property values, inspections, and land use records. Planned use of a particular property usually must be cleared through the local government, and the required forms may include a listing of company officials.
5. Papers of corporations. Groups that incorporate for any reason — for example, to purchase a professional team or raise money for youth boxing programs — usually must fill out state papers on which they list names and addresses of corporate officers.
6. Public purchasing records (these include bids).
7. Government hearings reports and records (these often include evidence presented in testimony).
8. Federal, state, and local taxation records (some sales and income tax records may be public).
9. Law enforcement and other criminal and civil court records at local, state, and federal levels.
10. Federal, state, and local license records.
11. Political candidate records such as campaign contributions.
12. Health care records of public agencies and hospitals.
13. Education spending and other administrative records.

Federal records may not be quite as accessible to a reporter, but that does not mean they are impossible to obtain. A phone call to the state bureau or office of the particular branch of federal government will usually determine whether a record is public, where it is filed, and how it can be obtained.

Using Personal Interviews

Once records are obtained (and this may take weeks in the case of federal forms), the information is synthesized and questions are then raised. The reporter working on the case decides who can best answer these questions and draws up lists of whom to talk to and what to ask. Interviews tend to fall into two categories, informational and confrontational.

The informational interview is usually conducted with a person who is not the actual target of the investigation but who can provide pertinent facts or leads. For example, a reporter checking out an organization formed to provide an inner city youth track program may find, from corporate papers filed annually for the three years of the corporation's existence, that the name of the officer who served as vice president for the first two years is missing on the third set of papers. The reporter could contact this person and ask for assistance in finding out what the group is up to.

The interviewing stage, more than any other stage, involves journalism ethics: how an interview is arranged, what basis is given for it, and how it is used. The reporter must decide how far he or she is willing to go in order to get an interview, asking, for example, "Will I lie to the source, claiming I am a member of a government office, to get an answer to a key question?" Once such questions are resolved, the reporter must make sure the interview is meaningful. Three keys to a good interview are preparation, control, and information (Williams 1978). A good reporter will have detailed knowledge not only of the story elements but also of the background of the source. Sometimes an interview can be helped by bluffing, or "verbal poker." A reporter after a certain fact can sometimes get an answer by acting as if the information is already known and confirmation is all that is necessary. Control can be maintained by being courteous and restrained even while asking pointed questions and by refusing to be disconcerted by counterquestions or challenges from the source. Listening is the best way to secure information, analyzing answers against previous information and asking follow-up questions for clarification.

The confrontational interview is sometimes called the key interview or target interview because it is conducted with the target(s) of the story. This interview has two purposes: to let the target comment on the information already collected and to obtain additional information.

It is frequently difficult to arrange this interview. The person being investigated has likely been tipped off that he or she is the target of a story with a possibly negative aspect. Although not knowing exactly what the reporter is searching for, he or she will have some idea about the information the reporter has already compiled. Just as reporters have tipsters, so do people being investigated. If initial efforts to reach the person do not succeed, a letter can be sent, even by registered mail, to make sure the target has an opportunity to get on the record. In fact, the most important argument in convincing the target to go ahead with the interview is: "I've already got statements saying you [did this and that]; don't you think your side of the story should be represented?" or "This story is going to run whether or not you contribute; shouldn't your side of the story be heard before it runs?" If the source still refuses, the efforts to contact him or her should be registered with the editor to prove that repeated interview attempts were unsuccessful. It is a good idea, for the reader's sake, to document these efforts by including them in the article. Once the target interview is arranged, many newspapers require two reporters at the interview to corroborate any statements. A tape recorder is a good tool in a solo interview, but some sources refuse to allow their use.

Some other tips for the target interview:

1. The reporter should look over all the notes and have files of information readily available to show to the target (but never take along the only copies of key information).

2. The reporter should open the conversation with courteous, brief, and general statements about the story and, avoiding accusatory comments, try to get the target talking about it.

3. When it comes to the tough questions, such as: "Have you indeed made illegal payments to athletes on scholarship?" the reporter must keep control. Any overly critical tone could end the interview. Questions should be asked clearly and the source allowed to respond.

4. If the conversation becomes too heated, the partner in the interview can interject a question or two, taking some of the pressure off the previous questioner. This is the "good cop/bad cop technique," one questioner pursuing a hard line, the other a softer one.

A team of writers for the *Los Angeles Times* recently used interviews as the primary method behind a two-week investigation into cheating on drug tests required for eligiblity by athletes at the University of Southern California. The newspaper interviewed more than 15 players; most would not permit their names to be used, but one who went "on the record" described ways athletes beat the testing program at the school over the previous six years. The story, which said football players "regularly cheated" by devising elaborate schemes to substitute urine and masking drugs, was initiated after former USC quarterback Todd Marinovich was arrested on charges of misdemeanor possession of cocaine. However, the school vigorously disputed the report, offering results of a four-week investigation that revealed no evidence of the cheating (Associated Press 1991). The full story, by *Times* staff writers Elliott Almond, Jerry Crowe, and Lonnie White and *Times* associate sports editor John Cherwa, is reprinted at the end of this chapter.

Writing the Story

The basic method of writing a good story, outlining for clarity, is even more necessary in writing investigative stories. A good outline, with major topics and subdivisions, will show whether the story will work the way it is envisioned.

Investigative stories, generally, are factual, and this listing of facts often makes a long and complicated piece. The newspaper may break up an investigative story into a series of stories that are run over a period of days. This not only makes more digestible stories but allows reaction to the initial stories to be run along with the later parts of the story.

Williams (1978) suggests answering the following basic questions before writing: (1) What is this story about? What am I trying to prove? (2) Who gives a damn? Where, among the many interests (taxpayer, union member, church deacon, business executive, parent) of my reading public, is the primary audience for my story? Why will my primary audience care? To which of their interests does the story appeal?

After outlining, the reporter should write down the main theme of the story. Because it is generally complicated, it should be kept free from extraneous material. The old rule of lecturing holds: Tell them what you're going to tell them, tell them, then tell them what you've told them.

Material needed to understand the story but which only complicates the lead-in can be held until later in the story or handled in a sidebar. If the story involves many people, a "who's who" sidebar box, with biographies and pictures of the central figures, would be appropriate, for example.

Once the main narrative is written, the reporter decides on the lead. There are several options: (1) a hard lead, in which, in a paragraph or two, the important information is summarized. The drawback is that in many instances, too much important information packed into a few paragraphs bogs down the story; (2) an anecdote lead, which relates to the reader; (3) a soft lead, which intrigues readers but gets into the main narrative much more slowly; (4) the bullet or dash lead, which allows many minor facts to be presented in readable fashion.

In an Associated Press Sports Editors annual writing contest evaluation by judges from the Associated Press Managing Editors, the best sports investigative reporting was cited because it provides readers a thesis, describes and maintains a sound reporting methodology, provides strong examples of the points being made, offers direct quotations to provide specific support from credible sources for generalizations made in the story, summarizes findings for readers in a box or itemized list within the story, and contains strong declarative writing with no waffling (Associated Press Sports Editors 1986).

Once the story is written, the editing process begins. Not only do sports department editors look at the story, but generally the managing editor and executive editor see it, and they may even turn it over to the company attorney for inspection. All material, therefore, should be kept in a good filing system so their questions can be answered immediately. Sometimes the very existence of the story depends on the reporter's being able to convince the editor that the information has been well substantiated. This task may be hard for someone from the sports department who has never been involved in an investigative piece, who comes from (as some editors perceive it) a "soft" news department.

Analysis of an Investigation

The following 2,800-word investigative story from the *Los Angeles Times* focuses on drug-test abuses in college football. The story shows the depth of description and research necessary in the two-week project involving four people. Three staff writers—Elliott Almond, Jerry Crowe, and Lonnie White—and associate sports editor John Cherwa produced the story about the newspaper's investigation. In reading the story below, note the method the reporters used in writing the story to back up generalizations. Note how the writers described procedures the athletes used to bypass the test and "mask" their illegal drug use, with specific steps described by identified sources. Also notice how the reporters got reactions from the University of Southern California, where the alleged abuses were found and note the amount of detail in the story. And finally, from a writing perspective, study the organizational plan of the story. As a long story, it poses particular problems. Subheads in the story solve many of them by dividing the article into sections.

SOURCE: *Los Angeles Times,* Home edition, page 1, part C
DATE: Sunday, February 3, 1991
AUTHORS: *Times* staff writers Elliott Almond, Jerry Crowe, and Lonnie White and *Times* associate sports editor John Cherwa
HEADLINE: Systematic Cheating on Drug Tests at USC; College athletics: McGee acknowledges the problem, says that task force will try to tighten enforcement

In the aftermath of quarterback Todd Marinovich's arrest for cocaine and marijuana possession, the *Times* has learned of a pattern in which some USC football players regularly cheated on their drug tests.

A two-week investigation has shown that some USC football players have learned how to get around drug testing by devising elaborate schemes to substitute "clean" urine for their own and also by using masking drugs.

Two days after Marinovich's Jan. 20 arrest in Newport Beach, USC took an official step toward addressing the problem. It formed a task force to investigate drug testing at the school. The group, chosen by Athletic Director Mike McGee, consists of Mike Garrett, Ron Orr and Barbara Thaxton, plus two others McGee declined to identify because they do not work for USC. Garrett is associate athletic director at USC, Orr assistant athletic director and Thaxton associate women's basketball coach.

The group, only getting started, has yet to offer any recommendations.

McGee, in an interview Friday, acknowledged that he was alerted to the problem more than a year ago but was unable to stop the practice.

"We heard in the fall of '89 that one of our athletes may have cheated on a test — not how it was done," McGee said. "At that point, we put into motion what we thought were some extra precautions that involved, in addition to a technician, a university administrator to be an observer."

Nevertheless, the word among USC football players is that the test can be beaten and that someone is always willing to teach how it is done. Interviews with more than 15 players indicate the following has happened with some regularity since the program was started in 1985:

— Urine believed to be "clean" is acquired from athletes and other students on campus.

— If little scrutiny is expected, the urine is brought to the testing area in a vial, bottle or package and simply poured into the testing cup when the observer isn't looking.

— If the player expects to be watched, a bladder pack filled with "clean" urine is strapped to a part of the body not visible, under an arm or under a shirt, for example, with a tube running to the pelvic area in order to simulate urination.

— The attention of testing officers is diverted by athletes, allowing other athletes to pour "clean" urine into the testing cup.

— A number of masking drugs, available at so-called "head shops" in Southern California, are purchased by athletes and these are taken with moderate success. "Head shops" are stores that sell, among other things, drug paraphernalia and non-prescription drugs allegedly to be used for health enhancement.

— If given 24 hours notice, athletes have consumed vinegar, cranberry juice and/or water in large quantities to flush illegal substances out of their systems.

Most athletes interviewed for this story would talk only on the condition their names not be used. An unwritten code of silence exists among USC football players since the Marinovich arrest. They fear being ostracized and fear having their name identified with drugs.

They also say that cheating on drug tests happens at every major university.

One player who was willing to address the subject on the record was Brandon Bowlin, a former USC defensive back.

"The situation was such that it seemed that they (tried to) catch those who they wanted to catch," Bowlin said, referring to the frequency with which some athletes were tested. "I didn't get tested all that often because I was a bit player. . . . But it was possible to get by on USC's drug test."

USC, among the first schools to institute drug testing, started testing all of its athletes in 1985. Initially, 10% of the athletes failed the test. USC says only 2% of the athletes now fail drug tests.

"Players get around drug testing all the time," said one former linebacker who has been out of USC's football program for two years. "(At USC) they were pretty flexible. They would watch you, but if you had the standard surgical tubing running down, you could fool them."

A former offensive player explained it this way: "(Players) would take someone else's . . . (urine) and have it in a bag that was taped to their back. They would then run an IV tube down between their legs. Then, they would have a clamp at the end that released the urine when you took it off . . . like you were really going to the bathroom."

Because there is no known study on beating drug tests, it is difficult to determine if this problem is unique to Southern California.

"There are a lot of drugs out there in Southern California," said one starter from last season's team. "I've been offered cocaine and marijuana a lot of times. People have come up to me at parties and just handed me a gram (of cocaine) for free. People want to give it to you and party with you because you're an athlete."

Another recent offensive starter said that USC testing procedures were so lax that it allowed cheating.

"Some of the guys knew how to beat the drug testing," he said. "They would take a small bag and put some clean (urine) in it and hold it under their arm. It didn't matter whose you had as long as it was clean. (USC) kind of slacked off in administering the test after a while, and the team knew it. The person who would be responsible for watching you would walk into the stall, but never knew if you cheated or not. I really don't think USC knew about this."

But, as McGee said Friday, USC was alerted to possible problems more than a year ago. Apparently, the problem was not easy to solve.

"What you had was a testing program that was run amok from the very beginning," said a drug-testing expert familiar with USC's program. "(USC) wouldn't follow scientific procedures. . . . The scientific collection aspects were not utilized in the testing program. I was never aware they did it in the appropriate manner. . . . (They) tried to do what was right, but they didn't have all the things at their disposal to make it work."

The recent events seem to have brought that point home to McGee.

"Maybe we don't have the latest understanding of techniques that might be used to cheat on tests," McGee said.

But McGee said if USC's program has deficiencies, so do others.

"You're saying our problems are in observation," he said. "My point is, we're not the only ones that have been fooled or not fooled." For instance, the NCAA was testing Trojan football players for postseason games.

"If I've said anything that makes you think we have all the answers, I'll be the first one to say we don't," McGee said. "But we are committed to a testing program. We think it has value."

Todd Marinovich

The rumors started about Todd Marinovich as soon as he arrived on campus in 1987, even though, at that time, he had never been arrested or charged with any drug-related offense. USC also says that Marinovich never failed a drug test.

But the rumors persisted and the athletic staff targeted him for the maximum number of tests — seven in the past year, four by USC and three by the NCAA.

McGee said there was one athlete on last season's football team who was tested seven times but would not identify him. "But he never complained about testing so much, even though he had recourse to appeal it," McGee said.

After Marinovich's arrest, USC officials privately said that he had been tested seven times.

Marinovich has maintained his innocence when it comes to drugs. Friday, during a telephone interview regarding his decision to apply for the National Football League draft, he said he has never taken drugs or cheated on a drug test.

But McGee acknowledged that Marinovich's arrest was the impetus to form the task force. That concern was echoed by Marvin Cobb, assistant athletic director and the administrator of USC's drug-testing program.

"After Todd's arrest, I received several phone calls from current and former student athletes," Cobb said. "They felt bad at what happened to Todd. And they felt guilty to a certain extent and wanted to make me aware of things that were going on at the point of collection by a small group of athletes.

"It actually fit with my suspicions. There were lots of rumors and there seemed to be cause to be suspicious."

Cobb said changes in testing are planned for next season and he hopes the Student Health Center will rejoin the testing process.

But currently, his concern is with Marinovich.

"I haven't had a chance to talk to Todd, but I feel it is really important to be honest with himself at this time," Cobb said. "And my prayers are that he does what is best for him."

Testing Problems

The USC athletic department took over responsibility of collecting urine samples in 1989, but the problems started well before then. Student Health Services was initially given the task of collecting samples, but it was far too understaffed to handle 50 football players at once.

Frequently, only two employees were there to administer the tests. A student trainer was assigned to complete the necessary paperwork.

"They were overrun," said the drug-testing expert familiar with USC's program. "They would take one (player) back to the bathroom (to be tested) and two or three others would show up in the bathroom and say they couldn't hold it anymore. . . . 'I've got to go now.' And so, the guys couldn't possibly watch all of them at the same time."

When the athletic department took over the testing, no one from American Chemical Laboratories of San Diego, which analyzed the tests, was asked to train the new collectors. USC's athletic department did not realize this service was available.

Nondice Ginpher, a technical manager of American Chemical, when asked to describe in general terms her company's program, said the firm trained all its clients in the proper procedure and how to catch cheaters. She suggests that the collector must watch the individual urinate in a cup. The cup is then sealed in front of the person and legal tape is placed over the cap. Ginpher said the laboratory will reject any sample with torn tape.

A chain of custody is established for each sample in which paperwork notes the date, time and place of collection. The paper is signed by the collector and the person who submits to the test. The sample is identified with a number. Only a designated person can match ID numbers with names.

Each person who handles the specimen during transport also must sign for it. The urine is stored in a locked facility at the laboratory.

Ginpher suggests that wash basins should be turned off so that no one has access to water to dilute samples. She cautions that even the most trustworthy person can be fooled.

"People have managed to bring into the restroom Clorox, rubbing alcohol and other masking agents," Ginpher said. "When it comes into the lab, we can smell it. Salt has been touted as a way to foil a drug test. I know on the market they sell herbs and compounds that will mask the presence of drugs in the urine. There is even clean urine for sale.

"That's one reason for observation. It is easy to smuggle urine and swap it out. There's always somebody who will try to beat the system. I don't think that much gets through, however. It boils down to you setting up the best collection system you're capable of and eventually you are having to trust somebody along the line to see that it is done right."

One Man's Dilemma

In the fall of 1989, USC's drug-testing program fell into the hands of Marvin Cobb, an assistant athletic director who once was a standout football and baseball player for the Trojans.

Drug testing was part of Cobb's responsibilities when he was hired in 1986 to replace Stan Morrison, the USC basketball coach and assistant athletic director who helped implement the program.

Players said that, at first, Cobb administered collection alone, but later was assisted by Ernie Bullard, USC's onetime track and field coach.

Although McGee says the administrators were qualified to handle the program, it was a difficult endeavor.

"If you could imagine 50 football players all anxious to use the bathroom and a full set of paperwork to be completed on each, you can see it is not a simple task, even for two people," Cobb said. "And if a student athlete is intent on not being caught, he can be very creative."

Even before Marinovich's arrest, Cobb said he had planned to change the collection procedure. Primarily, he was going to make sure that athletes were not hiding foreign urine.

He said that, in light of recent developments, even more changes are needed. For instance, he is recommending that the school use trained observers who will continually watch athletes deliver their specimens.

Despite deficiencies, Cobb wholeheartedly defends the program. He said it has benefited many more athletes than people realize.

"Probably one of the most difficult things that I did was help an athlete stop using crack cocaine," he said. "I've dealt with cases of athletes being compulsive gamblers, alcohol problems . . . with eating disorders."

Because he is on the front line, Cobb said athletes have sought his advice for myriad problems.

"Sometimes they self-disclose or come to tell me about a teammate, a roommate or even someone in their family. Just the existence of the program has helped a lot of student athletes maintain abstinence."

Once You're Caught

USC has an elaborate three-strike plan to deal with athletes who test positive. However, implementation of the plan was shaky at first.

One former offensive starter tested positive two times in a six-month period and received little or no counseling.

"Nothing was done and I'm not sure why," said the drug-testing expert close to USC's program. "They just didn't follow through. I know they confronted him over it and just told him not to do it again. That was it. Drugs just don't quit because you ask them to quit. You've got to have some type of intervention and structured counseling. There wasn't any."

That problem appears to have been corrected. The current plan is that when an athlete tests positive for drugs for the first time, he or she is suspended for one week and required to attend counseling sessions. That athlete also must submit to drug tests for the remainder of his or her college career.

Only USC administrators and the athlete are notified of the positive test. The athlete is not ostracized because the results are kept confidential.

"Just seems as though players wouldn't hear about it right away," said a former USC defensive back. "When someone was caught, it was up to the individual player to let everyone know."

The counseling for the athlete is a basic drug-awareness program, created to discourage any further drug use. The dangers of drug use are also discussed, usually one-on-one with a counselor.

When an athlete tests positive a second time, he is given a longer suspension and is required to attend even more counseling sessions. That athlete also might be required to take a weekly drug test, depending on the evaluation.

If an athlete tests positive for a third time, he or she is dismissed from school.

"The first year, we had three athletes (dismissed)," McGee said. "Two of them tested positive three times and one was charged with distribution of an illegal substance. The person is dismissed, just as if he tested positive.

"It was in the second year that the message was really understood and then we had small instances of positives. We even changed the level of testing. In year three, I think we relaxed a little. Halfway through the year, we started seeing some positives again. We started thinking about other things. We didn't hammer on drug use as much. We then made a conscious decision to redouble our efforts. We have seen some positives, but they are a fraction of that from the first year."

McGee said the cost of testing athletes is not a factor.

"I'm not saying we're perfect," McGee said. "That's one of the reasons we're going back to look at it."

The examination process will be painful and emphasizes McGee's dilemma.

"I don't want to catch them, but I do want to catch them," he said.

References

Almond, Elliott, et al. 1991. Systematic cheating on drug tests at USC. *Los Angeles Times,* February 3, Home ed., p. 1, Pt. C.

Associated Press. 1991. USC drug testing. Associated Press sports wire, February 4, n.p.

Associated Press Sports Editors. 1986. *APSE 1985 Contest Report.* Auburn, Ala.: Associated Press Sports Editors, 64.

———. 1991. Writing contest guidelines 1991. Associated Press sports wire, January 25. n.p.

Behrens, John C. 1977. *The Typewriter Guerrillas.* Chicago: Nelson-Hall.

Benjaminson, Peter, and David Anderson. 1990. *Investigative Reporting.* 2nd ed. Ames: Iowa State University Press.

Bolch, Judith, and Kay Miller. 1978. *Investigative and In-depth Reporting.* New York: Hastings House.

Collins, Don. 1988. The anatomy of an investigation: How to conduct your own. In *1988 APSE Convention Report.* Auburn, Ala.: Associated Press Sports Editors, 7.

Dennis, Everette E., and Arnold H. Ismach. 1981. *Reporting Processes and Practices: Newswriting for Today's Readers.* Belmont, Calif.: Wadsworth.

Dwyre, Bill. (1991). Telephone interview with executive sports editor, *Los Angeles Times,* March 25.

Editor & Publisher. 1985a. Wildcat boycott: "Boosters" of the University of Kentucky basketball team protest *Lexington Herald-Leader* expose on payoffs to players by alumni. 118 (November 9): 9, 38.

———. 1985b. Investigations should continue, editor says. *Editor & Publisher* 118 (June 8): 93.

Fitzgerald, Mark. 1985. Investigative reporting on sports: Is it a no-no? *Editor & Publisher* 118 (July 20): 16, 29.

———. 1987. More feuding in Dallas. *Editor & Publisher* 120 (March 14): 12.

Healy, Jerry. 1985. Blunder in Tucson: Sports editor and sportswriter resign after story containing incorrect information about coach is published. *Editor & Publisher* 118 (April 13): 13, 28.

Schudson, Michael. 1978. *Discovering the News: A Social History of American Newspapers.* New York: Basic.

Shaw, David. 1989a. Writers do little digging: Sports sections fumble many off-field stories. *Los Angeles Times,* June 24, 5–8.

———. 1989b. Taking sports seriously: It's over the fence, onto page 1. *Los Angeles Times,* June 23, 1–4.

———. 1989c. Ground-breaking coverage is sometimes suspect: The Rose affair: Testing new territory. *Los Angeles Times,* June 24, 30.

Ullmann, John, and Jan Colbert, eds. 1991. *The Reporter's Handbook: An Investigator's Guide to Documents and Techniques.* 2nd ed. New York: St. Martin's.

Williams, Paul N. 1978. *Investigative Reporting and Editing.* Englewood Cliffs, N.J.: Prentice-Hall.

11

Reporting the Business of Sports

The late George Halas may have been exaggerating when he said: "I was asked not so long ago if I were twenty-four now instead of sixty years ago, would I have my old eagerness to make a career in professional football. I said, as a player, yes. But as a coach, manager and owner, no. Football has largely turned from a personal sport into an impersonal business. The personal relations which meant so much to me are no longer so strong."

We say Halas may have been exaggerating because professional sports, by their very nature, have always been a business. The bottom line in professional sports, and increasingly in collegiate sports, is money. Halas' point, however, is well taken. The golden days Halas longed for are over, replaced by a world of computer spreadsheets, accountants, taxes, budgets, agents, and lawyers.

In the 1920s, when Halas founded the Chicago Bears and helped to form the National Football League, an entire team could be fielded — equipped and paid with a few thousand dollars (Halas 1979). But as sports grew in popularity, so did the dollars involved. Fueled by publicity from newspapers, sports began a healthy growth period. Radio broadcasts helped spread the word, and then came the golden goose, television.

Television's love affair with sports, especially major professional sports and college football and basketball, was the most important factor in creating a sports-oriented American society. Television, unlike newspapers or magazines, paid for the exclusive "rights" to broadcast the sports event and in turn passed on the cost to advertisers. Businesses that advertised found sports programs an effective way to sell their products to a target audience, particularly to males in the late 1940s and 1950s.

Broadcast rights started off small. Halas got only $900 per game in 1947 for his team's first television appearances. By the early 1990s, however, the Bears and other teams were receiving millions per season to be part of the NFL's lucrative league-wide television contract.

Television's millions descending upon sports had a great impact. Professional athletes, in particular, saw the large dollar amounts paid to owners for rights and decided they should share the wealth, something owners were reluctant to do. But the athletes had very little bargaining power because restrictions, called "reserve rules," kept the athletes tied to their teams for their entire careers, unless a trade occurred. This gave players little or no opportunity to realize their true worth, or market value, by offering their services to the highest bidder.

In the late 1960s, players began challenging these reserve rules by forming players' associations, or unions, to fight for their rights, by filing lawsuits in federal courts, and by hiring savvy agents and attorneys to help bargain over complicated contracts. By the 1980s, to even the most casual observer, professional sports appeared to be like any other business. The rights to broadcast professional sports continued to rise to staggering levels. For example, CBS-TV paid Major League Baseball a total of $1 billion for exclusive rights from 1990 through 1993 (Rodriguez 1990b).

Even amateur athletes are aware of how much money their talents can bring event organizers and sponsors. In 1990, the 1992 Summer Olympic Games organizing committee in Barcelona had sold television rights for a total of $610 million, or 50 percent more than all revenue that the 1988 Games earned for the organizing committee in Seoul. The American NBC television and radio network was committed to $401 million of that total, with the rest coming from other networks around the world. The price for these spectacular events keeps rising; the 1988 Winter Olympics television rights were sold in 1984 by the Calgary Olympic organizing committee for $309 million to ABC-TV. It cost ABC $91.5 million for the 1984 Winter Games in Sarajevo, Yugoslavia, and $225 million for the 1984 Summer Games in Los Angeles.

On the college level, meanwhile, the focus of money was not on individual athletes as much as on winning football and basketball programs that began to share in the same type of television rights wealth as their professional counterparts. Athletic departments learned that winners attracted fans and their dollars, which led to a race for top high school prospects to build their programs. In fact, this is not new. Football recruiting competition began in the 1920s, with the rivalry for Red Grange. Reporter Paul Gallico (1964) writes:

In their frantic attempts to acquire similar attractions [to Grange] the universities impale themselves front, back and sideways on the horns of the dilemma that had been created—how to coax, lure, rent, hire, or buy football stars who would be drawing cards, while at the same time managing to keep their fingers off the swag. During this process they fractured amateur codes into so many pieces that no one has yet been able to put them together again.

The pressure to win that was put on athletic directors and coaches by university administrations, fans, and alumni led to recruiting scandals such as payoffs and even academic transcript forgeries to keep players eligible. The dollar squeeze on athletic programs was increased in 1972 by the federal government's requirement for equal athletic programs for women (through Title IX).

The Big Business Revolution

The period of the late 1960s and early 1970s, more than any other, was the time of a sports business revolution. But in reality, it was more of an evolution, as the changes in sports began when the first athlete was paid to play a "game," and when the first fan paid to see the athlete.

The changing face of sports, both on professional and collegiate levels, posed a dilemma for modern sports journalists in the 1970s and 1980s. Should they continue to cover sports as in the past, emphasizing on-the-field events? Should they change the focus of coverage to include what happens off the field? The answer wasn't always an easy one.

Although many sportswriters had seen the importance of writing about philosophical, psychological, sociological, and legal aspects of the modern sports world, economic issues had largely been ignored. Many attempts to deal with business issues in those years were sketchy, factless, or emotional diatribes against the "foolish" sports owners who paid high salaries and the "greedy" athletes who collected them. Few publications tried to educate their readers about the history of sports from a business point of view. Sports journalists used the excuse that they were not capable of writing business stories, or that these stories did not belong on the sports pages. Many journalists and sports editors wished to ignore the business aspects, hoping, apparently, that they would just go away and quit spoiling the "game."

But the business of sports will never go away. Sports are big business. Sports on television and radio and in newspapers and magazines are even bigger business. And that holds true, not only for professional sports, but for big-time college programs with million-dollar budgets. Even some high school athletic programs have major budgets involving hundreds of thousands of dollars and dozens of full-time or part-time employees. And amateur sports are finding their way into the business world also. Amateur sports organizers, who long cried they were the victims of athletic poverty, have found ways to tap into another lucrative area of the sports business, that of sponsorships, in which corporations pay a fee for the right to associate their service or product with a sports team, league, or association.

The business of sports, no matter how sportswriters try to ignore it or wish it away, increasingly intrudes into the actual sports event, affecting the field. Unhappy players argue directly with managers about contracts in the dugout or in the locker room, sometimes in front of reporters or cameras. Players are traded from one team to another, and new players join a team after becoming free agents in order to boost clubs to playoff caliber. New teams and leagues are created for the sake of the dollar. In short, economics has become a significant part of sports. Sportswriters can no longer ignore economics and business any more than they can ignore win-loss records.

Origins of the Sports Business

There once was a period when sports was just a game, with athletes participating merely because of the enjoyment. But the time when sports were indeed "pure" didn't last long. City baseball teams were organized in America by the 1840s and 1850s, according to John Betts (1974). It took only until the late 1860s for the first professional teams to be formed and, by 1871, leagues of professional teams were organizing.

With the professional athlete came problems. Fixed games, wars between rival leagues, and player raids were common a century and a half ago. George Gipe (1978) says heavy betting on baseball was a habit in the 1850s, with one game in 1857 the object of so much betting that even the umpire had a few dollars on the outcome.

Sports began to grow rapidly after the Civil War. Many factors came into play. Before what Gipe calls the "revolutionary" period of growth in sports from 1870 to 1900, America was largely an agrarian country. During the industrial revolution, industry drew both European immigrants and farm workers to East Coast urban population centers. Elaborate factory machines evolving in the industrial revolution provided more leisure time to a productive working class. Railroad travel allowed professional and collegiate sports teams (and their fans) to travel from city to city. The telegraph allowed the results of sports events to be transmitted almost instantly. Newspapers and magazines, which had followed the attitude of upper-class America and looked down on sports activities, began paying more attention to readers' interests in sports activities and results.

Agrarian and religious anti-sport attitudes began easing, no longer restricting participation as either players or spectators. By 1900, Betts (1974) says, an athletic impulse swept over the country and became a permanent part of the social scene, winning the general approval of the American public. And the dollar figures involved in sports grew proportionately.

Printing presses did much to spread the word about sports in newspapers and special sports magazines, but nothing had an effect like radio and, later, television. Betts (1974) has assessed the impact of radio: "Radio came of age in the hectic 1920s, and sport was soon seized upon as an entertainment feature. Although the sports craze of those years was given its greatest encouragement by the metropolitan and local press, broadcasting for the first time brought the drama of ringside, diamond, and gridiron into homes from coast to coast." Radio not only provided publicity; stations and networks soon began seeking exclusive rights to broadcast events, paying teams and leagues for these rights with money from advertisers.

Bert Randolph Sugar (1978a), a former advertising executive, notes that the Gillette razor company turned to sports to help its struggling business in 1929. In 1935, Gillette, obviously satisfied with the relationship, sponsored its first boxing match. By 1939, one-fifth of Gillette's annual advertising budget of $203,000 was allocated for the acquisition of radio rights, air time, communication lines, and talent for its broadcast of the World Series between the New York Yankees and Cincinnati Reds.

But even with radio, the profits from ownership of a professional team and the financial rewards to winning college teams were minimal. Income was limited to gate receipts, concessions, and radio rights. All three revenue categories could be measured only in thousands of dollars. This determined who could be involved in a sports franchise. The owner of a professional team tended to be an upper-class businessman who looked on his involvement with sports as a civic venture, a hobby, or both.

When television money came into sports, the makeup of the professional owner and the college program changed. Corporate executives—like media conglomerate owner Ted Turner, shipbuilder George Steinbrenner, and pizza mogul Tom Monaghan—saw the potential in sports ownership. And although few professional sports owners actually expected to make or enhance their fortunes with their investments, there is little doubt that colleges saw the big dollars they could earn from sports like football and basketball.

Sports leagues found willing owners and undertook wholesale expansions. The 1960s, 1970s, and 1980s became an alphabet lovers' dream of new leagues and teams. When existing franchises or expansion franchises were not available, a businessman like Jack Kent Cooke set up his own league. The American Football League (AFL), created in the 1960s, and the United States Football League (USFL), created in the 1980s, challenged the established National Football League (NFL). The World Football League (WFL) existed in competition with the NFL briefly in the 1980s after the AFL merged with the NFL. The American Basketball Association (ABA) challenged the National Basketball Association (NBA), and the two eventually merged. The same process occurred when the established National

Hockey League (NHL) and World Hockey League (WHL) joined forces. Rival leagues created bidding wars over athletes, especially those just coming out of college who had yet to sign binding contracts with reserve clauses. The only leagues to survive were those able to secure television contracts to fund the rising salaries. The AFL survived intact to join the NFL, for example, largely on the abilities of New York Jets quarterback Joe Namath and the television contract that he attracted (Curran 1965).

While rookies and players who jumped leagues, ridding themselves of their reserve clauses temporarily, saw their salaries go up, the wealth was not being shared with players who were tied to their teams by long-term contracts. Eager to get what they felt was their fair share of an increasing broadcast rights pie, other players began organizing, seeking professional bargaining help and hiring union executives to form players' associations. Established players like St. Louis baseball star Curt Flood challenged the reserve rules, filing court suits to negate them. Still other athletes tried individual representation, hiring agents to negotiate their contracts. In 1966, for example, major league baseball players acted as a group to hire economist Marvin Miller to champion their cause.

Success was not immediate. Flood's fight to stop an involuntary trade from the St. Louis Cardinals to the Philadelphia Phillies in 1969 ended in a decision against him in U.S. Circuit Court. But others following Flood were successful, such as basketball player Oscar Robertson. Robertson's suit was settled out of court. It contended that the NBA's common draft, its option (or reserve) clause, and the then-proposed merger with the ABA violated antitrust laws. Robertson scored first in the case when he successfully obtained an injunction against the NBA-ABA merger, putting pressure on the owners to settle out of court because each day without a merger cost them in ever-increasing player salaries, especially for rookies. When an agreement with owners was finally reached, the way was cleared for collective bargaining among players that allowed the merger and ended what had been lucrative leverage used by some players to increase their salaries. A new player freedom clause came into existence that allowed players to become free agents after they had fulfilled their contractual obligations.

Other players, like pitcher Jim "Catfish" Hunter, sought other legal remedies. Hunter challenged his contract with Oakland A's owner Charlie Finley, charging that Finley had failed to live up to all obligations. Hunter invoked special arbitration, arranged in the previous bargaining agreement between owners and players; the decision in Hunter's favor shocked the owners. That allowed the star pitcher to offer his services to the highest bidder, the New York Yankees. A year later, two more pitchers, Andy Messersmith and Dave McNally, took their contracts to arbitration, declaring simply that the option clause was not valid. When the arbiters again agreed, baseball owners saw the handwriting on the wall—change the reserve system or face turmoil through its repeal in the courts and through arbitration.

In 1976, a four-year agreement was reached between players and owners, allowing for such things as free agency after a certain length of time in the major leagues, no option or reserve clauses in contracts, and for veteran players like Flood, the ability to turn down a trade if they did not like the team or location to which they were traded.

The 1980s were turbulant in terms of player-owner relations. It was, in reality, an era when sports and sportswriters began to realize they were covering labor-relations stories. Labor-relations news in sports? Labor-management issues? Unions? Those had been subjects for the business section. Now they were also sports stories. There were player strikes. Owner lockouts. A modified form of free agency, which still allowed players free agency but allowed teams losing free agents to receive some compensation from the clubs that signed the free agents, became standard practice, also. Professional basketball and football leagues also experienced a turnaround in the rights owners held over players. But in football, what many consider a weak players' union has not been able to wrestle the same rights as did baseball and basketball players.

College football, the first intercollegiate sport to become general public entertainment, underwent its own revolution in the 1960s and 1970s (see Rooney 1980). Some athletes criticized the autocratic approach to athletics at a time when they and their fellow students were protesting the war in Vietnam and demonstrating over civil rights issues. Several athletes and professors, including Jack Scott, Dave Meggysey, George Sauer, and Chip Oliver, wrote stinging critical works about college football and other sports (Spears and Swanson 1978).

The Mid-1990s Sports Business

On almost every level, sports is a business. Professional team owners and college athletic directors have complex budgets, lawyers, marketing and advertising strategists, accountants, insurance experts, and professionally trained staffs. With tax write-off advantages, which owners used to help their own financial situations diminished by court rulings, professional sports must make a profit or, like any other business, perish. Professional athletes collect salaries not only in cash, but in deferred, tax-free payoffs, loans, large insurance policies, and other fringe benefits; players' associations bargain for disability pay and retirement benefits.

Millions of people attend professional and college sports events, while millions more read newspaper sports sections, listen to radio broadcasts, and watch televised accounts of sports events. The money generated has required that sports activities be managed more and more like major businesses, all the while retaining their peculiarities such as government protection for what many believe is monopolistic behavior that would not be tolerated in other business areas. This, to some degree, sustains the myth that these activities are only "games."

Table 11.1 shows the tremendous size of television sports audiences. Professional and major college football, the Olympics, professional and major college basketball, Major League Baseball, and auto racing draw millions of viewers in addition to the large numbers in attendance each year. These numbers are likely to be staggering to the casual observer and point to the necessity of considering the big business nature of sports, especially those with large television appeal.

Table 11.1.   1988 Sports Events Ranking (average audience size)

	Men 18+ years		Women 18+ years	
	Rank	Avg. Aud.	Rank	Avg. Aud.
		(000s)		*(000s)*
NFL football	1	11,110	3	6,330
Olympics, Winter	2	8,690	1	10,640
Major League Baseball	3	6,620	4	4,570
Olympics, Summer	4	6,410	2	7,020
NBA basketball	5	5,790	5	3,330
College football	6	5,040	6	3,020
NCAA basketball	7	3,790	10	2,170
Auto racing	8	2,710	13	1,660
Multi-sports series	9	2,490	11	2,000
Golf	10	2,260	12	1,660
Horse racing	11	2,170	7	2,320
Bowling	12	2,140	9	2,190
Other sports events	12	2,140	8	2,240

SOURCE: *Nielsen Television Index (NTI) 1988–89 Sports Report,* Nielsen Media News, Nielsen Media Research, Northbrook, Ill., July 1989, p. 3.
Reprinted with the permission of Nielsen Media Research

PROFESSIONAL SPORTS. The changes in the world of sports in the 1970s often led to confused, even angry, sports reporting, filled with generalities, and, in many cases, stories of doom that suggested advancements such as free agency would lead to the economic destruction of sports. It never happened. The generalities are being replaced by the realities of sports:

Sports is a business. Often, business decisions have a marked effect on the field or court. The trade of professional basketball player Ricky Pierce by the Milwaukee Bucks to the Seattle Supersonics in 1991 for Dale Ellis is an example. Pierce, considered one of the best sixth men in the National Basketball Association, had a contract dispute with his team in the middle of the season. The Bucks, despite their appreciation of Pierce's contribution, traded the popular player, rather than renegotiate his contract. That's the sports business.

Professional athletes are not overpaid. It was commonly written in the

BASEBALL SALARIES GOING, GOING . . .

The average salary of a major-league baseball player in 1991 was $851,492, a 42.5 percent increase from 1990.

*In thousands

Year	Salary
1970	29,303
1975	44,676
1980	143,756
1985	371,571
1990	597,537
1991	851,492

NOTE: Average salary as compiled by the Major League Baseball Players Association. Beginning in 1979, salary deferrals without interest are discounted at 9 percent per year.
    Beginning in 1987, signing bonus are increased at 9 percent per year.

SOURCE: AP

HIRAM HENRIQUEZ / Miami Herald Staff

Huge player salaries are one reason that sports today cannot escape being a business (Reprinted with the permission of the *Miami Herald*).

1970s and 1980s that athletes were not worth the large amounts of money they were receiving. Critics contended they were overpaid. This is simply not true. Athletes are worth whatever they are paid because, in simple terms, they are getting it. The "worth" of an athlete's paycheck has nothing to do with the importance of an athlete's place in general society. But the free agency system is a voluntary one. The Boston owner who agreed to pay pitcher Roger Clemens approximately $5.38 million ($21.5 million over four years) or the Oakland owner who paid José Canseco $4.70 million in 1991 obviously felt that the stars were worth it.

Professional owners are not unwise to pay big salaries. The corollary to the misapprehension about too-high salaries is that owners are thought stupid for paying high salaries. The owners who paid Roger Clemens, Michael Jordan, and José Canseco see, in fact, a double value in big-money athletes. Not only can they help their teams to better win-loss records (and winning teams draw much better than losers), but they are individual attractions bringing fans to games by their presence. This occurs, for example, in every arena where Jordan plays in the NBA.

Athletes are no longer worth their salaries when they no longer draw fans or help their teams win. There are, indeed, cases in which a professional athlete, near the end of a career, is given a contract for a large salary and does not earn it. But owners, like all businesspeople, sometimes make mistakes, and injuries or other unforeseen circumstances can also cut short an athlete's career.

Ticket prices are not determined by player salaries. As in many other entertainment activities, sports tickets are generally priced by market demand. If an owner feels the most a ticket will sell for is $15, that's what it will be priced. If there is a high demand for tickets and market research shows ticket prices could be raised to $19 without hurting the gate, the owner may raise the price, regardless of the team's salary situation or any other expense factor. Many people have pointed to contracts of expensive free agents as the cause of subsequent increases in ticket prices, assuming cause and effect, but the two events seldom have a direct relationship. For example, a big-money player may raise a team's salary level by $1 million, while a ticket price increase may bring in twice that amount. The reason a ticket price increase may follow a free agent signing is simply that the team is more attractive with the big-money player and owners are guessing that fans will be willing to pay more to see the team. Winning teams are also more likely to raise ticket prices, as demand on their tickets allow for higher priced tickets than losing teams.

Some college athletes are professionals-in-waiting. This is especially true in basketball and football, which have no true minor leagues like those in baseball. Few professional-to-be athletes in these sports come out of schools with bachelor's degrees, partly because they find it nearly impossible to finish school within four years, but also because they hope to go into professional sports as a career. Prep athletes, who understand this system, add to the rich-get-richer sequence of college athletics by heading to schools with records of producing athletes chosen by professional teams.

COLLEGE SPORTS. College programs, too, succeed or fail because of the bottom line. They are ultimately judged by their bottom line as well. A report on the financing of college athletics (Atwell et al. 1980) said: "The pressure is considerable on college and university chief executive officers in these institutions to produce winning teams. Winning not only enhances public relations, but is also often necessary to produce gate receipts that account for more than half of the income needed to support the athletic programs of the 180 institutions that participate in NCAA Division I football." The pressure to produce a winner on the college level has led to a well-documented series of college recruiting violations in enticing high school talent. Morgan Wooten, coach of the top boys high school basketball program at Washington (D.C.) DeMatha High School, says a recruiter once offered him $5,000 to persuade two of his players to attend a certain college (Wooten and Gilbert 1979).

What are the rewards for college sports? A good example of what winning produces is recent fees paid by television networks to college football. In 1990, the ABC television network sports division and cable network ESPN paid the College Football Association, made up of many of the nation's top conferences and teams, a total of $300 million for the rights to televise games from 1991 to 1995 (Rodriguez 1990a). Weeks later, the University of Notre Dame signed its own television deal with NBC for a reported $30-plus million for the same time period (Rodriguez 1990a).

HIGH SCHOOL AND AMATEUR SPORTS. Nothing, including sports, is immune to inflation when it hits the nation's economy. High school athletic programs found this out the hard way in the late 1970s and early 1980s. Increased costs occurred in areas such as travel, with rising fuel costs; insurance, with the increase in lawsuits; and labor, with increasing coaching salaries and benefits. These changes forced many programs to trim costs, or in a number of cases, drop some sports.

Big sports money occasionally flows down to the high school and other amateur levels. The Kinney Shoe Company, for example, has been a sponsor of state and national cross country championships, bringing together the top high school runners in the United States. The increased appetite of nationally televised cable sports networks led to many high school games being broadcast throughout the country, and even to so-called minor amateur sports, such as soccer, negotiating multi-year contracts with cable networks.

Researching the Sports Business Story

PROFESSIONAL SPORTS. Whom can a reporter trust for reliable sports business information? It is important to remember that a sports business story must be treated like a business story. Reporters covering a factory employee strike would not think of covering it by talking only to management representatives, for example. Full coverage requires listening to all sides of the story. The same holds true for honest, balanced coverage of sports business stories. An article including comments only from ownership (owners, league officials hired by owners, general managers) and other club officials (such as coaches and their staffs) on a business-related issue is just part of the story. Another side—the active and former players, players' association spokespersons, and agents—must be contacted for comment. Almost any issue regarding sports economics or business will elicit differing opinions from ownership and players. Experts can be used by either side in a dispute and can be quoted in articles. These experts might include neutral university-level business or law professors who specialize in labor, occasionally sports labor, issues. Sportswriters should also ask neutral experts to discuss and interpret the issues. Many colleges publish a list of faculty specialties. Contact your local school's public relations office for help.

Writing about sports business, especially on the professional level, is no simple matter, even when sides are clearly delineated. Traditionally, ownership has gotten the better deal from the news media because it has been easier for sportswriters to side with the "establishment." But with only a few exceptions, professional sports teams are private companies not required to file annual reports or to make public other revealing business information. On the one hand, owners and front-office managers may complain about poor coverage of their side of business issues. On the other hand, most team officials are unwilling to provide factual information, including their financial accounting books, to reporters.

Reporters covering a business sports story may have to become detectives, turning to any available avenue of information. Several professional sports teams are publicly owned. The Green Bay Packers, for example, are publicly held and as such are required by local, state, and federal governments to file certain business documents that are in the public domain. Many teams play in leased public facilities and must comply with some local, state, and federal government disclosure statements. Reporters can get a general idea of revenue amounts through public reports. Included are gate receipts and other income producers, like radio and television rights. Some expenses, including player salaries, can also be deduced from published sources.

More and more books give glimpses into the business side of sports. For example, the late Chicago Bears owner George Halas' (1979) autobiography gives a fascinating look at an early professional football team budget. Skimming other sports books, including histories, biographies, and collections of sports stories and sports columns, can yield nuggets of information about the sports business (Durso 1971, Johnson 1971, Auf der Maur 1976, Sugar 1978b).

It would also be wise to study sports management and sports administration. Academic programs on these subjects have begun at universities and colleges, such as Ohio University, and materials prepared for use in course work may prove valuable for a reporter. Textbooks give outlines of the makeup of sports teams, both on the professional and college levels, looking at budget and finance. They discuss revenue items such as advertising sales, ticket sales, concessions, and other game revenues and public relations, as well as the use of computers in sports administration.

The late 1980s and early 1990s have brought the business side of sports to the forefront in magazines and specialized sports newspapers. Even a

More and more women, such as the NBA Miami Heat Vice President Pauline Winick, have become executives and take important roles in the management of sports teams. (*Photo by C. W. Griffin, the* Miami Herald.)

publication devoted to the business side of sports at all levels, *Sports Inc.,* was produced briefly. Other magazines or specialized newspapers can prove beneficial to reporters seeking business coverage hints. These include *Sports Illustrated* and *The Sporting News.* Non-sports publications can often be helpful. *Broadcasting* gives reporters a good idea of the money involved in television and radio rights. *Advertising Age* spells out the dollars involved in the ties between sports and the advertising world. Business magazines, such as *Fortune, Forbes,* and *BusinessWeek*, touch on sports business issues at times and can contain story ideas and comments.

Court records and government hearing records may prove to be other reliable sources of information. Books and newspaper and magazine articles can be based on misinformation and hearsay, but court cases involve legal documents and sworn testimony. Information from government hearings can also be relied on, as sports representatives seldom mislead the government by providing false information, for fear of later interference or regulation. In 1976, for example, the U.S. House of Representatives held hearings on professional sports that, while not resulting directly in legislation, generated a three-volume record of testimony of owners, athletes, and experts familiar with the inner workings of the sports business (U.S. Congress 1977).

Players' associations frequently print newsletters to keep their members informed about the workings of the organization, and many will include newspapers on their mailing lists. Former athletes who become player agents after their playing days are finished can prove helpful in providing multiple perspectives for economics stories.

COLLEGE SPORTS. Concern for the size of college sports, with the resulting professionalism, is nothing new. In 1905, President Theodore Roosevelt, concerned about a win-at-all-costs philosophy and brutality that he felt were increasingly infecting college football, convened a conference and told colleges to take action or he would put an end to the whole enterprise. This meeting led to the formation of the National Collegiate Athletic Association (NCAA), which governs most of college athletics. There are several other administrative bodies that schools can now join. Many small colleges belong to the National Association of Intercollegiate Athletics (NAIA), and junior and community colleges belong to the National Junior College Athletic Association (NJCAA) (Hanford 1979).

Despite these organizational efforts, the financial entanglements get more and more complex. And the dollars have become bigger and bigger. The College Football Association's $300 million deal with ABC and ESPN and Notre Dame's reported $30-plus million deal with NBC illustrate this point.

Several determinations must be made before attempting sports business stories on the college level: Is the school public or private in nature?

What is the level of the institution? What is the source of funding for the sports program?

Public versus Private Status. The ownership status of a sports organization makes a significant difference in a sportswriter's access to information. Public sports organizations are common at the university and high school levels but are rare at professional and other amateur levels. Public organizations are publicly owned. State or local schools are literally owned by taxpayers — the public. Some "publicly owned" professional teams are actually owned by stockholders who purchased shares of ownership on the open market. These teams, and amateur teams from public institutions such as schools, must file documents that are public property and therefore are available to the public for review. Private institutions such as most professional teams and some schools are operated as businesses and are not likely to voluntarily release financial information unless required by law. The difference is often frustrating for sportswriters seeking information.

Type and Level. Each of the three major college governing bodies, NCAA, NAIA, and NJCAA, differentiates among levels of athletic competition. Generally, the levels, or divisions, are labeled by Roman numerals (I, II, III), with level I the highest. Division I usually includes schools considered major colleges, with programs that recruit nationally, provide scholarships, and have full-time paid coaching staffs, travel budgets, and usually high-caliber facilities. Division II schools typically commit less to their programs financially, restricting travel to a regional basis and giving limited, or no, scholarship help. Division III schools usually do not give any athletic scholarships. The situation is a bit more complicated in college football, where the NCAA differentiates between two levels in Division I, calling the biggest schools — including those such as Miami, Notre Dame, Oklahoma, and Colorado — Division I-A, and others — such as Alabama State, Eastern Illinois, and Yale — Division I-AA.

Most of the abuses in the collegiate athletic system have been at the Division I level, where television money and large crowds are involved. A study by the American Council on Education (ACE) of the intercollegiate athletic system classified programs and came up with six categories (Atwell et al. 1980). Although not a formal system, these categories provide a way of looking at college athletics that can be helpful to a reporter.

1. Semiprofessional. About 260 institutions were classified in this category. They hold membership in Division I and are distinguished by highly competitive football and basketball programs that are expected to produce substantial gate receipts.

2. Ivy League. Only eight universities belong to the Ivy League. The principal distinguishing characteristics of these schools is that they do not

award athletic scholarships but still maintain a competitiveness that is at a higher level than most of the remaining kinds of institutions.

3. Small colleges. At least 250 institutions fall into this classification. Their athletic programs have similarities with other models. Most are private, liberal arts schools with athletic budgets not exceeding $150,000.

4. Mixed. At least 250 institutions are classified in this category. Their athletic programs have some characteristics of the semiprofessional program, but they have significantly lower recruiting budgets and small athletic staffs. Unlike other small colleges, they do offer aid based solely on athletic ability and do generate some income and aspire to be nationally competitive in one or two sports.

5. Historically black. Almost all the 100-plus predominantly, or historically, black colleges and universities offer athletic programs of various types that correspond to other models. Because of the history and unique financial problems of black higher education in America, the status and function are treated separately by ACE.

6. Community colleges. About 700 two-year institutions participated in intercollegiate athletics at the time of the survey.

The positive view of the semiprofessional programs has seldom been emphasized. Instead, these athletic programs have received unbridled criticism, from both within and outside the academic community. Solving the financial and ethical problems of semiprofessional intercollegiate athletic programs depends on the ability of the higher education community to understand the commercial role and the positive function of these programs as they relate to institutional goals.

Funding College Programs. The source of funding is also critical. As with professional teams, private colleges are not likely to make their ledgers available to supporters, while publicly funded ones are usually required to keep theirs open for public accountability. There are three major sources of income to a college sports program:

1. Gate receipts and television. These two areas combine for the largest revenue sources. Football is usually the income leader, with basketball second. Money generated in these sports would, at a major college, support most of the rest of the athletic program.

2. Private giving and fund raising. In 1980, the ACE study considered this the most probable new source of athletic revenue, for although many schools have actively tried to increase gate receipts, there is a natural market limit on the price of a ticket. Most major universities have set up scholarship funds and booster clubs to raise donations from corporations and private donors. At the University of Miami, for example, the "Hurricane Club" was listed as the second-leading source of athletic revenue. The major source was gate receipts (37.3 percent), with the club second (17.3 percent), and television and radio rights third (15.2 percent).

3. Student activity fees and public funds. Many universities assign a portion of each student's activity fee to the athletic programs. This has led to some protests because students not involved in athletics criticize the mandatory use of their non-tuition fees for sports.

Table 11.2 displays the approximate costs in a recent fiscal year of one school that plays NCAA Division I-A football. The table compares the current budget to the costs if the number of players was reduced by returning to single-platoon play. The savings would be almost one-fourth of the budget.

Table 11.2.   Cutting Athletics Costs

Budget line item	Current	One platoon
Salaries/wages[1]	$1,301,750	$ 930,000
Scholarships	1,010,480	753,000
Physical plant costs	720,000	720,000
Distributed expenses[2]	710,000	555,000
Overhead[3]	483,000	375,000
Team clothing/uniforms	260,000	150,000
Team travel/autos/lodging	210,000	170,000
Game operation	200,000	200,000
Recruiting expenses	200,000	160,000
Training ex./room/board	200,000	125,000
Individual/general travel	110,000	50,000
Telephone	100,000	70,000
Printing/publishing	90,000	90,000
Team supplies/misc.	70,000	40,000
Officials' fees/travel costs	50,000	50,000
Repairs/maintenance	50,000	30,000
Training/medical supplies	45,000	30,000
Advertising	40,000	40,000
Hospital/medical supplies	40,000	30,000
Coaches' clothing/supplies	35,000	20,000
Mailing/postage/shipping	30,000	25,000
Drug testing	20,000	15,000
Insurance	20,000	15,000
Office supplies	20,000	10,000
Office equipment/furniture	20,000	10,000
Film/photography	15,000	15,000
Rented equipment	11,000	5,000
Individual consulting	10,000	10,000
Programs	10,000	10,000
Other equipment	10,000	5,000
Auto repairs	5,000	3,000
Dues/membership	2,000	2,000
Special stadium repairs	2,000	2,000
Total	$6,100,230	$4,710,000

SOURCE: Douglas S. Looney, "One Is More Like It." *Sports Illustrated* 73 (September 1990):35.
   One big-time athletic director calculates that one-platoon football would enable his school's program to cut its annual budget by 23 percent. The figures assume 60 scholarship players, compared with 95 permitted in 1990.
   [1] Projected staff cuts would leave five assistants instead of the current nine.
   [2] General athletic department expenses, such as tickets and public relations, that are charged to football.
   [3] Special "auxiliary enterprise" fee owed to the university by football.

HIGH SCHOOL SPORTS. With much less revenue available, high school programs are not often equated with sports business stories. However, many of the same pressures to win that college coaches have felt have led to "recruiting" scandals on the interscholastic level as well. And rising costs, particularly of liability insurance, have led to many high school programs being trimmed or dropped.

Most high school athletic programs are governed by one or more regulatory bodies on a statewide level. Again, schools may be divided into categories, usually reflecting school attendance or public-private status.

AMATEUR SPORTS. The term "amateur" once meant an athlete who participates in a sport without compensation, but today's amateur athletics movement is hardly without intrusion from the business of sports. The father of the modern Olympics in the late 1800s, Pierre de Coubertin, asked that the Games be staged in as Spartan a manner as possible and that only true amateurs be allowed to participate. But this Olympic ideal caused problems. What is amateur? How much assistance should an athlete receive? The controversies began quickly but have yet to be completely resolved nearly a century later (Killanin and Rodda 1976).

The opportunity to host the Olympic Games has become a multimillion dollar quest. But the rewards, as proved by the 1984 Summer Games in Los Angeles, can he worth the price. The Games cost the city of Los Angeles organizing committee $545 million but brought in an excess of $223 million over expenses and had a $3.29 billion economic effect on Southern California. Officials in the city of Atlanta had similar expectations as they promoted the 1996 Summer Games as much as five years before the opening ceremony was scheduled to take place.

The Olympic Games have become financially stable for the same reason that professional and major college sports have found economic success: television rights. In 1960, CBS paid just $50,000 for the rights to broadcast the Winter Olympics from Squaw Valley, Calif. The same network paid $300 million for the rights to the 1994 Winter Games in Lillehammer, Norway. Meanwhile, the Summer Games have also escalated rapidly. Rights to the Summer Games in Rome in 1960 brought $394,000. The 1992 Summer Games in Barcelona, Spain, meanwhile, have brought $401 million from NBC, but much more from the world's television networks.

In order to accommodate television and corporate sponsors, the most fundamental change in Olympic history was announced in 1986. The International Olympic Committee voted to change the cycle of the Games after 1992. The Winter and Summer Games would be two years apart rather than in the same year. Another Olympics issue that has changed drastically because of economic factors is that of athletic eligibility. The 1980s, again, brought the most sweeping changes, as it became possible for athletes to receive money to train and still retain their amateur eligibility, and for athletes designated as professionals to compete along with non-professionals in some sports, such as basketball.

Sports Business Story Ideas

Once a sportswriter has developed background on the issues, story possibilities should become apparent. There are more and more possible story ideas for reporters wishing to include the sports business in beat coverage or in feature coverage of a sport. In a general way, a newspaper might simply background a particular sport's amateur roots and how it has developed. Or stories could be written on the role of radio and television in the current sports world, or on the role of newspapers themselves in the growth of professional and college sports.

PROFESSIONAL SPORTS. The role of agents could be explored, looking at how athletes choose them and how they perform their duties. Players' associations, once a staple of the daily sports page, have receded to the background again. How have they changed from the "revolutionary" days of the 1970s? Are they more or less effective than in that time? Ownership in sports is an area providing many story opportunities. Why are owners involved with sports? What do they get out of it? What is the source of investment money? What are the personal and/or business satisfactions of ownership? Tax breaks for sports owners and athletes, as well as government subsidies of sports through the building of stadiums and arenas, are areas of potential exploration. Studies of lease arrangements between team owners or event managers and local governments are another potential area.

COLLEGE SPORTS. Even more questions need to be answered on the college level than the professional level, which has had keener attention from the press: How are college programs funded? Should students, with their student fees, generate the money whether they participate in athletics or not? Should, as one series of stories suggested, college football and basketball coaches make a higher salary than the institution's president? Other potential stories involve the role of the student athlete: How many actually get a degree? Should college athletes "share in the wealth" and be paid for the revenue their talents bring to the institution? College booster clubs and their roles are also at the center of potential stories.

HIGH SCHOOL AND AMATEUR SPORTS. It is difficult to make generalizations about high school sports because of the different means of organizing programs. But most are funded from local taxes. Finances are seldom an issue in high school programs, except when school districts run into economic problems and extracurricular activities are trimmed or sometimes even dropped.

How "amateur" are today's amateur sports? What do the new, more liberal policies mean to the Olympics athlete? What do companies feel they are getting for their sponsorship associations with the Olympics?

Who Does the Sports Business Story?

Traditionally, the true sports business story or series of stories has largely been ignored, especially on small newspapers. But ignoring the sports business story is, in effect, ignoring reality and cheating readers of the true story of what may indeed be shaping the on-the-field results. The newspaper that decides to tackle business issues has several alternatives for coverage: allowing sports department staff to handle the stories, assigning staff of the business or other news sections to handle the stories, or combining personnel from more than one department. The last alternative is often the best. In most sports departments, few reporters are trained to handle a business story. This lack of background in business areas may handicap them when they are first attempting business stories. And business reporters, who are better equipped to undertake such stories, do not have sports reporters' contacts. Sports reporters seeking information through court records or other government sources should not be afraid to enlist the help of reporters on those beats as well.

Who in the sports department should handle the business story? Newspaper sports staffs are usually too small for one person to devote full-time effort to business stories, so the story ideas must be assigned according to beat load. Sports reporters also find advantages in teaming up on assignments. Sometimes, however, the sports beat reporter may find that the business story, something many sports sources are not used to, may cause problems in their ability to cover their beat throughout the year. Then, possibly, a reporter from another beat could be assigned to the story, using the contacts of the regular beat reporter.

Writing the Story

Writing the story is a tough assignment for most sportswriters. Most will feel a certain amount of uncertainty because of a lack of familiarity with terms, information, and sources who know a great deal more about the subject. But, if taken a step at a time, reporting a story about the business side of sports will get done.

Joe Strauss, a sportswriter for the *Atlanta Journal* and *Atlanta Constitution,* demonstrated that the story can be done effectively if it is written for readers who do not have a strong knowledge of business practices. Strauss, who covered the Braves for two seasons for the Atlanta newspapers before transferring to a national sports beat, took on the responsibility for his readers of translating complicated business issues and making them understandable when he wrote a story about the Atlanta Braves' financial concerns for the 1991 season before the season even started.

As the team was reporting for spring training in Florida, Strauss was meeting with Braves officials to gather financial information about the team for Atlanta area fans. His story, which points to the large expenses the team has encountered in a number of areas, tells readers that the Braves will lose money during 1991 even if the team has a successful season on the playing field (which they did).

Strauss' story, below, employs high-caliber sources. He interviewed baseball commissioner Fay Vincent. He talked at length with Braves president Stan Kasten. He interviewed the players' association experts about the effect of high salaries that placed the Braves in a category of losing on the bottom line even if they won on the field. And, of course, he interviewed the team's front office general manager. Note the choice of language in the story: There is very little spreadsheet terminology understood only by accountants. There are no four-syllable MBA-level explanations. The story explains the situation in simple dollars and cents. exploring what this means and how it might be remedied. To further help readers understand the situation, the story also included a full-color graphic consisting of two multicolored pie-shaped graphs. These graphs showed the proportions of income and expenditures anticipated for the 1991 season and fiscal year.

SOURCE: The *Atlanta Journal/Atlanta Constitution,* final edition, pages
            D1, D6
DATE: Sunday, March 10, 1991
AUTHOR: Joe Strauss, staff writer
HEADLINE: Even if the Braves win, they're certain to lose; Club's on-field
            optimism contrasts with estimate of $4 million loss in '91

It will be some time before the Atlanta Braves know whether their $30.1 million off-season investment in the free agent market will pay off on the field, but already the acquisitions of Sid Bream, Terry Pendleton and five others have helped draw the Braves even with the three-time defending American League champions in one category:

Both clubs figure to lose about $4 million this season.

The A's have projected a $2 million-to-$5 million loss, despite their expections that they'll duplicate last season's attendance of 2,900,217, third in baseball to the Toronto Blue Jays and Los Angeles Dodgers. The main culprit is a payroll in excess of $40 million.

Figures obtained from Braves and baseball industry sources indicate that the Braves' losses will approach or exceed $4 million. The main culprits are a payroll that projects to be doubled from last year—from $11.2 million to about $22.7 million—plus attendance that hasn't toppled one million since 1987.

"I'm sure that we can show [a profit], but if a club drawing 2.9 million is going to lose money, what are you going to do? What does that say about the industry?" said Braves president Stan Kasten.

What it says is this: Salaries skyrocketing because of free agency have made the business of baseball a losing proposition for at least half the industry, particularly clubs in smaller media markets. The Braves are one of a dozen or more teams that commissioner Fay Vincent projects to lose money this year.

"I'm concerned about Atlanta, but not as much from a financial standpoint," Vincent said. "I have been concerned about Atlanta because of a lack of attendance . . . They have some assets and revenue that separates them from Seattle and Cleveland and other clubs whose situations aren't as robust."

Chief among those assets is support from parent Turner Broadcasting, which causes many in the industry to view the Braves' profit/loss situation as a moot point. Though the club has shown a loss for each of the last seven years, Turner Broadcasting emerged from red ink in 1990 to show its first annual profit in five years. After suffering a net loss of $70.7 million in 1989, TBS realized a $4.6 million after-tax profit, according to a report issued to shareholders.

"With TBS, asking how much the Braves make or lose is like asking how much Mickey Mouse makes or loses for Disney," a Players Association executive said. "It's irrelevant. It's only one line on a corporate profit/loss statement."

The Braves' relationship with Turner is inextricably tied to Turner's relationship to baseball. Although TBS will pay the Braves $20.5 million this year for the rights to broadcast 114 games, industry sources say the Braves have to send $12.5 million of that money to Major League Baseball as compensation for WTBS infringing upon other cable markets. So the Braves' actual take from WTBS is only $8 million.

The Braves can take heart from one aspect of their projected deficit: It's a lot smaller than last year's estimated loss of more than $13 million. That figure, however, included a one-time $10.8 million payment to the players' union as its share of a $280 million settlement regarding collusion by owners against free agents. So, discounting that figure, this year's deficit could be double last year's.

The reason is no mystery. Salary expenses have increased nearly $12 million largely because of new general manager John Schuerholz's foray into the free-agent market. The philosophy is a stark contrast to the patient build-from-within credo of his predecessor, Bobby Cox.

"We've lost money the last couple of years, which is symptomatic of what we've done on the field," said Kasten. "There are ways we could lose less money by stripping our payroll à la Houston. But we're certainly not interested in that."

In 1990, the Braves' payroll of $11.2 million was the lowest in the National League and the third-lowest in all of baseball, ahead of only the Seattle Mariners and Chicago White Sox. This season's projection of about $22.8 million would have placed the Braves second to the Boston Red Sox in last year's market.

The salary figure includes $3 million in signing bonuses awarded four free agents this winter.

"None of this happened by accident," says Schuerholz, who asked for—and received—a free financial hand to improve a club that has finished last in four of the previous five seasons.

Over the winter, the Braves guaranteed eight free agents $30.1 million for the next four years. Third baseman Terry Pendleton was the most expensive, leaving the St. Louis Cardinals to sign a Braves-record $10.2 million contract for four years. First baseman Sid Bream came from the Pittsburgh Pirates for a three-year, $5.6 million deal. Right-handed reliever Juan Berenguer, who left the Minnesota Twins, received $2.1 million over two years, and catcher Mike Heath was given $2 million over two years to leave the Detroit Tigers as a second-look free agent.

In addition to the newcomers, several holdovers will be making far more this season than last. Pitcher Charlie Leibrandt, one of the players granted "second-look" free agency as part of the collusion settlement, decided to remain with the Braves after they committed $8 million to him over three years compared to $1.3 million in 1990. Center fielder Ron Gant, who was not eligible for free agency but was for arbitration, avoided a salary hearing by agreeing to a one-year deal for $1.195 million. Gant made $150,000 in 1990.

The Braves hope richer players will translate into better attendance, which will translate into more revenue. They're optimistic, but it won't be easy.

The Braves ranked last in the majors last season with $7,821,366 in gross gate receipts, and last in actual attendance for the third consecutive season with 980,129.

Though their actual attendance—as measured by turnstile count—increased over the 1989 total by 4,801, they sold 2,071 fewer tickets. Which means the increase in fans is attributable solely to a decrease in no-shows.

Attendance in Atlanta has not escaped Vincent's notice. "Nobody likes to see the attendance at Braves games," he said. "It's a downer when other teams come in there."

Vincent last season even expressed concern that TBS showing so many Braves home games might hurt attendance, but others counter that winning is a simple cure for that ailment. The last time the Braves won a division title, 1982, the club attracted an Atlanta record of 2,119,935 the following season. Plus, the other two superstation teams, the Chicago Cubs (WGN) and New York Mets (WWOR), have not suffered attendance woes.

Schuerholz, 50, is seen as a key figure in the drive to revive attendance. He has been given more control over the club's overall operation than any man since owner Ted Turner's self-imposed exile began in 1985. He has immersed himself in all aspects of the organization, including the complex relationship between the Braves and their parent company.

"It's cause for hand-wringing to determine why there has been a lack of success here, not why there have been [financial] losses," Schuerholz said. "I don't think it's fair to start measuring the profitability of this organization until we create a quality product. If we have the quality product in place and it's a loss situation, then it's cause for concern."

Reprinted with the permission of the *Atlanta Journal* and the *Atlanta Constitution*

References

Atwell, Robert H., Bruce Grimes, and Donna A. Lopiano. 1980. *The Money Game: Financing Collegiate Athletics.* Washington, D.C.: American Council on Education.

Auf der Maur, Nick. 1976. *The Billion Dollar Game: Jean Drapeau and the 1976 Olympics.* Toronto: Lorimar.

Betts, John R. 1974. *America's Sporting Heritage: 1850–1950.* Reading, Mass.: Addison-Wesley.

Curran, Bob. 1965. *The $400,000 Quarterback or the League That Came In from the Cold.* New York: Macmillan.

Durso, Joseph. 1971. *The All-American Dollar: The Big Business of Sports.* Boston: Houghton Mifflin.

Gallico, Paul. 1964. *The Golden People.* Garden City, N.Y.: Doubleday.

Gipe, George. 1978. *The Great American Sports Book.* Garden City, N.Y.: Dolphin.

Halas, George, with Gwen Morgan and Arthur Veysey. 1979. *Halas by Halas.* New York: McGraw-Hill.

Hanford, George H. 1979. Controversies in college sports. *Education Record* 60 (4): 35–66.

Johnson, William O. 1971. *Super Spectator and the Electric Lilliputians.* Boston: Little, Brown.

Killanin, Lord, and John Rodda. 1976. *The Olympic Games: 80 Years of People, Events, and Records.* New York: Macmillan.

Rodriguez, Ken. 1990a. UM helps new deal for CFA. *Miami Herald,* February 10, 1D.

_____. 1990b. Network replaces Musburger with Hall of Fame broadcaster. *Miami Herald,* April 6, 7D.

Rooney, John F., Jr. 1980. *The Recruiting Game.* Lincoln: University of Nebraska Press.

Spears, Betty, and Richard A. Swanson. 1978. *History of Sport and Physical Activity in the United States.* Dubuque, Iowa: Brown.

Sugar, Bert Randolph. 1978a. *Hit the Sign and Win a Free Suit of Clothes from Hal Finklestein.* Chicago: Contemporary Books.

_____. 1978b. *The Thrill of Victory: The Inside Story of ABC Sports.* New York: Hawthorn.

U.S. Congress. House Select Committee on Professional Sports. 1977. *Inquiry into Professional Sports.* 94th Cong., 2d sess. Parts 1–3.

Wooten, Morgan, and Bill Gilbert. 1979. *From Orphans to Champions.* New York: Atheneum.

12

Sports Reporting and the Judicial System

Generations ago, in the era of Grantland Rice, athletes and athletic clubs only occasionally resorted to the legal system to resolve problems. But in the past two decades, it has become almost as common to find a sports reporter in the courtroom as in the locker room. As American society has become more litigious, so has the sports world, and in the criminal justice system as well as in the civil courts.

Journalists must deal with a jurisdiction problem when sports stories enter the legal system: Who covers this kind of story, the sports journalist or the courtroom reporter? Because of their expertise, courtroom reporters have usually been sent to handle sports-related cases. But this is changing. As more and more sports reporters are skilled in the courtroom, they take the assignments.

There is also the placement dilemma. Some stories will land in the sports section. Some will go on the front page or on the front of the local section. On occasion, such stories may be run in the sports section although they have been written by a city desk reporter. Because of the increasing need today to interpret and write about complex legal matters that involve sports, even the beginning sportswriter should have a basic background that allows him or her to write about sports cases that wind up in the judicial system. This chapter discusses the types of cases most commonly found in the judicial system involving sports and athletes and the available sources of background. The information should assist the beginning reporter in getting up to proper "legal" speed.

What sorts of stories involve the legal system?

● The beauty pageant contestant raped in Indianapolis by heavyweight boxer Mike Tyson filed a lawsuit against Tyson, seeking damages for assault, battery, false imprisonment, and emotional distress. The attorneys for 19-year-old Desiree Washington sued Tyson in 1992 for unspecified damages in U.S. District Court in Indiana. At the time the suit was filed, Tyson was serving a six-year sentence for raping Washington in his hotel room in July 1991.

● Heavyweight boxing champion James "Buster" Douglas fought promoter Don King in the courtroom in summer 1990, but after three weeks of trial in U.S. District Court, the parties reached an out-of-court settlement that allowed Douglas to defend his title against Evander Holyfield later in the year.

● One baseball card collector sued another over possession of a rare card featuring President George Bush. The case entered a Champaign, Ill., courtroom in 1990.

● The University of Miami athletic department sued the contractors who built its football practice fields. University officials felt the construction was faulty, cost the team practice time during its 1988 season, and may have led to its only loss to Notre Dame, leaving the team ranked No. 2 nationally behind Notre Dame. The case was heard in a county court in Miami.

● A popular high school basketball coach was charged with vehicular homicide after he allegedly struck and killed the child of one of his former players with his automobile. The coach lost his job and was tried in a county criminal court in Florida.

● Pete Rose, baseball's legendary hits king, entered federal court in Cincinnati for tax evasion charges. Rose was sentenced to five months in an Illinois prison and to six months of public service in several Cincinnati schools.

● The mother of Loyola Marymount University basketball player Hank Gathers filed a $32.5 million wrongful death suit against Loyola Marymount, former coach Paul Westhead, and doctors after the star player dropped dead on a court during a game. Gathers, who once led the NCAA in scoring but had a heart condition, played despite his knowledge of his medical problem.

There are hundreds, if not thousands, of examples like these every year. Sportswriters need not become as knowledgeable as attorneys or court officers but should become familiar with the judicial system — with the procedures, the environment, and the sources necessary to cover cases — in the event an occasional court-related assignment is made.

Sports journalists are more than ever alert to questions of libel, invasion of privacy, and other legal problems that sometimes result from covering legal matters. Libel may result from inaccurate reporting, such as carelessness in identifying defendants and plaintiffs. Invasion of privacy can be a concern even before an incident ever goes to court. And related to this is the "right of publicity" of professional athletes on live television. That is to say, these athletes now enjoy the same rights of publicity as other entertainers and can exploit their names, images, and public personality (Day 1988).

Libel remains a major problem even for sports journalists. For example, in 1991 the United States Supreme Court refused to stop a libel suit against the *Lexington (Ky.) Herald-Leader* that arose from its Pulitzer Prize–winning stories on recruiting violations at major universities in 1986. The court let a ruling stand that forces the newspaper to defend itself at trial. An assistant coach named in the story sued the newspaper for two references to him in a series of articles on recruiting in October 1985 that won a 1986 Pulitzer Prize. The newspaper wrote that the coach offered money to a high school basketball star if the star signed a scholarship letter with the coach's school. Early court arguments centered on whether the coach was a "public figure," but an appeals court ruled he was not for the purpose of the suit. Proof of false and negligent statements is generally easier for private citizens. The coach had not coached since the articles appeared in reprint form. The case was scheduled to go to trial later in the year.

Herb Appenzeller, athletic director at Guilford College in North Carolina, has studied the athlete and the law. In his book, *Athletics and the Law* (1975), he wrote:

> A new day has arrived in both athletics and physical education. Interest in athletics at all levels, from little league to professional play, has reached unprecedented proportions. This is the era of crowded stadiums, Monday night televised football, instant replay, multi-million-dollar contracts and record participation.
>
> On the other hand, law and athletics are becoming synonymous as lawsuits are filed in alarming and record-breaking numbers. Athletes in locker rooms discuss such things as personal rights, due process, equal protection and the guarantees of the First, Fourth, Fifth, and Fourteenth Amendments. Judges and juries are called upon to consider every possible type of case, and school officials are becoming frustrated over the claims and contentions brought forward by athletes, coaches, and spectators alike.

Sports reporting requires at least familiarity with all the areas Appenzeller mentions, and perhaps even more. Suddenly, stories about athletes and the legal system are not just about contract disputes. Appenzeller notes a distinct trend toward more athlete litigation, more disruptive behavior, and changing attitudes toward married athletes, training rules, and even good conduct codes. There are concerns about athletic team travel (after disasters such as the loss of the entire University of Evansville basketball team in an airplane crash), the changing role of women's athletics and programs, the role of state athletic associations and rules, and possible federal legislation. Some believe this justifies developing a specialty within sports journalism. Former network television commentator Howard Cosell writes, "Indeed, professional sports generally are undergoing the greatest upheaval and restructuring in their history and it is happening through the courts of law and through collective bargaining" (Sobel 1977 [foreword]).

Herb and Thomas Appenzeller (1980) emphasize this point, suggesting that athletes, coaches, administrators, officials, physicians, equipment manufacturers, operators of sports facilities, and even unsuspecting sports fans "share a common bond—the risk of sports litigation." They feel that awards resulting from civil action will "change the nature of sports as we know them. With so many lawsuits in sports, involving so many different groups, it is important for all sports administrators to know what to do and what to expect if a lawsuit develops."

Enter the sports reporter. Because these events involve sports teams, personalities, athletes, and community interests, the reporter may cover such activities in court. There is often much at stake, with long-term implications of civil actions that seek damages, enforcement of rights, or redress for wrongs. Furthermore, criminal charges are being filed against athletes for incidents occurring during athletic contests, as well as violations of the law, such as drug dealing. Two decades ago, such a thing was unheard of in sports. But recently, names such as Len Bias, Mercury Morris, and others are as well-known for their drug problems as for their athletic achievements.

The type of story sports reporters often cover now has definitely changed. In one of the earliest such cases in 1975 Dave Forbes, a hockey player for the Boston Bruins, was charged with aggravated assault in Minnesota after striking Henri Boucha, a player for the Minnesota North Stars, with a hockey stick. The case, which ended in a hung jury and Forbes not retried on the charge, illustrates the trend toward criminal prosecution for the violence once taken for granted in hockey, football, basketball, and other sports (Binder 1975).

Regulation of Sports

Sports regulation occurs at all levels. There are rules for participant eligibility and rules for different degrees of ability and classes of performance. Rules and regulations for amateur sports are different from those for professional sports. Special financial relationships exist in professional sports that do not exist among non-professionals, although some amateur competition is becoming so sophisticated that it mirrors that of professionals.

Legal situations differ, depending on the amateur or professional status of an athlete or sport. Covering these sports and their various legal concerns requires the sportswriter's familiarity with the major differences, such as traditional player restraints among professional athletes (for example, the reserve clause in professional contracts) or eligibility questions for amateurs. Since the mid-1970s, generally, the field of sports has moved from a recreational nature to a level closer to legal scrutiny. Changes in regulation have been a major reaction to this changing situation. Attorneys John Weistart and Cym Lowell (1979) argue: "We certainly know much more about the legal implications of player restraints, collective bargaining, player contract depreciation, and amateur regulations than we did just a few years ago. As a result, predictions about the course of future development can be made with more confidence than could have been generated in 1972."

In the area of amateur competition, Weistart and Lowell identify more than two dozen categories of regulation. Among them are:

Rule making (by public and private institutions)	The right to participate
	Race and sex
Participation in "non-approved" events	Athlete and coach relationships
Scholarships	Tournaments and other major events
Workmen's compensation	Freedom from unreasonable regulation
Transfer of residence and eligibility	Enforcement activities
Federal income tax	Legislative intervention
Personal activities, such as marriage	Amateur athletic organizations and institutions
Definition of amateur athlete	
Grades and academic eligibility	

In the area of public regulation, Weistart and Lowell identify an equally large number of problem areas that may end up as court cases, such as athletic commissions, issue of licenses, discrimination by sex or race, and management. These matters thus may become newspaper story material.

Professional sports include much wider bases of legal structure. Entire treatises have been written, such as Lionel Sobel's *Professional Sports and the Law* (1977) and its supplements and Robert C. Berry and Glenn M. Wong's *Law and Business of the Sports Industries: Professional Sports Leagues* (1986), that provide excellent background for reporters looking into professional sports problems. A major question in professional sports, and one of the oldest ones, is enforcement of athletes' contracts. As Sobel points out, many of these problems parallel those in the entertainment industry. What do they include? The major ones are no doubt familiar:

Judicial enforcement of contracts   Suits against clubs and teams
Arbitration in contracts   Contract breaking by athletes or em-
Contexts of enforcement   ployers
Commissioners' roles in arbitration   Jurisdiction over players
Exclusive rights to athletes' services

Perhaps the most important single category is baseball's antitrust exemption. This affects player restraint factors, such as reserve and option clauses, the draft system, and prohibition from tampering. Since the Curt Flood case, these factors are a changing aspect of professional sports contracts. Weistart and Lowell (1979) note attention should be paid, as well, to player discipline, exclusionary practices of sports associations, the antitrust aspects of ownership and location of franchises, and exercises of monopoly power over potential rival leagues.

Louis A. Day (1988) notes that as television and sports industries have become more important in our society in recent years, a new era of litigation has resulted over rights and revenues between team owners and their athletes. He says: "Lucrative TV contracts, which provide a large share of professional teams' gross revenues, have become the target of players and their collective bargaining agents who are seeking a share of these substantial revenues. This struggle has been intensified by the increasing power and militancy of players' associations and the rapid growth in recent years of sports on cable TV as a new source of revenue" (p. 62). Day says critical issues include (1) whether athletes enjoy a "right of publicity" to exploit their public persona and (2) whether U.S. copyright law, which protects the property of owners, precludes the exercise of the "right of publicity" by players. Day says athletes enjoy the same rights as other entertainers, but their rights are subordinate to the rights of the team. As Day notes, the growth in this area has only created new areas of legal concern and further litigation in existing areas that are "potentially more explosive" than traditional labor disputes that have confronted professional sports.

And professional football cannot be ignored. The federal courts permitted the Oakland Raiders to move to Los Angeles and use the Memorial Coliseum, former home facility of the Los Angeles Rams. This case involved antitrust laws, too; it was eventually decided that the National Football League had violated antitrust laws in attempting to block the move for the 1982 football season. In the early 1990s, of course, there was considerable legal attention given to the prospects of Al Davis' moving his team back to Oakland.

Although these are the major areas relating to regulation of sports, they are not the only ones. There are cases involving collective bargaining and professional sports, federal and state income taxation of sports activities, sports injury liabilities, and many other legal questions. Reporters are wise to prepare for covering a civil case in court by reviewing current discussions of these topics. The community library may have such books, or they may be available in a newspaper's library. A reporter should ask the newspaper's librarian for assistance. An area law library also will probably have background books or articles.

Courts: The Environment and Actors

A civil case or action is a lawsuit based on a private wrong (as distinguished from a crime against society or the "state") or a lawsuit to enforce the rights of an individual or group through remedies of a private or non-penal nature. A criminal case or action is one brought in the name of the state against a person who allegedly committed a public offense. Both can originate at any level in the court system. In the United States, most court cases begin in state courts because the U.S. Constitution reserves all powers not specifically delegated to the federal government to state governments. These two judicial systems are parallel in many ways, in terms of structure if not jurisdiction.

It is important to know how these courts are set up. Reporters dealing with one case may watch it progress through a state or federal system from the level of the trial court. After the trial is completed, the case may go to an appeals court, which is an intermediate-level court (some states do not have intermediate appellate courts). Following an appeals court decision, the case may be appealed again to the court of last resort, the final judicial authority, ordinarily called a supreme court. This system varies from state to state, and there may be different trial and first appellate court levels. State supreme courts can be more specialized; in a few states, some supreme courts handle only civil cases, while others handle criminal cases. By comparison, the federal courts have a much more uniform system.

Most state courts have a similar structure despite the many variations. Often the differences are in name only. The major court of original jurisdiction is the circuit court, also called the district court, superior court, or a similar name. Below this court are county courts, which are limited in the cases they hear; these include justice of the peace or magistrate courts, as they are mostly called. Between the justice of the peace courts and county courts are probate courts and any municipal or city courts that exist in the county.

The appellate level of a state court system is kept busy with cases originating in the county or district courts. Only about half the states have intermediate appellate courts, which are designed to reduce the case load of the state supreme court.

The state supreme court is the highest state court in most states. After a state supreme court hears a case, if one or both parties desire it, and there is some basis for federal jurisdiction, the case enters the federal court system by being appealed directly from the state supreme court to the U.S. Supreme Court without returning to the federal court of original jurisdiction. There is a court in just about every county of every state.

The type and seriousness of cases vary, of course, and on this basis the jurisdiction is determined. Cases that are not serious, such as misdemeanor traffic offense cases or civil suits over small amounts of money, originate in justice of the peace courts. The more serious cases, those involving felonies and civil suits with larger monetary claims, originate in state district courts. The sum claimed that determines jurisdiction varies from state to state.

Jurisdiction of appellate courts also varies from state to state. Most cases are heard in other courts first, but in some states an action can originate in an appellate court, such as a writ. A writ is an order issued from a court requiring the performance of a specific act or restraining the performance of an act.

The federal court system consists of the district courts, appellate courts, and the Supreme Court. The American judicial system includes several other important courts beyond these three basic ones. Feeding into the appeals courts are special district courts with local jurisdiction, such as those in U.S. possessions and several quasi-judicial administrative agency courts, such as tax courts, the National Labor Relations Board, and the Federal Communications Commission. Feeding directly to the Supreme Court are not only the appeals from state supreme courts but also cases from the Court of Claims, Customs and Patent Appeals Court, and Customs Court.

Many cases involving athletes, teams, and other sports-related people will go to federal court because of the interstate nature of professional sports. But other cases will begin in state courts. It is difficult to generalize about when a sports journalist might end up covering a trial. The best advice is to be prepared to go into a courtroom at any time.

At this point grand juries must be considered. Both state and federal court systems use grand juries with generally similar systems. Attorneys William C. Ballard, Gregg D. Thomas, and Carol Jean Locicero (1990) write: "The grand jury's primary role is to determine whether sufficient evidence exists to justify indicting an accused individual." In many states, such as Florida, grand jury indictments are required only in the most serious cases, such as capital offenses like murder. Grand juries work in secret, which is a problem for reporters who wish to cover their activities in progress. When disclosure of information is prohibited, revealing leaked information gained through unnamed sources can become a complicated business. The possibility of a reporter being subpoenaed to tell a court the name of the source necessitates discussion with editors and other newsroom management about the best way to proceed. Caution is the key.

Generally, if a city attorney, district attorney, or state attorney decides there is cause enough to prosecute a case, he or she will present it to the state grand jury (normally a larger number than the six or 12 people on a court jury). The grand jury then interrogates witnesses and principals and votes whether an indictment should be handed down. Grand juries also have an investigative function, inquiring into civil administration, conduct of public employees, and similar matters.

Federal grand juries consist of 16 to 23 people, with 12 needed for indictment. There are subtle differences in state and federal grand jury procedures, so a reporter must research individual states.

In all courts, with all types of juries, court officials play an important role as far as the reporter is concerned. In many situations, these officials are the best information sources. Following are the main court officials in court structures (see Bush 1970):

JUDGE: Chief officer of the court, the legal umpire
CLERK: Secretary of the court
COURT COMMISSIONERS/MASTERS/REFEREES: Judicial-clerical assistants to judges, generally on technical cases
ATTORNEYS: Representatives of private parties or the government
OFFICIAL REPORTER: Stenographer of the court, who takes the court record
BAILIFF: Court police officer or sergeant at arms, who keeps order
INTERPRETER: Language translator

For more information about the legal system, see *The Reporter's Guide to Legal Terms, Courts, Court Agencies,* and *Courthouses* (for a current copy, write to the Communications Department, Pennsylvania Bar Association, 100 South Street, P.O. Box 186, Harrisburg, PA 17108).

Key Sources in the Court System

Most individuals who hold the positions mentioned above should be good sources of information for a sports journalist covering a case. Some will be more helpful than others; some will not want to help at all. And there are helpful sources besides these court officials.

The judge, the chief officer of the court, makes all important decisions about the court's activities both in and out of the courtroom. During trials, he or she makes procedural decisions and exercises powers given by a constitution or by statutes. The judge decides questions of law, while juries decide questions of fact. A judge can be a valuable information source. Most will readily talk with reporters. Some judges are appointed and some elected, and, sometimes because of this, their willingness to cooperate will vary. Despite their codes of ethics that prohibit discussing a case in progress, some judges such as those in the lower courts will do so. These interviews are always done out of court and often off the record; the reporter must weigh the value of the information to decide whether such an interview will be worthwhile.

Although the judge is the most important court official, the people who work for the judge, either directly or indirectly, are the best sources. In addition to the clerks and deputies, the bailiffs, the court reporters, and others who work in the court know what is going on and can help if they are cultivated as sources and trust the reporter.

First and foremost among sources, usually, is the court clerk (as well as deputy clerks). These individuals are the court record-keepers or secretaries. In a large court system the clerk is an administrator; most duties are left to deputy clerks, which makes these people vitally important to reporters because reporters often use court records in researching cases before, during, and after a trial. It is the clerk's duty to keep the records and assist individuals in locating them once the records are filed. Duties of clerks vary, as do the responsibilities of deputies, but overall these people also assist in drawing jurors; issuing court documents, such as summonses or subpoenas; keeping any trial exhibits and evidence; handling funds, such as fines and other fees; and assisting the judges. They keep calendars of upcoming court activities, which are available to the public. In covering a case involving a sports figure or team, the sports reporter will be well-advised to get to know the clerk's office personnel (Krantz 1983).

Attorneys are prevented from discussing cases in progress by their professional codes of ethics, but many will discuss their client's side of a controversy. However, a reporter who contacts one side is obligated to approach the other side to be fair. For example, if the plaintiff, or the plaintiff's attorney, is interviewed, the reporter should try to interview the defendant or the defendant's attorney. In a criminal case, if a reporter hears the state's case by interviewing a prosecution attorney, he or she should also seek to hear the defendant's side. If a reporter is confused or just wants expanded background on strategy or a legal point, many attorneys will be helpful. They will discuss matters up to a point, but usually will refuse to comment on the quality of performance of other attorneys and on the guilt or innocence of a defendant.

Each case varies; a reporter should approach new situations with care. Business colleagues of people involved in a case (partners, associates, and co-workers) are often good sources of information. It is also wise to contact family members, who may cooperate with tactful reporters. And, as Professor Ralph Izard (1982) points out, reporters always depend heavily on tips. They are less dependable, but can be useful and frequently come from people connected with the courtroom either on a one-time or a regular basis. Izard makes another observation worth noting. He says there are three types of information sources in any courtroom reporting: First are most court records and documents, which are available by law as open public records. Some records, such as juvenile records, are generally closed.

Second are the in-court sources, what the reporter sees and hears while observing courtroom activities during the trial. Third are the out-of-court sources, what is said and done outside of court regarding the trial or hearing. A reporter who keeps these three categories in mind and uses each in some way in covering a trial or hearing will likely do a thorough reporting job.

The Courtroom and the Trial

Journalists experienced in reporting about the legal system know that many critical decisions and activities take place before the trial begins. In fact, the vast majority of both civil and criminal cases never get to the courtroom. Many civil cases are settled out of court when agreements are reached between parties, and many criminal cases are plea bargained, a process in which the accused agrees to plead guilty to a lesser charge. This avoids the expense and uncertainty of a trial. Estimates are that between 75 and 90 percent of all cases are resolved in some manner before going to trial. Criminal and civil trials do not follow the same procedures.

CIVIL ACTIONS. The civil case begins with a person, group, or institution filing a complaint with a court clerk, which creates an adversary situation. Civil law has been developed to solve a legal problem created by some action, either real or perceived. When the cases involve matters such as athletes' rights, contracts, or coaches' investment activities, an interesting sports story is created. The document, usually called a complaint, summarizes the situation for the court, outlining the contested events or issues. The party mentioned as the defendant is informed through formal notification in a summons issued by the court. There may be other requests of the court at the time the brief (concise statement of the plaintiff's case) is filed, such as issuing a temporary restraining order (to keep things as they are) or a preliminary injunction. The complaint may be answered by the defendant through a second brief, which makes counterclaims and disputes facts. If there is no answer, the case is lost by a default judgment, but this is rare.

In civil cases judges often hold pretrial conferences to get the case under control, perhaps by limiting the issues involved. As the trial date nears, attorneys for both sides prepare arguments and evidence to convince a jury. Even at this point, settlements may be reached. These settlements eliminate the need for a trial; they occur out of court, often in a judge's chambers or an attorney's office.

Civil trials are held under the direction of a judge, who sometimes also decides the outcome. In most civil cases, though, a jury is present. Depending on state law, the jury can be waived in some cases and requested in others.

In the courtroom, proceedings begin with opening statements by each side. The side that has filed the complaint presents evidence and witnesses first. The defendant may cross-examine the witnesses and dispute the evidence. Then the side being sued may offer evidence or witnesses in support of its case.

Reporters covering civil cases may report each step as the case develops. But many wait until the decision is announced to write their stories, giving the case one-story coverage. If a jury is involved, it will deliberate in private and then report its decision. In civil cases, unanimity is not generally required. A 9–3 or even 8–4 decision (or 5–1 or 4–2, with a six-person jury) is not uncommon. A judge deliberates in private, in most circumstances, if no jury is involved. And, as stated earlier, the final option may be to appeal if either party is unhappy with the result. After a decision for monetary compensation, for example, an appeal may be filed to reduce the award.

CRIMINAL ACTIONS. Baltimore courts reporter Lyle Denniston writes, "The most visible court in America is the criminal trial court" (Denniston 1980). Less sports-related legal activity has occurred in criminal courts, however, than in civil courts. Many of the examples earlier in the chapter were civil actions, but this may be a trend of the past. Sports competition violence has now entered the courtroom, leading to the need for sports journalists to familiarize themselves with criminal procedures as well.

The criminal court hears a case against an individual or group of individuals filed on behalf of the state, or other governing unit, because a person or persons have been accused of violating one or more laws. The trial is only one portion of the entire criminal justice process, which is quite complex and cannot be fully discussed here. Excellent treatments of it are included in books such as John Kaplan's *Criminal Justice* (1978). These books should be consulted before covering a criminal trial or the events in the justice process that occur before and/or after the trial.

The criminal trial process begins with an investigation by a police agency and a complaint filed by the district attorney's or community prosecutor's office. As a result, the person or persons may be arrested on the charges listed in the complaint. Or a grand jury indictment may be handed down, resulting in an arrest. After the person is arraigned, a plea is entered. Then the trial date is set. If the accused person pleads guilty, the case will not go to court again except for sentencing. A not-guilty plea leads to a trial.

The trial actually begins with jury selection, unless the defendant waives a jury trial. Once a jury has been picked to the satisfaction of the prosecution and defense, in most cases both sides make opening arguments. Next, the prosecution presents evidence in terms of documents and other materials and introduces witnesses with testimony favorable to the state's accusations. The defendant's attorney has the chance to cross-examine, of course. Then the defendant has a chance to introduce evidence and witnesses, with the prosecution cross-examining.

When each case has been presented to the court, the two sides make closing arguments in summation. The jury is then instructed by the judge about how to consider the charges and evidence. The jury retires and eventually reaches a verdict, and the decision is announced in court. A series of closing motions are made, and sentencing follows at that time or at a later date. Appeals may be made, as in civil cases, if the defendant judged guilty chooses to do so.

COVERING THE TRIAL. As mentioned earlier, some trials are covered in one story, with all information held until a verdict or decision is reached. The reporter might have to be present throughout the whole case, to collect and synthesize material. If this is not possible, a single story still requires skillful use of records and sources. Many cases, of course, start and finish in only one day, but others can run from a few days to a few weeks and require some advance strategy for reporting. If a case is covered as it develops, insignificant details take on greater importance. It is not unusual in a major case for one witness' testimony to last a whole day or more. Covering a major trial can be time-consuming and expensive; how to do it is a serious editorial decision.

WRITING THE TRIAL STORY. When a legal issue or other matter comes to the sports section it involves an athlete; a team, league, or institution; fans; or a combination of these. Just because the story is written for the sports section does not mean it should be handled in any less serious manner than if assigned by a city editor for the local news section or front page, and the sports journalist should not write it any differently. A sports reporter inexperienced in dealing with judicial matters must remember that such stories should be approached with utmost caution, double-checking all sources for accuracy of facts and of quotes. These stories can lead to libel cases, and with good reason, because careless errors can defame the people involved. One example is a simple mistake that might be made by a beginner: reversing the names of plaintiff and defendant. Another might be writing stories without full and complete identifications, because there may be two or more people in a community with the same name.

The reporter must be able to understand and correctly use the language of the courtroom and to translate for readers terms used by lawyers and judges. When motions or pleas are made or other noteworthy activities take place, the reporter must write about them so that readers can grasp their significance.

Researching Legal Issues

A reporter doesn't need to be a legal scholar, but there are helpful references and legal research procedures for the sports reporter covering the courts on occasion. The newsroom library may have one or more of these references; the local public library, or a college library, will probably have a good collection of basic law references. A local law library will have all up-to-date references. Many universities and colleges with law schools and independent law schools will grant permission for short-term use of the library if a reporter asks the law school library director or an administrator in advance. And many law school librarians will assist a reporter in finding materials.

Another good institutional library to consider is the local government law library. In some states there is a public legislative reference service that contains materials for basic legal research, particularly in areas in which laws may be proposed. County and city governments also often have small legal libraries for public use, but their existence and quality varies from community to community, and most are created for the convenience of the local court system. The reporter can determine if such a library exists by asking in the county or district court clerk's office.

Some of the most helpful of the many tools for legal research follow (see Gordon 1984):

1. Legal encyclopedias. These books are commercially published and are coordinated with the publishing company's other legal publications. Two of the major encyclopedias, and their common abbreviations in legal periodicals, are *Corpus Juris Secundum* (C.J.S.) and *American Jurisprudence* (Am.Jur.). They are available in most law libraries. (See Gulick and Kimbrough 1989, Mack 1990.)

2. Digests. These books provide users with a paragraph summary of each case on a specific topic that was decided within the time frame and the court jurisdictions covered by the specific volume. For example, there is a volume on the U.S. Supreme Court, a "General Digest" for all American courts.

3. Law textbooks and casebooks. Known as treatises, these are the books law students read on specific topics such as communication law or mass media law. These law textbooks give an excellent introduction to a given topic such as constitutional law or contracts. They direct the reader to specific major cases, which are summarized, and judges' opinions are often presented. These are good to start with because they might save searching through other books. These treatises are often updated with supplements.

4. Legal periodicals. Any law library has hundreds of legal periodicals, which sometimes provide the type of shortcuts discussed in law textbooks. These law reviews and other periodicals refer to other publications

as well. The *Index to Legal Periodicals* (Rosen 1926) covers more than 500 periodicals and is updated monthly with quarterly and annual cumulations. Another good reference is the *Current Law Index,* which includes more than 700 periodicals. It is updated on a monthly basis. Legal periodicals are quite specific in nature; there are periodicals devoted to just about all categories of law. A number of legal periodicals have been published on the subjects of sports and entertainment, such as *Entertainment and Sports Law Journal* and *Marquette Sports Law Journal.*

5. Reported decisions. These are commonly called "reporters," collections of reported court decisions provided by public or private services to libraries and interested people who pay for the service. These reporters are collections of opinions from a court or series of courts, generally in chronological order. Almost all appellate courts are served by reporters. Major legal publishing companies produce reporters, such as West Publishing Company (St. Paul, Minn.). West publishes *West Law Finder,* which identifies the case reporters that publish in full the opinions of the various appellate and some federal trial courts. Reporters are also published by interest groups and other people active in a specific area of the law. In sports, reporters representing the most current sports law cases have appeared in recent years with the increase in sports litigation. One example is the *Sports Law Reporter: Current Cases and Decisions in the Law of Sports,* published monthly since 1978 from Bronxville, N.Y. These publications are expensive and not likely to be added to any sports department's subscription list; however, most law libraries have them.

6. Case histories. These are reference books that trace the legal history of any court decision up to the most recent citation of the original case. They are difficult for beginners to use at first, mainly because of the codes and abbreviations used. The most commonly used book is *Shepard's Citations,* published by Shepard's Citations, Inc., Colorado Springs, Colo., with supplements.

7. Dictionaries. Dictionaries are helpful in defining certain legal terms. A widely used law dictionary especially useful in translating law into meaningful language for the layman is *Black's Law Dictionary* (1990). Another good reference is the *Law Dictionary for Non-Lawyers* (Oran 1975).

8. Local journalism law professors. Many universities and colleges with mass communication and journalism programs have a faculty member who specializes in media law research. Law school faculty members sometimes assist in legal research.

Many more reference sources are available. The reporter must use some initiative, of course, to locate background for a specific case. A good overall reference guide is *Legal Research in a Nutshell* by Cohen (1985).

For conducting legal research, the major legal publisher, West, has set up a key number system of case referencing (explained in *West's Law*

Finder). This consists of lists of numbered topics with subcategories that cover every point of law in a reported case. Thus, a case on rights of college athletes would be classified under a general heading of civil rights, and if other points are involved, under those as well. As legal scholar David Gordon (1984) says, this system is a giant series of pigeonholes, each with a topic title and a key number. When the editors at West review a new case, they decide in which pigeonholes the legal points in the case should be placed. These numbers are consistent in most of West's publications, so the researcher can find cases with ease once the key number system is learned. To do research, the researcher must come up with a case and then work either forward or backward to find others. Gordon advises: "If you get bogged down, ask for help. Law students and law librarians usually take pity on neophyte researchers, and are willing to provide guidance, as long as you don't take unfair advantage of them."

Judicial System/Sports Stories

From the wide variety of such stories, we have chosen two representative ones that have been covered well, beginning with a rather amusing civil suit case story written by Norm Cohen for *Newsday.*

SOURCE: The *Miami Herald,* first edition, page 1D
DATE: Monday, March 5, 1990
AUTHOR: Norm Cohen, *Newsday*
HEADLINE: Bush in hand: A baseball card whodunit

Judge Wapner could have a field day with this one. It's a civil lawsuit over possession of a card that no one was supposed to have in the first place. And although it's no federal case, the president of the United States is at the center of the controversy.

Call it "The Case of a Bush in the Hand Is Worth a Whole Lot of Trouble." The litigants first entered a Champaign, Ill., courtroom Feb. 23.

The plaintiff, Jim Danner of Champaign, alleges that on or before Dec. 18, Lee Hull, a friend who runs a memorabilia shop, offered to sell him a 1990 Topps George Bush baseball card for 15 cents.

Hull, who isn't supposed to have the card in the first place, says that Danner is dreaming.

And Topps, which isn't involved in the suit, contends that whoever has the card is in possession of stolen merchandise. Topps still has to figure out how the picture of the president found its way to the central Illinois town.

Hull says that it came from a wax-pack box he purchased from an unidentified woman in December.

Topps says that this is impossible, because only 100 cards were made, and all were given to the president last month.

Danner says Hull promised to sell him one for 15 cents.

"I never offered the card to him for 15 cents," Hull said. "It's never been offered for sale. The thing is, even if I had offered it to him for 15 cents, why didn't he buy it? Didn't he have the cash in hand?"

To put everything in perspective, we must go back to last year, when a member of the Bush clan supposedly asked why President Grandpa — a baseball star at Yale — was never on a baseball card.

Rather than allow the president to wallow in embarrassment, Topps came up with a plan to put Bush on cardboard. The finished product, numbered USA 1, shows Bush in the traditional Yale University captain pose. He's clad in his uniform and leaning against a wooden fence before a mural of trees in the basement of Yale's field house.

"Only 100 cards were made, and they were all presented to President Bush," Topps spokesman Ken Liss said.

Yet Hull says that he found one in a wax pack.

Liss claims that is impossible, since the regular baseball cards are printed in Duryea, Pa., and the Bush cards were printed in New York. Topps has demanded that Hull return the card, but he has refused.

Hull has said he has no intention of giving the card to Topps, although, thanks to Danner's lawsuit, he couldn't even if he wanted to.

Hull had to turn the card over to the Champaign County clerk and post a $25,000 commercial bond. No trial date has been set.

Topps could make the whole stink disappear by running off a few million of the Bush cards and making them available through a mail-in offer or by including one in its end-of-season update set, provided there is a baseball season to update.

"Absolutely not," Liss said. "The whole idea was to make these special cards for the president. There's no chance that we would make any more."

Reprinted with the permission of *Newsday*

SOURCE: The *Miami Herald,* final edition, page 5D
DATE: Tuesday, December 11, 1990
AUTHOR: Mike Phillips, *Herald* sportswriter
HEADLINE: Bell's trial delayed again

The state won't decide the guilt or innocence of former Carol City High boys' basketball Coach Ernie Bell until next year.

Bell, who was arrested Aug. 7, was granted his third continuance Monday and won't return to Circuit Court Judge Arthur Rothenberg's courtroom until Jan. 22.

Bell, 50, is charged with one count of vehicular homicide in the death

of 3-year-old Shaquetta Green, the daughter of one of Bell's former basketball players. Green was struck and killed March 24. Bell also is charged
with one count of leaving the scene of an accident involving a death.

Sam Rabin, an attorney representing Bell, asked for a continuance
Monday because Bell was recently released from the hospital and his doctor, Dr. S. Carrington, recommended bed rest.

Reprinted with the permission of the *Miami Herald*

References

Appenzeller, Herb. 1975. *Athletics and the Law*. Charlottesville, Va.: Michie.
_____, and Thomas Appenzeller. 1980. *Sports and the Courts*. Charlottesville, Va.:
Michie.
Ballard, William C., Gregg D. Thomas, and Carol Jean Locicero. 1990. The grand jury
system. In *Reporter's Handbook*, by the Florida Bar Association, Florida Press Association,
and Florida Association of Broadcasters. Tallahassee: Florida Bar Association.
Berry, Robert C., and Glenn M. Wong. 1986. *Law and Business of the Sports Industries*,
Vol. I. Dover, Mass.: Auburn House.
Binder, Richard L. 1975. The consent defense: Sports, violence and the criminal law.
American Criminal Law Review 13 (Fall): 235.
Black, Henry Cambell, Joseph R. Nolan, and Jacqueline M. Nolan-Haley. 1990. *Black's
Law Dictionary*. 6th ed. St. Paul, Minn.: West.
Bush, Chilton R. 1970. *Newswriting and Reporting Public Affairs*. 2d ed. Philadelphia:
Chilton Books.
Cohen, Morris L. 1985. *Legal Research in a Nutshell*. 4th ed. St. Paul, Minn.: West.
Day, Louis A. 1988. The pro athlete's right of publicity in live sports telecasts. *Journalism
Quarterly*. 65 (Spring): 62–70.
Denniston, Lyle W. 1980. *The Reporter and the Law: Techniques of Covering the Courts*.
New York: Hastings House.
Gordon, David. 1984. Research techniques. School of Communication, University of
Miami, Coral Gables, Fla. Mimeo.
Gulick, George S., and Robert T. Kimbrough, eds. 1989. *American Jurisprudence*. Roch-
ester, N.Y.: Lawyers Co-operative Publishing.
Izard, Ralph. 1982. *Reporting the Citizens' News*. New York: Holt, Rinehart and Win-
ston.
Kaplan, John. 1978. *Criminal Justice: Introductory Cases and Materials*. Mineola, N.Y.:
Foundation Press.
Krantz, Dick. 1983. Covering the courts. In *The Reporter's Handbook: An Investigator's
Guide to Documents and Techniques*, ed. John Ullmann and Steve Honeyman. New York: St.
Martin's.
Mack, William, ed. 1990. *Corpus Juris Secundum*. St. Paul, Minn.: West.
Oran, Daniel. 1975. *Law Dictionary for Non-Lawyers*. St. Paul, Minn.: West.
Rosen, Stephen, ed. 1926. *Index to Legal Periodicals*. New York: Wilson.
Sobel, Lionel S. 1977. *Professional Sports and the Law*. New York: Law-Arts Publishers.
Weistart, John C., and Cym H. Lowell. 1979. *The Law of Sports*. Indianapolis: Bobbs-
Merrill.

13

Precision
Sports
Journalism

Sports journalists often generalize about the attitudes and opinions of sports fans and athletes in their communities. Many of these generalizations find their way into newspaper columns or stories. Consider the following hypothetical situation: A sports journalist spends an evening with friends at a local restaurant. In their conversation, it is apparent that these people do not support the coach of the community's college football team, which has a poor record. Will alumni pressure and other public opinion pressures combine to force the coach out of his job? The reporter decides to write a story for the next day's sports section about the lack of support.

These impressions may be accurate, or the story may only be fueling a rumor. How can a reporter be certain? Often, such generalizations are not even close to accurate; they are not representative of the opinions of more than a few individuals in the community who have access to a reporter. An alert reporter would not be swayed by influences, but it is not uncommon to find reporters talking to fans at various gathering places in the community—restaurants, taverns, arenas, ticket offices—to get a feel for the mood of the public on issues involving sports and sports people. Reporters need to know their readers' reactions to local teams. If attendance is low, sports journalists may feel interest is also low. When fans write letters in reaction to stories, the reporters and editors make deductions about how the fans feel. There have been many different traditional indicators of what fans and readers think about teams, personalities, and issues. But in addition to talking with fans, reading mail, listening to telephone callers, or looking at various economic indicators, sportswriters can use another method for evaluating local or national public opinion about sports and athletes — public opinion polls.

The *Washington Post* and ABC News recently conducted a poll to determine what the American public thought about a growing problem: drugs and sports. The *Washington Post*–ABC News poll sought to determine whether Americans support drug testing for athletes, especially professionals, and whether those tests should be mandatory. The poll was conducted because many experts believe drug use is a serious problem in professional sports. The professional leagues took their own actions on the issue, but the two news organizations felt it was an important enough issue to measure national public sentiment.

The study revealed that three-quarters of those polled felt testing should be done and two-thirds felt it should be required of all participants. The poll interviewed more than 1,500 Americans over a five-day period. The poll asked questions about penalties for athletes found to be using drugs. It also asked respondents for opinions about college and other amateur athletes and drug use. As a secondary focus to the poll, the news organizations also asked Americans whether they felt gambling was a problem in professional sports.

Issues in sports often reflect the larger problems of our society, such as drug use, gambling, and violence. Often, questions arise about how best to approach the problems in our diverse and complex society. Sports and social problems are not strangers. Sports and polls are not strangers, either. Major daily newspapers and wire services have used polls in sports in different forms for years. These polls have generally been non-scientific polls of special groups, such as writers, coaches, or players. And most of these polls have resulted only in ratings of the best amateur football, basketball, baseball, and racing athletes and teams. The systems would be most effective if the entire membership of a group was polled — a census — but this is rarely the case.

The news media have used more sophisticated public opinion polls. These polls have been conducted for several decades, primarily in political contexts. The best known is the Gallup Poll, but other national polls such as the Harris Poll or state polls occasionally conduct polls on sports topics, also. Recent subjects of those polls have included public participation in sports, the public's favorite sports to follow, and the public's favorite sports to attend.

Many major newspapers conduct their own national or regional polls. Some newspapers poll extensively on local matters, such as education, crime, and mass transportation; others have not attempted such reporting. Since Philip Meyer wrote *Precision Journalism* (1979) and more recently *The New Precision Journalism* (1991), more polling has been used to report community opinions. Meyer convincingly shows that reporters can conduct their own polls to determine reliably attitudes of people in their communities.

The poll is a natural for sportswriters accustomed to the informal opinion indicators he or she has traditionally used. Should a city build a new baseball-football stadium? Does a community want to spend tax dollars on a public golf course? Should the city build tennis courts? How many? Where? Should the county limit parties in the parking lots of the stadium before games? Should alcohol be sold? Are concession prices too high? Should players strike? How important is television to local sports fans? What are the most popular local sports? How should renovation of the high school stadium be funded? Do fans participate in any sports? These are only a few examples of the questions that sports journalists generate daily.

A sports reporter must understand the correct use of the public opinion poll, both to make sense of the work done by outside interests providing poll results and to be able to originate polls. Sports reporters are often given poll results by organizations and are encouraged to base stories on these data. It is not unusual, for example, for an athletic director of a major university or college to send a press release to area newspapers giving opinion survey results, such as alumni support of construction of new seats for a stadium. A reporter not aware of polling techniques may use the story without considering the source of the information or the methods used to obtain it. A poll taken at halftime at the hot dog stands during the homecoming game is quite different from one sampling alumni, conducted by telephone or mail, and the results may be equally different.

Unfortunately, individuals often conduct polls and surveys like the "homecoming poll" and attempt to generalize their results as legitimate indicators of public opinion. The term "poll" used throughout the rest of this chapter refers to a statistically valid scientific procedure. A poll is a method of drawing a sample from a population, and a representative poll should give every member an equal chance of being selected into the sample. This point will be discussed in more detail later in this chapter.

"Non-scientific" Polls Cause Problems

In the late 1980s a worrisome trend developed in polling. It remains a problem today: the use of 900 area code telephone numbers for polling. These are numbers that have a user-based fee attached per call, in contrast with 800 numbers, which are free to the caller but paid for by the recipient of the call. Usually, the 900 call fees are low, about 50¢ to $2 per call for most surveys and polls (the fee appears on the caller's phone bill at the end of the month). Research has shown that polls using the 900 numbers contain substantial errors even though some readers might hold them in high regard (Gerhard 1990).

A number of newspapers and television stations, looking for shortcuts to measuring opinion on an issue, have turned to these inexact and biased devices. These organizations often want to "measure" local sports fans' opinions without going through the correct procedures to do so. Perhaps the most frustrating point about these 900 polls is that the sponsors are well aware of their scientific shortcomings, and although they often label them as non-scientific, they use them anyway. In sports, it could be argued that these polls are more for entertainment and amusement, but most social scientists would say that they are still misused.

The main problem is that these polls yield misleading or incorrect results. First, these polls use a self-selection sampling approach, reducing the generalizability of the findings to the larger population for statistical reasons. Second, these polls also introduce a possible socioeconomic class bias in that only those willing, and able, to pay the toll will call. Third, they permit repeat calling, or "voting."

Furthermore, these polls make the news organizations that conduct or sponsor them appear to be profit-seeking by charging "voters" for their opinions. The sponsoring organization splits revenues from the calls with the telephone company. The bottom line on 900 polls is simple: avoid them. Even those organizations savvy enough in measuring public opinion to issue regular disclaimers (such as "this is a non-scientific poll") still cause problems with these polls by using them and therefore lending an air of legitimacy to them. Ultimately, the news organization's credibility may be hurt.

Conducting an Opinion Poll

There are a number of important considerations in originating and conducting a poll. Many of these decisions must be made long before the first survey question is posed. Charles Backstrom and Gerald Hursh-Cesar (1981) list the major steps in setting up and executing a poll. A brief discussion of these steps will follow.

1. Hypothesizing (predicting the results through statements of relationships of key variables)
2. Designing (developing procedures and methods to gather data)
3. Planning (setting up a project budget, figuring materials and personnel needed)
4. Financing (arranging support for the survey itself)
5. Sampling (choosing the group to be surveyed and the sample to be interviewed)

6. Drafting questions (to be used in the questionnaire)

7. Constructing the questionnaire (ordering questions on the questionnaire and developing the questionnaire format)

8. Pretesting the questionnaire (determining whether questions elicit desired data)

9. Training field interviewers (teaching beginning interviewers the skills needed to interview successfully)

10. Briefing interviewers (telling them how to use the questionnaire, how to follow instructions and properly record responses)

11. Interviewing (securing data consistently from sample/survey respondents)

12. Controlling (supervising the interviews)

13. Verifying (assuring that data collected from interviews are accurate)

14. Coding (preparing codes to questionnaire responses for analysis)

15. Processing (organizing data manually or electronically for tabulation)

16. Analyzing (interpreting data for meaning)

17. Reporting (presenting the new information in the most understandable form for the reader)

THE HYPOTHESIS AND RESEARCH QUESTIONS. The hypothesis is a prediction about events. A reporter might expect citizens to oppose community funding of construction of a new sports and entertainment arena after talking with people informally, but a poll would determine the actual community sentiment. The hypothesis helps to formalize, in specific terms, what the poll will measure. In research such as polling, it is also helpful to write general questions, called research questions, to help focus on these informational goals. They are much like an outline. A questionnaire that asks these questions and tests the hypothesis will provide the maximum useful information.

General questions could include: What do residents of your city think about building a new sports and entertainment arena with public funds? How do residents prefer the arena construction be financed if public money is not used? And the hypotheses might be: (1) taxpayers support construction of the new arena; (2) taxpayers do not favor a special assessment to finance the sports arena; or (3) taxpayers prefer outside funding in the form of a private investment to finance the arena.

Too often, research bypasses this first step, and the result is useless questions, poorly planned analysis, and other flaws that lead to extra work and expense.

DEVELOPING THE QUESTIONNAIRE. Survey questions require as much or even more preparation than customary news interview questions. Research is critical in drafting to construct questions that yield the most information. Avoid leading questions that encourage a specific answer. Questions must be neutral and fair, or the information they provide is useless for an objective story. The planner must consider, as well, what type of questions to ask. Open-ended questions allow more freedom of response on the part of the respondent but take more time to analyze: "How should the city finance the construction of a new sports and entertainment facility?" Closed-ended, or multiple-choice, items limit the range of answers but are easier to analyze: "The new sports and entertainment arena planned for the city can be financed in several ways. I am going to read you a list. Which do you prefer: a 1¢ sales tax, a state grant, a special tax assessment, private investor funding, or an event ticket tax?" Remember, it is much more difficult to write a question understood by hundreds of people than by a single, known respondent.

Once the questions are in final form, the next consideration is the order of the questions. Usually, it is better to rank questions from the most general to the most specific on a given topic. Instructions to interviewers must also be placed on the questionnaire. A general format for a questionnaire might include these five parts: (1) An introduction (to place the survey in context for the respondent), (2) screening or "filter" questions (to determine if the respondent qualifies for the survey) and interviewer instructions, (3) substantive questions (the objective of the project) and interviewer instructions, (4) demographic questions (to reveal data about the respondent) and interviewer instructions, and (5) a conclusion and expression of gratitude to the respondent for participating.

PRETESTING THE QUESTIONNAIRE. After the proposed questionnaire is created, it must be determined if the questions actually elicit the desired information. The "pretest" saves the planner from guessing and serves as a last-minute check against ambiguities and wording or sequencing errors. Pretesting can be done in a relatively short time. It is conducted with respondents who have a background similar to those in the sample. A safe pretest usually involves about two dozen respondents interviewed in the same manner as proposed in the actual survey. Afterward, it is useful to talk with them about the questionnaire and the questions. Are the questions clear and understandable? If not, the questionnaire should be revised and pretested again. Some questionnaires go through several drafts before they are ready to be used.

DESIGN. When planning the survey, it is extremely important to determine what should be learned from the project. Equally important is the project design. There are three main ways to collect information: through telephone interviews, through personal interviews, and through the mail. Each has advantages and disadvantages. The majority of newspapers that conduct surveys use the telephone: It is quick, and the media need news in a hurry; it is less expensive because it requires less fieldwork; and it is accurate, shown by researchers to be as reliable as the other two methods.

A reporter designing a survey should set up a table of pros and cons for each method, evaluated in light of available resources. If the budget permits, it is advantageous to use an independent interviewing firm to conduct the fieldwork, leaving the questionnaire creation and other work to the sports reporter. If not, then the reporter must consider how to get interviewers, telephones, and other resources needed to complete the survey.

Sometimes local colleges or universities have survey centers or faculty members who conduct surveys who will help for a lower price than a commercial organization will charge to conduct a poll. This is an option if a reporter has a small budget for survey expenses.

CRITICAL DECISIONS. Designing and planning the poll involves a set of critical decisions about resources. Most editors require an assessment of costs before agreeing to a study. A well-executed professional survey in the 1990s could cost well over $25,000, but a smart reporter with reliable in-house resources, or a low-cost local college or university, can cut these costs and come up with a survey for less than $3,000. Budget preparation may include the following factors: questionnaire duplication and supplies, interviewers' time and cost, telephone tolls or fees, computer analysis time, data processing time, supervisors' time.

There are still other considerations. Will other newspaper personnel assist in the project? How many interviewers will be needed? Where will they come from? Who will supervise and train them? When will the fieldwork be started and completed? By what date should the stories be ready? Most reporters who plan and execute polls set up timetables for projects so that all people understand when they will be needed and when copy must be ready.

FINANCING. With the budget made, the reporter can talk seriously with his or her sports editor or department head about funding for the project. A well-thought-out budget, with a rationale for all items, is a distinct advantage when seeking funds. Some newspapers, however, do not have the financial resources for such an undertaking, and some can only partly finance it. In these cases, the reporter must use ingenuity but should not give up. Institutions such as area colleges or universities often have classes interested in working on such a project. Or interested community groups may be willing to lend support, such as labor. Grants from independent groups are often available for projects. Persistence will pay off.

SAMPLING. Much has been written on sample design, or sampling (see

Slonim 1960, Kish 1965, Babbie 1973). The idea is really quite simple. A population (for example, adult sports fans in a state or county) is defined by the survey planner. Sample design is the procedure by which the reporter/planner determines the part of this population to survey. A small sample, if well selected, will be representative of the entire group and allow the reporter to generalize from the sample to the entire population. This is usually the only practical means of gathering information from a population; all adult sports fans in an area cannot be questioned. In some cases, such as all coaches in a state coaching organization, a group is small enough so that all of its members can be contacted.

There are two types of sampling: probability and non-probability. Most polls use probability sampling, a procedure guaranteeing random choice of respondents. This does not mean that just any person is interviewed at random, but that each member of the population of possible respondents has an equal chance of being included in the sample. There must not be any biases in the sample selection design that reduce any member's chances of being selected. Such samples are difficult to achieve, but are respected by professional pollsters.

The advantage of probability sampling is that it makes possible an estimate of the accuracy of the survey. Statisticians have worked out procedures to determine the probable difference between the responses of all members of the population and the responses of only a sample of the population. This difference is called the margin of error. The chances of error are reduced as the size of the sample is increased. A sample of 200 individuals from a population of 10,000 is not as reliable (it has a higher margin of error) as a sample of 400. The margin of error for a population of 10,000 individuals or more ranges from a maximum variation of plus or minus 13.9 percent if a sample of only 50 people is interviewed, to plus or minus 2.5 percent if 1,500 people are interviewed.

If a survey of 400 people found that 45 percent supported construction of a new arena whereas 43 percent did not (with 12 percent undecided), the range of accuracy of this survey is not sufficient to be certain of the outcome. With a margin of error of plus or minus 5 percent, the supporting group actually ranges from 40 to 50 percent and the opposition group ranges from 38 to 48 percent. This is literally too close to call. A smaller sample from the same population, of course, would cause the error to be even larger and the findings even less certain.

If the *Knoxville News-Sentinel* sports department interviewed a sample of 1,500 adults taken from the population (more than 10,000) of the University of Tennessee football season ticket holders about preferred starting times of home games, the actual responses (if all of the population was measured) might vary as much as 2.5 percent above or below the predicted responses. So a reporter learning that 49 percent of the survey sample favored night games over early afternoon games and 48 percent favored early afternoon games, with 5 percent undecided, could not make a judgment about ticket holders' opinions either way because of the closeness of the figures and the range of the margin of error, assuming the sample was well designed and unbiased.

A four-step procedure determines the error for any probability sample. Using a pocket calculator with a square root key, just follow these steps:

1. Enter 0.25
2. Divide by your sample size (400 in the above example: $0.25/400 = 0.000625$)
3. Punch the square root key ($0.000625 = 0.025$)
4. Multiply by 1.96 ($0.025 \times 1.96 = 0.049$, or 4.9%)

Wilhoit and Weaver (1980) offer a handy table of margins of error based on sample size for large populations. Other books on survey research provide similar tables.

TRAINING INTERVIEWERS. In a well-executed survey, the interviewing technique is taught to the interviewers, particularly if they have no previous interviewing experience. If a project takes the low-budget route, it will be likely that interviewers are inexperienced. They must be trained. The influences of an interviewer on a respondent, which can be significant, must be controlled by proper procedures. Several experts have written excellent discussions of survey interviewing (for example, Stewart and Cash 1991). Briefing interviewers, an extension of the training session, involves the specific survey instrument. A thorough briefing session includes a demonstration interview and an explanation of how to record responses and deal with situations that may arise during an interview. One key to professional survey interviewing is consistency, conducting all interviews under the same circumstances as much as possible, and in the same manner.

CONTROLLING AND VERIFYING THE INTERVIEWS. To achieve the necessary consistency, there must be an effort to control data collection in the field. This is easier in a telephone survey than in door-to-door interviewing, and it is not possible to control mail surveys because they are self-administered. Uncontrolled interviewing is asking for trouble; inconsistent questioning, voluntary explanations, and other situations can lead to unreliable results. Once control is achieved (e.g., by monitoring interviewers, providing thorough training, and seeking standardized interviewing environments), the project director may turn his or her attention to verification, also an extremely important step. The information must have been collected when the interviewer reports it was done. Fraud is infrequent, but on occasion the temptation is too much for an interviewer and it happens. Also, the project director must be able to verify whether the information collected is accurately recorded. On important surveys, every interview may be verified. Other projects selectively verify randomly selected interviews. Some sort of verification process must be done, however, to give credibility to the project. As in any type of reporting, accuracy is the most important consideration. Verification is a major step toward a greater degree of accuracy.

CODING RESULTS. Coding is the first step toward processing the data collected in the field. Answers are recorded by a numerical code that is entered into a computer. For simple polls, data processing may also be quite basic, with a single digit representing each response. Such coding may be done in several ways:

1. Marginal coding leaves a space at the left or right of each question for the numerical code to be inserted.

2. Optical scanning sheets (the common test answer sheet) are a labor-saving device for coding. Responses are coded by shading in rectangular preprinted areas.

3. Some survey researchers train interviewers to record answers on coding sheets as they interview, bypassing the time-consuming postinterview coding. These scanner sheets also bypass another time-consuming step, computer card keypunching. Short, simple questionnaires do not need computer card data entry. But most surveys require computers at the coding stage.

4. The most sophisticated survey research operations use telephones linked with personal computer terminals for direct data entry, bypassing many of the data processing steps. In this system, called computer-assisted telephone interviewing or CATI, a personal computer using specially written survey software displays the questions, and the interviewer, with a telephone headset, directly keys the answer code into the terminal. Such systems are quite expensive and may be out of the financial reach of some newspaper budgets. However, some newspapers have marketing or research departments with such a facility. Furthermore, local colleges and universities often have such setups available for lease by the public.

If you take a do-it-yourself approach but know little about computers, the more realistic method for data analysis is still marginal coding or optical scanner sheets. Although more time-consuming, it is practical for beginners and more affordable for low-budget projects.

PROCESSING RESULTS. Data can be processed in numerous ways. With very simple polls, it can be done using a desk calculator or other non-computer method. But the widespread availability of personal computers makes analysis much easier. Spreadsheet programs such as Lotus 1–2–3, Microsoft Excel, or inexpensive statistics programs can be used. With more complex polls, a computer data processing expert is of immense assistance, providing advice for processing and analysis. Some newspapers, even those that conduct their own extensive polls, often leave the processing to a research department or an outside source, such as a local college computer center. But this is costly and may not be possible if the budget is small.

ANALYSIS OF RESULTS. Once the data are processed and the computer programs run, the all-important analysis occurs. What do the numbers tell? Can any conclusions be drawn? Were the hypotheses supported? The meaning of the numbers is then interpreted for the reader in the subsequent story. Often, reporters will go beyond their own expertise for analysis, taking the findings to other experts on the issues for their interpretation of the results.

EVALUATING AND REPORTING POLLS. More often than not, a survey done by someone else must be evaluated by a reporter for news value. It is not unusual, for example, for an outdoors editor to receive a press release from the state conservation department presenting attitudes of residents toward proposals on hunting and fishing regulations. Or an editor may be given the results of a consumer survey on participatory sports by a corporation's promotion and marketing departments. This situation is even more common on smaller newspapers and other publications that lack the resources to do their own public opinion measurement. G. Cleveland Wilhoit and Maxwell McCombs (1976) tell reporters this situation requires two decisions: (1) What does the reporter or editor do with the poll when it comes in from an outside source? Publish it in some form, file it for reference, or throw it away? (2) How does the reporter or editor evaluate the credibility of the poll?

Even without the interest or resources to conduct a poll, a reporter must understand what goes into a good poll in some situations. Certain technical information about a poll can be a tip about its news value. And organizations such as the The National Council on Public Polls, for example, have established disclosure criteria for what should be reported about public opinion poll methods. The NCPP lists seven criteria, which are used as guidelines in the Associated Press stylebook (Goldstein 1992):

1. How many people were interviewed? How were they selected? Generally, AP advises, only polls using random sampling are reliable.

2. When was the poll taken? As the AP stylebook notes, "Opinion can change quickly in response to events."

3. Who paid for the poll? Was it a special interest group? An independent polling organization? A newspaper?

4. What was the sampling error for the poll and for subgroups mentioned in the story? In related areas, there are other concerns also: How many people were in the group to be contacted? How many responded? The degree of accuracy of the poll should be reported, as well, in terms of

margin of error. The larger the sample, of course, the less error in the results.

5. How was the poll conducted—by telephone or in homes? Polls conducted on street corners are troublesome and should be avoided.

6. How were the questions worded? The wording and sequence of the questions may be factors in the results. And most important, questions should be reported in exact words.

The answers to these questions will be helpful to the reporter and editor and, in the end, to the informed reader.

An expansion of criteria for evaluating and presenting polls was produced by G. Cleveland Wilhoit and David H. Weaver (1980), emphasizing the need for reporters to understand and use public opinion polls in a professional manner. It, like *Precision Journalism* and *The New Precision Journalism* (Meyer 1979, 1991), is an excellent reference.

Analysis of a Sports Poll

The *Washington Post* is one of the major daily newspapers in the United States that regularly conducts polling. Occasionally, the polls cover subjects of interest to sports fans. In the following example, the *Post* conducted the poll on its own, looking closely at athletes and drug use. The story is based on a poll conducted days after University of Maryland All-America basketball player Len Bias died from an overdose of cocaine. College Park, of course, is just a few miles from Washington. The story, national in caliber, sent shock waves through Maryland and Washington, and was very timely. Writer Barry Sussman asks Maryland residents about the perceived widespread nature of drug use among athletes and the possible penalties for those found using drugs. Analysis focused on demographics such as race, age, gender, education, and political orientation.

SOURCE: The *Washington Post,* page B3
DATE: June 28, 1986
AUTHOR: Barry Sussman, *Washington Post* staff writer
HEADLINE: 44% in poll think many U-Md. athletes use drugs; Most Marylanders indicate that problem is no worse than at other big schools

About half the adults in Maryland think the use of illegal drugs such as cocaine is widespread among athletes at the University of Maryland, but only three in every 100 think the problem is worse there than at other large schools, according to a *Washington Post* public opinion poll.

Residents see the drug problem as so complex that they are sharply divided over whether it is possible for university officials to prevent athletes from using the drug. By a 2-to-1 margin, Marylanders surveyed said they would reject a rule banning players from competition if they are found to be using cocaine for the first time.

The Post's poll began last Saturday, two days after All-America basketball player Len Bias died from using cocaine, and was completed Wednesday. In all, 1,656 people age 18 and older were interviewed at random by telephone across the state.

Concern that drug use is common among Maryland athletes grew day by day as details of Bias' death became known. On Saturday 39 percent of the people interviewed believed that the problem was widespread; by Wednesday that figure climbed to 49 percent.

On the average over the five days of the survey, 44 percent believed that the use of illegal drugs such as cocaine was a widespread problem among the school's athletes. Eleven percent believed such drug use was not widespread, and 45 percent said they were unable to venture an opinion.

With only a few exceptions, all groups in the population—men and women, high school dropouts and those with graduate degrees, younger people and older ones, blacks and whites, political conservatives and liberals—had uniform views on the nature of the drug problem.

There was virtually no difference among any of these groups, for example, in the proportions thinking the situation at Maryland is worse than at other large schools. Overall, only 3 percent felt that way, and 6 percent said drugs such as cocaine were used less by Maryland athletes than by athletes at other schools. The great majority, 70 percent, saw no difference in the pattern at Maryland and other places, and 21 percent offered no opinion.

There also were virtually no differences in views on whether it was "realistic or unrealistic to expect the University of Maryland and other large schools" to prevent athletes from using drugs such as cocaine.

In all, 47 percent called such an effort "unrealistic," 41 percent said it was "realistic" and 12 percent had no opinion. However, younger people—those between the ages of 18 and 34—were slightly more inclined to think the use of drugs such as cocaine could be stopped.

The survey asked whether athletes found to be using cocaine for the first time at Maryland should be banned from sports there, or whether whatever decision is made should "depend on the circumstances." Among all people interviewed, sentiment ran against a blanket ban, 62 to 31 percent.

On that question, one group—people who thought of themselves as conservatives—tended to be tougher, dividing 41 percent in favor of a ban and 50 percent against.

Theoretically, a poll this size has a margin of sampling error of less than 3 percentage points. That does not take into account other undeterminable sources of error that may occur in polls.

The next story is a portion of a major package based on a public opinion survey of professional football fans in South Florida. The effort was a team project by reporters from the sports department and city desk. It is a thorough presentation on an issue that was very controversial among sports fans at the time: cost and interest in attending Miami Dolphins games at the relatively new Joe Robbie Stadium between Miami and Fort Lauderdale.

SOURCE: The *Miami Herald,* final edition, page 1D
DATE: Friday, November 2, 1990
AUTHOR: Greg Cote, *Herald* sportswriter
HEADLINE: Why JRS isn't a full house; Dolphins pan prices, parking

The Dolphins are winning again but there are empty seats at Joe Robbie Stadium most every game, and empty seats on your living-room couch because the games aren't on local TV.

Miami has lost 16,000 season-ticket holders during the club's four years at Joe Robbie Stadium. Only two teams in the 28-club NFL have had a longer run of blacked-out home games than the Dolphin streak that will reach 20 with Sunday's visit by Phoenix.

Why?

Attendance last season plummeted to the franchise's lowest average since 1980. There is an upturn so far during this 6-1 season and, indeed, the blackout streak figures to end when the Los Angeles Raiders visit Nov. 19 on Monday Night Football—fewer than 5,000 tickets remain. But the Raiders game throbs as an aberration. More typical is Sunday's cold-ticketed Phoenix game, which is expected to draw only about 56,000 to the 73,083-seat JRS.

Why?

"I'm scratching my head," Dolphin President Tim Robbie said. "As well as our team is doing it shouldn't matter who we're playing; we should be doing better. It's disappointing."

The Miami Herald sought answers to Dolphin attendance problems by conducting a telephone survey of self-described pro football fans in Dade and Broward.

Results show an overwhelming belief that ticket prices are too high; continued dissatisfaction with stadium parking and traffic; and an indication that a large number of South Florida pro football fans—perhaps one of three—are not Dolphin fans.

● Eighty-four percent of surveyed fans thought ticket prices were too high. The range is $28 to $22, and the average of all tickets is $26.21—the NFL's sixth- or seventh-most expensive, Robbie said.

● Seventy-four percent agreed with the statement, "Parking and traffic are awful at JRS." The percentage was slightly higher among fans who had never been there, suggesting perception may be worse than reality.

● Sixty-five percent called the Dolphins their favorite team, meaning a third of the club's core of potential customers favored other teams, led by the Giants, Raiders and 49ers.

"A poll like that here and we'd get at least 95 percent support," said Denver Broncos President Pat Bowlen, whose club is one of five to have every home game sold out and shown on local TV since the blackout era began in 1973.

The Broncos have a 15,000-fan waiting list for season tickets. When a ticket-holder moves away, he places an ad to sell the "rights" to his ticket — typically for $5,000.

In Miami, the waiting list also numbers about 15,000 fans — except that it's the club waiting for the fans, not the fans waiting for tickets. That's about how many season-ticket holders have disappeared. And it is the season-ticket base that largely determines sellouts and blackouts.

The Dolphins must sell out only their 62,000 regular-price seats within 72 hours of a kickoff for the local blackout to be lifted. In 1987, the first year at JRS, 53,000 were pre-sold through season sales. This season: fewer than 36,000.

"The main reason has been our record," Robbie said, referring to four straight seasons out of the playoffs. "There's going to be more demand on season tickets following this season, assuming we keep playing like we've been playing."

There also remains a perception that the ambience at a Dolphin game isn't as lively as at the Orange Bowl. Fifty-five percent agreed with the statement, "The Orange Bowl atmosphere was more fun."

Countered Robbie: "Winning makes for a fun event. All this talk about the Orange Bowl being louder and having a better atmosphere is a bunch of nonsense. In recent games we've proved that."

There is evidence that lingering dissatisfaction — including that over ticket prices and parking — may not be as justifiable today as when the stadium opened.

The Dolphins' across-the-board $26 ticket was the NFL's highest average in 1987. Now seven teams have a higher lowest-priced ticket than Miami's $22 ticket. Surveyed fans said $17 would be a fair price — but no NFL team has an average ticket that cheap.

Parking and traffic? Robbie said that was a problem during the transitional 1987 season, but "the perception that there are still parking and traffic problems here is an erroneous one."

But the perception remains.

Attendance is up, from last year's average of 55,958 to 66,817. But the expected crowd Sunday reminds that problems remain, and surveyed fans show cost and hassle are keeping them away.

Typical is Bob Wyner, 71, a security guard from Hollywood, a Dolphin fan "since Griese." Wyner does not go to games. Asked what it would take to get him to one, he replied, "A limo. Because parking's horrible, I've heard."

Joseph Swiderski, 70, retired night-club owner from New Jersey, goes to four or five games a year and said, "Prices and parking are ridiculous. I went to Giants games for years and it was never that bad."

Prices also are too high for Judy Pincus, 44, a school teacher in North Miami Beach, who said, "Parking is bad. It's too far to walk from my car to the stadium."

Victor Perez, 18-year-old student at Braddock High in Southwest Dade, goes to a few games a year, said the parking is "getting better," but he doesn't attend more games "usually because of the prices"—about $40 per game for him.

The Dolphins won't lower tickets to $17, but, of the parking/traffic perception, Robbie said, "As the team continues to do better and people come out, that can resolve itself."

Neither does Robbie fret over indications that a third of local football fans are not first Dolphin fans.

"We have so many transplants," he said. "Look at the crowd when we played the Jets. We have season-ticket holders who root for the Dolphins every week, except when the Jets come to town. That makes it even more important for us to put a good product on the field so people will come even if another team is their favorite."

The transient phenomenon may hurt Dolphin attendance most, Robbie said, when attractive television games featuring teams like the Giants and Raiders compete against a Miami home game.

The Dolphins have polled expatriated season-ticket holders to learn why they left and similarly heard price and parking complaints, Robbie said. The club hired a full-time marketing chief in August and plans what Robbie calls an "aggressive" off-season campaign to bolster season-ticket sales, attendance and the likelihood of lifted blackouts.

From a strictly financial view, it may be as advantageous to the club for a game to nearly sell out after the blackout deadline passes as to be shown locally. Lifted blackouts often mean thousands more no-shows, which means thousands in decreased concessions revenue.

"On the other hand," said Robbie, "to have people at home able to see a crowd rooting for the Dolphins rather than against them, and to see everyone whooping it up—that type of exposure can be very positive."

Positively, that type of exposure has been very rare.

What We Asked

The Herald surveyed 200 fans in Dade and Broward to find out why the Dolphins are having so much trouble filling Joe Robbie Stadium. Four out of every five described themselves as fanatic or moderate pro football fans, yet fewer than half said they have attended a game at JRS.

What the Fans Said

The main reasons fans cited for not attending Dolphin games:

● Only 65 percent said the Dolphins were their favorite team.

● A total of 74 percent strongly agreed or somewhat agreed that parking and traffic are "awful" at JRS.

● A total of 84 percent strongly agreed or somewhat agreed that ticket prices are too high. The average person responding said $17 would be fair rather than the $26.21 current average ticket.

How This Survey Was Done

Telephone interviews were conducted Oct. 26-28 with 200 adult fans of professional football from Dade and Broward counties. The error margin for a sample of this size is plus or minus 6.9 percentage points.

Respondents for this poll were randomly chosen from a list of more than a thousand randomly selected South Florida residents who were surveyed 18 months ago regarding sports coverage in *The Herald*.

The survey was designed and the results analyzed by Associate Editor/Research Stephen K. Doig. Also contributing to this survey were Betty Grudzinski and Nancy Leve of *The Herald*'s marketing research department, and Tara Connolly of *The Herald* sports department.

Dolphin tickets range from $28 to $22. The Phoenix Cardinals have the most expensive seat in the NFL ($50) and the Detroit Lions the least expensive ($7.50).

Reprinted with the permission of the *Miami Herald*

The original article included a table of ticket prices for all National Football League teams and a chart that listed specific survey questions and responses by percentages.

Team Rankings, Not Polls

For the first time in many years, the issue of team rankings and polls raised its ugly head in 1990 and 1991. The 1990 and 1991 college football seasons had no clear dominant team, and a number of schools held the top ranking throughout the season. The pages of sports sections across the country are filled with these non-statistical rankings of teams each season. Perhaps the most widely publicized are the ratings of the top college and high school teams. Two of the most popular ratings, the Associated Press sports journalists and sportscasters poll and the United Press International poll, rate the top college football and basketball teams on a weekly basis. In recent years, these two polls have been joined by numerous others, forcing fans to make decisions about which poll is to be most respected—usually, of course, the poll that rates his or her favorite team highest. Sportswriters are frequently caught in this trap, referring to the highest rating of the local team in their stories.

Detroit Free Press sports columnist Michelle Kaufman (1990), writing during the chaotic 1990 college football season, said it well when discussing the impact of these polls:

> College football polls are no longer the playful lists they were intended to be when the AP introduced its poll in 1936. Nowadays, rankings determine bowl bids, multimillion-dollar payoffs and national champions.

Reprinted by permission of the *Sporting News*

Serious stuff.

But examine the polls, and you'll find that they are about as credible as professional wrestling. Is anyone truly an expert on 106 major college football teams?

Consider: Brigham Young beat Miami handily. Miami is No. 8, BYU No. 10 in the latest AP poll. Auburn dropped from second to fourth after a victory, a 17-16 squeaker past mediocre Mississippi State. And Wyoming won its first nine games before losing to Colorado State Saturday and couldn't get past No. 19.

The AP voting board consists of 60 sports reporters. Some writers come from big papers — the *Miami Herald,* the *Boston Globe,* the *Chicago Tribune.* Others work for lesser-known publications — the *Waterloo (Iowa) Courier,* the *Honolulu Advertiser.*

The UPI rankings are decided by 56 coaches, about 10 per geographic region. Some coaches sit down each Sunday morning, peruse the summaries and make their choices. Others have members of their staff (or family) do the voting.

It must be remembered that these are rating devices, *not true polls.* It is unfortunate that the word poll is almost always used to describe them. "Ranking" is a more accurate word. The AP, UPI, and ESPN rankings are from non-scientifically drawn samples of sportswriters, broadcasters, and Division 1-A coaches. Their purposes may be worthwhile, but more sophisticated sampling designs would establish greater credibility and accuracy of opinion among these highly specialized groups.

Some newspapers have begun generating their own rankings. The *New York Times,* for example, uses a computer ranking system that does not mislead readers by claiming to "poll" a group to determine rankings.

A disproportionate emphasis is placed on these non-scientific rankings, with unfortunate consequences. For example, in Division 1-A NCAA football, which has no playoffs, the rankings determine the national champion each January 2. The 1990 college football season is a good example of the chaos caused by the proliferation of non-scientific rankings. At the end of the season, after all the bowl games were played, at least three different schools were ranked No. 1. In the AP writers rankings, Colorado was at the top. The UPI coaches rankings placed Georgia Tech at the top. The *New York Times* computer ranked Miami first.

Even scientific polls will not settle the issue, however, when opinion is divided. It only makes the division of opinion less doubtful. At the end of the 1990 football season, in early 1991, *Newsweek* magazine commissioned a Gallup Organization national survey of 759 sports fans across the country. The poll was conducted immediately after the January 1 bowl games. *Newsweek*'s poll found 21 percent of fans supported Colorado, 21 percent supported Georgia Tech, and 11 percent supported Notre Dame (Leerhsen and Nelson 1991).

With a little additional preparation in sampling writers and coaches, uncertainty could be eliminated in the validity and reliability of these polls. The first step is determining what population is appropriate to evaluate team rankings. For example, to develop high school rankings during a football season, a sports department must decide whether to survey coaches, players, or journalists. If coaches are chosen, the reporter directing the poll would compile a master list of all coaches in the state at a particular level. These lists are commonly available at low cost from high school athletic associations. The reporter would choose names at random from the list for the weekly survey, either using the same names each week for a panel approach or selecting a new sample each week. These individuals could be contacted by telephone to obtain their ratings for the top 20 or 25 teams. A panel approach offers the advantage of the respondents preparing lists on a regular basis, which speeds up the process. Once information is collected by telephone, the tabulation is simple, requiring only a desk calculator to assign points to each team in the reverse order of their ranked positions.

Sports Journalism and Polls

Use of surveys and polls in sports journalism is clearly on the increase, and careful use of polls is also growing, just as it is in other news departments of the newspaper. Many newspapers have discovered polling applications, and others are trying their own polls. As polls become more economical and reliable with the merger of inexpensive personal computer and telephone systems, sports journalists will use them more to determine the opinions of fans on critical issues affecting their communities. Small daily and weekly newspapers, which cannot necessarily afford such elaborate reporting tools, will find inexpensive ways to approach opinion measurement in sports news (for example, getting help from nearby colleges or pooling limited resources with other newspapers). As polling comes to be a routine reporting tool for sports, the standards for sports polls and surveys will become more rigorous in the years ahead.

References

Babbie, Earl R. 1973. *Survey Research Methods.* Belmont, Calif.: Wadsworth.

Backstrom, Charles H., and Gerald D. Hursh-Cesar. 1981. *Survey Research.* 2d ed. New York: John Wiley & Sons.

Gerhard, Michael E. 1990. A newspaper's 900 telephone poll: Its perceived credibility and accuracy. *Journalism Quarterly,* Autumn, 508–13.

Goldstein, Norm, ed. 1992. *The Associated Press Stylebook and Libel Manual.* New York: The Associated Press.

Kaufman, Michelle. 1990. Polls as credible as pro wrestling. *Miami Herald,* November 4, 14D.

Kish, Leslie. 1965. *Survey Sampling.* New York: John Wiley & Sons.

Leerhsen, Charles, and Margaret Nelson. 1991. Win one for the clipper. *Newsweek,* January 14, 59.

Meyer, Philip. 1979. *Precision Journalism: A Reporter's Introduction to Social Science Methods.* 2d ed. Bloomington: Indiana University Press.

_____. 1991. *The New Precision Journalism.* Bloomington: Indiana University Press.

Slonim, Morris James. 1960. *Sampling.* New York: Simon and Schuster.

Stewart, Charles J., and William B. Cash. 1991. *Interviewing: Principles and Practices.* 4th ed. Dubuque, Iowa: Brown.

Wilhoit, G. Cleveland, and Maxwell McCombs. 1976. Conducting a survey. In *Handbook of Reporting Methods,* ed. Maxwell McCombs, et al. New York: Houghton Mifflin.

_____., and David H. Weaver. 1980. *Newsroom Guide to Polls and Surveys.* Washington, D.C.: American Newspaper Publishers Association.

5 State of the Art

Kansas City Star sports copy editor Charles Coulter (left) works at his computer terminal in the newspaper's office while other staff members behind him discuss the next day's editions. Coulter represents the growing number of minorities working as sports journalists in the 1990s. (*Photo by Daniel Starling.*)

14

Technology and the Sports Journalist

Consider these possibilities:

● Full-color photographs every day

● Computer-generated graphics merged with computer-provided statistics

● Stories filed by cellular telephone connected to a laptop- or notebook-sized computer

● Research for stories conducted by one computer linked to another

● Team press releases arriving within seconds instead of days, over a facsimile (fax) machine

● Live local team games several thousand miles away shown on television screens in the sports department through cable and satellite links

● Sports stories and pages assembled and produced on a computer screen

● Much-needed photographs or documents arriving within a few hours from hundreds of miles away by overnight delivery services

● Beat reporters seldom going to their newspaper offices, choosing to work from home with personal computers and telephone modem links

● Reporters working from remote locations using electronic (computer) "E-mail" or recorded telephone "voice mail" to gather telephone messages and memoranda

This is the high-tech world of sportswriters in the mid-1990s. Sports journalism, like other departments of the newspaper and other mass media, has been substantially and forever changed by technological and communications developments. Just about everything that sportswriters do now is improved and speeded up by the computer, telephone, and satellite link.

The telephone radically altered reporting methods earlier in this century. As the 20th century began, communication by mail and telegraph was replaced by field reporters who telephoned stories to rewrite specialists at news desks. Today, the computer, as the telephone did, is revolutionizing the way sports journalists communicate. Communication theorist Marshall McLuhan wrote in *Understanding Media* (1964) that technological innovations change the communication process. He stated that the typewriter created "an entirely new attitude to the written and printed word." The "explosive character" of the typewriter had an immediate effect on regulating mechanics of writing such as grammar.

Sports journalists in the 1990s live in a world of powerful palm- and notebook-sized personal computers, pocket-sized appointment and address computers, fax machines, satellite- and microwave-based communications (such as television, radio, and telephone), and cellular telephones. The vast technological changes that the newspaper industry has experienced in the past two decades alone have been the direct result of the introduction of the computer into newsrooms and composing rooms. Once a cold room with tile or wood-block floors filled with the constant clatter of manual typewriters, the newsroom is now a carpeted "news center" filled with programmable telephones, cable-connected television monitors, and dozens of personal computers. Newswriting, reporting, editing, graphics, and full-page composition are controlled by the computer. Beyond the newsroom, the computer also is the nerve center for marketing, circulation, advertising accounting, advertisement layout, employee payroll and benefits, and just about all other aspects of newspaper operation.

Powerful computer systems are the epicenter of the new technology. They have all but eliminated the glue pots, pencils, erasers, scissors, and manual typewriters common in newsrooms until the 1970s. And computers have made possible many improvements in what sports journalism is able to do for readers. More news is processed faster, with fewer errors, and closer to deadline than ever before.

Personal computers (PCs) or video display terminals (VDTs) serving dedicated, or proprietary, systems are found today in newspapers of all sizes. Personal computers offer more flexibility in what they can do and will gradually replace VDT-based systems, which originated in the 1970s and early 1980s. Proprietary VDT-based systems are too limited in what they do—word processing only. During the early 1990s, these systems are being phased out of newsrooms. Personal computers linked through local area networks (LANs) for one-location news operations or wide area networks (WANs) for long-distance news operations, such as those with bureaus, are the new generation of production technology (Davis 1991).

Newsroom computer systems are connected with various types of photocomposition hardware, producing greater speed and accuracy in typesetting and the rest of the production process. The traditional, front-end copy flow system involved typing by a reporter and then retyping by a printer at the keyboard of a Linotype machine. Electronic editing systems eliminate the second (error-prone) typing task. Reporters and editors have become, in effect, their own typesetters and proofreaders.

Electronic Reporting and Editing Systems

Why did the newspaper industry move toward PCs and VDTs and these numerous other technological developments? The majority of the reasons are economic. Central to it all is preservation of the reporter's original keystrokes, which leads to faster production, more accuracy, and increased reliability. Consider the following case:

An Associated Press sportswriter types a story about a Wimbledon tennis match on a laptop PC in a room near center court. The portable PC is a self-contained unit linked by modem to a telephone line to the AP bureau in London. There, the story, without being retyped, is edited and transmitted by satellite link to New York. At the AP sports desk in Rockefeller Center, the story is processed and sent along the national sports wire to newspapers subscribing to the AP service. At the *Chicago Sun-Times,* the sports slot (a desk editor who supervises the sports copydesk) will see the story as it moves on the wire by reading a sports wire storage queue directory. The story has been automatically fed into the *Sun-Times'* electronic editing system computer and electronically stored for the sports department to evaluate for the morning editions. If selected, the story is still in keyboarded form and does not require rekeying unless the sports slot or copy editor decides to rewrite it, combine it with another story, or revise it in some other fashion. But the story may well be in the same form in which it originated a few moments earlier at Wimbledon. When the sports slot is satisfied that the story is ready for publication, it is electronically transferred to the composing room, where no retyping is necessary. A photocomposition device takes the electronic impulses and transfers them into type by reproducing the characters and numbers at high speed on photographic paper. And at more modernized newspapers, the typesetting occurs within the computer system, and the page that contains the story is laid out electronically—a process called pagination.

Newspapers have the option of retaining their wire service printers for wire service and syndicated news service stories, in addition to using the electronic versions. Few news operations use hard copy today unless a hard copy is specifically requested.

The industry has covered much technological ground in just over two decades. As recently as 1970, *Today* (Gannett Newspapers, Cocoa, Fla.) became the first newspaper to use an electronic editing system (Mencher 1991). Barely a decade later, there were more than 21,000 VDTs in operation in the United States, according to the American Newspaper Publishers Association Research Institute (1980).

By the early 1990s, most newspapers were replacing the single-task VDTs with multitask personal computers. These devices are smarter in that they are capable of processing tasks on their own as well as serving as part of computer LANs or WANs. At some metropolitan newspapers, it is not unusual to find hundreds of PCs. The *Columbia Missourian,* a small daily staffed by students and faculty of the School of Journalism at the University of Missouri, is a leader in PC applications in newspapers. Nearly 300 PCs are in use in a sophisticated LAN at the *Missourian* and the School of Journalism. The newspaper staff and school faculty are also experimenting with electronic photography, electronic picture editing, and storage of photographs and other graphics. Smaller newspapers have also adopted these LAN systems, although generally with smaller storage capacities and fewer PCs.

Most newspapers using PCs, LANs, and WANs are now also using desktop publishing systems for page layout and paste-up. Sophisticated off-the-shelf software such as Aldus' PageMaker and Xerox's Ventura Publisher permits sports page graphics editors to produce pages on PC monitors at their desks (Truitt 1990). Similarly, photo editing and graphics have become computerized. Newspapers and wire services are shifting to electronic photography, by which cameras contain memories and images that are "shot," digitized, and transferred to a computer for long-term storage and editing. With these systems, there are no chemicals or paper for developing and printing (Truitt 1990).

Since the mid-1980s, news graphics have been produced with computers. The influences of *USA Today* are now well-known in this area—and well-documented in the research literature—throughout the industry. *USA Today* is widely credited for awakening the industry to regular use of full color, more spot color, and computer-generated graphics throughout the newspaper. With its satellite-based printing system, the newspaper remains available throughout the country with high-quality and up-to-date content.

Mastery of a PC or an electronic editing system should take little time. Most word processing systems are very easy to use. Graphics and pagination take longer to learn, but most programs are "user friendly." Basic operation may be learned in a few hours, and research has shown proficiency follows in a few weeks. Most beginning sportswriters learn basics of computer operation when in high school and college, but employers offer on-the-job training as needed. Regardless of where it is learned, computer literacy among sportswriters is important.

High-Speed Wire Services

Associated Press and United Press International are the two major news services that provide sports news to newspapers in the United States. As UPI has experienced financial problems throughout the past decade and grown much smaller in the United States, AP has become dominant as the major sports wire service. AP offers high-speed wire transmission service to sports sections of member newspapers through its "DataStream" technology. The system transmits 1,200 words-per minute from its base computer system in New York to bureaus and members. The printer of the 1960s produced copy at only 66 words per minute. The 1,200-words-per-minute speed has vastly increased the amount of copy that a sports editor sees in a day from the external sources such as AP, UPI, and other major syndicated news suppliers. Some newspapers no longer use the high-speed printers, preferring to have their computer directly transfer stories from the wire service computer. In this case, a reporter or editor sees the copy only on a computer screen. The volume from the wire services is staggering. AP generates about 150,000 words a day, or, in standard newspaper column measurements, about 3,750 column inches of type—not including statistics (Grimsley 1988).

AP also has a GraphicsNet system for newspapers seeking to use its sports and news graphics. One of the most recent services under development for newspapers seeking production assistance has been full-page agate delivery on Macintosh computer-based systems. This means, simply, that newspapers with limited personnel can use a completely assembled page of agate results when the system is fully in use. The full page includes graphics labels, headlines, and current statistics such as player performances, standings, and results. Newspapers using the service have the option to insert local results such as prep scores and statistics (Christian 1988 and 1990).

Computers in Sports Reporting

Not only has the computer been a factor in processing news, but it has become increasingly important in gathering news. Of course, as mentioned earlier, the faster process, allowing later deadlines and the possibility of updating and revising stories, affects newswriting and editing decisions. Newspapers have begun to consider conversion of space-consuming reference libraries to electronic storage accessible by computer. Such storage and retrieval systems may become the basis for all clip files in the future.

In addition to information storage and retrieval, sports reporters are increasingly gathering information from various outside computers. Almost all official statistics are computer calculated and stored. Major league teams file box scores and other vital statistics each night with the league offices, where new statistics are calculated and released. In a matter of hours, data are fed to the teams, which have new statistics to release before the next day's game.

Amateur athletic organizations, such as the National Collegiate Athletic Association, have gone to computers for recordkeeping. This system makes the information more accurate and more rapidly available, but it can also make the information less accessible to the reporter in some cases (Schiller 1978, Compaine 1981, Garrison 1983).

There are also attempts to establish public information centers based on computer systems. Such fast and accurate information networks would obviously be useful to reporters. Many major libraries already have computerized bibliographic data bases for research purposes. (For more information, see Marvin [1978] and Branscomb [1981].)

Commercial data bases are becoming popular among sports reporters who need quick and easy references to statistical information, scores, or standings. While their own newspapers' electronic libraries are a starting point, many do not keep information beyond what is published. When reporters need to go beyond that, or need current information fast, they use "on-line"—that is, connected computer to computer by telephone line—versions of news services' sports wires such as those available from AP and UPI. This is particularly valuable for a sportswriter on the road. Equipped with a laptop or notebook personal computer and a modem, a sportswriter can connect to his or her own newspaper's library, the current wire service storage queues, or a commercial data base for statistics. Most of these services are available for a fee and also charge by the time used on-line.

SportsTicker is an instant sports information commercial service used by many sports broadcasters, but it offers on-line services to sportswriters for a per-minute or per-hour rate. This 24-hour-a-day current information enables sportswriters who need new information to access scores of current sports events, schedules, trades and other player or team transactions, and other vital information about more than one dozen different sports. Sports-Ticker is the modern version of Western Union's original baseball ticket, started in 1909. The primary sports it covers are baseball, football, basketball, hockey, golf, boxing, bowling, soccer, and auto and horse racing.

Of most interest to sportswriters are SportsTicker's PC Plus and ON-LINE services. PC Plus is a menu-based service connected 24 hours a day to a PC by telephone, providing constant access and research capability to all SportsTicker information. ONLINE is a use-when-needed dial-up service that connects a reporter with a PC and modem anywhere to Sports-Ticker data bases that give current partial and complete game scores, trades, standings, schedules, and other "headline" sports news.

Reporting "on the road" has been made easier by portable PCs linked to the main computer in a newspaper plant. Reporters are able to file stories directly to the computer. The portable PCs—much like the larger, permanent PCs, with keyboards, video displays, and many text editing features—can link up from anywhere in the world where there is a telephone line connecting with the base system. The link is made through a standard telephone with a modem. Storage while typing reduces long-distance charges; a one-time send command permits entire stories to be transmitted in only minutes. These devices weigh about 15 pounds; notebook PCs weigh less than 10 pounds, some just five to seven pounds. Palmtop PCs weigh even less. These terminals have fast transmission speeds through modems (usually 1,200 or 2,400 baud). Special cassette tapes permit up to 16,000-word storage on some units. Personal computers—including laptops, notebooks and palmtops—can be equipped with modems that also receive and send faxes. This capability makes transmission of information to reporters on assignment or at home even more convenient.

Other Technological Aids

Another widely used development, originating in the mid-1940s, is the facsimile, or fax, machine. This is basically a photocopier connected to a telephone line. These machines operate in the same way that early wirephoto machines transmitted photographs by telephone line, only much faster and with much higher quality. The process is fairly simple, but there must be sending and receiving machines. When the sponsor of an event does not have fax service, newspapers may provide their reporters with fax machines if they are needed. All that is needed is a base fax machine at the sports department copydesk and one in the press box or nearby. The reporter places typed copy in the machine and permits the two machines to communicate with each other electronically. At the copydesk, a photocopy gradually emerges from the machine; it may then be edited. This process is particularly fast, taking just seconds for minimal quality reproduction — a little longer for higher quality — to transmit an average 8½-by-11 inch page. In moments, a complete story including box scores or other agate can be transmitted and ready for copy editing. Telephone dictation, the traditional method of handling late-breaking stories, might be as fast with an experienced reporter and a fast typist but is never as accurate as a high-quality fax transmission.

Many sports organizations, such as professional teams and major college athletic programs, provide fax services. Many, in fact, regularly transmit fax press releases to newspapers with special telephone numbers for fax transmission. They believe that some releases, such as game results, cannot wait for mail delivery and that telephone dictation is too time-consuming and error-prone, especially when several newspapers have to be reached. Enough of these services are now provided commercially that reporters seldom travel with fax machines. A typical university sports information department has fax service. On a Saturday, for example, the school's track, golf, and baseball teams all may be competing without reporters present. The coaches then call the sports information director (SID) or an assistant, and a results release is prepared. The sports information department calls the major newspapers and wire services across the state with the release, sometimes two or three at once, for the next editions. The stories are then edited and published.

Fax systems have become so sophisticated that many newspapers have special telephone numbers set up for SIDs and sports publicists to use; these numbers are automatically answered by the fax machine. Such services are becoming more visible at college and professional sports levels. Numerous companies lease fax services to reporters on a per-game basis. They may also provide portable PCs and other types of computer links on site with keypunch services available so all the reporter must do is provide a typed original of the story. This works well for a newspaper with a limited number of portable VDTs or other types of portable terminals that need direct transmission of the story to a typesetting system. Under deadline, such a service is worth the expense. Only 20 years ago, reporters were handing copy to typists operating teletypes for transmission of stories through telex systems or were dictating by telephone to their home newspapers. These new developments get more complete news to the reader faster than ever before.

There have also been numerous developments in the area of home and office computers. With Macintosh, IBM, Epson, Toshiba, and other companies making personal computers more affordable and portable, more and more journalists are exploring their applications to make the job faster and easier. With a home computer, for example, a sports journalist can easily compute statistics or reanalyze existing ones. Home computers, known as hardware in the computer industry, are accompanied by user-friendly software packages (programs) that enable a beginner to use these devices very quickly. A reporter need not be interested in computer programming in order to use a computer in the home, with an interface by telephone as an extension of the newspaper electronic reporting and editing system. Furthermore, personal computers feature word processing software programs that enable writers to work with an error-free hard copy printout from high-speed dot matrix or daisy wheel printers. Many writers who work a great deal at home are finding these relatively inexpensive word processing systems a significant asset in practicing their craft.

Cellular telephones have become essential reporting tools for reporters on breaking spot stories. These telephones make it easy to report to the desk instantaneously for instructions, to call sources while in transit, or to receive calls from sources. Although expensive, these phones help in planning and executing critical stories. Enterprising reporters have learned how to connect their laptop personal computers to their cellular telephones to permit them to file their stories from anywhere they might be — a cab, a locker room — when deadlines beckon.

Sports reporters who also serve as photographers will see their work change in the next decade as electronic cameras begin to replace film cameras. These cameras use disks, much like computers, and electronically store images in the same manner a computer stores a graphic image. Newspapers have been using video images for some time now. USA Today was the first newspaper to take color video images and reproduce them on the front page of a newspaper with high quality. The newspaper did this to publish color World Series photographs in the following day's edition in October 1987 (Rosenberg 1987).

AP is working to improve sports photo transmission speed, too, through its PhotoStream electronic darkroom service. Technology previously was limited to a photograph every eight to ten minutes, or about 140 a day. With new systems, wire services such as AP and UPI can transmit sports photographs in one minute. Color photographs, which once required a half hour to transmit, now require about three minutes (Christian 1990). This not only means greater selection, but better coverage much faster. PhotoStream service means editors and reporters can see and edit as many as a dozen photographs on a computer screen at a single time (White 1990).

Even the telephone and mail systems are more sophisticated for sportswriters. In the area of messages, communication has become more sophisticated because of applications of new telecommunications and computer technologies. Mail systems have become more flexible and much faster through electronic, or E-mail systems. Using LANs and WANs, or using mainframe computers linked through networks of telephone lines, reporters can communicate with editors and other journalists through messaging systems. With electronic mailboxes, communication from distant locations can be quicker and easier than conventional mail or even fax. Telephone message systems have been improved by voice mail, sophisticated answering machine systems that enhance a reporter's ability to be in touch with sources. Reporters can check messages from remote locations with personal access codes and communicate with sources more quickly.

Other Developments, Current and Future

There can be no doubt that the development of television over the last 40-plus years has had a significant effect on newspaper and magazine sportswriting. Many aspects of televised sports have compelled changes in published sports journalism, but one feature of television has been used by print reporters as a new reporting tool—the instant replay. Reporters benefit from being able to rewatch controversial or decisive plays and other moments in an event that they used to see only once (even film was not available on the same day). Instant replay provides reporters with increased detail for description in stories and opportunities for evaluation, resulting in better overall reporting and more depth and analysis in reporting.

Closed circuit television has also meant better reporting, even for reporters on the scene. At most major league baseball parks, press boxes are equipped with television sets for replays and closer views than most writers get from upper-deck press boxes.

Sports news, like the product of other news departments, is now assembled at a few newspapers by electronic devices called pagination systems. This technological development permits even faster production, and theoretically more time for reporting because of a later press deadline, by making possible not only keystroke (and labor) preservation but also electronic page layout and makeup. The first pagination systems were installed in newspapers on an experimental basis in the late 1970s; in 1982 the first complete system with graphics became operative at the *Pasadena Star-News*.

And newspapers are beginning to crossbreed with television. Televised text systems are being developed, and newspapers are purchasing interests in cable systems for transmission of their product over television into homes where television sports viewers can become television sports readers. Early in their development, cable systems transmitted computerized display pages with scores and edited versions of wire stories. These features, not localized to any extent, were only reproductions of external sources' outputs, such as wire service offerings. This was a step leading to teletext and videotext sports.

Since the 1970s, viewers in Great Britain have read sports on television. Football (soccer) scores are broadcast regularly on subscription services. These services offer information in color on standard television sets. Some special systems called videotext allow interaction, or viewer selection of the video sports pages. There are similar systems elsewhere in Europe, and several are being marketed in the United States.

Reporters, and anyone else with a computer for that matter, can purchase "read-only" time on data bases for research and news. Services such as AP, UPI, and most major daily newspapers are available on general information data base services such as Dialog, Knowledge Index, Lexis/Nexis, Vu-Text, CompuServe, and Prodigy.

These technological developments mean that sports reporting will become more global in this decade. Richard Rosenblatt (1990), national desk supervisor for AP sports in New York, says: "The theme for sports in the 1990s is more. More leagues, more games, and more athletes — professional and amateur. Sports will be *globalized* as pro football goes international and Americans discover the "other" football — soccer."

Rosenblatt (1990) says technology will be a key to covering the growth in sports in scope and geography. Greater speed over longer distances will force news organizations to depend on it. And with greater quantity, there will be a need for new ways to write and for readers to consume the large amounts of information. The answer? Writes Rosenblatt: "The trend in coverage is toward shorter stories, snappier leads and easy-to-digest information. Few sports fans will have the time to read 112 800-word stories on every professional team in the United States, not to mention international events."

References

American Newspaper Publishers Association Research Institute. 1980. *Special Report: Electronic Applications in ANPA-Member Newspaper Departments for 1979.* Easton, Pa.: American Newspaper Publishers Association.

Branscomb, Lewis M. 1981. The electronic library. *Journal of Communication* 31 (Winter): 143–50.

Christian, Darrell. 1988. Agate delivery in page form is due soon. *APSE Newsletter,* December, 20.

_____. 1990. Quicker photo delivery is on the way. *APSE Newsletter,* June, 10.

Compaine, Benjamin M. 1981. Shifting boundaries in the information marketplace. *Journal of Communication* 31 (Winter): 132–42.

Davis, William S. 1991. *Computing Fundamentals: Concepts.* 3d ed. Reading, Mass.: Addison-Wesley.

Garrison, Bruce. 1983. Impact of computers on the total newspaper. *Newspaper Research Journal* 4 (Spring): 41–64.

Grimsley, Will. 1988. AP and the sports explosion. *AP World* 3 (Fall): 3–8.

Marvin, Carolyn. 1978. Prospects for a public information network. *Journal of Communication* 28 (Autumn): 172–83.

————. 1980. Delivering the news of the future. *Journal of Communication* 30 (Winter): 10–20.

McLuhan, Marshall. 1964. *Understanding Media.* New York: Signet.

Mencher, Melvin. 1991. *News Reporting and Writing.* 5th ed. Dubuque, Iowa: Brown.

Rosenberg, Jim. 1987. Color video images make the front page. *Editor & Publisher* 120. (November 21): 36, 40, 47.

Rosenblatt, Richard. 1990. Sports will be globalized in the '90s with more games, leagues, athletes. *APSE Newsletter,* January, 12.

Schiller, Herbert I. 1978. Computer systems: Power for whom and for what? *Journal of Communication* 28 (Autumn): 184–93.

Truitt, Rosalind C. 1990. How smaller papers deal with changing technology. *presstime* 12 (June): 36–42.

White, Don. 1990. Photo system promises speed for the desk. *APSE Newsletter,* convention issue, 11.

15

Issues and Ethics in Sports Journalism

Important questions remain unanswered about the role of sports in society in the mid-1990s. Similarly, there are unresolved problems related to how the mass media report news about sports. The lessons of sports — discipline, competitiveness, teamwork — will not have any value unless society reconsiders its priorities. If, as veteran sportswriter John Underwood (1981) notes, the values learned in sports are often taken from the field to the boardrooms of corporate America, the whole system should be reassessed:

> Competition can't serve a society if it's antisocial. Winning at any cost and true sportsmanship are incompatible. The idea that athletic endeavor — win, lose, or draw — is essential to the clearheaded, well-rounded individual is a very old one, extending back to the ancient Greeks. The view that sports competition — especially of the team variety, with its blend of cooperation and self-discipline for the good of the whole — is beneficial, even necessary, to building and maintaining a healthy, productive society is less venerable.

Many American leaders — George Bush, Gerald Ford, Jack Kemp, Byron White, Bill Bradley — have learned some of life's basic lessons from sports and taken them to big league business and government. As Underwood and others point out, sports reflect the society in which they are played. And the journalist reporting sports also reflects society, including the negative side—violence, strikes, drug abuse, injuries, and discord. Some experts argue that values have changed in sports as well as in society. Perhaps people work less as a team, less for long-term goals in favor of short-term ones. Underwood suggests the bigness of sports has created some of the problems: big money, big television, big athletes, and big leagues. The effect of this, he notes, is widespread—but not all bad.

Chronicling the world of sports places some unusual pressures on sports journalists, pressures that did not exist in the days of the "gee whiz!" approach to sportswriting. Sportswriters in the 1990s must cover court cases involving athletes. They gauge (and must do it accurately) the opinion of the sports public on prominent issues. They must not ignore dissent among teams and coaches. They cannot look the other way when corruption, fraud, or plain cheating involves the home team or a beloved athlete. Sports journalists must try even harder to give the complete picture of what is happening in sports and the interactions of sports and society, as well as the impact of sports on society and of society on sports (Forbis 1988).

The Mid-1990s Sports Journalist

Contemporary sportswriters are highly motivated and willing to go the extra mile. *Los Angeles Times* sports editor Bill Dwyre (1981) writes about today's professional sports journalist:

> Sportswriting, when done on a major-league level and done right, is an abnormal profession carried on by abnormal people. The concept of nine to five work . . . is a joke to any sportswriter worth his weight. That's an eight-hour day. It is normalcy, routine, controllable—all those things that sportswriting is not, and never will be. . . . There are those who feel . . . that sportswriters are merely a group of people whose intellectual growth came to an abrupt halt somewhere between second and third base in the midst of a little league game. All that is left for these poor souls is the pursuit of their youthful days, and the only real outlet for that, which society will accept, is the profession. But that segment is rapidly being replaced by a segment of bright, dedicated, hard-working people who seem driven by a desire to give legitimacy to a profession still thought by most to have been conceived out of a journalistic wedlock.

Many people envy a sportswriter's life. The general public will never quite understand why covering games is as much work for a sports reporter as operating a drill press is for the factory worker. For that matter, a sports journalist's job may be even tougher in the long run than more routine ones because sportswriters' hours, scheduled around the timing of events out of their control, are so irregular and hard on a personal life. The increase in jobs on morning newspapers means more and more sportswriters are working the late shift, beginning in late afternoon and ending at midnight or even later. That makes a normal social life impossible for the single person and means the married reporter has a work schedule often clashing with those of a working spouse and school-aged children. And because Friday and Saturday nights are peaks for scheduled sporting events, many reporters find themselves working during prime social evenings of the week.

The most envied sports reporter, it seems, is the one who travels with a college or professional team. But such travel quickly loses its appeal after too many narrow airplane seats, stiff hotel beds, and bad meals. Traveling sportswriters actually spend 24 hours per day on the job because they are not able to go home after they finish writing. Instead, they have to follow the team to the next stop. A baseball writer, for example, from spring training in February to the end of the season in October, may be occupied 31 weeks with the team and home only 10 weeks. This travel can put a strain on a relationship. Several sportswriters have asked to be relieved of a glamorous pro beat because the job had finally gotten to be too much on their families, who asked them to change to routine office jobs. Thoughts of family turmoil may not be pleasant, but they are something that the sportswriter must keep in mind. One of the best solutions is something reporters are supposed to do best: communicate, letting family and friends know exactly what they are doing, why they are doing it at odd hours, and making sure family and friends are responding openly.

The situation has taken on such significance that the Associated Press Sports Editors has devoted time at national meetings to the stressful nature of their work. Inviting psychologists and other experts to offer ways to cope, these editors have held numerous workshops to learn how to manage time, relationships, and other problems that are more commonly associated with teachers, police officers, or doctors. Deadlines, budget decisions, and production demands have added new pressures on sportswriters (Shirley 1985).

Hal Bodley (1980), sports editor of the *Wilmington News Journal,* says this is the era of the three-piece-suit sports editor, who looks more like an attorney preparing a brief than a journalist covering a basketball game. Sports editors today are required to know as much about management as about football. They must be able to add up budget items as easily as game points. Bodley says, "No longer is this a person who runs the 'Toy Department.' This is an editor who is handling one of the most important departments of today's newspaper." Sports pages, he writes, are now also business pages, labor pages, conflict pages, and police-beat pages. Sports editors must not only know layout and design but must also be efficient managers of human (and other) resources. Most newspapers seek in sports editors what they seek in city, feature, and other main section editors. With higher staff salaries and much larger travel budgets, contemporary sports editors manage a sizable investment of their newspapers. It is a critical job demanding extremely well-qualified people.

Preparing Sports Journalists

The requirements for sports journalists have, like the occupation itself, changed dramatically in the past several generations. At one time, all it took was a serious interest in sports and an ability to understand the jargon. No one required a general college education for sportswriters, and many did not have it. Many began with just a high school education, or even less.

Sports journalists of the mid-1990s are college graduates and some have studied at the graduate level (Garrison and Salwen 1989b, Shirley 1985). They compete for higher paid positions that demand greater educational and professional backgrounds. In fact, most newspapers — at least the major dailies — will not hire full-time sportswriters who do not have some sort of college education underway or completed. Most high-caliber college journalism programs ensure that students have studied basic newswriting, reporting, copy editing, graphics or photography, mass media law, journalism history, and ethics. Areas of specialization such as feature writing and, at some schools, sports journalism and broadcasting are gaining increased attention, also. In most programs, only one-fourth of the courses are in journalism; the remaining three-fourths are based in the liberal arts — the social sciences, physical sciences, humanities — and other non-journalism areas.

How does a beginning sportswriter get started? Most work their way up, starting at smaller newspapers. Experience on high school and college newspaper staffs is valuable. To gain professional experience, many college students serve internships while in school and many work part time at local newspapers as clerks — processing agate, taking telephone calls, and so on. This experience often leads to full-time openings after graduation or when a position becomes available. It is a ritual on most sports desks called "paying your dues." Few sportswriters advance to top assignments without it.

It is never too late to improve an education, especially if it seems inadequate. Numerous organizations offer continuing education for beginners or for mid-career sportswriters and editors.

Farewell to Heroes

Sportswriters once held the philosophy that stars on the athletic field are bigger than life. These individuals were society's heroes. As John Consoli (1982) writes: "Many sportswriters considered it taboo to write about the locker room antics of the players, but today, many consider it standard operating procedure indicative of the new style of coverage of professional sports teams." He adds, "No longer is an athlete's performance on the field the only thing that is written about. Many times the athlete's conduct off the field becomes an even bigger story. Disputes among teammates and between players and owners get as many headlines as game results — sometimes even bigger headlines."

Is the era of the super sports hero over? Consoli and a number of sports editors whom he interviewed think so. Furman Bisher, longtime sports editor of the *Atlanta Constitution,* thinks it is, primarily because television has given athletes more exposure to the public than athletes received in the "golden age of sports" (Consoli 1982). Another reason may be the growing independence of the sportswriter. The Babe Ruths and Ty Cobbs of this generation are under closer scrutiny, and the readers and the viewers expect it. The sports hero is still with us, but fans know much more about the person as well as the athlete because of changes in reporting technology and philosophy. It's a good thing that most sports journalists no longer identify with a team and are more independent in their attitudes toward beats and sources.

Concerns about Reporters and Sources

Anyone who reads the professional publications in journalism — periodicals such as *Editor & Publisher* and *Columbia Journalism Review* — has seen articles describing the conflicts between sports journalists and their sports personality sources. Here is just a sampling of encounters in the past decade:

● The Toronto Maple Leafs hockey team barred *Toronto Globe and Mail* reporters from its press box during a feud caused by the newspaper's critical coverage of the team (Fitzgerald 1984b).

● The National Football League confiscated film from an *Orlando Sentinel* photographer, angering the editor of the newspaper. The photographer was on assignment for a Super Bowl practice session in Tampa, but after he took his photographs from a college campus building, NFL security personnel took the film (Fitzgerald 1984a).

● After Lisa Olson's locker room experience with the New England Patriot players became a focus of concern in and out of sports and journalism, legislators around the country began to propose state laws on the subject (Krauthhammer 1990, Kerwin 1990a and 1990b).

● Pro football writers were banned from practice sessions of the San Diego Chargers by coach Dan Henning for reasons — probably simple se-

Wisecracks Aside, Being a Woman Sportswriter Is Still a Great Job

By Michelle Kaufman, *Detroit Free Press* sports columnist

In case you're wondering, no.

It isn't fun interviewing naked athletes in the locker room.

Nor is it fun getting winks from the coaches, reading insulting letters from readers or hearing obscene wisecracks from men who call themselves "professional" athletes. It certainly wasn't enjoyable writing a story after a Pistons playoff game while a group of male reporters passed around a close-up photo of the crotch of a Chicago Bulls cheerleader.

Unfortunately, life isn't easy for female sports enthusiasts who choose a career in writing or broadcasting.

This summer [1990], *Free Press* intern Jennifer Frey was subjected to a crude, unsolicited comment from Tigers pitcher Jack Morris. As she asked Morris a question, he snapped: "I don't talk to people when I'm naked, especially women, unless they're on top of me or I'm on top of them."

Rather than apologize for Morris' insensitive remark, Tigers president Bo Schembechler wrote the *Free Press* a letter implying Frey was a voyeur. He added that "no female member of my family would be inside a man's locker room regardless of their job description."

He went on about the "sanctity and privacy" of the locker room.

If the locker room is so sacred, why doesn't anyone complain about male reporters, cameramen and hangers-on who mill around naked athletes before and after games? Is that a normal working environment?

Locker rooms are open to reporters because that's where athletes are available for interviews. If fully clothed football, baseball and basketball players were accessible immediately after games—as tennis players, golfers and women athletes are—everyone would be better off. But they're not, and reporters have deadlines. Sometimes as little as five minutes separates the end of an event and a deadline.

That being the case, male reporters demanded that they be given access to the locker room. Women reporters need equal access if they are to do an equal job.

While women sportswriters aren't the norm—there are about 400 in a nation of 1,800 daily papers—a woman with a notepad shouldn't be dropping jaws in 1990. ESPN has five women on camera, ABC has three, CBS two and NBC one. Three women are on *Sports Illustrated*'s 30-writer staff. The Association of Women in Sports Media recently offered a $1,000 scholarship for college women interested in sports journalism, and 31 women applied.

There are women, like me, who truly enjoy sports. The attraction is not the prospect of seeing nude men. We can do that in the privacy of our homes. I chose sports over other sections of the newspaper because it offers stories that combine human interest with business, news and entertainment.

Sports is one of the few passions that is enjoyed by the rich and poor, black and white, Jew and Arab. And in a world where kids sell crack, teenagers kill over sneakers and adults hold hostages over oil, a Sunday afternoon football game can offer tremendous therapy.

Women sportswriters studied as hard as their male colleagues and worked just as many hours on college publications. It's infuriating to read comments like Schembechler's or to hear colleagues say women are taking away their jobs.

There are only a handful of women sports columnists and another handful who are sports editors. If male reporters and editors don't realize that diversity is necessary to cover a city properly, then they're further behind than I thought.

It's a shame a young woman like Frey, a Harvard graduate, had to have her name dragged through the ugly summer episode. It's ridiculous that I once was the subject of a locker room joke in which a Miami Dolphins player danced nude behind my back while I interviewed another player. Even more nauseating was when an NFL coach interrupted an interview to ask for a photo of my eyes.

Frank Deford, a longtime *Sports Illustrated* writer now with *The National* sports daily, offended some women at the May Association for Women in Sports Media convention in Dallas. He suggested that young women reporters use their gender as an advantage in interview situations. While I don't plan to take his advice, his frankness was welcome.

"I know you struggle with yourself. The reason you have to is we (men) are pigs. It's nothing to be proud of, but that's us. Make us accept you, because it will make us better. It's not a matter of you breaking into a profession, it's a matter of you breaking down a culture. And that is eminently harder to do."

Source: *Detroit Free Press,* September 14, 1990, p. 11D.
Reprinted with the permission of the *Detroit Free Press*

crecy—that at the time were unclear to reporters. The reporters, from all area newspapers on the Chargers beat, were forced to use binoculars for weeks to watch practice from a hill on public property overlooking the practice site (Stein 1989).

These and countless other disputes have occurred because of the growing strain between sports reporters and sources (Sportswriters clash 1980). Over the past decade, teams, players, and those affiliated with the athletes and their organizations have made it increasingly difficult for reporters to get their stories—in effect, to do their jobs. Much has been written in the professional publications and in sports sections about the trouble. The frustration is that there seems to be no solution, at least no simple one, in sight.

Some teams have tried press guidelines. The Associated Press Sports Editors has called for more cooperation from teams for the free flow of information between athletes and the public, through journalists. In the wake of the Lisa Olson locker room access case, numerous discussions have been reopened that have tried to systematically deal with the rights of sports reporters and of their sources, such as legislation proposed and debated in Wisconsin in 1991 that would ban everyone from locker rooms except those connected to teams (Daily 1991).

When guidelines are proposed—and some states have begun to consider legislation instead of voluntary guidelines—they are not often easily agreed upon. Some rules hurt reporters on deadline more than others. Some hurt one form of news media more than others. Some rules may deny athletes rights such as privacy. It is not easy to make all parties happy.

Reprinted with the permission of King Features Syndicate

A growing gap, widened perhaps by the New England Patriots–Olson controversy, still endangers this strained relationship, and the situation may get worse before it gets better (Kerwin 1990a and 1990b). Other concerns about sources and sportswriters do not even center on the gender of a reporter or attitudes of athletes toward that reporter's gender. There is a more fundamental difference in the goals and motivations of reporters and sources underlying all of this. John Powers (1981) of the *Boston Globe* writes: "By nature [the reporter–athlete] relationship is adversarial and always has been. The professional athlete is paid to perform, the journalist to report and assess [the athlete's] performance. Friction is inevitable." Some journalists argue that part of the athlete's responsibility is dealing with reporters, whereas others feel this impinges on athletes' privacy. Sportswriters must understand that athletes are entitled to privacy, but athletes must also recognize the need for writers to convey information about them and their performances to interested fans.

Powers feels most athletes understand the levels of attribution in releasing information. He calls off-the-record reporting, out-of-context reporting, and inaccuracy the most controversial subjects involving journalists and athletes. Many athletes disagree with reporters on the basic role of the media and on what they (the athletes) perceive as negative sports reporting philosophies. Other parts of the problem, according to Powers, are the reporters' qualifications, athletes' sensitivity, media's power, athletes' lack of understanding of media, and athletes' general lack of interest in journalists.

Even before Powers produced his series for the *Boston Globe,* David Bush (1979) wrote in the *San Francisco Chronicle* about the problem:

> The problems of newspapers aren't confined to their dealings with political leaders, famous entertainers and the Supreme Court. The relationship between professional athletes and the press also is deteriorating, and if the situation doesn't improve, the ultimate loser will be those fans and readers who will see less than complete coverage of their favorite teams and athletes. The present emotions, on both sides, are formidable:
>
> ● Athletes increasingly refuse to cooperate with or talk to journalists, sometimes resorting to physical means to register their disapproval of a writer's prose.
> ● Coaches and management have been known to ignore or even attempt to ban an offending reporter.
> ● Locker room shouting matches have become commonplace.
> ● Mutual mistrust abounds.
> ● Apparently, neither the press, nor the athletes nor the front offices fully understand each others' roles, and this has further aggravated an adversary relationship.

Compounding this problem has been the philosophical change in sports journalism over the past two decades. Sports journalists traditionally promoted local teams. Now, cheerleading is not the professional stance of journalists who are covering sports, but some athletes and team managements still do not completely accept this new role (Huenergard 1979). It will take considerable effort on the part of journalists and sources to ease back to a position where each respects the responsibilities and rights of the other.

Growing Leadership of the Associated Press Sports Editors

A major player in setting the new course for sports journalism in the mid-1990s is the Associated Press Sports Editors. This organization, anchored by secretary-treasurer Ed Storin at Hilton Head, S.C., represents the sports section managers and their staffs of Associated Press–member newspapers in the United States and Canada. APSE's members are, thus, the assistant managing editors/sports, executive sports editors, sports editors, and assistant sports editors—the leaders in the industry today and tomorrow (Garrison 1989a, Shirley 1985).

A recent national study of APSE showed that the contemporary sports editor is white, male, and has about 14 to 15 years of newspaper experience, excluding years in college. Most are young—about 40 years old—and well-educated (70 percent college educated and almost 6 percent with an advanced degree) (Garrison and Salwen 1989a and 1989b, Salwen and Garrison 1989).

Criticism of Sports Journalism

Not everyone is happy with how sports journalists do their jobs. The managing editor of the *Kansas City Star,* Mike Waller, feels sports journalists are not fulfilling their potential (Huenergard 1981). First, he is critical of writers who do not report, waiting instead in cozy press boxes for the information or news to come to them in the form of neatly printed press releases provided by a sports information director or other press representative. He further asserts that writers often become too friendly with sources, eroding the boundary between professional journalist and subject. Waller also feels sports journalists should work harder to conduct themselves professionally, in person, with sources.

Jay Searcy, executive sports editor of the *Philadelphia Inquirer,* says there is too much pack journalism for the good of reporting. He sees too much commentary in straight sports news, says reporters write not for their readers but for their colleagues, and thinks that sports journalists too often sacrifice information for style in writing (Huenergard 1981).

Bob Broeg (1980), sports editor of the *St. Louis Post-Dispatch,* feels there has been too radical a shift from the cheerleading to the critical style of sports journalism: "If the prose of old was too fat, now it's almost too lean. If there was at one time too much 'gee-whiz' writing, now there is too much of an 'aw-nuts' approach." And Dick Kaegel (1980), the former managing editor of *The Sporting News,* wonders whether sports sections have overreacted to television, feeling the "television syndrome" may have led to too many features, columns, and other material at the expense of facts and figures. Should sportswriters assume readers get the facts of an event the same day it occurs from television and radio? He says no. Kaegel also gives the following criticisms:

1. There are too many columnists.
2. Feature stories are disguised as columns.
3. Some writing is so involved in writing that it does not tell a story.
4. Too many sportswriters try things out of their area of expertise (labor negotiations, drug investigations) and need help in learning new skills.
5. Sportswriters do not tell both, or all, sides of a controversy and forget there are two teams in a competition, not just the home team.
6. Too often quotations are depended on to build stories rather than writing skills and well-informed analysis.

One of the most serious criticisms of coverage of women's sports has been its inconsistency. The fact that women's sports are still dwarfed by men's coverage remains a serious problem as well. Studies by the Women's Sports Foundation have repeatedly shown this bias toward men's sports (Maman 1987).

Special interests never seem to be satisfied, either. For example, groups within the thoroughbred racing industry sponsored a national study that determined newspaper sports pages did not offer sufficient coverage of the industry to satisfy interests of racing fans (Gersh 1986).

Sports, the Beleaguered Section

Sports journalists must tailor editorial policy changes to their individual markets, and the changes should be tested and refined before being implemented. Wick Temple, managing editor of the AP, served as an AP sports editor before moving up. Aware of the shortcomings of sports journalism, Temple (1980) says sports section editors have come to realize that "in metropolitan markets and a good many in smaller cities . . . show business is an important ingredient of the sports page." Commentary and opinion are needed on the contemporary sports page, Temple argues. In the future, sports sections should have a strong, personalized column or perhaps more than one, he says. They also need "comprehensive, often gadfly reporting on the life and times of the home team and its players, coaches, wives, and dogs." They should have a "mass of agate and notes columns so that the avid sports fan can find at least something in his daily paper about everything that transpired yesterday." Temple and many other authorities in sports journalism agree that the sports section has changed remarkably since 1970. In the 1990s, it must deal with shrinking space for news stories, along with more and more teams. "Now the battle [of space and coverage] is over. The other side won," Temple says. "So [editors] have tried to determine what their individual audiences want most, and then report, write, and package that as well as it can be done. Then they cover the rest of the sports world on the agate page."

Critics also point to the imbalance in coverage of men's and women's sports (Stein 1991). There are more women's teams now than ever before, involving more women as athletes and fans. But studies show news media stories about men's sports are often as much as 20 times more frequent than stories about women's sports, that women-only stories consist of only 3.5 percent of all stories, that women seldom make the front page of sports sections, that more than 90 percent of photographs are of men, and that more than 200 times the space is devoted to men's sports (Stein 1991). Some efforts have been made to rectify the women's sports coverage imbalance. Whether eliminating some men's sports coverage to provide space for women's, or tightening it up, or expanding the newshole (the amount of space available for news), something must be done in response. It is not an easy problem to solve.

Minorities and Sportswriting

There is increasing concern today about the lack of minorities in sports journalism. Like the rest of the newsroom, newspaper sports departments entering the 1990s had far fewer blacks, Hispanics, and Asians on their staffs than were represented in their local populations. Although the industry has worked to change that since the mid-1960s, solutions do not come quickly. At one time, there were simply no minority sports journalists. Now, of course, minorities are being hired and are rising within the ranks. But the rule, rather than the exception, is that there are usually only one or two minority group members on a given sports department staff, if any at all.

The problem is not being ignored. APSE has focused on it for several years, questioning its own ability to solve the problem. One member (Shapiro 1990) wrote that there was much discussion on the issue of minority staffing but wondered whether there was much hiring. He doubted it. A non-scientific survey of APSE-member newspapers at its Portland meeting in 1989 showed sobering figures:

● Only 153 minority group members out of 1,430 employees at 34 newspapers of at least 200,000 circulation.

● Only 80 minority group members out of 894 employees at 45 newspapers with circulations between 75,000 and 200,000.

● Only 19 minority group members out of 403 employees at 40 newspapers of less than 75,000 circulation (Shapiro 1990).

APSE developed a program in 1990 to increase the number of minority sportswriters and sports copy editors through U.S. college and university journalism programs with internships and other part-time opportunities. APSE noted that in 1990 there were only 20 minority copy editors in sports departments nationwide. This, wrote *St. Petersburg Times* executive sports editor Jack Sheppard, "is an indication of the vast opportunity for improvement" (Sheppard 1990).

Minority sportswriters have unique problems. They face racism and old-fashioned thinking, often from team or organizational management, which is an additional barrier to their successful work. Some professional organizations, such as the Professional Golfers' Association, as late as 1990 still held events at private clubs that enforced discriminatory white-only membership policies.

African-American journalists and other minorities often have credibility problems. National Association of Black Journalists seminars relate that black reporters often experience whites who do not take them seriously. In addition, black sources frequently do not respect the independence of black reporters. The first problem centers on consistent underestimation of the abilities of black journalists by their white sources. The second, perhaps even more anguishing for minorities, is the expectation by minority sources of minority reporters to automatically be boosters of minority causes and positions (Fitzgerald 1986a).

African-American and Hispanic women are still very rare in sports journalism, especially at newspapers and magazines. They not only face the frequent chauvinism of unenlightened males, but also face the problem of being racial or ethnic minorities. Many minority women say they have overcome the obstacles through ingenuity, skill, or nerve (Turner 1991). Although they often fight the same access battles of other women, the compounded problem of being a minority female makes the task trying at best and nightmarish at worst. Some black female sportswriters, in fact, complain that the combination of being a minority female erases opportunities before individuals can prove themselves. This is a cause for the low number of black women who write sports, one analysis determined (Turner 1991). But it can work to advantage, also. Often, black athletes feel a special bond or a protectiveness and camaraderie from the writer's struggle to make a career where there is not supposed to be one (Turner 1991).

For minority sportswriters, it is often an awkward position to cover minority athletes. Minority reporters are often criticized for being a part of a system that exploits minority athletes rather than trying to change it. Sports sociologist and University of California–Berkeley professor Harry Edwards made that point at a recent meeting of the National Association of Black Journalists. Edwards and critics like him say that minority sportswriters focus too much on the outcome of the game and not on a system such as professional football or basketball that makes large fortunes from the efforts of minority athletes. "There are some things the white media simply does not have the ticket to say," he says. "Let the black athletes know that the black press is not going to stand up and defend them when they snort and shoot up [because] they are role models" (Fitzgerald 1986b).

Covering Women's Sports

With the increase in popularity of spectator sports, women's professional sports leagues and associations have developed, and new or existing amateur organizations have experienced substantial growth in sports such as golf, tennis, basketball, and softball. But as noted earlier, the coverage is still not there (Stein 1991).

Peggy Gossett (1981), former sportswriter for the *Palm Beach Post,* says that sports journalists must look at a number of issues involving women's sports, on both the professional and amateur levels. In dealing with professionals, Gossett says it is important to determine what and how much should be covered and whether agate results should be published and how frequently. A relevant concern, she says, is how popular these sports are with readers (some editors use attendance as a measure) and how they compare with men's professional sports when competing for valuable news space.

Many of the same questions that reporters and editors must face when dealing with women's professional sports also apply to coverage decisions about women's amateur sports. How and how much should they be covered? What is the interest level of readers? What are the newspaper's community responsibilities in men's sports coverage?

Many of these questions are being debated within sports section staffs across the country. There are no sure indicators on which to base the decisions, and most sports sections re-evaluate their coverage of women's sports in their areas regularly, because the growth of organized sports for women at professional and amateur levels still is erratic. How to deal with this new type of sports news is an issue that will continue to be studied in the years ahead.

Because of inequities and inconsistency of coverage, many women athletes, women sportswriters, and women readers are dissatisfied with coverage provided today. Increased public awareness of women's sports has stimulated interest, but sports sections have not always responded favorably, maintain critics such as the Women's Sports Foundation and the Amateur Athletic Foundation (Maman 1987, Stein 1991). But sports editors argue their decisions are based on knowledge of readers' interests. Dave Smith, executive sports editor of the *Dallas Morning News,* summarizes the major argument for the imbalanced coverage: "We cover women's high school and college sports but we don't give the same number of columns (of space) to women's sports because we believe our readers are more interested in professional sports." Smith said he would like more research done on readership patterns to resolve coverage issues such as this one (Stein 1991).

Other Important Developments

This is an era of experimentation and change in sports journalism. Sportswriters are writing, but they are also talking on radio and television. SportsChannel America, the cable sports network, features four Chicago-area sportswriters participating in a roundtable talk program each week (Telander 1990). Sportswriters for the *Orlando Sentinel* host a regular cable television network program. And sportswriters at the *Philadelphia Inquirer* and *Daily News* were once part of the regular programming of Philadelphia's sports radio station, WIP, until editors decided the activity created potential ethical problems such as conflict of interest (Haughton 1989 and 1988). The *Quincy (Mass.) Patriot Ledger* allowed its sportswriters on the air as hosts for a call-in talk show in the late 1970s ("Sports" talk show 1978).

At the beginning of this decade, a daring experiment to create a national sports daily newspaper began and failed. Other countries in Europe and South America, for example, have had national sports-only newspapers for years. These financially successful publications, plus the success of the new national newspaper, *USA Today,* led a group of individuals to create *The National.* Bankrolled by a Mexican media magnate, *The National* began limited publication in early 1990 with hopes of gradually going nationwide in distribution over the first two years. It closed only a year after it began. The newspaper recruited some of the nation's best columnists and sportswriters for its 275-person staff based in New York. The newspaper's editor-in-chief, Frank Deford, was recruited after a long and distinguished career at *Sports Illustrated.* The executive editor, Vince Doria, was recruited from his job as sports editor of the *Boston Globe.* The big-name writers included Dave Kindred, Mike Lupica, and Charles Pierce. Each tried to build regional and national followings from cities such as Atlanta, New York, and Boston.

Early financial problems led to layoffs before the end of the first year even though *The National* became increasingly available across the country, guaranteeing circulation of 200,000 to advertisers although it did drop its

Ethics and the College Sports Journalist

By Bruce Garrison, *University of Miami*

Ethics affect college sports journalists just as they are a factor in the life of working professionals. There are at least eight different ethical situations that college sports journalists regularly face:

1. Social responsibility. College sports journalists have a responsibility to the student body and other readers/audiences. This means reporting should cover *all* sports on campus, not just the major team sports. This should include participation sports such as intramurals as well.

2. Privilege. Sportswriters have certain advantages over others interested in sports. There are at least seven kinds of special privileges given to sports reporters but not given others at the event on many college campuses, perhaps even more. These include major event passes, preferred and guaranteed reserved seating, locker room access, field/court access, close-in reserved parking, statistics/rosters and other information, and free use of food-beverage and communication facilities.

3. Cheerleading. Many college sports reporters readily and openly root for their school team. But should they? Does this influence the way they report "bad" news about the team? Undoubtedly. Ideally, reporting should not be influenced by school loyalty or favoritism.

4. Fairness. All sides should be represented in controversies. Journalistic norms dictate that stories should be reported by offering views of

all sides. How much college sports reporting truly achieves this goal? Are there differences in how this is achieved, or even attempted, for on-campus and off-campus stories? In rather ordinary events such as intramurals or even crucial football conference games, do college sports reporters always want to be fair?

5. Conflict of interest. There are reporting situations in which a student sportswriter will try to serve more than one master. This raises questions about personal involvement with sources or subjects of stories being reported. Although it might seem to be an obvious advantage or convenience to report about a club or team you play for, this seems unfair and biased to readers.

6. Reporter-source relations. College sportswriters also risk getting too close to sources, just as happens with their professional counterparts. For students, there is a similar line that should not be crossed when it comes to relationships with sources. Once that line is crossed, news decisions become quite difficult, and credibility with readers or audiences suffers. Ultimately, reader/audience trust is lost.

7. Source-provided transportation. For college sportswriters, financially successful varsity programs will offer transportation and other travel assistance. Especially for resource-poor college media, this is a problem. What is expected by the athletic department in return? Good news? Do a free plane ride and motel room compromise reporting? They do. A student writer will always quietly wonder, "If I rip the team this week for losing, will I get to go on the next trip?" Readers wonder, too.

8. Commercialization of events. On an increasing basis, amateur sports have been heavily influenced by commercial sponsorship. Football bowl games are only one example. The growing interdependence of college and professional sports and the beer industry is another example. Some colleges and universities permit sponsors to buy field or court-level signage and other visible support. Some schools even sell the name of an event such as a tournament. How much sponsorship creeps into written or photographed coverage before becoming unwanted, unpaid advertising and promotion instead of news?

SOURCE: Bruce Garrison, "Ethics, sports & college journalists," *College Press Review* 28 (Spring 1989): 28–30.

slow-selling Sunday edition after 11 months (Wollenberg 1991). A tabloid, the newspaper featured strong national story reporting and writing while de-emphasizing local coverage, full-color graphics, and a magazine style. But the newspaper could not survive a tough period in the industry. Distribution and sales were two concerns, of course, but advertising revenue was even more critical (Wollenberg 1991). As most newspapers suffered at the beginning of this decade from reduced advertising revenue, *The National* did also. It was eventually forced to close because of low revenues from both advertising and circulation.

Nearly a decade before *The National* experiment, Gannett Newspapers' *USA Today* quickly rose to offer a leading comprehensive national sports section, winning numerous national awards for its quality and presentation of sports journalism.

In response to the growing competition from other major newspapers that circulate on a national basis, Gannett and *USA Today* experimented with a new baseball weekly based in Washington in 1991. *The Sporting News,* owned by Times Mirror since 1977, underwent a major content and format makeover in its coverage of baseball, basketball, hockey, and football in 1991 upon celebrating its 105th birthday. *TSN,* headquartered in St. Louis, had a circulation of about 625,000 in 1991 (Rawlings 1991).

Growing Concern about Ethics

Because of a growing concern for professional standards, professional performance guidelines for sports journalists are being adopted at more and more newspapers of all sizes. The news departments of most newspapers have been operating under mostly unwritten ethical guidelines for many years. Many professional organizations, such as the Society of Professional Journalists, have become concerned with the unsuitability of some professional news reporting activities, as have many sports departments. As a result, codes for specific departments, including sports, have been generated. Many newspapers, of course, have written codes of ethics for all staff members that include portions devoted to the particular problems of the sports journalist.

Just what are journalism ethics? Generally, ethics are the self-discipline of dealing with right and wrong, with moral duty and obligation. As far as mass media professionals are concerned, ethics are anything but abstract, Bernard Rubin (1978) tells us. No ethical standards are built into the mass media, but "the ethics of each responsible communicator contribute to the making of professional codes of conduct to which most media people can subscribe."

Ethics in sports journalism are no different. APSE felt strongly enough about the topic to devote much of its first convention in 1973 to developing a code of ethics, which was adopted in 1975. Many newspapers have adopted guidelines similar to the APSE code. These codes address serious problems and issues and are reviewed and modified as new problems and issues arise. APSE met and discussed updating the code at national conventions in 1990 and 1991. Debates were long and not easy to resolve on some of the most important points.

APSE's code today focuses on acceptance of free goods and services, outside activities of sports section staff members, selection of award winners, use of other reporters as sources for stories, promotions and sponsorships of sports events by newspapers, and gambling. Specifically, the problems exist under these types of situations:

● Regarding teams that offer free travel and other assistance on road trips, APSE's code explicitly states that travel should be paid by the newspaper.

● Sportswriters should not be involved in outside activities that are in conflict with their assigned sports work. This includes not writing or scoring for teams they cover, APSE says.

● Staff writers who appear on radio and television should be identified as newspaper representatives, APSE maintains. It is the affiliation that gives the writer credibility in many cases.

● Sportswriters should not accept gifts of $10 or greater value, except when such gifts are also available to the public, to retain their independence and to avoid the perception of bias, APSE says.

● APSE also expects members not to accept free tickets from teams. These should be paid for by the newspaper. Non-working sports reporters attending a game should pay for those tickets, or the newspaper should pay for them.

● Sportswriters should not vote for player awards that result in monetary gain for the athletes, APSE believes. It creates a conflict of interest, especially for beat reporters.

● APSE does not advocate use of other reporters as sources in stories. APSE instead argues that the reporter should independently verify information.

● Sportswriters should be careful in the use of unnamed sources. This can risk story credibility.

● In-house promotions and sponsorship of sports events or teams should be acknowledged by disclaimers that sponsorship does not affect the reporting of the event, APSE argues.

● Gambling is improper and should not be permitted even in areas where it is legal. Legal gambling should be limited to events that a sportswriter does not cover and should be discouraged, APSE says.

A Collective Conscience on Ethics

By Bill Dwyre, *Los Angeles Times* executive sports editor

It was somewhere in the midst of filling out Glenn Guzzo's questionnaire on ethics that it really hit me. All the chest-thumping that we've been doing the last few years about how we've cleaned up our ethics act is probably a lot of baloney.

Guzzo's questionnaire, one of the best I've ever seen on the topic, was jarring because of its quality and approach. He and his APSE ethics committee didn't just ask a bunch of the old-hat, predictable questions that would bring old-hat predictable results and insulate us from the real truths we probably don't want to hear.

No, his questionnaire was based on research of actual situations, things that happened at newspapers where the sports section is run by the guy you met last year at an APSE function who seemed bright and in tune with all the right moves we have made in the sportswriting industry.

Yes. Guzzo's survey, plus a couple of other things on APSE's current agenda, have convinced me that, while we may have learned to excel at the art of telling each other all the right things at our annual social/professional gatherings, the fact remains that once we get back home again in Indiana — or wherever — we all too often turn our backs while our troops fill their pockets with the literal and figurative goodies of the trade.

Being Catholic, I have done what the nuns taught. I examined my conscience. I want to point some fingers here, but I ought to look at home first.

I remember the good old days, back when I was sports editor of the *Milwaukee Journal*. I took such pride in being hardnosed about this stuff.

One of my all-time favorite things used to be having my baseball writer, Mike Gonring, keep track of all the hot dogs and colas he ate in the press box at Milwaukee County Stadium so that I could make some ridiculous calculation at the end of the season and send a check to Bud Selig, then and now president of the Brewers.

Getting that check, usually a figure something like $827.16, was an annual lowlight for Selig, who never quite knew what to do with it — whether to debit it or credit it or set up some special fund for convicted former sportswriters. He would call up and bitch and it made me so happy, every year. He'd usually start out the conversation by saying: "Dwyre, what in hell am I supposed to do with the 16 cents?"

Back then, I would frown very heavily on staffers calling up the PR person to buy tickets to events. I used to snarl something about standing in line like the rest of the public.

At the 1976 Olympics in Montreal, I put a quarter on the machine every time I took one of those press room colas. I wasn't gonna let those slick Canadians think they could get me to write nice things about their Olympics by filling me with free colas.

Bob Hammel of the *Bloomington Herald Telephone,* who became a good friend in the time we spent together in Montreal, still lists that in his top ten stupid things he's witnessed in sports, which is saying a lot when you consider all the years he's covered Bobby Knight.

But now, I've mellowed. I don't ask my writers to keep track of hot dogs in press boxes, and I don't mind when staffers call the team to buy tickets for games. And I can drink a press room cola without even gagging. Well, unless Hammel is there.

Basically, I'm much less feisty about the little things. I tell myself I don't have the time to keep the letter of the law on ethics. I rationalize that I should spend my time on higher priorities.

But it also occurred to me that if the president of APSE is dealing with the issue of ethics like some sort of Hollywood airhead (is that redundant?), then where are some of the others in the organization on the issue, others I am supposed to be leading?

Happily, I think the collective conscience of APSE remains. And happily, I think that this June's national convention agenda addresses that beautifully.

Remember, ethics are a matter of wide scope. At Portland, we will deal with:

● The ethics of some of our writers becoming radio and TV stars: which comes first, the newspaper chicken or the broadcast egg?

● We will be led by Sherry Jonson in a discussion of the various applications of the Freedom of Information [Act] laws, and how we can legally, as well as ethically, dig out the dirt at universities where much of the higher learning is being done on the football fields and basketball courts.

● We will open up to the entire membership, for the first time, our much discussed writers group committee work, and some of the situations and issues already discovered by Ed Storin and his group will have you dropping your jaw.

● And we will open with a session led by lawyer, media critic and media consultant Michael Josephson, who will take a carefully selected panel through an ethical test case that, while being hypothetical, will be designed to ring all too true to too many in the audience.

So Portland's APSE convention, whether by design or merely good instinct on the part of convention chairman Steve Doyle, should provide the shock treatment needed by APSE.

We have gone from an organization living mostly off the innovation and farsightedness of Dave Smith and his fellow founding fathers to an organization wandering a bit and thrashing about to find its own identity to an organization of deep pockets and time-tested formats.

Which is a nice progression as long as the current state doesn't also translate into an organization of fat cats, unwilling to undertake any real introspection.

Portland is a time to pull ourselves up by the bootstraps a bit. The agenda Doyle has for us serves that purpose well. It is time for us to spend less time telling each other how far we've come in turning out quality sports sections the last few years and more time figuring out ways to do some spring cleaning on ethics.

If we don't, one day soon, we'll pick up our papers one morning and read a story about a sportswriter who was gambling on the team he was covering, or how some such thing could ever have happened.

And deep in our hearts, while we are still pursuing, with zest and delight, stories on situations such as Pete Rose's, we'll know that, by our own collective indifference at APSE, we will own a little piece of the guilt and shame.

SOURCE: Bill Dwyre, "A collective conscience on ethics."
APSE Newsletter, May 1989, pp. 1, 3.
Reprinted with the permission of Bill Dwyre and APSE

The revised 1991 version of the APSE code is reprinted in the appendix.

Among the other matters of concern to sports journalists are improper use of passes; sportswriters acting as official scorers, accepting money for writing for sports publications such as game programs, and not paying for press box services such as food; bargain group memberships; and use of the sports journalist's position for personal gain. The APSE code of ethics says: "Guidelines can't cover everything. Use common sense and good judgment in applying these guidelines in adopting local codes covering your own situations" (Adelizzi 1981).

Professional performance codes must be continually modified to reflect new concerns and changing conditions. Without such monitoring, codes are quickly outdated and ineffective. But most important is the desire to follow the guidelines. Any standards a publication chooses for professional performance must be adopted on the individual level. At present, unfortunately, many publications still do not have such codes or even seem to follow unwritten ethical standards. Perhaps even more serious for sports journalism, many sports journalists have not become sensitive to the need for professional performance standards for the improvement of their work, their newspaper's work, and the profession at large.

A growing concern, too, is the lack of enforcement of these codes. There are few purely legal reasons to honor the codes — except in the case of fraud or gambling, of course. Employers can enforce the codes through performance appraisals, raises, and ultimately the decision to continue employment. But few companies do today.

Because the news media's relations with the public are fragile and because a newspaper's, or reporter's, credibility is hard to build once it is lost, ethics are a matter of current and future concern for all sports journalists. (For an additional discussion of the situation, see Solomon [1980].)

In addition to sports journalists' concern for ethics, growing attention is being given to ethics in sports itself. In 1990, for example, the University of Rhode Island's Institute for International Sport named a 17-person group to conduct a three-year study of sports ethics. The study is expected to result in codes of ethics for several sports organizations. Members of the group conducting the study include coaches, former athletes, and athletics administrators (Associated Press 1990).

Professionalism as the Goal

For many years, sports journalists have sought professionalization of the field for a number of reasons, especially to upgrade the status of the sports journalist from overgrown kid to serious reporter and editor. It is a slow, tedious process that is still a long way from complete.

Among its news-side colleagues, sports reporting is frequently viewed as a part of the occupation "conceived out of journalistic wedlock" (Dwyre 1981). Sports journalists have long been criticized for hackneyed writing, cheering for the home team, gladly accepting "freebies," serving as a source of scrapbook material for the stars, an unwillingness to report in-depth issues, and a host of other sins (Garrison 1989a, Koppett 1981, Surface 1972). These criticisms raise questions about the role of sports journalists and their proper place in journalism.

Despite the lingering stereotypes, there is evidence that newspaper sports journalism is changing and becoming serious. Sports journalists were once quite different from their colleagues in news, features, and opinion. Not only was the subject matter different, but the approaches taken to reporting the stories varied considerably. Sports journalists of yesterday covered games, personalities, and little else. While professional- and college-level sports always had business, legal, social, and other considerations, these seldom found their way into sports reporting. During the past two decades, however, these differences have begun to blur as sports journalists have become more skilled and better educated. In addition, the advent of television sports, which can report the play-by-plays better than print media, highlighted the need of newspapers to stress the behind-the-scenes accounts of games and sports figures. Yet it is debatable whether sports journalism is becoming more respectable and whether it is a "profession" at all (Garrison 1989a, Isaacs 1986, Neff 1987, Surface 1972, Temple 1977).

For nearly a century, the field of journalism has been marked by an aspiration to attain professional status (Janowitz 1975, Osiel 1986). Although a minority view, exemplified by Merrill (1986), argues that professional status threatens journalistic autonomy and diversity and may lead to external controls, the lure of professionalism seems overwhelming. With the recognition of professional status comes greater respect from other established professions and the public (Johnstone et al. 1972–73, Weaver and Wilhoit 1986).

Not everyone finds the trend toward increased professionalism in sports journalism desirable. Michael Novak, a professor of religion, writing in *Columbia Journalism Review* (1976), argues that the new seriousness in sports journalism has sapped the writing of its past religious fervor. "Some 'chipmunks'," Novak writes, "would prefer to be working on some other section of the paper, covering financial or business news, or investigating politics. There is some plausibility to their new conception of sports reporting: the growth of sports as a plaything of millionaires, for example, badly needs to be investigated. Still, it seems astonishing to read writers who seem not to love their subject." Novak specifically chided *Los Angeles Times'* media critic David Shaw for his enthusiasm for the "new breed of sportswriters" with their "quality of writing," "questioning minds," and "master's degrees." Research on journalistic professionalism suggests that the new breed of professionally oriented journalists is marked by generational differences. The younger, better-educated journalists are thought to represent the new breed with professional aspirations, whereas the journalists of an earlier generation represent the "buffalos" (Coldwell 1974, Nayman et al. 1977, Weinthal and O'Keefe 1974).

Among the most important criteria that provide an occupation or field with power are those that make the field exclusive. Medicine and law are viewed as "true professions" and "success stories" because, unlike journalism, they monopolize a systematic body of knowledge and restrict entry into the field to those with requisite knowledge (Allison 1986). In the traditional professions, those aspiring to professionalism must meet minimal educational levels, achieve certification to practice, and adhere to written, formalized codes that the profession enforces. Although many journalists agree that the educational preparation of journalists is inadequate, few would advocate setting minimum educational requirements for employment (Isaacs 1986). Generally, an occupation must be able to meet eight criteria before it becomes a profession (McLeod and Hawley 1964). It must (1) perform a unique and essential service, (2) emphasize intellectual techniques, (3) have a long period of specialized training for the acquisition of a systematic body of knowledge based on research, (4) be given a broad range of autonomy, (5) place greater emphasis on service than on private economic gain, (6) develop a comprehensive self-governing organization, (7) have a code of ethics that has been clarified and interpreted by concrete cases, and (8) have practitioners who must accept broad personal responsibility for judgments and actions.

Evaluating the present state of sports journalism against each of these criteria, it is clear that sports journalism is moving in the right direction, but it has not arrived. There is no doubt sports journalism has provided a unique and increasingly essential service to the public. There is increasing dependence on intellectual techniques beyond basic writing activity. Most sports journalists in the 1990s have a college education; increasing numbers have also earned advanced degrees in journalism or another field. Sports journalism has always had a degree of autonomy in the newsroom, with independent copy and reporting desks, but it is becoming even more autonomous as more sports journalism organizations develop. As demonstrated by conferences and day-to-day performance, sports journalists are responding to the eighth criterion, responsibility for activities, in a positive fashion in many communities as well as nationally. In isolated cases, unfortunately, some reporters still perform irresponsibly.

Service to the community is a strong point. Sports reporters have usually been devoted to their readers' needs and also have often been underpaid for this service. In some cases greed and/or frustration overwhelmed individuals who ignored their service responsibilities and sold out. Increased salaries, which provide at least parity with other sectors of the newsroom, may eliminate much of this.

APSE has filled the void of leadership in the field in the past two decades. No other quasi-professional organization exists, but APSE does not include "rank-and-file" staff writers as members. The self-governing criterion is an area for still further development, because these organizations lack any authority for disciplining members as medicine can, with its strong American Medical Association. Perhaps little can be done here; licensing is a factor in such enforcement, and most journalists oppose any such suggestion. The development of codes of ethics has been a recent response to the last criterion listed. However, the codes are still general in nature, and in most cases are difficult or impossible to enforce. But the organizations (new and old), plus the codes sports journalists are trying to adhere to, indicate movement toward greater professionalization. How well journalism as a whole meets these standards can be debated at length. They are a good measure of how sports journalists compare with other professions and with other journalism subdivisions, as well. Professionalism is not just specific behaviors; it is also a state of mind. We hope both will be manifested by sports journalists in the years ahead.

A recent national study determined strong support by management-level sports journalists for a stated desire to attain professional status, including a ringing endorsement of written codes of ethics and a willingness to go to jail to protect one's sources. The sports journalists, however, showed mixed support regarding some education-related issues, including whether a college education should be mandatory for practicing journalism. The results point to a desire to appear and act as a professional without taking the next step into a "true profession" — setting standards for entry into the field. This may be because U.S. journalists have long been leery of the use of such minimal entry standards by autocratic governments to limit freedom of the press by restricting who may be a journalist (Garrison and Salwen 1989a and 1989b).

It could be argued that it is easy to give verbal support to endorsing professionalism, ethical codes, and ethical behaviors. Verbal endorsements for such matters give the impression that sports journalism is moving toward professional status. There are only rewards to be gained and no negative consequences from verbally endorsing professionalism and lofty ethical standards. Endorsing mandatory educational requirements, however, can have implications for sports journalism.

The Garrison and Salwen (1989a and 1989b) interviews with sports editors found there was some fear that mandatory educational requirements could change the makeup of newsroom personnel, limit the pool of applicants, and threaten existing jobs. For example, George Solomon, assistant managing editor/sports for the *Washington Post,* once said that editors searching for quality sportswriters cannot overlook those without

After an important district playoff high school football game has ended, the head coach of the Osceola County, Fla., High School Kowboys, Greg Johnson, answers questions from competing sportswriters Rick Pedone of the *Osceola News-Gazette* (left) and Frank Carroll of the *Orlando Sentinel* (right) and a third unidentified reporter (partially obscured). (*Photo © by Mike DiBari.*)

academic credentials: "Many times a person can be gifted in creative ways but not hold a degree. Newspapering is still one of the professions left where a person can excel and not have an interest in obtaining a degree. . . . It is more and more important these days to get a broad education to be aware of the world and many different subjects."

Nevertheless, endorsements of less consequential statements dealing with education also indicated mixed feelings for journalism education, including whether a college education provides necessary components for a career in journalism. There was modest to strong support for other education-related matters involving the need to return to school to brush up on skills, and strong endorsement for the "five W's" writing style stressed in beginning journalism classes.

Clearly, codes of ethics are a major element in established professions such as law and medicine. These respondents understand the value of such standards. Many metropolitan daily newspapers — including the *Miami Herald,* the *Orlando Sentinel,* the *Washington Post,* and the *Rochester Times-Union/Democrat and Chronicle* — have their own written ethics policies that include references to sports reporting. Former APSE president Steve Doyle, assistant managing editor/sports at the *Orlando Sentinel,* states: "I think there has been a lot of improvement in the esteem of sportswriters. In the 1960s and early 1970s, there were a lot more Oscar Madisons and a lot fewer Jim Murrays. People want to be held in the same high regard as other professional journalists. . . . For example, our ethics are 180 degrees from what they were. Now we actively campaign to avoid ethical problems."

References

Adelizzi, Joe. 1981. AP sports editors calling new plays. In *Sports: An APME Continuing Studies Committee Report,* Toronto, 1981. New York: Associated Press Managing Editors.

Allison, Mariana. 1986. A literature review of approaches to professionalism of journalists. *Journal of Mass Media Ethics* 1 (Spring-Summer): 5–19.

Associated Press. 1990. Sports ethics. Associated Press sports wire, September 10, n.p.

Bodley, Hal. 1980. Today's button-down sports editor. *Bulletin of the American Society of Newspaper Editors* 637 (November): 15.

Broeg, Bob. 1980. Sports prose. *Bulletin of the American Society of Newspaper Editors* 637 (November): 19–20.

Bush, David. 1979. Athletes vs. writers — Fans may lose. *San Francisco Chronicle,* July 23, pp. 45, 51.

Coldwell, Thomas. 1974. Professionalization and performance among newspaper photographers. *Gazette* 20:73–81.

Consoli, John. 1982. Shop talk at thirty: Have sports writers ended the era of heroes? *Editor & Publisher* 115 (June 5): 44.

Daily, Matt. 1991. Bill to ban reporters from locker rooms debated. Associated Press sports wire, February 26, n.p.

Dwyre, Bill. 1981. The new breed of "driven" sportswriters. In *Once a Year,* no. 85. Milwaukee: Milwaukee Press Club.

_____. 1989. "A collective conscience on ethics." *APSE Newsletter,* May, 1, 3.

Fitzgerald, Mark. 1984a. Editor fumes after NFL confiscates film. *Editor & Publisher* 117 (February 11): 16, 35.

_____. 1984b. Out in the cold. *Editor & Publisher* 117 (February 11): 18.

_____. 1986a. Black journalists face special problems with sources. *Editor & Publisher* 119 (September 6): 12.

_____. 1986b. Sports reporters get failing grade in covering collegiate athletics. *Editor & Publisher* 119 (September 6): 12.

Forbis, Barry. 1988. Objectivity in a college town: Can it be achieved today? In *APSE 1988 Convention Report.* Auburn, Ala.: Associated Press Sports Editors, 7.

Garrison, Bruce. 1989a. The evolution of professionalism in sports reporting. In Roger Jackson and Thomas McPhail, eds., *The Olympic Movement and the Mass Media: Past, Present, and Future Issues.* Calgary, Alberta: Hurford Enterprises.

_____. 1989b. Ethics, sports & college journalists. *College Press Review* 28 (Spring): 28–30.

Garrison, Bruce, and Michael Salwen. 1989a. Newspaper sports journalists: A profile of the "profession." *Journal of Sport and Social Issues.* 13(2): 57–68.

Garrison, Bruce, and Michael Salwen. 1989b. A survey of sports journalists. *Editor & Publisher* 122 (January 14): 36, 48.

Gersh, Debra. 1986. Thoroughbred racing coverage: Study says it's getting the short shrift on newspaper sports pages. *Editor & Publisher* 119 (November 1): 20, 38.

Gossett, Peggy. 1981. Women's sports. Paper presented at the Southern Newspaper Publishers Association seminar, University of Miami, Coral Gables, Fla., November.

Haughton, Jim. 1988. Taking to the airwaves. *Editor & Publisher* 121 (December 30): 18–19.

_____. 1989. Sportswriters and talk-show radio. *Editor & Publisher* 122 (December 30): 14–15.

Huenergard, Celeste. 1979. No more cheerleading on the sports page. *Editor & Publisher* 112 (June 16): 11.

_____. 1981. Sportswriters rapped by KC managing editor. *Editor & Publisher* 114 (May 2): 72.

Isaacs, Norman E. 1986. *Untended Gates: The Mismanaged Press.* New York: Columbia University Press.

Janowitz, Morris. 1975. Professional models in journalism: The gatekeeper and the advocate. *Journalism Quarterly* 52:618–22.

Johnstone, John W. C., Edward J. Slawski, and William H. Bowman. 1972–73. The professional values of American newsmen. *Public Opinion Quarterly* 36:522–40.

Kaegel, Dick. 1980. But how are dailies covering sports? *Bulletin of the American Society of Newspaper Editors* 637 (November): 20.

Kerwin, Ann Marie. 1990a. Harassment in the locker room. *Editor & Publisher* 123 (October 6): 10, 42.

_____. 1990b. Interview room called "unrealistic." *Editor & Publisher* 123 (October 13): 11–12.

Koppett, Leonard. 1981. *Sports Illusion, Sports Reality.* Boston: Houghton Mifflin.

Krauthhammer, Charles. 1990. When discrimination makes sense. *Washington Post,* October 14, CompuServe ed., n.p.

Maman, Pat. 1987. Women's sports seeking consistency in coverage. In *APSE Convention Report.* Auburn, Ala.: Associated Press Sports Editors, 7.

McLeod, Jack M., and Searle E. Hawley, Jr. 1964. Professionalization among newsmen. *Journalism Quarterly* 41 (Autumn): 530.

Merrill, John C. 1986. Professionalization: Danger to press freedom and pluralism. *Journal of Mass Media Ethics* 1 (Spring-Summer): 56–60.

Nayman, Oguz, Blaine K. McKee, and Dan Lattimore. 1977. PR personnel and print journalists: A comparison of professionalism. *Journalism Quarterly* 54:492–97.

Neff, Craig. 1987. Portrait of a sportswriter as a young man. *Gannett Center Journal* 1 (Fall): 33–38.

Novak, Michael. 1976. The game's the thing: A defense of sports as ritual. *Columbia Journalism Review,* June, 33–38.

Osiel, Mark J. 1986. The professionalization of journalism: Impetus or impediment to a watchdog press? *Sociological Inquiry* 56:163–89.

Powers, John. 1981. Athletes, reporters both have gripes. *Milwaukee Journal,* June 24, 10.

Rawlings, John. 1991. Exciting look, serious news: We *will* deliver. *The Sporting News* 211 (11): 11.

Rubin, Bernard. 1978. The search for media ethics. In *Questioning Media Ethics,* ed. Bernard Rubin. New York: Praeger.

Salwen, Michael, and Bruce Garrison. 1989. A survey of sports journalists—Part II. *Editor & Publisher* 122 (April 22): 56, 58, 127.

Shapiro, Leonard. 1990. Minorities: Still talking, but are we hiring? *APSE Newsletter,* April, 13, 15.

Sheppard, Jack. 1990. Communication with authors, September 1.

Shirley, Bill. 1985. The sports editor: Once regarded as a stogie-smoking bunch of rapscallions, the boys in the toy department have joined the real world. *Los Angeles Times,* July 7, pt. 3, 3.

Solomon, George. 1980. No more cash envelopes. *Bulletin of the American Society of Newspaper Editors* 637 (November): 23.

Sports talk show run by Massachusetts daily. 1978. *Editor & Publisher* 111 (May 27): 48.

Sportswriters clash with coaches, owners. 1980. *Editor & Publisher* 113 (December 6): 38.

Stein, M. L. 1989. Welcome to "Scribes Hill." *Editor & Publisher* 122 (October 21): 14.

———. 1991. Survey: Women's sports coverage shortchanged. *Editor & Publisher* 124 (February 16): 18, 51.

Surface, Bill. 1972. The shame of the sports beat. *Columbia Journalism Review* 10 (5): 48–55.

Telander, Rick. 1990. Not just pretty faces. *Sports Illustrated* 72 (5): 71–83.

Temple, Wick. 1977. Sportswriting: A whole new ballgame. *Bulletin of the American Society of Newspaper Editors,* September, 3–6.

———. 1980. The problems in the 1980s. *Bulletin of the American Society of Newspaper Editors* 637 (November): 12–13.

Turner, Renee D. 1991. Black women sportswriters and the locker room wars. *Ebony* 46 (4): 170–78.

Underwood, John. 1981. A game plan for America. *Sports Illustrated* 54 (February 23): 62–80.

Weaver, David H., and G. Cleveland Wilhoit. 1986. *The American Journalist: A Portrait of U.S. News People and Their Work.* Bloomington: Indiana University Press.

Weinthal, Donald S., and Garrett J. O'Keefe. 1974. Professionalism among broadcast newsmen in an urban area. *Journal of Broadcasting* 18 (2): 193–209.

Wollenberg, Skip. 1991. *The National.* Associated Press sports wire, January 30, n.p.

Associated Press Sports Editors Ethics Guidelines

1. The newspaper pays its staffer's way for travel, accommodations, food and drink.

> **(a)** If a staffer travels on a chartered team plane, the newspaper should insist on being billed. If the team cannot issue a bill, the amount can be calculated by estimating the cost of a similar flight on a commercial airline.
>
> **(b)** When services are provided to a newspaper by a pro or college team, those teams should be reimbursed by the newspaper. This includes providing telephone, typewriter or fax service.

2. Editors and reports should avoid taking part in outside activities or employment that might creat conflict of interest or even appearance of a conflict. This includes:

> **(a)** They should not serve as an official scorer at baseball games.
>
> **(b)** They should not write for team or league media guides or other team or league publications. This has the potential of compromising a reporter's disinterested observations.
>
> **(c)** Staffers who appear on radio or television should understand that their first loyalty is to the paper.

3. Writers and writers' groups should adhere to APME and APSE standards. No deals, discounts or gifts except those of insignificant value or those available to the public.

> **(a)** If a gift is impossible or impractical to return, donate it to charity.
>
> **(b)** Do not accept free memberships or reduced fees for membership. Do not accept gratis use of facilities, such as golf courses or tennis courts, unless it is used as part of doing a story for the newspaper.
>
> **(c)** Sports editors should be aware of standards of conduct of groups and professional associations to which their writers belong and the ethical standards to which those groups adhere, including areas such as corporate sponsorship from news sources it covers.

4. A newspaper should not accept free tickets, although press credentials needed for coverage and coordination are acceptable.

5. A newspaper should carefully consider the implications of voting for all awards and all-star teams and decide if such voting creates a conflict of interest.

6. A newspaper's own ethical guidelines should be followed, and editors and reporters should be aware of standards acceptable for use of unnamed sources and verification of information obtained other than from primary news sources.

> **(a)** Sharing and pooling of notes and quotes should be discouraged. If a reporter uses quotes obtained secondhand, that should be made known to the readers. A quote could be attributed to a newspaper or another reporter.

7. Assignments should be made on merit, without regard for race or gender.

Guidelines can't cover everything. Use common sense and good judgment in applying these guidelines in adopting local codes.

Index